IRIS MURDOCH:
WORK FOR THE SPIRIT

FOR
DILYS AND WALTER
CARRINGTON

# IRIS MURDOCH:
# WORK FOR THE SPIRIT

*Elizabeth Dipple*

1982
THE UNIVERSITY OF CHICAGO PRESS

The University of Chicago Press, Chicago 60637
Methuen & Co. Ltd, London EC4P 4EE

Library of Congress Cataloging in Publication Data

Dipple, Elizabeth.
Iris Murdoch, work for the spirit.

Bibliography: p.
Includes index.
1. Murdoch, Iris – Criticism and interpretation
2. Philosophy in literature.   I. Title.
PR6063.U7Z64      823'.914      81-52553
ISBN 0-226-15363-0       AACR2

Good art, thought of as symbolic force rather than statement, provides a stirring image of a pure transcendent
value, a steady visible enduring higher good, and perhaps
provides for many people, in an unreligious age without
prayer or sacraments, their clearest *experience* of something
grasped as separate and precious and beneficial and held
quietly and unpossessively in the attention. Good art which
we love can seem holy and attending to it can be like
praying. . . . Good art . . . provides work for the spirit.


A reading of Plato helps us to see how good art is truthful.
Dream is the enemy of art and its false image. As pictured in
the *Republic*, the higher level is reflected as an image in the
lower level. The high-temperature fusing power of the
creative imagination, so often and eloquently described by
the Romantics, is the reward of the sober truthful mind
which, as it reflects and searches, constantly says no and no
and no to the prompt easy visions of self-protective self-
promoting fantasy. (Like the daemon of Socrates which said
only 'No'.) The artist's 'freedom' is hard won, and is a
function of his grasp of reality.

*The Fire and the Sun*

# THE NOVELS
## OF IRIS MURDOCH

*Under the Net*, 1954
*The Flight from the Enchanter*, 1955
*The Sandcastle*, 1957
*The Bell*, 1958
*A Severed Head*, 1961
*An Unofficial Rose*, 1962
*The Unicorn*, 1963
*The Italian Girl*, 1964
*The Red and the Green*, 1965
*The Time of the Angels*, 1966
*The Nice and the Good*, 1968
*Bruno's Dream*, 1969
*A Fairly Honourable Defeat*, 1970
*An Accidental Man*, 1971
*The Black Prince*, 1973
*The Sacred and Profane Love Machine*, 1974
*A Word Child*, 1975
*Henry and Cato*, 1976
*The Sea, The Sea*, 1978
*Nuns and Soldiers*, 1980

# CONTENTS

# PREFACE

This book can be read in two ways, has a double structure and is indeed intended for two audiences. For those who have read all of Murdoch's novels or are critics of her work, a straight reading through is in order, and a warning must be given of the book's deliberately shifting structure. The shift occurs with Chapter V, and is part of my attempt to increase the usefulness of this study for both scholar and reader. I also wish to address those general but serious readers who have read only a few novels and wish to have some help in seeing how they work and where they fit in Murdoch's career. These readers should also be warned, for this is not to be construed as a Murdoch handbook. Use of the index and table of contents will assist those whose knowledge of Murdoch's novels is incomplete in finding where the books they have actually read are addressed. Most of the books are given fairly extended readings, and there is a brief bibliography at the end suggesting further studies, particularly on the subject of the early novels which are treated less complexly than the last eleven. Although this study argues a strong thesis, it can also be dipped into, and perhaps its length may encourage either a slow reading or a piecemeal one. My purpose throughout has been to show the depth of Murdoch's massive achievement, and although the role of critic as evangelist may seem questionable, it strikes me as necessary, given the current tendency to under-read and underestimate Murdoch's work. I do not at any point dodge the often troublesome issue of reading any Murdoch novel for the first time; it can be for some a difficult and often unbalancing, even irritating experience, and one that I myself cringe under: but I do argue strenuously against those who judge her lightly because of the uneasiness of such readings. These are not novels for instant consumption and easy judgement, and their effect can be calculated finally only as one thinks about them and studies them. The purpose of this book is to encourage readers to approach Murdoch's work seriously in the light of study and rereading.

It is essential here to warn the reader of this study's designed omissions. A dominant influence on Murdoch's early working-out of her ideas was obviously Simone Weil, who appears only in patchy references in this study, and is much overshadowed by my stressing the greater mark of and argument with Plato which define so much of Murdoch's mature apprehensions. Given the ambitions of my work, a great deal of material had to go, and I deliberately chose certain areas that I could not develop. The influence of Weil was elsewhere done extremely well, especially in A. S. Byatt's excellent book (1965), but in other articles too, and I have therefore taken it as assumed, even though my own admiration for this radiant mystic tempted me to add a lot more to this already long study in order to make this allegiance clear. Similarly, because I do not find the effect of Sartre on Murdoch's work very extensive, I felt free to omit it in the face of so much commentary about it, and in many ways I have a serious quarrel with those who say that she has ever sounded like him.

The most serious charge against the limitations of my study must have to do, no doubt, with my refusal to conjecture about Murdoch's life, about which I know only the standard hearsay. That she has no doubt been influenced by her husband, the admirable critic John Bayley, I do not question, although I think that equally obviously he has profited by her thought, and trying to sort out which is which would be silly and hubristic for someone in my position. The entire Oxford circle has in fact been scarcely mentioned, partly because I know nothing about the mechanics of their conversations, interests, etc., and partly because I am not at all bent on giving a full account of influence and communality. A critical biography would of necessity have a different intention: I write as a reader of novels, not as a student of the personality rather than the mind and imagination of the writer. In general my point in this book has been that criticism of Murdoch is still at a naive stage, and I regretfully participate in this naivety. I ardently hope that many other studies of an entirely different nature from mine will soon emerge.

Murdoch's range of allusions is enormous, and I have had to excise many of them from my discussions, concentrating on those directly related to the kind of reading I was giving specific novels. In the process of writing this book, I frequently found myself longing for space so that individual novels in their full richness could be laid out before the reader: my reluctant self-discipline will no doubt irritate readers who will all too often find their favourite references unremarked. This is most notable in certain mythological implications, in echoes of poets, in quotations from or references to Kant and Wittgenstein, and in a direct tapping of Simone Weil's materials. To a degree, I have dealt with these when I could, but not to the extent possible, for a variety of reasons that I have explained in various places throughout the text. The enormous cultural richness one feels in reading Murdoch can be served in only a limited way in any given study, and I have concentrated specifically on references that serve my thesis, mercilessly throwing away (but never forgetting) those that would simply add freight.

In order to slant this study towards the moral and religious contexts of Murdoch's achievement, I particularly regret having very much slighted her political connotations and the wide-ranging subtlety of her treatment of sex in its association with social secrecy, lying and contemporary violence. Again, these were subjects which took up a lot of my time in the early stages of writing this book, and I reluctantly omitted most of the material in the belief that it was the province of another study. The book that should be written on these subjects, in my opinion, constitutes the next serious task of Murdoch criticism.

Above all, I wish in this preface to make my point of view not merely one that is implied throughout this text. I chose to write on Murdoch because I admire her work, and because, after I recovered from my recoil against the novels in the late 1960s, she seemed to me increasingly to be working through her novels to explain and analyse a situation in contemporary literature and thought which troubled me, because of both my mental inclination and my training in Renaissance studies. In thinking about her work and writing this book, I offer not a contribution to the current critical debate about contemporary fiction and literature which has such figures as Raymond Federman in one camp and my colleague, Gerald Graff, in another, but a somewhat parallel argument which agrees completely with neither. I am far from averse to experimental fiction, and hope for a brilliant continuation of the experimental novel as constituted by Joyce, Beckett and Nabokov. However, such a continuation seems far away from immediately contemporary experimentalists, particularly in America, and instead we are in the middle of the collapse of central ideas about the vital uses of literature and hence, by implication, all aesthetic experience.

I do not at all mean to encourage or endorse the simple-minded and essentially anti-art didacticism loudly advocated by John Gardner, but it is nevertheless true that the pointless and, for me, unreadable self-indulgence of writers of enormous talent, like later Barth, Barthelme and Pynchon, has caused the collapse of a major category of usefulness and significance. The result echoes on the level of fiction-writing what the post-structuralist extremists have been doing in 'creative' criticism; my particular point is that both of these coterie enterprises parallel, as literature and its satellites always do, the problems of cultural knowledge and especially theories of personality in the post-modern world. Murdoch's work is partly used as an instrument here; her definitions, her illustrations through character, plot, causality, symptomatology, and final effect, are seen in this study as a serious talismanic device for dealing with the problems that I think she too recognizes, and with more clarity than most of us. Her novels constitute a Platonic *zetema* which emphasizes the idea of the significant and pointed uses of art in describing our contemporary dis-ease, and fighting against it.

# ACKNOWLEDGEMENTS

In the process of writing this book, I have been fortunate in having friends and Murdoch fans who read my work and gave me advice, from those who read only relatively short passages, such as Dilys Carrington, Joyce Brewster, William Wilkins, Karin Strand, Albert Cirillo, Marcia Osofsky, Brenda Rosen, Trudy Murray and Daryl Hine (the last of whom offered three distinct insights which I incorporated into the main body of my argument), to those who read most of the manuscript with discernment and valuable suggestions: Catharine Stimpson, Lynne Wilkins, Penny Hirsch, Zivile Bilaisis, Daniel Calder and Marjorie Weiner. Marjorie Weiner also typed and retyped the chapters and helped me with the technical aspects throughout. My special thanks, and they cannot be too enthusiastically expressed, are due to Wayne Donnelly who read the whole manuscript, commented on it, tightened the prose and tried to banish solecisms. His editorial work was unflagging and his criticisms always just.

I would like also to thank the College of Arts and Sciences at Northwestern University, which allowed me a quarter leave from my teaching duties when I was starting this book.

Iris Murdoch herself talked to me once during the early stages of the book, and repeatedly, with the faithfulness and generosity which all who know her report, answered my letters and tactfully tried to keep me on a few occasions from going too far off the track. This does not mean that the ideas or contours of the book are hers; rather, I report my gratitude for her charity on a project that does not in any way have her particular stamp of approval: she has read practically none of the manuscript. This book is offered not as a biographical curiosity about Iris Murdoch, but as a way of looking at her novels. I hope that as such it does not disappoint her or her readers.

# AN INTRODUCTION TO MURDOCH'S WORK

The courage to insist on the almost intolerable demands of excellence is lamentably missing in most contemporary fiction, but it is towards these demands that Iris Murdoch's best work strains. An additional problem – the distance between the serious work of fiction and the inaccuracy of most readers – troubles the aesthetic life as it does the moral realm, as Murdoch well knows, encouraging the reign of the mediocre and allowing the artist to relax in ways foreign to this novelist's endless energy and commitment. Plagued by generalizations based on her early novels, Murdoch's reputation has been too often idly denigrated by readers who no longer take the fictional enterprise seriously, and believe that a novel, however difficult, can be adequately mastered in a fast reading. As Murdoch's work developed past her first slickness and faltering nerve in the earlier novels, the demand placed on the reader has become increasingly great, and the rewards of hard work and attention commensurately rich. In considering Murdoch's last dozen novels, one can profitably turn for instruction to the eloquence of Vladimir Nabokov as he lectured to Cornell undergraduates in his novel course in the 1950s:

> I use the word *reader* very loosely. Curiously enough, one cannot *read* a book; one can only reread it. A good reader, a major reader, an active and creative reader is a rereader. . . . When we read a book for the first time the very process of laboriously moving our eyes from left to right, line after line, page after page, this complicated physical work upon the book, the very process of learning in terms of space and time what the book is about, this stands between us and artistic appreciation. When we look at a painting we do not have to move our eyes in a special way even if, as in a book, the picture contains elements of depth and development. The element of time does not really enter in a first contact with a painting. In reading a book, we must have time to acquaint ourselves with it. We have no physical organ (as we have the eye in regard to a painting) that takes in the whole picture and then can enjoy its details. But at a second, or third, or fourth reading we do, in a sense, behave towards a book as we do towards a painting. However, let us not confuse the physical eye, that monstrous masterpiece

of evolution, with the mind, an even more monstrous achievement. A book, no matter what it is – a work of fiction or a work of science (the boundary line between the two is not as clear as is generally believed) – a book of fiction appeals first of all to the mind. The mind, the brain, the top of the tingling spine is, or should be, the only instrument used upon a book.                                    (*Lectures on Literature*, 1980, pp. 3–4)

The contrast between reading and the attentive study involved in rereading marks the difference between frivolity and seriousness, and although Murdoch has been extremely patient under the steady barrage of misestimation and refusal to take her novels seriously, this study is dedicated to an opposite approach which attempts to be proselytizing and yet critically just within the naive boundaries implied by such a paradoxical task.

One of Murdoch's insistent themes involves attention, even though she knows, as do her characters, that in the artistic as in the moral life one will be misjudged. Thus Bradley Pearson in *The Black Prince* is jostled and denigrated by his fellow characters when they are allowed to write postscripts to his autobiographical tale, and only the discriminating reader, willing to follow Murdoch with attentive discipline through the tortuously difficult paths of thought in the final development of the novel, can keep himself from being thrown into a moral maelstrom which belies the book's central dark study. Similarly, Anne Cavidge in *Nuns and Soldiers* must listen at the end of the book to vicious misreadings of her monumentally disciplined character and behaviour as she sits alone in a pub which represents the warmth and mediocrity of ordinary human society. The patience of these two characters in the face of those who judge them parallels the patience of this truth-seeking, serious writer who not only continues to write seriously, but progressively deepens and expands the task of her art. This present study attempts to illuminate the nature of Iris Murdoch's task.

Her ostensibly bourgeois mode has called out hostility from both conventional novel readers and critics who find such a style recalcitrantly old-fashioned in comparison with the fashionable post-Joycean coterie fiction often described as the mainstay of American post-modernist thought. The conventional reader is dismayed by the puzzling texture and anti-consolatory aspects of the work, whereas the experimentalist critic (I draw a distinction between readers and critics here: readers are not part of the experimentalist coterie) lacks the patience to deal with any aspect of the realist frame. Although Murdoch argues against Plato on several points, it is nevertheless clear that her sense of the integrity of art reflects his injunction that fantasy and sophist lies be avoided: the world Murdoch knows best is always her subject, and if this means a proliferation of civil servants and middle-class types, her uncanny achievement shows how little the contours of an original and varied series of novels are limited by such necessities.

A patient study of Murdoch's work reveals how deceptive the bourgeois surface in fact is, and how ironic her deployment of its materials. Although she operates structurally from situation and character, the process of her best books involves a subtle peeling-off of layers of bourgeois complacency and prejudice. Her primary tools are a devastating accuracy in the detail of human character and an enormous allusive frame which pushes the reader toward a willingness to see how large her intentions are. When the allusions fail, as they tend to in early novels like *A Severed Head* and *The Italian Girl*, the result is overplotted, tricksy books where the profound laws of causality central to Murdoch's thought are lost in clever satire. When these allusions to mythology, art and religion are functioning at a high level of imaginative power, however, their syncretic force is such that they become images assisting the novel towards profound and unnerving ends. These ends are religious in impact, but the novels never succumb to the warm fuzziness of consoling or salvational piety. Great mystics are invoked, especially Julian of Norwich and occasionally St John of the Cross, and Christ actually makes a personal appearance in one novel, but the real direction of the fiction works through the characters of the workaday world which realism has always used as its basis: as a character in *Nuns and Soldiers* describes the process, the problem for Murdoch is 'to try, to invent, to work through our nature against our nature' (p. 69). The goal is spiritual discernment; the enemy, debasement of the religious task.

The fact that ultimate reality, even the cosmos itself, lies behind the drifting and often frenetic bourgeois surface is the vast secret of Murdoch's best fiction, and the sheer nerve and ambition required in the projection of such a stage on which to place traditional realism make her fictions risky in the extreme. There can be no doubt, for example, that it is correct to read *A Fairly Honourable Defeat* as an oblique commentary on the combat of good and evil and the defeat of the Christian Trinity, and yet its psychological verisimilitude deflects the allegorical loftiness of its conception. Similarly, Murdoch's often studied references to sainthood are seen in her serious work as an ironic chimera, a product of bourgeois optimism and atavistic memory of a golden age long since past. As she studies the realms of ethics and spirituality in novel after novel, it becomes clear that such conceptions as sainthood are too sadly far from the realist world of our present, and the mediocrity of our response to her hard, cool moral discriminations can keep us from pursuing them in their final implications.

Art itself at its highest can be seen as equally elusive and impossible, largely because of its commitment to trickery and magic, yet the infinite usefulness of great art provides the base of Murdoch's connotative artistic practice. In *The Nice and the Good*, she evokes a painting which can be read as a central reference against which her work can be placed: Bronzino's *Allegory* in the National Gallery in London, in which Venus and Cupid are frozen in an elegant eternal kiss while Time either reveals them by removing the blue veil or prepares to annihilate them by shrouding them from sight. This image of beauty, idleness, sexuality and *luxuria* is puzzingly positive and negative as it uncovers and displays, yet threatens concealment. Certainly much of Murdoch's work can be seen as an exposure of *luxuria* and decadence, but the sense of its hidden beauty, the problems of eternality and transience, the statements of lack of quality and duration in human activity, love, or recognition of truth, are all part of the power of her endlessly complex accomplishment.

Moreover, no contemporary writer struggles more ironically and ferociously against the impossibility of art than Iris Murdoch. Explicitly in her critical and philosophical essays and in interviews, she argues the case for all art, not just the novel, even as she points out the near hopelessness of twentieth-century theories of fiction and the inability of the contemporary writer to achieve the excellence which characterized his great, especially nineteenth-century predecessors. She is evidently convinced of the sorry incapacity of the late Romantic mode of the late twentieth-century, where the negative twin sources of empiricism and existentialism have narrowed the novel's achievements to solipsistic celebration of the mediocre. Unable to restore the power and largess of an earlier period in the history of the novel, the contemporary novelist is trapped by the theories and preoccupations of a milieu which encourages self-concentration from both writer and reader, and against this entrapment Murdoch's own fervent and prolific practice fights in open warfare.

Ostensibly a realist who has been criticized nervously by some British critics for continuing boringly in a bourgeois mode as opposed to following American, French and East European experimentalism, Murdoch has soldiered on through twenty novels from 1954 to 1980, the limit of this study. In the process of writing these twenty novels her style has changed and her authority grown. Her extensive achievement in radical thinking about the novel as a genre as well as in her use of it as a vehicle for those ideas has involved a participation in subtle and difficult ways with an oblique method of experimentation. This method is basic to an understanding of her work and entirely unlike the current post-Joycean fashion which has become such a coterie project and so unreadable by whatever general novel audience remains in our culturally fading times. Murdoch palpably believes in texts and a novelistic tradition, and sees the form as she does all art as having an important function within human experience and knowledge. Determined to separate herself from a limited didacticism like that now advocated by the American John Gardner, who, imitating late Tolstoy, would reduce all worthy fiction to moral *exemplum* and primitive parable, Murdoch nevertheless through her sophisticated practice of the genre illustrates a strong sense of the powerful uses of fiction.

She argues in *The Fire and the Sun* (1977), her book on Plato, for the supremacy of art over dialectic, and although the philosophical impulse present in Murdoch's fiction at the level of allusion from the beginning remains, it is very much in a secondary position and is scarcely seen by the casual reader. Nevertheless, one must necessarily perceive her basic modifications of realism in terms of a religious apprehension which has its roots in Plato. When Murdoch argues for the value of art, she uses a fundamentally Platonic vocabulary even as she rejects much of Plato's view. Her stance on fiction specifically is hard to get at because she dislikes the limitation of theories, and one must find out her basic thought patterns from the novels themselves where her ideas about the uses of fiction are put into practice. The novels constitute a subtle indirect teaching of the connection between the external other of Platonic reality and traditional literary realism, and in spite of her tricks and confusing surfaces, this is where the life and essentially experimental aspect of her fiction reside.

Murdoch tends in interviews to speak slightingly of the tricks and games of fiction, and often refers to the fact that the novelist is always making jokes. Her readers automatically respond to her enormous capacity for game-playing, and we know by now that the possibility of a surprising new turn is present right up to the last word of any of her novels. This gaming aspect has often looked like a limited experimentalism, especially when it involves obvious tricks like the point-of-view altering postscripts in *The Black Prince* or the lingering refusal of closure in *The Sea, The Sea*, and in a small way it is. But for Murdoch's work this whole issue of games is bound to her negative apprehension of the artistic endeavour and to the large paradoxes which tease her work and, as she argues in *The Black Prince*, all art into ironic and comedic frames. Murdoch's work is plagued by contradiction and her best fiction reflects it: on the one hand her *oeuvre* illustrates her commitment to reality and her practice of a firm defensible realism; on the other hand her games, tricks and ironies indicate her reluctant acquiescence to the artifice and unreality of the form.

In the novels, her artist characters are almost always negative and opposed by firm realists or spiritual beings whose hold on external reality is in sharp contrast to the vagaries and idealism of the artist, and her fictions constantly reflect on their own impossibility. One of the most frequently used, dangerous words in Murdoch is magic; she associates it not only with human misuse of theories, ideology and religious materials, but also with the chimerical delights of the surfaces of art. The novelist is bound to use magical devices to enchant the reader and produce form, and Murdoch is no mean practitioner, but for her this is all a subservience to the patina and not reflective of the deep uses of fiction. Her irony about her materials separates her from most of her British contemporaries but does not quite manage to align her with American experimentalists. In spite of her radical distance from them, her nearest relatives are Saul Bellow, Isaac Bashevis Singer and, in a small way, British writers fundamentally interested in magic – John Fowles and Muriel Spark. The difference lies in the fact that for Murdoch, as for Singer, magic is a tool which must be used ironically and not believed in; the real area of significant fiction, and the one that relates to its primary task, is for Murdoch unmagical realism as it was practised by Shakespeare and the great nineteenth-century novelists, and towards them she aims.

Much has been written and conjectured about the contemporary British novel, where experimentalism is limited by strong realism and good story-telling, where in fact pure experimentalism is shunned. Murdoch would seem to be aligned with this current tendency, but her work does not reflect the same weariness within the tradition and failure of nerve which characterize her compatriots. She makes it clear that her realism reflects a conviction about the uses of art, and in opposing it to her necessary 'magical' materials – both technical and ideological – she forges a distinctive product which tries to steer clear of the mediocre art produced when devices are foremost as they are in most contemporary experimentalism and in some British realism.

Murdoch's strongest area of experiment lies in the fact that she is a writer with enormous content, and no one can read many novels without being haunted by the need to uncover that content. No simple tale-spinner, she plays the role of the invisible writer teasing her reader into thought and thereby engaging him in the deeper purposes of an all too often frivolous genre. The quality of thought in Murdoch has produced alienation in some readers, but it is the most tantalizingly serious aspect of her novels and must be examined as such. There is complete consistency of idea in Murdoch; once the thought patterns are worked out the reader can watch the technical expertise with which she plays them, yet each novel is entirely new and in a sense a continuation and elaboration of elements one thought one knew. Thus each novel presents a new milieu with new problems in depicting progress towards human consciousness and change. Denying the conventional solaces of the novel as a genre, Murdoch never presents the ideal end but concentrates rather on a real and stringent depiction of the errors and resultant causality which rule human affairs under the general aegis of chance. Inhibiting herself as much as possible from becoming the kind of realist that uses the novel as a forum for moral argument, she nevertheless makes it clear that art itself has a moral base and that its real function, apart from enjoyment, is truth-telling. The just reader of Murdoch must therefore acknowledge that his task is not simply to get through the pages in a state of greater or less pleasure and to register the structural design of the art object, but to *use* the book, to comprehend its intention which has to do with a serious transmission of knowledge and experience. This demand does not produce a purely or conventionally literary reading, for in spite of her literary powers Murdoch extends the potentialities of fiction beyond this sort of concern, and the quality of knowledge transmitted is in compelling competition with the pleasures of the act of reading.

It is fairly evident that when Murdoch argues for the superiority of art over dialectic, she is arguing something close to intuition rather than logical cognition, and for this kind of teaching, fiction elevated and subtly changed as it is in Murdoch's practice is an ideal agent. One can gather from Murdoch's essays and novels that she is above all interested in the degree and sort of knowledge attainable by humankind, and that she believes the knowledge available must be treated as experience and not as abstract intellectualism. The experiential base of literary realism is therefore an ideal vehicle, not because it can include preaching which Murdoch abhors, but because it is centred on the particular and on detail. For Murdoch, knowledge is a process of particularizing, of making experience more and more explicit rather than abstracting it into theory. The particularity of description and event which the novel as a genre allows gives her the breadth she needs, and her work can be seen as a progressive illustration of a life the reader shares with his fellows and contemporaries. The natural mode for such particularization is expansion and amplification, and as Murdoch's style develops, this is certainly her direction. It may also help explain what has been called her comparative failure in drama where the brevity and limit of the form impede this development of richness. The urge towards particularization also defines many of Murdoch's strengths, for in detail, allusion and moment-by-moment richness, her later style is unequalled by her contemporaries. Her concentration on the inner life and experience of her characters keeps her mature novels far from the utilitarian subservience to plot which characterizes some of the early ones, and the Murdoch of her serious twentieth-century reputation will be the Murdoch of these rich extended fictions.

Intrinsic to her study of the particular is the contrasting temptation so many of her characters have towards gnostic breakthroughs and towards the kind of knowledge that demands theories to explain it. This desire for knowledge is aligned to her persistent presentation of all characters in a state of metaxy and longing where they despairingly contrast their limited and all too particular present with various grand ideals towards which they aspire – innocence, romantic love, God. In *The Fire and the Sun*, Murdoch pointed out that the main problem with religion is that it materializes God, and all her characters long for such materialization of the ideals that govern their own lives. The narrator of *The Black Prince*, Bradley Pearson, says that the question 'What does the artist fear?' reveals much about that artist's work, and in Murdoch the materialization of God and all attendant magics and ideals is doubtless the thing she most carefully excludes from her novels. This does not mean that her characters do not play with God and magic in many forms, but the point of the books is to deny and exclude the satisfaction and consolation that would come from the possibility of the existence of the broad and splendid general thing rather than the limited particular. One is nevertheless reminded in Murdoch's work of the reverse alchemy of Baudelaire's claim in the *Journaux Intimes* – 'Dieu est le seul être qui, pour régner, n'ait même pas besoin d'exister.' (God is the only being who does not even have to exist in order to reign.) – because it is indeed true that there is an external other, unknowable but deeply sought after in Murdoch's work which governs much of that work's tenor and compels the mind of the reader on to a secret religious track.

All Murdoch's characters are world-immanent beings who, in spite of an inclination towards ideals and knowledge, are forced to concentrate on ordinary action in a realistic world where muddle reigns. It is evident that for Murdoch the transcendent is too easily deceptive and distracts human beings from focusing on the truth of the particular and immediate, the truth that is available without tricks or game-playing or magic and that is so well served by realism. However, realism as strict reportage is not what Murdoch is after, and her modifications of realism in the direction of Platonic reality are illustrated by the strategies explored in the following two chapters. Murdoch's characters are not allowed transcendence and their seeking of an ideal end is always brutally smashed, but they do know about virtue or holiness, and the best way of describing this is through the Platonic idea of the good. This religious apprehension lies at the core of Murdoch's work and removes it from simple realism into a more serious realm where an external other presents the reader with an idea against which the fiction can profitably be placed. Refusing manifestations of the divine, Murdoch nevertheless operates ironically within a limited idea of a theurgic universe where the idea of the good, which must be sought in a stringent way without hope of reward, is seen as the basic human access to the spiritual life. The other frenetic areas of spiritual activity deliberately distract from this central apprehension in the actual reading of the novels, and I have therefore begun the next chapter with an outline of the few characters of the good who exist in Murdoch's work and who are basic to an understanding of it. Following Murdoch's inclination, I work from the particular to the larger ideas, showing the subtle and difficult processes by which this novelist extends the novel form to include a teaching which is beyond the bounds of the genre as practised by her contemporaries.

## II

## REALITY AND REALISM

Characters of the good: Theo in *The Nice and the Good*,
Bledyard in *The Sandcastle*, Tallis Browne in *A Fairly
Honourable Defeat*, Brendan Craddock in *Henry and Cato*
– Platonic reality and literary realism

Iris Murdoch's generosity in thinking about her characters means that they all
– except for a few real demons – are given some hold on good, some access to
truth. Often this comprises only a very small corner of a capacious personality: one thinks, for example, of Miles Greensleave in *Bruno's Dream*, a
monster of self-concentration, who can arrive mentally at this illuminating
conclusion: 'He knew, and knew it in fear and trembling, that good art comes
out of courage, humility, virtue' (p. 179). Knowledge does not lead him to
these qualities, nor is the reader ever convinced that Miles can write good
poetry even when the creative Eros comes to him. But he has a momentary
grasp of truth which could, if pursued, begin to transform him. Because
almost all of Murdoch's characters share, at least momentarily, in this
tendency towards the luminous, the question of how a 'good' character is
handled in her work becomes very important. Her allegiance to the rigours of
reality means that the novels are populated by the generally imperfect,
egotistic and even demonic characters of our contemporary bourgeois world.
But good characters do occur – a whole range of them – and the reader must
perceive them clearly to gain access to what her fictional world would have us
know.

*The Nice and the Good* (1968) posits an important central distinction: the
nice are *not* the good, although our love of comfortable social relationships
and sheer moral laziness tend to make us choose the easy way of equating the
two. John Ducane, deceptively placed at the centre of the novel's action, does
not, on examination, qualify as a character of the good – that is, a character
whom the percipient reader can see as under the tight, even appalling, moral
discipline which is required in Murdoch's subtly worked frame. He is nice,
and learns a great deal, but let us look harder to discover what can be seen of

the good. This can be done only by following the progress of a minor, off-centre character, Uncle Theo, whose formal impact on the novel's complex design is minimal. He functions as a vital signpost to, rather than as an exemplar or successful illustration of, the good. Much of his compelling strength in the book comes from the complementarity of his melancholic Jewish refugee friend, Willy Kost, and his energies are generally absorbed by his guilt over his past and his longing for redemption. Theo's bondage to the consoling image of forgiveness must be broken – as indeed it quietly is in the last few pages of the novel – before one can reliably perceive his dimensions or the way towards which he points.

Theo's closest relationships are not with his placid, self-confident brother or the sophisticated crew of the main action, but with Willy Kost and simple household beings: Mingo the dog, the inseparable, prodigious, nature-loving children, Henrietta and Edward, and Casie the servant. He is a superbly designed eccentric – ageing, smelly, shuffling in the background of the scene where the characters' lives are focused. Occasionally he has a brisk fight with Casie, sending her into rages which cheer her considerably, but generally his is an attenuated personality, and his inclination is to withdraw to his dirty, cage-like room with Mingo, whose canine personality he seems to emulate. Most of the major characters ignore him, although the nice Mary Clothier, who shares with John Ducane the illusion that one should actively interfere to help others, has tried and failed to penetrate to the heart of his life, his problem, his past. She in fact gives us the central insight into his behaviour. Puzzled by his neutrality and invisibility in the crowded scene of the Dorset household, she wavers between two opinions: one, that his animal placidity deprives him of energy, like a spider in the corner; the other

> more unnerving theory according to which Uncle Theo's invisibility was something more like an achievement, or perhaps a curse. At these times Mary apprehended his laziness and his relaxation not exactly as despair but as something on the other side of despair of which she did not know the name. It was as if, she thought, someone had had all his bones broken and yet were still moving about like a sort of limp doll. It was not that she caught, through the mask of Uncle Theo's behaviour, any momentary flash or flicker from some other region of torment. There was no mask. It was simply that the ensemble of Uncle Theo's particular pointlessness could take for her the jump into a new *gestalt* which showed him to her as a man who had been through the inferno and had by the experience been deprived of his will.                                                    (p. 87)

That he has indeed been through the inferno, and been broken by it, we will not discover until the last few pages of the novel, but when Mary early on urges him to go to see Willy, he rather oddly describes himself and Willy as neurotic egomaniacs. Self-effacing though he is, this description is, in a sense, true; both are so trapped by absorption in their guilty pasts that any step forward is blocked.

Some chapters before Mary's brooding analysis of Theo, the hero John Ducane, feeling his inadequacy, longs for the 'power . . . that comes from an understanding of suffering and pain' (p. 54). He has been talking to Willy, the melancholic, permanently depressed, concentration camp refugee, in whom he sees this power. Ducane wants it so greedily that he longs to be able to pray for it: 'But he did not believe in God, and the kind of suffering which brings wisdom cannot be named and cannot without blasphemy be prayed for.' The charismatic Willy, whose brooding on past horrors draws the pity and the love of the inhabitants of Trescombe Lodge, is locked into suffering, like Uncle Theo, but publicly so. He is for the other characters their sacred sufferer, their scapegoat, and on his cottage window ledge they leave gifts – binoculars, books, flowers, birds' nests – 'rather in the spirit of those who place saucers of milk outside the lair of a sacred snake' (p. 91).

When Theo, whose grief and its source are private, finally visits Willy, the charismatic man and the invisible one are seen to share a certain kind of truth, of which Theo is the spokesman:

> Even what we are most certain of we know only in an illusory form . . . Such as that all is vanity. *All* is vanity, Willy, and man walks in a vain shadow. You and I are the only people here who know this, which is why we are bad for each other. We have to chatter about it. You and I are the only people here who know, but we also know that we do not know. Our hearts are too corrupt to know such a thing as truth, we know it only as illusion. (pp. 123–4)

Willy carries on his life by working on the preparation of a text of Propertius, which he sees as a futile but real exercise of love; Theo, on the other hand, rails, like Shakespeare's Jaques, against the vain sexuality of the other characters. At this point Theo's sense of the good does indeed look autocratic and peculiar: Willy is right to chide his railing against everybody for not being saints. Theo's reply is 'Yes, yes, yes. And when I stop railing I shall be dead. It is the only thing I know and I shall cry it out again and again, like a tedious little bird with only one song' (p. 125). This statement suggests the idea of the death of self necessary for the good to function, but it is much more negative and self-indulgent than that which Theo will later see. That the good is stringent, hidden, resistant to absorption by even the suffering personality is evident throughout this scene, and the Lear/Gloucester-like embrace of the two guilt-ridden, haunted men is doubtless the best reflection Murdoch can give us of the frivolity of Ducane's desire for suffering as an access to wisdom.

Theo also suffers from the ancient problem of the separation of the many from the one. In Chapter 18 as he sits on the beach beside Pierce (the fifteen-year-old *Kouros* he loves secretly and silently), he fingers the stones of the shingle: 'Their multiplicity and randomness appalled him. The intention of God could reach only a little way through the opacity of matter, and where it failed to penetrate there was just jumble and desolation' (p. 152). He is contrasted to the luminous twins, who delight in the multiplicity of stones and are bothered only by being unable to confer their loving special attention on each one. That the very opacity of the world is part of its necessary quality, that its contingency and randomness must be accepted, and that he cannot entirely do so, are part of Theo's problem. Not until the last few pages of the novel do we learn that his derailment had been caused by his attempt at an easy solution: to take vows in a Buddhist monastery had long ago seemed to him a way of changing, pursuing the single truth, becoming good. After his failures there, the rest of his life had been a discipline in the hard path, but always with the hope of the redemptive, healing touch of the old Buddhist master as a possibility.

The last three scenes in the book turn from the ironically novelistic happy ending to the lesser characters who have not been stage-front for a long time – Willy, especially Theo, finally the marvellous twins. It is only here at the end that we learn how far Theo has travelled from his derailment and how much he can manage in a newer vein. It is important that the scene of Willy's confession to Theo precedes the letter about the Buddhist master's death and Theo's rumination on it, for it is not this letter but Willy's confession that produces his greatest insight. In his first scene with Willy, Theo had said that no one should hear such a confession, nor does he have any intention of telling his own tale of defeat and guilt. But Willy, released from the prison of his guilt by an erotic encounter with Jessica Bird, for the first time tells of his complicity in the death of two fellow prisoners in the concentration camp. Theo knows that Willy, in passing on his guilt, is not really talking to him, and therefore he tries hard to concentrate on something else of great importance – the seagull with the broken wing which the twins had brought to him and which he mercifully drowned.

Many of Murdoch's images develop from the experience of nature; they recur again and again, generally performing the same functions. Birds occur fairly constantly, evoking classical and Christian spiritual connotations. In the context of this book, where the dead caged pigeons in Radeechy's black-magic cellar are an image of evil's dead horror and cruel destructiveness, the drowning of the seagull is particularly poignant. The twin Henrietta, in tears, had earlier reported the incident to her mother Paula, but as Theo revives it to keep himself from eavesdropping on Willy (and gaining power over him by wrong knowledge), it achieves new strength. The light, soft bird as the human spirit, its calm beauty maimed and reduced to a bedraggled, dead bundle, becomes a sad image of life in the world and a shadow of Willy's confession.

The railing Theo is gone; now he describes the good that this novel is committed to illuminating:

> He thought, what is the point here, what is the point. What can I say to him. That one must soon forget one's sins in the claims of others. But how to forget. The point is that nothing matters except loving what is good. Not to look at evil but to look at good. Only this contemplation breaks the tyranny of the past, breaks the adherence of evil to the personality, breaks, in the end, the personality itself. In the light of the good, evil can be seen in its place, not owned, just existing, in its place. Could he explain all this to Willy? He would have to try.        (p. 344)

He knows that the breaking of the personality comes not from the curse of defeat, guilt or evil, but from the clear light of the good. Not, of course, that this light is his.

A few pages later the story of his own defeat in the monastery emerges for the first time as part of Theo's ruminations over the death of 'the old man'. The tale comprises his search for a discipline that would really be an easy spiritual solution to the universal problem of relentless egotism; it tells of his failure to transform himself or to face the real issue – a failure ultimately signalled by the homosexual seduction of a boy and the boy's subsequent death. Like Cato in *Henry and Cato* (1976), his initial love for and joy in the religious life had been the joy 'of a child at play'. But as he was drawn further into the rigours of Buddhism,

> Theo had begun to glimpse the distance which separates the nice from the good, and the vision of this gap had terrified his soul. He had seen, far off, what is perhaps the most dreadful thing in the world, the other face of love, its blank face. Everything that he was, even the best that he was, was connected with possessive self-filling human love. That blank demand implied the death of his whole being. . . . Perhaps it was to calm the frenzy of this fear that he had so much and so suddenly needed to hold tightly in his arms a beautiful golden-skinned boy as lithe as a puma.        (p. 348)

Although Theo has come very far in the quest for the good and the need to change the greedy self, in that he has made himself a neutral character on the human scene and can refuse to use the power he might have over Willy, he has, until hearing of the old man's death, held on to his guilt and dreamed of the external healing sweetly administered by a superior soul. Now he must drop this last illusion, this romantic dream of forgiveness in a green valley, and go it alone, without any illusion whatever. A choice to go back to the monastery to wait for death must be made knowing the fullness of his limitations, without any ameliorating fantasy. Most importantly, he would go to watch others, to be part of a human community. This kind of 'action without fruits' is vital to Murdoch's depiction of the good:

> The image of return had been the image of a very human love. Now it was the image of that other one. Why should he stay here and rot? Perhaps the great mountain of himself would never grow less. But he could keep company with the enlightenment of others, and might regain at least the untempered innocence of a well-guarded child. And although he might never draw a single step closer to that great blankness he would know of its reality and feel more purely in the simplicity of his life the distant plucking of its magnetic power.          (p. 349)

The stripping of illusion and the stepping away from the ego-satisfaction of success, as well as the projected refusal to suffer comfortably with comfortable people in Dorset, are part of what the good character, in Murdoch's stringent definition, seeks. But we leave him with no decisions made, in human, loving communion with the irascible Casie. This minor character would surely have gained more weight had the novel ended with him and his knowledge, but it significantly does not. We turn from his abstraction ('Metaphysics is devilish', he says to Willy in their first conversation) to the innocent, love-filled twins, for whom the idea of the one good need not abolish the many, as they gaze at one of their magical flying saucers, filled, they think, with good people who are clever and mean no harm.

In this novel only Theo knows what good is (in this respect he is similar to the rather underdeveloped character of the scholar Max Lejour in *The Unicorn*), knows the 'appalling demand' it makes, and with guilt behind him and no false consolation before him, he may be able to move forward, hopelessly, towards it. To distinguish the nice from the good demands the acerbity that Theo's progress illustrates. Under such stringent definition of the good and its disciplines, the possibility of a good character – not just one with inclinations towards the good or in the process of becoming so – must seem remote. Indeed, given Murdoch's sense of the infinite unattainability of good, the idea of a 'good' character must be modified and seen as a person 'of the good', a person who goes as far as possible towards an unseeable goal. The production of such a character is not an easy job.

However, Murdoch on occasion has been able to project what could be called a character of the good of the highest order – one whose mind is not disjunct from or selfishly unconscious of his milieu, whose knowledge and humility lead him into areas of human development rare in our civilization. The high moral constitution of these occasional characters makes them, generally, fairly minor rather than gloriously heroic. Indeed, we are told repeatedly that the highest human state – our *a priori* notion of a saint – is not really attainable because such a person would be invisible, utterly neutralized by the perfection of his undestructive self-lessness. ('A saint would be nobody's spoiler.' 'A saint would identify with everything' – *The Black Prince*.) In all her novels, only one person is clearly identified as a saint by a genuinely trustworthy reporter: the priest Brendan Craddock in *Henry and Cato* calls his mother one. He describes her as almost invisible – but she is not a character who lives and speaks in the book, and therefore she is, to reader and Cato alike, truly invisible, mythic, an object of hearsay like God himself.

But just beneath the absolute level of sainthood for which so many of Murdoch's characters yearn in horror and despair is this maximum human achievement – the good person whose self-discipline pushes him towards the possibility of 'acting for nothing', who is after no ego satisfaction or reward, who perceives reality as well as foundering mankind can. I count only three of these characters in the first nineteen novels (the twentieth novel, *Nuns and Soldiers*, presents a peculiar case which will be discussed in the last chapter of this book): Bledyard in *The Sandcastle* (1957), Tallis Browne in *A Fairly Honourable Defeat* (1970) and Brendan Craddock in *Henry and Cato* (1976). It is simplest to talk about them chronologically, and also instructive, since the firmness and authority with which Murdoch presents them develop from the sketchiness of Bledyard to the conviction of Brendan Craddock.

Bledyard is Bill Mor's fellow schoolmaster in Murdoch's third novel. Like Brendan Craddock, he exists under the unconsoling, unrewarding, severe discipline of a religion – in his case, pious Anglican Christianity. He is dutifully and lovingly attached to the community; he participates faithfully in the all too human rituals of school church services; he does his schoolmastering carefully, although he has neither power nor charisma in the classroom and is considered a comic butt by the boys; as art master he participates, honestly and devastatingly, in the community response to Rain Carter's portrait of Demoyte; and, most significantly, he challenges Mor (as he no doubt would anyone) when he perceives the wilful, destructive pattern of the Rain–Mor affair. He does so with the sharpness and objectivity of the truth-teller, without regard for his own position in Mor's eyes. He describes his criticism in Christian terms as bearing witness (as another striver towards the good, Edgar Demarnay, will do in *The Sacred and Profane Love Machine*), and he is a vehicle for some of Murdoch's central truths about the greedy egotistical energy of modern man's selfish will to be 'free':

What has happiness got to do with it? You do not know even remotely what it would be like to set aside all consideration of your own satisfaction. . . . The gifts of the spirit do not appeal to the imagination. . . . But real freedom is a total absence of concern about yourself. . . . You will prevent her from being a great painter.                                        (p. 217)

In the context of the genre of *The Sandcastle*, such an attitude is surprising. Generally considered one of Murdoch's weakest books because of its women's magazine theme, this novel's apparent, rather debased aspect of popular romance does not raise audience expectations for such a scene; and a frivolous sensibility (which so many even sophisticated novel readers often find ungovernable) feels instantly that even if morally correct, Bledyard is essentially in the wrong, being against romantic notions of love and open freedom (or, more correctly, permissive anarchy), the specious goods that guide this genre. Two scenes reinforce this negative response to Bledyard, or at least keep the reader in doubt. One occurs after the scene with Mor, immediately preceding the breathtaking account of Don Mor and Jimmy Carde's doomed attempt to climb the school tower. It is the occasion of Bledyard's annual school lecture on art, in which he announces, hilariously and truistically, that faces are things in the world, and is tormented by giggling boys and crazy slides in the projector. Rain, one of many Murdoch characters trapped by a retarding childishness, leads the adult laughter in a scene which shows dramatically how little Bledyard is regarded in his world. His gauche mannerisms and avoidance of stylish gestures deny him the authority and charisma a lecturer needs. That this lack is a virtue achieved by humility is not easily perceived, and the reader tends to be further convinced of Bledyard's inaptness for the world.

The other scene that makes him seem wrong-headed or unreliable is rich in complexity; the occasion is Everard's lunch for Rain Carter early in the book. Here Bledyard monopolizes the conversation with a thoroughly unsettling attack on the impiety of portrait painting and representation – on, basically, the whole mimetic base of western art:

> 'What is the first and most fundamental truth which an incarnate being must realize? That he is related on the one hand to God, who is not a thing, and on the other hand to other things which surround him. . . . But . . . when we are in the presence of another human being, we are not confronted simply by an object –' He paused. 'We are confronted by God. Who is worthy to understand another person? . . . who can look reverently enough upon another human face? The true portrait painter should be a saint – and saints have other things to do than paint portraits. . . . We should be shocked at any representation of a human face.'                                                              (pp. 77–8)

Again it is Rain, the portrait painter, who gives the conventional response: 'He argues insistently and coherently and with the appearance of logic – but somehow it's just all wrong, there's some colossal distortion.'

There is indeed a colossal distortion, but it lies at the root of the central colossal problem any truth-seeking artist must deal with. Plato, on whom Murdoch published an illuminating essay, *The Fire and the Sun* (1977), was suspicious of the authenticity of most art and wary of the artist who practised mimesis. All religious anti-spectacular criticism against drama (Augustine, many other Church Fathers, all Puritans) comes from the same kind of thinking. The problem has to do not only with Platonic reality or religious justice, but also with the precise issue Bledyard points to: the imperfection and impiety of the merely human artist, whose subjectivity or jealous belittling reduces the fullness and complexity of the person portrayed. Bledyard's contention partakes of philosophical and theological discipline, yet there *are* transcendently great portraits, some great drama (Shakespeare certainly and probably Aeschylus would be on Murdoch's list), great novels, great mimetic poems. Moreover, Bledyard's intelligence, skill, judgement and teaching are all largely absorbed in art. The paradox of his position is important to Murdoch's work, as it was to Plato's.

This often comic, humble man, whose most serious comments appear hilarious because of his stammering word repetitions, has other, more evident qualities that make even the most careless, genre-obsessed reader aware of Bledyard's real, rather surprising authority. He is admired by his colleagues as a man; he has a minor reputation as a painter, although he seems no longer to indulge this talent, and Rain had especially looked forward to meeting him; he is a gentleman with inborn style and well-trained grace, as Mor observes in remarking his ease in wearing evening dress and socializing with the rich and influential at the final dinner; and much more crucially, he is right in criticizing Rain's portrait of Demoyte for sacrificing the fundamental truth and spirit of her subject to form and decoration. We last see her, chastened after the defeat of her romantic affair, repainting the portrait, her creative, erotic energy channelled properly – away from the meretricious delights of story-book fantasy. Partly because of Bledyard, whose full view of the world is only hinted at, her own and Mor's wills have not prevented her from trying to become a good painter.

And yet, in the process of the book, how minor and uncharismatic Bledyard has seemed. His presence transforms the novel – but only if the reader can pay attention to him and is not distracted by the conventions of form. The idea of using Bledyard in this subtle way is a splendid one and the novel, in this respect at least, is better than many have thought it.

Tallis Browne plays a larger role in *A Fairly Honourable Defeat* (1970), but like Bledyard he appears minor and powerless, out-of-step and irritating. Nowhere in Murdoch's work is the problem of presenting a 'good' character more interesting and puzzling than in the case of Tallis. In interviews, Murdoch has pointed to a fairly obvious allegory of Christ, Satan and the human soul, in which Tallis plays Christ to Julius King's powerful Satan and Morgan's horrible human soul. His father Leonard plays an embittered God the Father, and his dead sister's dream visitations represent the changing wisdom of the Holy Ghost. This allegorical idea need not be central, nor is it necessary to understand the novel in these terms. Indeed the allegory can obscure our view of Tallis, and the mythology involved can make certain scenes feel bizarre or contradictory. One thinks, for example, of Morgan talking to her sister Hilda about her marriage to Tallis, from whose dream image she wishes (*inter alia*) to free herself. She admits that she has probably never thought about the real Tallis, but that her feelings for him, resembling human pity for an animal, were somehow unnerving:

> Everything about him wounded me. I mean, through him I was vulnerable to the whole world. It was like grieving over an animal. And it wasn't quite pity either, it was much more than that. Just by existing he tore my heart-strings. . . . But Tallis has no myth . . . in some ways Tallis is a sick man. He's perfectly sane, but his sanity is depressing, it lowers one's vitality. My love for him was always so sort of nervy, and he hadn't the instincts for making things easy and nice. Tallis has got no inner life, no real conception of himself, there's a sort of emptiness. I used to think that Tallis was waiting for something but later on I decided that he wasn't. Sometimes his mode of being almost frightened me. He's obscure and yet somehow he's without mystery. (p. 48)

Contrasted to this are Julius's vitality and carefully orchestrated mythological presence; he conjures a real excitement which affects everyone. That Morgan perceives Tallis as weak, without myth, and Julius as strong and full of mythic charisma does not prevent her mythologizing them herself, as cosmic Christ and Satan; she remarks that if the two met 'It would be frightful, destructive, like some huge catastrophe in outer space' (p. 50). There is a problem here, either in Morgan's perception or in Murdoch's attempt to combine the mythic power of allegory with her stringent approach to the good. Tallis cannot go both ways, that is, he cannot be as strong as Morgan's image implies and yet without the powerful sense of self that produces a mythology of character. As Morgan sees Tallis generally, he is so empty that his 'mystery' cannot logically exist. The reader, too, has difficulty perceiving the mythic dimension, and when he and Julius meet accidentally at Simon and Axel's, Tallis acts not cosmically but simply, although with a shudder, shaking hands with a sweet but, to the onlookers, shocking spontaneity. Morgan's conjuring up of mythological memories of rabbinical accounts of the war in heaven or of Milton's Book VI of *Paradise Lost* does not really fit with what the realist novelist describing the good man must depict.

Again, as with Bledyard, we confront a paradox in character and idea; the solution must involve more than simply demythologizing, subtracting the mythical dimension so that simple human mimesis can do its work. The sheer power of evil lies at the heart of this novel, and its most impressive identification in western tradition is with the vital, charming image of Satan. Murdoch's realism embodies the small but very real opposing power of good, not in the mythological aggrandizements of Christ's divinity, but in an honest depiction of what the good man devoid of myth might look like in and to the world. We cannot and probably should not forget Tallis's mythic other side, however, for Julius recognizes and is affected by it. It cannot precisely fit in the framework of realism, but functions well as a peculiar complementarity.

The other problem in thinking about Tallis appears to be Murdoch's irresolution about whether knowledge is necessary to develop the human soul or whether a good character has his goodness unconsciously, rather like an inherited gene. In considering this brief catalogue of maximal characters, I initially placed Tallis in a secondary category, together with Hugo Belfounder in *Under the Net* (1954) (first novel, first good character) and Ann Peronett in *An Unofficial Rose* (1962). These two characters, like those in the primary group, represent the kind of good that human personality can at its best demonstrate, but their unawareness makes them undynamic and of a touchstone simplicity. In them there is no feeling of passionate, unenvious achievement (the adjectives are Plato's, as rendered by Murdoch), none of the instructive strain or tension of analysis, no consciously articulated gnosis. Both of them spontaneously perceive and accept the muddle of the world, but they do not describe it in the analytic, often Platonic way which is so much at the heart of Murdoch's thinking. They are simply admirable, and that they exist is a relief in the darkness of much of Murdoch's world (although Ann glows with a rather pallid light). They passively give other characters, as well as the reader, a background against which to set their own observations and knowledge. But we learn more from the primary group who strain towards the good and in doing so illustrate the active nature of the quest for reality.

Tallis, like Ann, muddles unpretentiously along, accurately and unromantically describing and devastating the self as he does so. At no point does he indulge in abstract talk, as do Bledyard the art critic and Craddock the theologian. He does not, as they do, use the materials of his profession (he is a lecturer in the social sciences and a charitable social worker and could easily bring these into theoretical focus) to expand his consciousness of what is true of life in the world. And yet he knows – indeed appears exhausted from carrying with him the burden of all knowledge. He knows that he cannot get back to the innocence that formerly existed between him and Morgan, which for him symbolizes some workable past. The pain of a world gone stale, the corruption of bourgeois life, the perception of the dreadful difficulties of those he tries to help through his myriad hopeless organizations, the concern for the sad lives of the Pakistani immigrants who room in his decrepit house, are all aspects of his knowledge. His house is a kind of microcosm of a universe 'gone wrong from the start', as Leonard puts it. Inhabited by immigrants, by moribund Leonard and by the drop-out undergraduate Peter, who represents a future without values or definitions but full of neuroses, it is also replete with supersensible manifestations from the spiritual world – scuttling undefined shapes, demons which Peter can feel and Tallis watches, and especially the spirit of his sister, whose power and definition change subtly as the book progresses and Leonard nears his death. Similarly, Tallis's mind echoes not only with contemporary ideas, but with what is described as 'words out of some lost and ancient past' (p. 96).

The most important characteristics of Tallis's knowledge are that it lacks precise articulation and it engenders no major attempt to alter the status of others or the conditions perceived. Tallis is described as having 'lost touch as far as Peter is concerned', as Hilda puts it brutally: 'The scales have fallen. People get over Tallis. I'm sure Morgan has' (p. 15). Indeed, in any relationship Tallis combines an unglamorous presence (Leonard calls him stupid) with hopeless, impotent love. He can nevertheless comfort Peter in distress, weep for and protect Leonard, tell Morgan the truth about her dangerous games with him and later with Peter. Here is his analysis of Morgan:

> There's something absolutely wrong here . . . you don't understand the meaning of the words you use – . . . I think you are mistaken about your nature. You need deep belongingness and connections and stability. . . . I think you're hopelessly theory-ridden.                    (pp. 189–90)

But he cannot effect change, or maintain the change he may once have managed. Morgan describes her loss of ego (that most dangerous power in Murdoch's world) in her early relationship with him:

> When I married you I felt I was killing myself. It seemed somehow wonderful at the time. But I couldn't kill myself. I couldn't even love in the end, down in that deep sea. I have to be outside, in the open, in the clear air, on the high places, free, free, free.                    (p. 190)

While many readers may be inclined to applaud Morgan's insistence on 'freedom', such freedom in this case clearly amounts to nothing more than selfish egotism; the momentary loss of self she now repudiates was in fact a progress towards the good. Tallis perceives her error, but instantly stifles his perception: 'It sounds like sense, . . . but somehow – Oh how stupid you make me feel' (p. 190). His hesitation looks partly like fumbling refusal to analyse – Tallis is not 'hopelessly theory-ridden' – and partly like an obscure pure knowledge which cannot be fitted into words. Morgan admits Tallis's power, but he has few instruments he can use.

When it comes to an issue which openly demands analysis, like Peter's thievery, it is interesting to watch Tallis's activity. He tells Peter simply that stealing is wrong and that he should cut it out, but refuses the analysis Peter asks for. He then puts the question to Rupert, who offers a well-designed, inclusive explanation of how the idea of theft came to be seen as incorrect and how it can be logically perceived. Finally Tallis asks Julius, who removes the idea from a moral frame and explains its pros and cons from a utilitarian point of view. Tallis offers a fascinating contrast to these two theorists (most of us are theorists) in that his knowledge is spare, uncluttered, muddily or not at all explained, and yet directly on target, clear and to the point. Tallis tells Hilda and Rupert that Peter's case is probably beyond all their capacities and requires psychoanalysis, which he ordinarily derides. As usual, he is right: we last hear of Peter under treatment in California.

In spite of Tallis's knowledge, Peter is unaltered, Morgan remains alienated, and Leonard must die. At the end of the book, Tallis is still pointlessly labouring, has no rewards, writes undemanding, newsy letters to Hilda in California, carries on with his bleak life. If this catalogue only were considered, his character, although obviously and impotently good and hence useful for this discussion, would be of limited interest. His real power and fascination come in his dealings with evil, where in a few dramatic scenes knowledge and activity coalesce with stunning success. The first occurs in a Chinese restaurant where a defenceless black man is being worked over by a gang of brutal white thugs. Simon tries to interfere, Axel scolds, Julius watches while his eyes shine with pleasure – and Tallis steps forward to slap the leader with tremendous force, breaking the spell of violence and putting an abrupt stop to the evil being enacted. It is a splendid scene, and if Julius had not recognized Tallis before as the High Incarnation (he confesses earlier to being disappointed in him), he certainly does now.

This spontaneous knowledge and simple action characterize Tallis. That he alone can cut through evil is seen here, and even more powerfully later when Julius comes to him to tell of his elaborate, demonic game to destroy the smooth fabric of Hilda and Rupert's marriage and humiliate Morgan. He comes freely and with a kind of inevitability to Tallis, after Hilda has gone weeping and alone to her cottage in Pembrokeshire, and tells him the whole thing, partly confessionally, partly cynically. Tallis instantly perceives its evil, and forces Julius into a phone box to explain the game to Hilda. His speed and instant comprehension of how to begin undoing the damage are so positive and powerful that the devastating outcome is almost averted. Hilda's selfish delight in wanting to preside over a reconciliation combines unfortunately with the terrible interference of chance elements, with the result that no salvaging of the situation is possible. But it is significant that only Tallis can perceive so well and act so powerfully and effectively. It is also he alone who sees, in a later scene with Julius, the concentration camp mark on Julius's arm – the mark of the suffering Julius has undergone, which he now pushes on to others with a kind of cynical amusement.

This peculiar paradoxical combination of power, knowledge, refusal of analysis and impotence is certainly a way of dealing with the Christ character in an allegory of a defeated, powerless, dying Trinity. But it is even more fascinatingly a way of dealing with the problems of the transcendent idea of the good as perceived in a character who lives totally and without illusion in the confusing complexities of the world. Tallis thinks constantly and honestly, and he lives absolutely in a world which he lacks the vitality to change. I find him strangely successful as a character, probably more so than Murdoch herself does. The paradox of power and impotence, of the clarity of his knowledge and the 'muck-heap' (p. 96) of his mind, is a true one, reinforcing his opacity (a condition Murdoch in her essays claims to aspire to in her characters) and his rich realism.

Brendan Craddock in *Henry and Cato* (1976) is more a development of Bledyard than of Tallis, the latter being partially connected with the idea of unconscious good. Like Bledyard, Brendan is very minor in the action of the book, and like him he exists under the discipline of religion. Of the characters in Murdoch's novels who are most capable of good, Brendan is the most immediately attractive to the hero-seeking reader, partly because he lives in a less contingent, less tawdry atmosphere (his elegant flat, Spanish ivory crucifix, firmness of place in the Church), but largely because this is one of Murdoch's negative, heart-sickening novels (compare *An Accidental Man*, *The Sacred and Profane Love Machine*), where the reader's longing for a sympathetic character, only moderately flawed, is generally disappointed. In these extreme novels, a character like Brendan can feed our need too richly and almost push us into a rather ecstatic misreading. He is, however, entirely consistent with the idea of the quest for the good.

Almost unknown to most of the characters except the priest-convert Cato Forbes, against whose spiritual flaws he is cast as a foil, Brendan enters the plot only through his attempts to help Cato and through his brief reminiscence of Henry's brother, the dead Alexander: 'I wonder if he was drunk when he killed himself? He seemed to me a man filled with desperation' (p. 139). Compared with Henry's wild jealousy of Sandy and Gerda's blind love, this is the clearest and most sympathetically trustworthy image we have of this ambiguous, still powerful shade. But Brendan's real task is to clarify our understanding of Cato's spiritual state and help the reader see Cato as living not in hell, as his sister Colette believes, but in a dark purgatorial present which he may or may not work his way out of. Brendan presents the tradition, the history of spiritual darkness – St John of the Cross's dark night of the soul – not as a theological catchword but as a living and terrible reality.

He appears from the first as a wise man, respected as a theologian in his order. He comes to us with an authority, based on the respect he has earned in his closed and rather mandarin group, that neither Bledyard nor Tallis has, and that Uncle Theo could not dream of. From the beginning he is cerebral, not in the slightest way unconscious, apparently without passionate, emotional or selfish involvement in the world. His discipline has taken him very far indeed, and his resultant insight is immediately impressive. As one of Cato's early mentors in the priesthood, he warns against the exaltation of Cato's religious vision; he eschews the delights of popular priesthood like 'Charisma Forbes: the swinging priest' (p. 29). He is austere but always helpful; though he is an attractive and relatively young man, his careful avoidance of charismatic effect reminds us somewhat of Bledyard's self-effacement.

As Cato loses his faith and begins to succumb to his illicit, absorbing love for the delinquent Beautiful Joe, he first would avoid Brendan, but then craves an audience in the wild hope of receiving permission to keep both delights – belief in God and the mission boy. When in failure he finally leaves his derelict Ladbroke Grove mission, Cato automatically goes to Brendan's elegant flat with his rather standard tale of lost faith. Brendan instantly perceives Joe at the root of the matter, and receives Cato's line with a powerful interpretation of Christian theology. He stresses Cato's selfishness and self-glorifying illusions. Particularly unconventional, and apparently new to Cato, is Brendan's statement that unselfing and death are equivalent:

> Being a priest, being a Christian, is a long long task of unselfing. You are just at the very beginning, Cato, you are now meeting the very first real difficulties. . . . The spiritual life is a long strange business and you've got to be quiet and docile enough to go on learning. You're doing the strong man wrestling act, you're still at the heroic stage, you want to do everything yourself. And now that you've got an inkling of what's really involved you're appalled, or the ego in you is appalled. It's like a death sentence. It is a death sentence. Not pain, not mortification, but death. That's what chills you. That's what you experience when you say there is no one there. *Up till now you have seen Christ as a reflection of yourself.* It has been a comfortable arrangement. . . . You are in a dream state. Ordinary human consciousness is a tissue of illusion. Our chief illusion is our conception of ourselves, of our importance which must not be violated, our dignity which must not be mocked. All our resentment flows from this illusion, all our desire to do violence, to avenge insults, to assert ourselves. We are all mocked, Christ was mocked, nothing can be more important than that. *We are absurdities, comic characters in the dream of life, and this is true even if we die in a concentration camp, even if we die upon the cross. But in reality there are no insults because there is nobody to be insulted.* And when you say

'there is no one there' perhaps you are on the brink of an important truth.
(pp. 143–4; my italics)

That the self is nothing, that Christ himself might be nothing, are both ideas far from Cato's mind – and he cannot absorb them. When he goes on, rather wildly, to say, 'I'm the only person who can save [Beautiful Joe]', Brendan coolly calls his game: 'you are being totally frivolous and self-indulgent. It's a dream, Cato, you are only saving him in a dream' (p. 145). Cato can't see or face Brendan's truth; he sees himself as a magnificent being caught between an evident truth (his love for Beautiful Joe and the boy's apparent need of him) and a fable (Christ). As he leaves the flat in the middle of the night, a weary Brendan is waiting for him at the door, aware of the psychological error he has made. He has a lecture on the *Timaeus* at nine in the morning and appears to be remembering some of that elegant dialogue's illustration of random necessity as opposed to tractable form: Cato's behaviour can be seen as the intractable random energy of human vagary, whereas Brendan's theology is the close-fitting, truthful form. Brendan understands that he has been stupid in trying to fit the one to the other by dictate and control, but Cato, in the grip of his neurosis, cannot be persuaded to stay. He leaves behind his symbol of priesthood: the little wooden crucifix, the only thing Brendan later says he will take with him to India.

Much later in the story Cato returns to the flat after his ordeal of imprisonment, darkness and fear, during which he produced not heroics but only self-centredness and cowardice, and which he ended in a frantic burst by killing Beautiful Joe accidentally in a violent attempt to save Colette, the angel of faithfulness Cato's cowardice had summoned. He sees himself as damned, a resident of hell, and he knows, as he told Henry:

> After one has committed a murder . . . one realizes that there are no barriers, what one thought were barriers, were simply frivolous and selfish complacent illusions and vanities. All that so-called morality is simply smirking at yourself in a mirror and thinking how good you are. Morality is nothing but self-esteem, nothing else, simply affectations of virtue and spiritual charm. And when self-esteem is gone there's nothing left but fury, fury of unbridled egoism. (p. 294)

This time Brendan's convincing statement of the nature of reality (it carries the same devastating truth as before) can be passed on to Cato rather more successfully, because the starting-point is no longer the fascination of Cato's ego for its own satisfactions. Beautiful Joe is no longer alive; the charming future in the north is obliterated by Cato's myriad personal failures. The starting-point now is guilt. The reader whose bourgeois life is seldom subject to such examination tends to interpret the situation as does Colette or Henry: Cato's guilt and suffering have cast him into hell, and he must receive consolation from Brendan, the only possible instrument. But Murdoch here, as always, denies the dangerous ease of consolation. Brendan presents a version of Christian theology which intensifies and changes as his argument goes on; in fact, the rest of his long and even ironic conversation with Cato is a concentration of Murdoch's most sustained thinking on the subject of truth. Much of this must be quoted, not only for its importance in this novel, but because it gives rapidly and directly so much of the process through which the human character steps forward towards the good – that 'blank face' Uncle Theo speaks of.

Let me generalize this process beyond the limited context of Cato: I am convinced that Murdoch sees this as truth-telling beyond a fictional plot. The first step is knowing that we do not understand the game we have been playing, even when the game has to do with a spiritual calling. We should remember Tallis's comments to Morgan as well as Uncle Theo's errors. The ego must be broken by the loss of even the best in it, followed by the knowledge that the guilt human beings cling to also has to do with vanity and self-esteem. Murdoch is at her impassioned best in such truth-telling passages:

> You say you've been years in the game. It seems to me you don't know what the game is. . . . Falling in love is egoism, it's being obsessed by images of oneself. It's the greatest pain and the greatest paradox of all that personal love has to break at some point, the ego has to break, something absolutely natural and seemingly good, seemingly perhaps the only good, has to be given up. After that, there's darkness and silence and space. And God is there. Remember St John of the Cross. Where the images end you fall into the abyss, but it is the abyss of faith. When you have nothing left you have nothing left but hope. . . . Try at least to use it now in relation to yourself. . . . Repentance isn't a bit like obsessive guilt. . . . Your guilt is vanity, it's to do with the self-esteem you were talking about, which you haven't really lost at all, it's only wounded. (p. 336)

That death is the real issue and that Cato now has the material for contemplation at hand is the next point. Murdoch often refers to Socrates' injunction that men should study dying, and here is Brendan describing this most unfaceable of issues:

> We live by redemptive death. Anyone can stand in for Christ. . . . Death is what instructs us most of all, and then only when it is present. When it is absent it is totally forgotten. Those who can live with death can live in the truth, only this is almost unendurable. It is not the drama of death that teaches – when you are there facing it there is no drama. That's why it's so hard to write tragedy. Death is the great destroyer of all images and all stories, and human beings will do anything rather than envisage it. Their

last resource is to rely on suffering, to try to cheat death by suffering
instead. And suffering we know breeds images, it breeds the most beautiful images of all.                                                    (p. 336)

These beautiful images of suffering – for Cato the dead Beautiful Joe, for both
of them Christ on the cross – lead Brendan forward to his next giant step, and
here we are leaving behind Cato and his still limited ability to see the truth. It
is by now quite evident that, just as the delinquent Beautiful Joe and the
frivolous Henry had counted on Cato the priest as an image-preserver and
symbol of the religious life, so Cato had relied on the traditional theology
of Brendan and imaged him as the ideal priest who believes unshakably in
Christ's suffering as well as 'the resurrection and the life'. When Brendan
rejects the imagery of a personal God because 'one lives with the game and
things change', Cato is simply appalled.

Brendan remains completely consistent. If one must go beyond the image
of suffering, if it is part of human illusion, then in spite of the great sign-
posting documents – the New Testament, Plato – one must give everything
up, keep 'oneself from slipping back into all sorts of illusions, it's a way of
keeping near the truth, even when, especially when, the truth cannot be
formulated' (p. 338). Brendan's step forward involves abandoning even the
intellectual speculation which has brought him to such an advanced spiritual
development:

> I was getting too addicted to speculation. I sometimes felt that if I could
> hang on just a little longer I would receive some perfect illumination
> about everything. . . . I know that if it did come it would be an illusion –
> one of the most, oh, splendid. The original *felix culpa* is thought itself. . . .
> The point is, one will never get to the end of it, never get to the bottom of
> it, never, never, never. And that never, never, never is what you must take
> for your hope and your shield and your most glorious promise. Every-
> thing that we concoct about God is an illusion.          (pp. 338–9)

As this dialogue goes on, Brendan is packing, preparing to go on a retreat
before leaving permanently for Calcutta. He is giving up his country, his flat,
his elegance, his books, his intellectual place in the Church, his power over
Cato and the glorious image of Christ so important to his priesthood, which
is symbolized by the beautiful Spanish ivory crucifix which he now hands
over to Cato, a man in the process of learning reality but much further behind
him in the quest. Brendan has evidently graduated from the images of Plato's
*Timaeus* to the grim, unillusioned *Laws*, and no longer needs the magic of
images. As Murdoch puts it in *The Fire and the Sun*:

> In the *Laws* God appears as a theological device, as quasi-philosophical,
> quasi-theological speculation, or as an absence prompting bitter jokes.
> Escape from the Cave and approach to the Good is a progressive discarding

of relative false goods, of hypotheses, images, and shadows, eventually seen as such.

(pp. 64–5)

The one thing Brendan retains is the ability and need to pray. As often in Murdoch's fictions, a primary biblical text is chosen, the literal interpretation of which comprises its intense real meaning. It explains Brendan's step precisely: 'Whoso he be of you who forsaketh not all that he hath, he cannot be my disciple.' He does this, going as far as a human being can go.

We cannot forget, however, that Brendan is a specialized character – a man with a head start, as he claims, through his saintly mother, and one whose detachment from the world is extraordinarily advanced when we meet him. The built-in discipline of his vocation as scholar-priest removes him also from much of the great stage where life is lived. Yet for all Brendan's authority and his self-denying step forward, Cato can still justly remind him, 'Theology is magic. Beware' (p. 339). Brendan certainly functions as a version of 'The Great Teacher' of Lucius Lamb's first and last poetry in this novel, but in the next Murdoch novel, *The Sea, The Sea* (1978), the fascinating magic and power of religion become a dangerous central issue, and it would be wrong to generalize Brendan's route or insist on the primacy of the theological way. At any rate, a character of Brendan's achievement must step off stage, out of the bourgeois world, and leave the very human, unachieving psyche of Cato to carry on, the ivory crucifix – now ineffectual as a charm or as a useable image for him and reduced to only an art object – bumping in his pocket as Beautiful Joe's gun had done in the first paragraph of the book. If this circular structure indicates a step forward for Cato, it is a very minor one, for he is even more wretchedly self-occupied, if better taught, by his terrible failures and Brendan's wisdom. Brendan cannot be emulated easily nor should he be considered simply as a model: Murdoch's moral or spiritual nudge is largely cerebral. A major point has been made, but the novel is really about Henry and Cato, its titular heroes, not about Brendan.

Brendan is an interesting device, as are all of Murdoch's 'good' characters, a sort of background against which the larger generality of human failure and attempt can be set. Consistently in the novels since 1966, and fairly frequently before, the characters have inclined towards lengthy ruminative examinations of themselves and what they perceive as the real, so that the novels are a continuing experimental dissection of the nature of human personality. Often this rumination becomes public, in conversations of the sort Cato and Brendan carry on (or Bruno and Nigel or Lisa in *Bruno's Dream*, or Carel and Marcus in *The Time of the Angels*, or Charles and James Arrowby in *The Sea, The Sea* – the list could go on and on).

That human beings are thus relentlessly preoccupied with the search for clear knowledge is one of Murdoch's most driving recognitions – and no doubt the source of the too frequent and incorrect claim that she is only a philosopher who writes philosophic novels. She is indeed a very clear-thinking modified Platonist, and certainly a philosopher, but in his small way Beautiful Joe is one too – so is any kid on the street, or any one of us who participates in and needs any theory of life. When Murdoch writes philosophy professionally she uses a different voice, and certainly none of the devices, techniques or games that characterize her novelistic world. In fact, her recent book on Plato, *The Fire and the Sun* (1977), argues for art against Plato's mistrust of it, and points firmly to the differences between art and philosophy as well as their necessary connection. Art is a rival of philosophy; it can in many ways do more; it is the more universally available; its exalted play is more effective.

But it is notably true that Murdoch is a great user of devices, and philosophy at various levels is very useful – from the device of using pointed philosophical detail from Wittgenstein, Kant, Plato (to mention only the main ones) to the basic idea that underlies all her novels: that of human aspiration to the real, the true, the Platonic good. The characters with which I have begun to illustrate what the good is in Murdoch's work and how it can be approached are, as I have indicated, themselves devices. Their powerlessness and minor status are essential, and surprising in only one sense, one that has much to do with the history of the novel. The good are not heroes, nor are they anti-heroes. As ardent readers of nineteenth–century fiction (most readers have cut their teeth on it) with its largess and general belief in the idea of hero and heroine, we are believers in a simpler good in every respect than Murdoch would have us look towards. Indeed, for all the advance of experimental fiction in our century, we have not in fact gone very far away from the central idea of the attractive, heroic character whom we roughly characterize as good – by which we tend to mean attractive, amusing, like us. Our growth in cynicism, irony and game-playing has developed the potent idea of the anti-hero, the unattractive man in the midst of a large idea (Murphy, Humbert Humbert, Leopold Bloom – all disarming in their own way), but literary critics, as well as most authors, fit them into a concept of comedic sophistication which is seen in itself as good. As a result of the highly elaborate play principle of much of the best contemporary fiction, the impulse has been to throw the idea of the good back to the level of conception – the characters become less and less important while the highly self-conscious technical skill of the author receives an attention which borders on moral judgement: the writer becomes the hero. One could argue that the problem lies in the perpetual ambiguity of the word 'good', but I think in fact that it is more fundamental than that.

Good literature always evokes a serious response, an attention that involves more than aesthetic judgement. When we read a novel, we know we are looking at a version of life in which large issues affecting the basic way in which we view the world come into play; and when we judge a book to be good, we are saying quite a lot about ethical response as well as technique and form. The old New Critics were useful in reminding us that tenor and vehicle go together, but inclination of mind, educated taste and especially moral energy are also very important. I would suggest that the experimentalism we are now educated to experience is part of a turning of value from the nineteenth-century stress on character to a peculiar sort of contemporary egotism: the egotism of the writer, on whom judgement is invited, and the egotism of the reader, who is asked to join in a match of wits. Placing the value there involves stressing form almost to the exclusion of character as an illustration of intelligence and achievement. But the spectre of character analysis is far from laid, and experimentalists still have difficulty with audiences who hanker after the moral value of character. Nabokov, for example, was surprised to discover that readers considered *Lolita* a mimetic book and hence immoral – it took a while for his game to be joined in the proper way: marvellously clever writer versus competitively clever reader. *Lolita* is a usefully illustrative novel too in that Nabokov felt compelled to say after its publication that he had 'no moral in tow'. The weaning of novel readers away from moral ideas has not been easy, and indeed it is ironically true that one of the most telling effects in *Lolita* – Humbert Humbert's final ability to lose his solipsism and love the real Lolita when the nymphet aspect is destroyed by time – is a moral idea. The pull away from morality is far from complete, even for an author who protests it so vocally.

In our tradition, the aim of the novel was persistently moral until the twentieth-century. Dickens, Tolstoy, George Eliot assumed absolutely that their task as novelist involved the transmission of a well thought out, scrupulous moral viewpoint. This morality involved not only an inclination towards an idea of good, but also the ethical necessity of seeing all characters clearly, realistically and lovingly. Recoil from this idea has led not only to a displacement of value, as in the experimental novel, and a focusing on the writer in the act of writing, but also to a loss of centrality in the novelistic tradition. The late twentieth-century, post-modernist writer (and critic) must begin with a sort of void where moral focus once existed so powerfully. Indeed, that moral focus also tended to contribute to firm ideas about form, and much of our elaborate preoccupation with freedom from forms comes from its loss.

The fragmentation of the novel's largest basic idea means that any novelist must create his own kind of structure: one can safely say that a really good twentieth-century novelist who has found his style never looks like any other contemporary novelist, whereas for all the eccentricity and originality of the nineteenth-century, in a very real way the genre had a large unity. In her literary criticism and interviews, Murdoch shows herself to be constantly aware that writers in our century cannot write the way nineteenth-century writers could, that there has been, for all the proliferation of formal experiments, a terrific dwindling in modes or types (she claims there are only two main types: crystalline – small, narrow – and journalistic novels) and a general falling-off. All Murdoch's criticism shows a strong crusading spirit, a sense that better can and should be done. In her article, 'Against Dryness' (1961), she typically sums up what she perceives as the novel's task in our late Romantic time:

> literature . . . has taken over some of the tasks formerly performed by philosophy. Through literature we can re-discover a sense of the density of our lives. Literature can arm us against consolation and fantasy and can help us to recover from the ailments of Romanticism. If it can be said to have a task now, that surely is its task. But if it is to perform it, prose must recover its former glory, eloquence, and discourse must return. I would connect eloquence with the attempt to speak the truth.

This and all of her other essays align literature with the quest for truth and an altering of many current intellectual conventions.

The clear path Murdoch has chosen as a writer is at first glance the rather old-fashioned one of realism. The stress on the author so characteristic of experimentalism she would doubtless dismiss as fantasy and interference with the main business at hand. On the one side, she continues the nineteenth-century tradition of literary realism; on the other, she is creating a mode she would like to see as an influence on the twentieth century. Her realism does not look like Tolstoy's or Dickens's, but she is closer to them and to James and Proust than she is to Joyce or Nabokov or Borges, or even to a journalistic novelist like Updike or a crystalline writer like Golding. Her commitment is to character; her idea of fiction is profoundly moral in the sense that she sees the transmission of realistically perceived character as exercising a moral function (all stringent examination of human worth is moral), that of reminding the reader of what Murdoch frequently calls the depth and opacity of human beings and the mysterious transcendence of reality. Her kind of reality (the sense of the world as existing objectively and powerfully outside us and our control) is one that the twentieth century has been trying very hard to obliterate, and there are many snares and paradoxes in talking about it, and even more in depicting it.

To understand Murdoch's achievement, one must first distinguish between realism, a literary term, and reality, the profound truth the questing mind seeks. The tradition Murdoch follows in assuming the nature of this latter reality is Platonic, and its *locus classicus* is the building of the world by the Demiurge in the *Timaeus*, a dialogue frequently mentioned in the novels. I do not mean to imply, however, that only the *Timaeus* is used, or that Murdoch is simply offering a commentary on Plato. Literary realism, on the other hand, must be described by its lengthy history and by the endless theorizing about it in the nineteenth and twentieth centuries.

For the sake of clarity, let us first examine Murdoch's relationship to this literary realism. The major theoretical problem in realism has been that of form and the determinism implied by form: *tranche-de-vie* realism must take into account that quotidian life has none of the beginning–middle–end format so necessary to the literary formalist (Flaubert disliked the formless prolixity of *The Pickwick Papers*), and to be genuinely realist and *a fortiori* to be naturalist is deeply contradictory to organization. The realist or naturalist author must enter the material and control it to a greater or lesser degree, and therefore as an idea realism is essentially at odds with itself. This problem has led to various fascinating experiments such as Sterne's or Proust's (the experimental novel began as a development of realism), and it also produced the idea of the large, crowded, often flawed novel (Dickens, Balzac, Dostoevsky) which Murdoch admires for its adherence to truth.

The impulse behind literary realism is the attentive perception and depiction of the history of characters and milieux, and many great realists and theorizers on realism like Balzac or Tolstoy were committed to their task as historians, transmitters of the great currents of a time and portrayers of the sort of characters specific eras of history produce. Anti-realists have always argued that the realist is not a transmitter but an interpreter; it is nevertheless true, as James Arrowby says in *The Sea, The Sea*, that although we do not and cannot know what the French aristocracy was really like in the late nineteenth and early twentieth centuries, we believe Proust. To put it another way, the writer who pays creative attention to his civilization will be able to persuade his contemporaries and future generations that his fiction is an image of life, that it follows the real.

From the beginning of her career as a novelist, Murdoch has adhered to this kind of historical realism. Several times, in the earlier novels particularly, her extraordinary fecundity in the gamesmanship of plotting takes over too completely, and the characters are left with limited dimension. From *The Nice and the Good* (1968) onwards, however, her balance has been consistently better and her style as a novelist firmly established. That she is a realist means that she adheres to a commitment to look clearly, which necessarily in our time almost completely destroys the nineteenth-century ideas of the hero as a good man or of the central action of the novel constituting a consoling moral *Bildungsroman*. Realism has always known that the closed happy ending is not congruent with life as it is experienced and can only awkwardly be forced in, but the inclination towards the exemplary character has been and remains great. All readers of fiction yearn to identify with a fictional protagonist and expend considerable moral energy in doing so; most writers oblige by producing characters who reward the reader's sympathy by being admirable, even if they do so in suffering: consider Hardy's Tess or Sartre's Roquentin, about whom Murdoch has had so much to say.

In her literary criticism and philosophical work alike, Murdoch has emphasized that our contemporary inclination is towards ego satisfaction of all sorts, including our Romantic belief in the ego-obsessed, suffering existential hero or the self-satisfied, sincere person who sees himself as sufficiently developed and in control of a world which he perceives adequately, even completely. She implies that the hero we long to identify with in our period is not so much the morally good person (so often mawkishly and sentimentally debased) of the Victorian era, but one of these suffering and/or self-satisfied types. I would suggest that we will take any kind of hero/heroine we can get – the conditioning of most novel readers is as much Victorian as contemporary – and that we are simply astounded when we do not get anything at all, but confront a novelist like Murdoch who is trying to get past mere reader-winning conventions to a radically truthful concept of how people act. This partly explains why the typical feeling one has on finishing Murdoch's best novels is so often puzzlement and discontent.

In the process of her novels, Murdoch does much by example to redefine realism and to establish herself as a very authoritative and stylish novelist. Redefine is perhaps an inadequate word, because the direction of her decisions about realism, for all their highly original turnings, is in a way reminiscent of the route taken by the very greatest realists. It is clear, not only from her book on Plato but also from the materials of many of her novels, that she would include mimetic artists working in any medium in the list of realists. Some confusion may come in here; usually literary realism refers specifically to certain powerful historical developments peculiar to the novel. Murdoch, on the other hand, would apply it to Shakespeare above all, to painters, to great artists of every period who took their mimetic function quietly and untheoretically for granted. In this assumption, she is akin to the spirit of Erich Auerbach in *Mimesis* (1953), and opposed to most polemical nineteenth- and twentieth-century theorists. We will thus err in reading her novels narrowly, through ideas of the history of the novel alone. Indeed, one of our greatest tasks in reading her work is not to limit ourselves to considerations of the genre, which can be so comfortably seductive.

As Murdoch sees it, then, the realist artist must depict what is, not what the client wants or is used to, or what philosophers and social scientists tell us to be true. As readers, it is our job to see clearly what is being shown us. Murdoch's aesthetic moral process involves total attention, a term she borrows in her theoretical work specifically from Simone Weil – although that radiant mystic's use of it is exactly the same as the attention pointedly asked for by Renaissance writers such as Spenser and Milton; Weil rightly saw it as necessary to all serious art and to human life itself. This attention – Keats called it negative capability – is the primary job of the artist, who must focus justly and sympathetically on the characters and situations to be described: Murdoch's great generosity to her characters is surely a result of this focusing. The secondary job is the reader's, and is almost as difficult: to quell illusions and conventional expectations and concentrate on what is being described. The novel – in fact most art – has become such a throw-away thing in our lives that we are not really very good at this skill, especially when a faculty almost foreign to us is called for. To be read justly, Murdoch's novels, even the less successful ones, require serious looking of a sort we would rather shirk. This rigour is happily, or perhaps dangerously, countered in her style by the obvious delights of her manifold talent – brilliant plots, clever turns, comedic underpinning, riveting characters, the now sure expectation that someone will die and the audience's participation in guessing who (I have never been right on the first reading, and although in *The Sea, The Sea* I guessed James, I did not manage to guess the circumstances correctly and missed Titus completely). One never doubts in reading a Murdoch novel that one is playing, although the serious nature of the game can indeed be the puzzle.

Murdoch's realism allows her to play games, but not any longer to overcontrol the characters, in spite of occasional earlier tendencies to do so. Since *The Nice and the Good*, that pivotal work, she has become very good at creating characters whose richness the novel only indicates and yet convinces us of. We get an overwhelming sense of a world subject to chance, with characters dismayed that their efforts to perceive its working are constantly brought up short. When Brendan says 'one will never get to the end of it, never get to the bottom of it, never, never, never' (*Henry and Cato*, p. 339), he reflects the world on which both novelist and reader must brood. This world is not obviously morally comprehensible, but it is fed by a perpetual conviction that there is some distant undefinable good which is the object of frustrated human pursuit. That object is not the self nor the perfection of the self – neither the Victorian positivist cry, 'I want to be good!' of Gwendolyn Harleth in George Eliot's *Daniel Deronda* nor the calm, limiting reason of modern scientific man – but an external, infinitely far-removed, transcendent idea on which the attention can be fixed without gratification or reward. Murdoch would have us see the defeat of the cult of human personality, its narrowness, its restless and irresistible concentration on itself.

To put it another way, a real attention to the world and a transmission of the characters in action (by action Murdoch comprehends internal and external, private mental activity and public behaviour) will show, inevitably, how destructive self-concentration is, how difficult it is to change, how full of danger and remorseless the world is. Some readers have found the novels simply depressing, but I would suggest that this reaction involves a refusal of the radical idea of realism Murdoch has developed. Realism involves seeing what is there, and behind and informing what is there is reality itself, a true perception of the world sought humbly by the meagre handful of characters with whom this chapter began.

This reality is a development of Platonic thinking, and is an idea alien to the conventional literary realism beside which Murdoch sets her theories of the novel. The presentation of this radical idea as an adjunct to realism comprises Murdoch's most profound alteration or addition to what we normally understand as mimetic realism. In the nineteenth- and twentieth-century realist novel, reality generally resides in the historical trappings and reflections of the period in which the characters play out their dramas. In Murdoch's work, the discovery of reality is both historical (generally, contemporary England) and transcendent – a curious and radical intermeshing which defines her idea of the operation of love. The hopeless quest for reality, for knowledge, for the good, so informs the quotidian texture of her novels that they must be seen in a serious religious and ethical context, not to reduce them to didacticism, but to elevate and emphasize their seriousness and her particular contribution to the ailing novel of our time.

That the characters who seek reality and can be defined as good are quite minor is a central ingredient of Murdoch's realism – few of us will go beyond our mediocre and largely comfortable lives, so naturally a 'literary realist' novel must concentrate on people like us. Besides, no drama develops around any of these good characters: Tallis cannot evince the excitement of Julius King, and Bledyard and Brendan Craddock lead narrow, disciplined lives. Instead of presenting good characters as consolations – nice, ordinary, decent people who end the game reputably – Murdoch forces us to make distinctions between the nice and comfortable and the good and nearly impotent. The good characters whose aim is reality are not easy, attractive characters with whom we identify, they are not central to the hurricane plots, and they are often irritating. We do not like being told we will never get to the bottom of things, nor that we must abandon all our sustaining images. The good these characters represent and strive for constitutes a kind of Platonic *zetema* – an insight into the structure of the disease of egocentricity which our human thirst for power feeds. These characters quietly show the way, but we will not follow, not until realism has taught us enough about pain and failure. As Bledyard puts it, 'The gifts of the spirit do not appeal to the imagination.'

That reality is dark and unreachable is the central fact, but discriminating realism is its shadow. The task is being able to accept the world we live in and not to settle for the one we continually create by our infinitely capacious illusions. Here is a Murdoch character, Bradley Pearson, on the subject of the real world which our desire for consolation tries to suppress:

> That this world is a place of horror must affect every serious artist and thinker, darkening his reflection, ruining his system, sometimes actually driving him mad. Any seriousness avoids this fact at its peril, and the great ones who have seemed to neglect it have only done so in appearance. . . . This is the planet where cancer reigns, where people regularly and automatically and almost without comment die like flies from floods and

famine and disease, where people fight each other with hideous weapons to whose effects even nightmares cannot do justice, where men terrify and torture each other and spend whole lifetimes telling lies out of fear. This is where we live.                                         (*The Black Prince*, pp. 298–9)

# III

# UNCONSCIOUS GOOD AND
# THE SUCCESS OF EVIL

Problems of realism: Murdoch's decisions and disjunctions – Characters of unconscious good: Hugo Belfounder in *Under the Net*, Ann Peronett in *An Unofficial Rose* –
The brilliance of evil: *The Time of the Angels*

The austerity of this primary group of good characters is almost hidden
behind the crowded forefront of Murdoch's novels – that forefront which so
frequently dazzles, impresses and engages the reader. The inclination of this
difficult, stringent austerity to fight through for a place on the stage only
gradually impresses the reader; often it confuses his ability to discriminate, to
sort out the various pleasures and pains, to see the rigours of the serious task
Murdoch sets for her audience. The surface of the books thus tends towards
an unnerving duality of ironic comedic entertainment on the one hand, and the
dark, stringent possibility of an unnameable good on the other; and much
authorial energy is rather puzzlingly devoted to deflecting attention from such
a rare, hard-earned, disciplined knowledge of good. In this disjunction,
Murdoch is evidently combatting the contradictions inherent in literary
realism even as she serves the various mastering ideas she perceives as essential.
Although Brendan Craddock rightly insists that the human mind cannot get
to the bottom of things, the novels, and particularly the characters, cannot
resist trying, often with verve and even gaiety.

As a novelist dedicated to the principle that great art must draw its
existence from the real world, Murdoch must balance that world carefully
against formulated ideological tendencies. From her earliest interviews she
has shown herself hostile to novels dominated by an idea or myth, and she has
been extremely critical of certain of her own early novels where such domina-
tion occurred (*A Severed Head*, *The Italian Girl*). In both interviews and
critical essays, she adamantly argues that the artist must curtail his control,
power and egotism, and that the creation of authentic art requires the constant, alert withdrawal of the artist's personal will from his materials. She has

repeatedly pointed to Shakespeare as the creator of the greatest literary art because of his absolute ability to pay full attention to his characters and freely to see what is really and complexly going on, without the imprisoning control of his prejudices or ideologies. The history of Shakespearean criticism proves the justice of her claims: every intellectual fashion attached to an interpretation of his characters has shown itself eminently disprovable – the Tudor myth, orthodox Christianity, the Elizabethan world picture, etc., etc.

But the example of Shakespeare also draws attention to the problem of saddling Murdoch, this highly articulate, well-trained ideologue, with the various formulae she has all too generously supplied to scholars and critics of her work. Good and useful critics like A. S. Byatt in *Degrees of Freedom* (1965) and Rubin Rabinovitz in his essay, 'Iris Murdoch' (1976), for example, present their studies of the early work under the general impresa of source-hunting and presentation of ideological apparatus. Murdoch's own essays, especially 'Against Dryness' (1961) and 'The Sublime and the Beautiful Revisited' (1960), have also been rich in the articulation of a vocabulary and apparatus for judging her novels. But however clearly she has spoken of the theory of the novel, there remains a sharp and necessary distinction between her prescriptions and analysis of the novel at large and the achievements and reader impact of her own stylized and stylish, constantly developing novelistic mode. Although no critic can or should want to relinquish the vocabulary Murdoch has supplied us with, there is no doubt that her achievements and particular intentions exceed the limits of her theoretical writings; criticism of her novels must, I think, break loose from the compelling frame Murdoch has given, even if it means the projection of a criticism which sounds (and is) much less interesting than hers.

In Chapter II, Murdoch's addition of the idea of a higher Platonic unreachable good was seen as a radical enrichment of the realist tradition. This good forms a very sturdy and even ominous moral backdrop to novels which she also tries to keep in an uncontrolled quotidian milieu. But before returning to that subject, it is necessary to deal more precisely with the contradictions within realism itself, beyond how it is opposed artificially in our period by experimentalism. Realism in practice illustrates how strain occurs between an insuperable universal authorial urge towards ideology and the transmutations of ideas which take place when powerful characters take over the novels. In looking over the historical struggles of realism, it is possible to see how Murdoch's work both participates in the struggles of previous great realists and is made new and particularized by her own decisions and innovations, for certainly her work provides major innovations besides her perception of transcendent reality.

To review briefly: original polemical statements of realism in the nineteenth century (obviously and unquestionably the great century of the novel) fought hard to assert that the realist writer was, in Balzac's term, merely a secretary or recorder of society, and that the author's production was, as Stendhal expressed it, 'a mirror in the roadway' which accurately reflected the traffic of life. Essential to this kind of thinking is the automatic and necessary retreat of the authorial voice. The desired product was large, 'baggy', prolix, uncontrolled. At its best, the idea produces the marvellous heterogeneity of description and the open-endedness Murdoch so admires in such writers as Tolstoy and Dickens and sometimes so brilliantly achieves in her novels. Under the aegis of realism Murdoch is quite successful at keeping autobiographical material at bay, and only cumulatively, after reading many novels, can one deduce her tastes (for stones, spiders, the sea) or come to grips with the compelling moral task that her whole written *oeuvre* is in the process of constituting.

René Wellek has described nineteenth-century realism as

> a polemical weapon against romanticism . . . a theory of exclusion as well as inclusion. It rejects the fantastic, the fairy-tale-like, the allegorical and the symbolic, the highly stylized, the purely abstract and decorative. It means that we want no myth, no *Märchen*, no world of dreams. It implies also a rejection of the improbable, of pure chance, and of extraordinary events, since reality is obviously conceived at that time, in spite of local and personal differences, as the orderly world of nineteenth-century science, a world of cause and effect, a world without miracle, without transcendence. . . . The term 'reality' is also a term of inclusion: the ugly, the revolting, the low are legitimate subjects of art. Taboo subjects . . . are now admitted into art.            (*Concepts of Criticism*, 1963, p. 228)

Clearly we are far removed from the historical simplicity of this view, and Murdoch attunes herself to all the ironies of the advanced contemporary realist mode within which she writes. No longer do we replace the romanticism of myth and *Märchen* with the romanticism of positivist views of science. But this early historical view made the whole idea of realism feel straightforward and possible, inasmuch as what was excluded was vast and mysterious, what included scientific and materially real. Murdoch is extremely interesting in allowing no exclusion at all: her category of the real includes all internal and external objects and ideas. The haunting of the mind by myths, fairytales, *Märchen* and allegories is as important in determining human behaviour as is the newest scientific statement, and all people are as desperately subject to chance as to cause and effect. The large range of inclusiveness is necessary to Murdoch's sense of realism, and her invigorating innovativeness excites many readers even as it enrages others whose commitment remains, even in our cynical times, strangely positivist. Of course Murdoch does not treat all her themes and subjects as equal or true, but she is determined to show their various powers over the minds of her characters. Instead of having a mad, superstitious sprinkling of contradictory ideas, fantasies and compulsions, her novels attempt the task of discriminating, of showing how the tenure of certain ideas affects behaviour, how cause and effect operate, what power chance has.

The absolute emptying of the author's personality and power from the work of art seen as a loving transcript of nature is of course patently impossible and its early pretentions of success produced argument, cynicism and finally the current extreme and very faddish anti-realist position. Contemporary theorizers of realism such as George Levine and J. P. Stern (those who do not howl with fashionable laughter at the whole long-standing enterprise or give themselves over to attenuated versions of Lukács) point to a second powerful movement in realism, involving an authorial voice and an ethical assessment of character and event which try to impose some order or feeling for the organization of the whole. This realism of assessment aligns it more closely to ideas of form, and, in its longing for ethical statement and formal control, is essentially at odds with the autonomous realism that Murdoch so much admires and in some ways models herself on. All literary realism gains vitality from the fruitful contradictions of the necessary coexistence of these two modes. Every realist writer must make his decisions in balancing, choosing, modifying and being defeated by this fascinating problem, which is best stated by evoking the paradox of formlessness within form. As a result, every good realist is, contrary to most readers' expectations, formally interesting, and although we may be engaged by the pleasure and excitement of superbly created characters, as critics and readers we are nevertheless obliged to fix our attention on the formal methods by which the author achieves the power and authority to transfix. Because no writer can be totally realist (there is no human mirror in the roadway) and still impose form, the whole realist idea is fraught with irony, open to attacks of subjectivity of the sort which are now the semiotic subject matter of the post-modernist style, and productive of the very interesting idea of the failed work of art.

The naive ideal of realism as representing a world ultimately governed by scientific materialism had of necessity to be seen as a polemical idea, not easily translatable into character and event. Historically writers saw that concentrating truthfully on the complexly composed human character meant that something like exaggeration (Dickens, Proust, James) had to occur or idealization would take over. To put it more precisely, the honest authorial voice had to deal with the fact that, as Murdoch put it in 'The Sublime and the Beautiful Revisited', science (or philosophy) subscribes to an inadequate theory of personality, and the good realist must expand that theory and instruct us in a world larger than the one our conditioning has taught us to believe in. This problem of presenting human character cannot avoid immersion in the difficulties of authorial responsibility and involvement, narration, moral intrusion, point of view, closure – all the terms comprising our vocabulary of form. From early on, then, the realist has had to be ironic and vexed over how his power to impose form can be subservient to his ethical task as writer and yet deliver truth.

Ethical consideration is automatically a part of realism, or the whole task of the good artist is instantly debunkable, the ironies of structure so great that fictional literature must be seen only as fantasy, games, fun, utterly separated from useful instruction. A good realist work has all the mesmerizing power of a game, and is of course entertainment. Yet realism in all its manifestations is one of our culture's most versatile and enduring modes, and the greater the structural problems of a great realist writer – Shakespeare, Joyce, Dickens – the more the attentive reader perceives of the moral quest that is apparently at its centre. This moral component, which our culture used to know very well and experimentalism wishes it to forget, involves the old Horatian *dolce-et-utile* idea of the ethical usefulness of literature. The realist's strenuous and probably impossible task is to present a structure adequate to the quality of the world or of an individual character. Shakespeare, for example, was inadequate to *Hamlet*, Dickens to *Little Dorrit*, and yet these superb failed works achieve by their failure. In the realist enterprise, the positive and perpetually serious issue is the context of the struggle itself: the need to impose a version of form when it is impossible, even dishonest to do so.

To return momentarily to Murdoch's vocabulary, let us note that she again and again uses the word 'accidental' to try to convey the quality of structure, of autonomy in character and action she aims to produce by removing her will from the scene. In describing the power of the greatest nineteenth-century realists (or any great artist of any period) to pay adequate attention to the unbridled, limitless nature of real human character, she specifically applies the word 'love' – the love of a creative mind concentrating on something wholly outside of itself and its own satisfactions. This attribute of love allows random and 'accidental' behaviour in complex, constantly surprising characters. It is a heavily loaded moral term (to which I shall shortly return), but it can, in its stress on the quality of attention required, introduce the tensions inherent in formal and ethical realism as opposed to the heterogeneous, descriptive sort of realism which the first realist theorizers, and Murdoch herself, argue for.

Certainly no realist work can avoid such disjunctive tensions without considerable sleight of hand and absurd fantasizing. Murdoch's own case is full of productive contradictions. In an interview with Michael O. Bellamy (1977), Murdoch pointed out that a version of this disjunction is indeed what she dramatizes allegorically (my terminology) in opposing false form-making artistic characters to truth-telling religious figures, as with Julius King versus Tallis Browne (*A Fairly Honourable Defeat*, 1970), Randall versus Ann Peronett (*An Unofficial Rose*, 1962) and Jake Donaghue versus Hugo Belfounder (*Under the Net*, 1954). Here is her account:

art is a harmless activity, but it represents a sort of temptation, a temptation to impose form where perhaps it isn't always appropriate. This is why, in order to make closed works of art, you have to be a poet in the literary sense; poetry is a stricter mode of speech – its artifice is more refined. *Morality has to do with not imposing form, except appropriately and cautiously and carefully and with attention to appropriate detail*, and I think that *truth is very fundamental here*. Art can subtly tamper with truth to a great degree because art is enjoyment. People persist in being artists against every possible discouragement and disappointment, because it's a marvelous activity, a gratification of the ego, and a free, omnipotent imposition of form; unless this is constantly being, as it were, pulled at by the value of truth, the art work itself may not be as good and the artist may be simply using art as a form of self-indulgence. So I think in art itself there is this conflict between the form-maker and the truthful, formless figure.     (p. 135; my italics)

If morality in a realist observation and description of the world has to do with not imposing form, the temptation of subjective mimetic art as well as the proliferation of inadequate or bad artists become very great problems. Notice, however, that Murdoch adds the qualifying 'except appropriately and cautiously and carefully and with attention to proper detail', and that she does not in this interview posit the failure of the artist who commits himself to truth-telling. Rather, she is warning against the temptation to be self-indulgent and ruin the enterprise. It is interesting that in the three sets of dichotomous characters mentioned in the interview, the three 'artist' types – Jake Donaghue, Randall Peronett and Julius King – are bad artists and increasingly demonic, whereas the three 'religious' figures – Hugo Belfounder, Ann Peronett and Tallis Browne – by refusing form and organization altogether enter the narrow ranks of Murdoch's characters of the good with varying degrees of literary success. Later in this chapter I will take up Hugo and Ann; I have already discussed briefly in the last chapter the problem of Tallis's humble dullness versus Julius King's powerful charisma.

One must say that in her work there is no real artist and no real saint; in fact the inclination towards saintliness is generally more productive than that towards art. Time and again when an artist figure appears (and notice that of the three listed in her interview only one, Jake Donaghue, is a writer), he is at best in the process of learning, as is Bradley Pearson in *The Black Prince* and probably Charles Arrowby in *The Sea, The Sea*. More often he is caught in his own egotism, like Miles Greensleave in *Bruno's Dream*, or trying to deny it and giving up on his work, like Muriel Fisher in *The Time of the Angels*, Barney Drumm in *The Red and the Green*, and both brothers in *The Italian Girl*, to name only a few. The characters of the good do not aspire to art, and are either wholly concentrated on other things, like Hugo and Brendan Craddock in *Henry and Cato*, or maddeningly shapeless, like Tallis and Ann and, most irritatingly, Kathleen Drumm in *The Red and the Green*. Critics have eagerly picked up Murdoch's own dichotomy of the saint versus the artist, but it is quite clear that her use of characters who aspire to these types is careful and subtle. The route to the good (sainthood, although we are frequently told there are no saints) involves absolute attention to detail, self-denial, removal from the centre of life, and knowledge that there is no end in sight, no reward, nothing to be achieved; the route to creative truth (becoming an artist, *inter alia*) is equally arduous and involves the same goals: discipline, self-denial and failure.

As Murdoch points out in the interview quoted above, 'people persist in being artists against every possible discouragement and disappointment'. In *The Black Prince*, Arnold Baffin explains:

> I am always defeated, always. Every book is the wreck of a perfect idea.
> . . . An alternative would be to do what you (Bradley Pearson) do. Finish nothing, publish nothing, nourish a continual grudge against the world, and live with an unrealized idea of perfection which makes you feel superior to those who try and fail.                          (p. 139)

In *The Fire and the Sun* and elsewhere in her critical writings, Murdoch talks of the 'pierced' work of art and of the idea of failure. The realist dilemma in all of its ramifications certainly leads to such a conclusion, arguing as it does through anti-formal declarations and yet functioning within decisions involving a false control. The impossibility of doing what adherence to realism demands is a great and discouraging problem. Added to the barriers of egocentricity and self-indulgence, which Murdoch sees as tempting so many writers and which are overcome only by stern commitment to the truth, these complex negatives mean that the cards are stacked against success. And when Murdoch uses the word 'truth', she is penetrating into a region beyond generalized historical and social accuracy, although her loyalty to such accuracy is also total. Like the idea of the good, truth in art is double in focus: on the one hand, it demands full attention (what she calls 'love') to all details of every aspect and creature of the quotidian; on the other, it implies the Platonic truth she partially images in *The Black Prince* as the dark creative Eros whose relation to the absolute is shadowy but real.

In the disciplined activity of the serious artist, this creative Eros connects to the ethical demands of truth-telling. The moral will towards truth may exist in the artist, but inattention can easily create the mediocrity which is both typical of most works of art and the bane of the impulse towards good that art has at its best. Bradley Pearson theorizes succinctly:

> As I said at the beginning, any artist knows that the space between the stage where the work is too unformed to have committed itself and the stage where it is too late to improve it can be as thin as a needle. Genius perhaps consists in opening out this needle-like area until it covers almost the whole

of the working time. Most artists, through sheer idleness, weariness, inability to attend, drift again and again and again from the one stage straight into the other, in spite of good resolutions and the hope with which each new work begins. This is of course a moral problem, since all art is the struggle to be, in a particular sort of way, virtuous.

(*The Black Prince*, p. 154)

Only genius and wariness against one's 'swooning relationship to time' can produce a work of art adequate to the germinal idea in the artist's mind, but the characters in Murdoch's novels generally are too besotted by the distractions of ego to be real artists equal to the task. Bradley Pearson progressively enacts the exception, and the process of *The Black Prince* and even its final ironies are Murdoch's comment on the nature of the artist.

This is not the place for a full discussion of that brilliant and subtle novel, but a few references to it may enlighten this discussion. Both Bradley Pearson and his loved and hated rival Arnold Baffin are mediocre writers who in opposite ways misuse the truth-telling sanctity of great art. Bradley is neurotically blocked in writing his great novel, whose hero, as he conceives it, will be a heightened, successful, infinitely wise version of himself; Arnold writes at great speed, going in for vague, imprecise mysticism which he cannot be bothered to think out. Bradley, a neurotic egotist, and Arnold, lazy and inattentive, both fail as artists, lacking the virtuous other-centred discipline art requires, although Arnold's books are popular bestsellers. The process of Murdoch's novel teaches Bradley the pain and final joy gained from loss of self and loving attention to the world, and it shows him how deeply all fictional structures must be rooted in the experienced real world.

Murdoch's technique here is extremely sophisticated, and an excellent example of the complex range and disjunctive duality which characterize her best work. First, she herself estimates art as it occurs in the real world, in one of the major works of a real, and in her opinion the greatest, author – Shakespeare. For while no character in Murdoch's fiction is presented as a genuine artist, Shakespeare did exist and his magnificent achievement illuminates the world. (In neither her novels nor her theoretical writing does Murdoch suggest the presence of a great writer or artist in our time. On the contrary, she often suggests a decline in twentieth-century novelistic style and implies that we are late-born and losers in the grand sweepstakes of art.) When Bradley articulates what art is and ought to be, he does so by a peculiar and original analysis of *Hamlet*. Murdoch's standards are lofty, yet real and very much of the world.

*Hamlet* takes Bradley as a suddenly inspired analyst in two directions. One is towards real life in the world, enacted by his love for Julian, who is always seen as a shadow of Hamlet. This development is a clever elaboration on how literature can alter the human psyche. As Murdoch plays it, the word is made flesh and lives among us. This idea is spelled out on the rood screen in one of the churches where Bradley and Julian take refuge, Saint Cuthbert's in Philbeck Gardens: 'Verbum caro factum est et habitavit in nobis' (The Word was made flesh and dwelled among us). In this church, the Christian idea is metamorphosed from its now lost original meaning to identification with both the real (Julian, an ordinary girl) and an anterior mythology from the pagan past, transforming the church into 'the cave of some doom-obsessed sibyl or of one of the more terrible forms of Aphrodite. Powers older than Christ seemed to have casually entered and made the place their own.'

Hamlet becomes Julian; Bradley's ideas of art become enmeshed in the physically real, and for the first time he loves not an abstraction which reflects himself but a real external being. Serious mythological connections of the sort indicated by the Aphrodite-haunted church constitute the second direction in which Bradley's psyche and experience move through the contemplation of Shakespeare's play. This second direction connects to Murdoch's radical idea of the good, has the same firm external basis, and is strongly linked to ideas of form and objective explanation. Behind the entire novel is the controlling image of the Apollo-Marsyas myth, first presented in the Editor's Foreword, signed by P. Loxias (Luxius, a version of Apollo), and in Bradley Pearson's repeated addresses to his 'dear friend' throughout his autobiographical ruminations and theorizing on the nature of life and art. Bradley keeps referring to the creative Eros as a true god, a 'veiled deity', which, indeed, this Apollo figure and 'impresario' is for the reader-sleuth. It is not until Bradley's impassioned statement on *Hamlet*, halfway through the text, that this gradually unfolding, controlling myth begins to clarify itself, and the artist appears as a mortal Marsyas, driven to the 'ground and author of his being'. In the context of the myth, art is a dangerous enterprise involving both pain and punishment:

> How does he [Shakespeare] dare to do it? How can it not bring down on his head a punishment which is as much more exquisite than that of ordinary writers as the god whom he worships is above the god whom they worship? He has performed a supreme creative feat, a work endlessly reflecting upon itself, not discursively but in its substance, a Chinese box of words as high as the tower of Babel, a meditation upon the bottomless trickery of consciousness and the redemptive role of words in the lives of those without identity, that is human beings.                    (pp. 163–4)

The touching myth of Apollo and Marsyas is for Murdoch an enactment of the nerve, defeat, pain and congress with the dangerous divine which produces artistic adequacy and even triumph. The mortal, oboe-playing satyr Marsyas is the image of the accomplished artist who, not content with mere popularity or reputation, goes infinitely and mysteriously further and challenges the divine, the god of art himself. Of course he loses the contest;

the god Apollo is the greater musician, and Marsyas' punishment is to be flayed alive, his skin hung out to the winds in what Murdoch calls 'the dance of creation'. The pain and masochism invited by daring to write at a level challenging to the divine itself are part of the love the great artist must suffer in the act of creation:

> *Hamlet* is words, and so is Hamlet. He is as witty as Jesus Christ, but whereas Christ speaks Hamlet is speech. He is the tormented empty sinful consciousness of man seared by the bright light of art, the god's flayed victim dancing the dance of creation. . . . Shakespeare is passionately exposing himself to the ground and author of his being. He is speaking as few artists can speak, in the first person and yet at the pinnacle of artifice. How veiled that deity, how dangerous to approach, how almost impossible with impunity to address, Shakespeare knew better than any man. *Hamlet* is a wild act of audacity, a self-purging, a complete self-castigation in the presence of the god. Is Shakespeare a masochist? Of course. He is the king of masochists, his writing thrills with that secret. But because his god is a real god and not an *eidolon* of private fantasy, and because love has here invented language as if for the first time, he can change pain into poetry and orgasms into pure thought. . . . He enacts the purification of speech, and yet also this is something comic, a sort of trick, like a huge pun, like a long almost pointless joke. Shakespeare cries out in agony, he writhes, he dances, he laughs, he shrieks, and he makes us laugh and shriek ourselves out of hell. Being is acting. We are tissues and tissues of different *personae* and yet we are nothing at all. What redeems us is that speech is ultimately divine.
>
> (p. 164)

Shakespeare's translation of himself into the work of art involves the death of that self and such total attention that the fictional creation, Hamlet, becomes in his speech the now painfully but perfectly perceived suffering soul of his creator and of all defeated mankind. That Shakespeare is Marsyas – flayed, suffering, defeated, dead to the self (drawn out of himself as his skin flaps to the wind) – is Murdoch's image of the genuine artist against which are set Arnold's tepid, quasi-religious sentimentality and Bradley's fastidious refusal to participate in the painful and real human relations that surround him.

The parallel between the moral life and the central problems of art is essential in Murdoch's thinking:

> Can there be a *natural*, as it were Shakespearean felicity in the moral life? Or are the Eastern sages right to set as a task to their disciples the gradual total destruction of the dreaming ego?　　　(p. 155)

That this world is a place of *horror* must affect every serious artist and thinker, darkening his reflection, ruining his system, sometimes actually driving him mad. Any seriousness avoids this fact at its peril, and the great

ones who have seemed to neglect it have only done so in appearance. . . .
Does this background forbid *refinement* in morals? How often, my dear
friend, have we not talked of this. And shall the artist have no cakes and ale?
Must he who makes happy be a liar, and can the spirit that sees the truth
also speak it? What is, what can be, the range of the sufficiently serious
heart? Must we be always drying these tears, or at least aware of them, or
stand condemned? I have no answer to give here to these questions.

(pp. 298–9)


In the full truth of Murdoch's fiction, the eastern sages are right; Shakespearean tragedy is more central than the felicity of his comedies; and any artist
must indeed be troubled or ironic over his own love of Sir Toby Belch's cakes
and ale. The firmness of Murdoch's thought in this direction is clear, but it is
equally clear that she perceives fiction, and indeed human activity, as
comedy, replete with pleasure, enjoyment and fun in spite of its pain and
failure. Although Murdoch mythologizes the work of the artist, she is also
driven in the opposite direction, and Bradley Pearson will later tell Julian that
'no high theory about Shakespeare is any good, not because he's so divine but
because he's so human. Even great art is jumble in the end' (p. 201).

No more instructive juxtaposition can be given to illustrate Murdoch's
disjunctive double point of view than Bradley's rendering of Shakespeare's
*Hamlet* as an ideological, mythically perceived, pointed work on the one hand
and as a jumble on the other. The drive towards strong analysis is essential to
the novel's instructive usefulness. Yet Murdoch perceives the tyranny of this
as well as its necessity, and knows that all theories automatically limit the
scope of the enterprise by imposing a probably false human order on the
chaos and random nature of real, lived life. The realist paradox of formless
form manifests itself in Murdoch's work by her careful decisions to distract
and crowd the forefront with the pleasures and confusions of contingent life.
At the same time she presents with generosity and considerable sympathy
characters likely to be doomed by their lazy refusals to analyse justly, to
suspend their egotistical desires so that their moral judgements can operate.
They see hazily the function of the moral faculty, but take on its rigours only
when forced to by the terrible cause–and–effect pattern of their activity.

For the reader as for the characters this powerful ideological base is only
gradually and painfully perceived, as it becomes evident that one is not
having as much fun as one had thought in this free-floating world with its
high comedic moments and rich detail. The disjunction of surface, separating
the accurate and witty realist description of place and character from the hard
knowledge of truth and the higher Platonic unreachable good, is in fact an
artful device: Murdoch's overbalancing of the realist, 'accidental' material
charms the reader into moral rumination almost unawares, and the progres-

sive necessity for clear, hard thought persists almost unobtrusively through all the paraphernalia of literary engagement.

Murdoch's handling of the paradox is very cool and authoritative. She embraces the realist dilemma and expands it to her own use, elaborating the unanswerable and playing all the ironies. Whereas the mediocre artist may push through difficulties in order to console and belie, Murdoch tries to see clearly, accepts the discouragements and limitations imposed by paradox, and enriches her style by her calm acceptance of the structural problems (she compares them to those of the Demiurge in *The Fire and the Sun*) in representing a broadly inclusive view of the world and the psyche. She is an impressive imposer of form, the area of her most experimental work and of her greatest self-consciousness. The Shakespearean ironic sense of artifice which occurs when denouements are openly and boldly wrenched into place or closure would otherwise be impossible (*The Sacred and Profane Love Machine*, *The Nice and the Good*) is as much a part of her interpretation of form as is refusal of closure or denial of expected form (*The Black Prince*, *The Sea, The Sea*); with every novel we discover new control and original formal structure, sometimes in defiance of, sometimes in acquiescence to, reality.

It is nevertheless important to try once again to give an accurate vocabulary to the central paradox of Murdoch's particular bending of realist style. Her ideal of art contributes to, but is paler than, her idea of the good, for her artist characters use art as a branch of the intense moral longing they feel and must try to express in terms of human relationships. We have then a few characters of good, some of unconscious good, many who in small and often bizarre ways point to the good. The continuous presence and intensity of this idea of the good constitute an anterior idea against which the actions of almost all the characters can be seen. But the degree of control such a powerful idea must have is troubling to Murdoch's overriding realist theory of fiction as 'accidental' and autonomous, since any strong and permanent anterior idea leads, as do Plato's forms or Augustine's fig-tree, to the conditions of allegory, where the permanent, objective presence of such a single-minded absolute can become a powerful pattern-shaper.

Almost all of Murdoch's characters, partly because of their modern conditioning, are autoreflexive and therefore unable to fulfil the demanding requirements of the good. Thus the formative idea of the good remains in the background, but with its power intact. As a thinker Murdoch is firmly opposed to autoreflexivity (egocentricity), which she sees as the motive force behind multiform confusions and human failures, yet this dominant psychological mode is directly equivalent to the concept of autonomy for the characters in the novel which she so much admires. The ideological resting-place of her fiction is permanently fixed on an imageless good which she is prone to identify either with Plato or with the mystical *via negativa* of St John of the Cross. Running contrary to this is her adherence to open autonomy of character and action, an autonomy central to her realist commitment and to the creation of complex characters, images, action, excitement and the proliferation of complications. This disjunction – even eccentricity – in Murdoch's style is strong and positive, but not easily talked about or even clearly perceived, and even her best critics find it difficult to put a finger on what fascinates or enrages. The result is too often a falling back on clichés about inadequate realism ('people-don't-act-this-way') or philosophical analyses using principally Murdoch's own vocabulary from her book on Sartre or her critical essays. I would urge that the elaborations of realism itself, in its own paradoxes and as Murdoch handles it, constitute the problem.

★

Since most readers are absorbed on the first reading with the issue of verisimilitude, it is sensible to begin there, and to go at it simply and even naively. Even though readers who prefer experimentalism are apt to accuse her of being old-fashioned, ordinary or tedious, the scene Murdoch registers again and again is middle-class English society in the late twentieth century; the only exception is *The Red and the Green* (1965), her novel about the Irish Easter Rebellion of 1916; *The Unicorn* (1963), although geographically obscure, is not historically remote. She records what she knows very convincingly – her failed writers sound like failed writers, her wine-sellers like wine-sellers, her clergymen like clergymen, her stage-directors like stage-directors. Surely one of the many reasons for her extraordinary popularity has to do with this success; building on the known, she can push forward convincingly into whatever reaches of the human mind she chooses. So absorbing is her depiction of middle-class society that the reader is quickly drawn into the *Gestalt* of the novels, even when he loathes what might be called the bourgeois decadence (see especially *A Severed Head*, *A Fairly Honourable Defeat*, *An Accidental Man*) of that society's general structure.

For all Murdoch's instant success in engaging her readers, a problem nevertheless arises from her skill in depicting this particular sort of society and her way of handling it. Although almost all readers of the contemporary novel come from the socio-intellectual world she depicts, some recoil, objecting in a rather confused and sometimes violent way, either to what they call her unrealistic plots or to the way the characters act. Some even claim that she is not only unrealistic but even evil (an extraordinarily emotive word, but I have frequently heard it used) in seeing human characters so unidealistically, so relentlessly. This problem probably would not occur for a writer who had not instantly become extremely popular, particularly in Britain, where almost everyone seems to have read at least a novel or two by her. And certainly it would not be a problem to a novelist who handled realism more easily and conventionally, who made decisions different from and milder than those which so powerfully motivate Murdoch.

The negative criticisms that spring from her popularity must nevertheless be looked at with some care, because Murdoch presents herself as a novelist with a wide appeal, convinced that art is for everyone. It would be easy, and wrong, to dismiss the objections of many readers as only the result of an incompetent clientele. Although Murdoch is in many ways a rather mandarin writer, deserving more thought than a 'quick read' can deliver, the novel has always been a popular genre and remains so, except in the case of many experimental novels (Donald Barthelme is not as widely read as Saul Bellow). In choosing to write realist novels, Murdoch set out to enchant at a level Virginia Woolf so aptly called that of the common reader – now defined as the fairly well-educated middle-class person who has been reading novels for a long time. Murdoch's enormous tale-spinning talents, ironic sophistication and infinite creative fecundity are almost disadvantages – staler, drier tales might be more generally acceptable for the kind of truth-telling she advocates, but they would not lead to such great popularity. Or the same talents could be applied to more frivolous ends, and popularity (plus the facile happy ending) would not be lost. It is the peculiar combination of popular appeal and a serious, religious approach to reality that leads to the kind of criticism she often receives. Certainly there is no middle ground – readers either hate her work or love it.

The chief complaints – that people do not act like this and that the plots are contrived – haunt the history of criticism of all literature, and realism in particular. The never-ending quarrel about Dickens's characters is a good example: is he depicting grotesques for effect or is this method a kind of realism? The argument any defender of Dickens does and must use is based on his own experience of the astonishing and bizarre people he meets and deals with all the time. Self-protective psychology makes the popular audience want to deny certain kinds of character and action, and although we experience very strange types indeed and are constantly suffering from the odd behaviour of our fellows, we often want them removed from a fiction which captivates its audience and which we therefore wish to see as entirely enjoyable and escapist. Not recognizing this tendency in themselves, some readers too often claim irritably that such characters and actions do not exist. The general reader of fiction would be more correct to say that as fiction loses its breadth in the twentieth century, what is wanted is a new and consoling, even fantasy-laden idea of separation, between a naive 'realism', containing solid, clear and limited characters, and absurdist fiction, where the peculiar, intense and grotesque, with their particular truth, can be locked away and more tidily grouped together.

But is Murdoch so faulty in the enactment of verisimilitude? All people experience irrational and even mad behaviour from others, and are often guilty of it themselves, and we know perfectly well that it would be difficult to imagine something that no one would do. Because of the demands of form, novels are naturally and inevitably selective; they deal with periods of human activity which are automatically and necessarily highlighted and pulled into rapid sequence. Even more important than the fact that people do act at least as strangely as Murdoch's characters is our knowledge that in a world of chance any external and contingent thing can intrude and alter lives, at both dramatic and undramatic moments. Murdoch has been criticized for convenient manipulations such as Harriet Gavender's death in *The Sacred and Profane Love Machine*: a timely shooting by terrorists at a German airport. Certainly it is a useful plot device, but hardly unbelievable: in the Renaissance there was a cliché that death has ten thousand doors, and subject as contemporary man is to violent death and terrorism, we must acknowledge that there is nothing unrealistic about this death. All interferences of chance in fiction – Shakespeare is full of them: the plague in Mantua in *Romeo and Juliet*, the timing that hangs Cordelia but not Lear before the messenger intervenes – are of course authorial devices, but they are not unlike our experience of chance in the world. Nothing inconceivable or unreal happens in Murdoch's novels, although some readers disbelieve or fault her. I think their criticism of both character and event has another source not connected to the words they use; their indignation lies deeper, and the accusations of lack of realism hide a deeper disturbance.

The clearest sources of this criticism are conventions of social behaviour and, even more powerfully, of traditional novelistic expectations. Rocking the boat of convention in fiction is not a very eccentric or peculiar activity, but Murdoch's straining and shifting of conventional expectations are further stressed by major characters who are not only unheroic, but also adamantly wrong-headed and strongly unsympathetic from the beginning – an increasing tendency in her novels (for example, Austin Gibson Grey in *An Accidental Man*, Bradley Pearson in *The Black Prince*, Blaise Gavender in *The Sacred and Profane Love Machine*, Henry in *Henry and Cato*, Charles Arrowby in *The Sea, The Sea*). The result can be a kind of frustration, a feeling of deflection from a viable centre. The central issue, however, lies in Murdoch's basic decisions about realism. Most of the characters with whom the reader identifies either are shown finally to be rather awful and hence unsatisfactory or are destroyed – knocked down and beaten at least – by their often sympathetically self-concentrated actions. In one of Murdoch's typically distressing sequences, Julius King, the Iago figure in *A Fairly Honourable Defeat*, says to Tallis that Rupert, who struggled unsuccessfully to be good, died of vanity. Like Othello, he actually died of evil – Julius's more than his own – and although the reader knows that Julius's assertion is in a sense correct, it is also clear that Rupert is an almost admirable, and certainly a serious, striving character until he falls into a trap rigged by Julius. The reader's frustration results in dislocated outrage – is Julius to be hated or Rupert despised? This dislocation, this awful, sickening knowledge that anyone can be destroyed partly, even largely, through his own weakness is claimed by Murdoch as part of the real world; and from analogy with tragic theory and the actual practice of a play like *Othello*, it is definable as a deep human truth.

The novel as a bourgeois form does not accommodate itself easily to a scheme where *all* characters are so vulnerable to destruction and betrayal as in Murdoch's fictional world. Even in an early novel like *A Severed Head* (1961) where the wit of the game is more powerful than the interest in individual characters, the clever plot turns on alarming betrayals; and a solid, seemingly trustworthy character like Martin Lynch Gibbons's brother Alexander gives the already frenetic plot another foul, funny, shocking turn by running off with the rapacious Antonia, with whom he has had, we discover with surprise, a long, deceiving affair. Because the end of the game here is not death, this tale, with its Chinese boxes of deception within deception and its witty satire of the sophisticated, psychoanalysed upper middle classes, feels less devastating to many than it in fact is. Under the amusements of the game, the sliding untrustworthiness of all the characters projects the reader into a terrifying world where he learns the frailty and vanity of all people by laughing, if he can.

The real world is one that most characters in Murdoch's fiction would dodge, but the ineluctable working out of cause and effect in their personalities, as well as their past and present actions, keeps them on a firm track towards a conclusion that only chance, the uncontrollable, frightening, indifferent element that governs much of human destiny, can change. As in the case of untrustworthy characters, the reader often wishes to fight the authorial power that invokes the results of chance. The protest is not, however, against any legitimate failure of verisimilitude on Murdoch's part, but against something seen as unfaceable – not an objection to the author as a writer but to the world that she perceives, insists on and transmits in her novels. Murdoch writes to tell what she sees in the sophisticated bourgeois society she knows so well, and many readers recoil from the horror of a world we also know too well. Murdoch's revelation is brave, even audacious, venturing into areas we fight to avoid.

That there is always a disjunction between the fictional world and reality is a fashionable and interesting critical argument; all writers are subject to their own consciousness, and even the most objective realist is carried away on his own hobbyhorse. In the pendulum swing away from the objectivity demanded by the dominating influence of T. S. Eliot, combined with the author-centred tendencies of the experimental novel and the growth of French structuralism, it is now, probably rightly, seen as unauthentic to overlook the specific drive of the writer. This revision is particularly apropos in considering what causes positive and negative criticism, centred as both are on taste and private judgement. In *The Sovereignty of Good* (1970), a collection of three related philosophical essays, Murdoch argues against Stuart Hampshire and the school of contemporary British empiricists and linguistic philosophers, putting forward the Platonic idea of the inner activity of man which should be and often is directed towards externals (the good, God or lesser concrete universals) rather than the dazzling self and its will. One point is very useful: 'it is not at all easy to mount an attack upon this heavily fortified position; and as I say, temperament will play its part in determining whether or not we *want* to attack or whether we are content' (p. 16). The temperament that leads Murdoch to attack strongly defended points of view in both philosophy and fiction, her decision to use realism as an instrument for leading her readers towards a view of reality, her strong Platonic bent, all colour her style and affect how her world can be presented. Her decisions, both general and particular, are not only central to an interpretation of her work, but interesting and curious in themselves. That she is so widely admired is proof of the attractiveness of both her temperament and decisions, but more important are the consistency and feeling of continuous unravelling that her work possesses.

Because of Murdoch's sustained presentation of human personality as unreliable and ultimately unknowable to itself and others, the reader counterbalances almost automatically by being alert to the signs of the good which Murdoch so obviously believes in and transmits in so many ways. This balancing in itself is rather paradoxical, an apparent forcing into the forefront of something which appears only in the background, but although the good characters are few, the range of truth allotted to many, even most, characters pulls the idea of good out of the obscurity and negativity of much of the action. Although the most striking action is external, often projecting brilliant and striking scenes – the tower climb in *The Sandcastle*, Effingham in the bog in *The Unicorn*, Pierce and Ducane in Gunnar's Cave in *The Nice and the Good*, etc. – its effect is internal, and much of the work of the novels is done in the perceiving, thinking, struggling mind. In this sense, Murdoch shows her novelistic affiliation with Henry James: that characters are subject to the infinite reverberation of every moment of their experience, that human beings are constantly haunted by value judgements they apply to all their activities, and that these judgements have both positive and negative poles are assumptions James and Murdoch share in their generally dissimilar styles.

For Murdoch, as for James, the negative pole dominates, and the defeat of good by evil – a fairly honourable defeat as she ironically calls it – is almost commonplace. Yet the yearning towards the good and its power over the often discriminating imagination of the characters when it occurs give it a primacy in Murdoch's world that makes its assertion crucial to our feeling about the novels. Its stringency, difficulty and remoteness from the centre where life is lived do not reduce the deep attention it elicits, and the unromantic part of the reader's response acknowledges its often touching and fascinating presence. One of the aspects of continuous unravelling in Murdoch's novels is her concentration on ways of talking about and revealing the good, the perception of the true, reality – the three are close to synonymous.

Herein lies her peculiarity within the frame of verisimilitude. The contrast between good and evil, abstract ideas given a local habitation in the novels, means that moral matter is constantly present, lying in wait as it were, but without solution or ease, and certainly uncomfortable in a mirror image of the secular contemporary world. Perhaps the best way of seeing the problem in detail is to move from a concentration on the gnosis of the characters of conscious good to the peculiar difficulties Murdoch encounters in handling characters of unconscious good, and to contrast these with the evil so startlingly and powerfully depicted in *The Time of the Angels*.

One feels that the characters of unconscious good ought to be as useful and instructive to the reader as those of conscious good. They occur in early novels, where Murdoch's talent and successes often pale in comparison to her mature style, and one character on the fringe of this unconscious good – James Tayper Pace in *The Bell* – strikes me as actually responding unconsciously to a wicked end: the rejection of another person. Murdoch is apparently of two minds about consciousness, since few morally active people are genuinely unconscious of the quality of their activity, as her realist inclination reflects. Unconscious good contrasted to conscious, intellectualized evil, as in *The Time of the Angels*, comes off rather wearily and ambiguously, and it is as well that Murdoch has left this mode behind. Indeed, the contrast between unconscious good and conscious evil asserts the primacy of the latter and gives it an unjustified power.

The characters of unconscious good – Hugo Belfounder in *Under the Net* (1954) and Ann Peronett in *An Unofficial Rose* (1962) – nevertheless provide an insight into what Murdoch understands by moral activity. Hugo's spontaneous refusal to believe that he theorizes and his natural attention to the humble minutiae of the world have the same moral import as Ann's continuous inability to express her will and her playing a profound and, from the point of view of survival of the ego, questionable role as a scapegoat and sacrificial victim for her husband Randall and daughter Miranda. Both Hugo and Ann have an access to good that is theirs just from long habit or obedience or simple inheritance, and in this respect they are unlike almost all the other characters in the novels, with the possible exception of Tallis.

Hugo is the more successful characterization of the two, because of his buoyancy and the fact that he stimulates creativity and a fruitful, if not wholly admirable, theorizing about the nature of art and reality in the two other most significant characters in the novel, Jake Donaghue and Anna Quentin. His simple, monolithic presence gives him the reliability that only the tiny handful of Murdoch's good characters possess – a reliability which has nothing to do with consoling sentiments but with a firm movement forward in a consistent direction towards the rigours and renunciations required by the perception of reality. Anna responds to what she instantly and instinctively sees in him (Hugo tells Jake that she took just one look: the automatic transfer from sex to symbolism is obvious in this novel) by loving him hopelessly and besiegingly. Her unavailing love can be seen as the symbolic longing of the plaintive human soul for the unattainable good, illustrated by her final beautiful song on the radio, often seen by critics as parallel to the negress's song in Sartre's *La Nausée*.

The more theoretical Jake had originally seen Hugo as a force against which to pit his own abstract intelligence in a quasi-Platonic dialogue, later polished, altered and published in book form under the title *The Silencer* which becomes for Jake a failed important document. But although Jake had first used Hugo as a whetstone for his own articulation, he finally recognizes Hugo's otherness, his pure functioning as a symbol of major dimension. Hugo represents inarticulate intelligence which exists as a catalyst but does not participate in language. A famous (against his will: Hugo does not seek either fame or money, both of which automatically flow towards him) maker of fireworks and films, the dazzling Hugo retreats finally to obscurity, a God figure created by Jake and Anna, withdrawing quietly from participation and immersing himself in the simplicity of the watchmaking trade, concentrating on the detailed, real and subtle workings of the instruments of time. But even his retreat fails to cut him off from the elaborating, fecund, overly creative mind of Jake, for whom he becomes an even greater symbol:

> I began thinking about Hugo. He towered in my mind like a monolith: an unshaped and undivided stone which men before history had set up for some human purpose which would remain forever obscure. *His very otherness was to be sought not in himself but in myself or Anna.* Yet herein he recognized nothing of what he had made. He was a man without claims and without reflexions. Why had I pursued him? He had nothing to tell me. To have seen him was enough. He was *a sign, a portent, a miracle.* Yet no sooner had I thought this than I began to be curious again about him. I pictured him in Nottingham in some small desolate workshop, holding a watch in his enormous hand. I saw the tiny restless movements of the watch, I saw its many jewels. Had I finished with Hugo?
>
> (p. 268; my italics)

When immediately after this speech Jake follows his persistent need to see this being beyond articulation, he finds that he too, the man of words, is like Hugo deprived of the means of communication. He rushes to Hugo's flat on Holborn viaduct, an astonishingly elegant, ill-guarded nest full of *objets d'art*, the debris of human creativity (only the bedroom reflects Hugo's Spartan taste), but finds it full of roof starlings that had come in through the open windows. Jake finds among other things letters from Anna and Sadie, packets of money and a pearl necklace probably bought as a present for Sadie. Sadie is the spirit of materialistic intelligence Hugo had vainly courted in the sustained symbolic round dance which is one of the organizing structures of this novel: Hugo (the good) is loved by Anna (the richly illusionist human soul) who is loved by Jake (the theorizer, pattern–maker, intellectual artist) who is loved by Sadie (materialistic intelligence) who is loved by Hugo who renounces materialism and withdraws. All the characters relate to Hugo apart from this circular, frustrated, erotic situation, and his withdrawal leaves a void in the human organization. The sense of the removal of a great presence, combined with the ubiquitous soiling by bird dung of the once elegant flat, forms an image of the desolation of an abandoned world. But Hugo, although gone from the scene in which life must be lived and where the socialist politics of Lefty will take over, still exists elsewhere, as an apprentice watchmaker in Nottingham. Jake attempts to communicate with this 'portent', but finds himself without words: 'In the end I just drew a curving line across the page, and signed my name at the bottom of it, adding the address of Mrs Tinckham's shop' (p. 271). Nevertheless Hugo had been the trigger for the book of words and theory. His copy of *The Silencer*, left behind with everything else, goes with Jake as he sets out towards the excellence and use of himself he had previously dodged.

That Hugo was a catalyst rather than an active theorizer in the discussions he and Jake had had about the nature of reality, and that he never presents a clear theoretical explanation of anything, in a way argue for the power of being as opposed to becoming. It was an old argument for Socrates and his rivals, that of unconscious being as opposed to the articulate spawning of image and illusion which characterizes Plato's sophist, the theorizer, the person who is bound as Plato was, as the novelist is, as the character Jake is, as the novel reader automatically must be (why else do we read such illusionist stuff?) to words and created symbols instead of looking at reality itself. Neither Jake nor Anna *sees* Hugo; both create a mythic structure around themselves, and the myth becomes greater than its source.

As we read *Under the Net*, however, we do not see Hugo as a god or as the embodiment of one of Plato's forms, but as a real character full of odd, worldly successes. Even here symbolism stalks him. An unintentional impresario, he presents first fireworks and magic devices like Belfounder's Domestic Detonators (miraculous means of breaking through barriers), then turns brilliantly to the fantasia of a film company called Bounty Belfounder. His success with these bright, ephemeral modes introduces the problem of lack of duration which will become so compelling in Murdoch's fiction. He renounces the bedazzlement of the momentary fireworks or the fleeting images on the screen for watchmaking, for a new concentration on continuous time and hence duration. Hugo's activities are to him humble undertakings, and both the money that automatically falls into his hands and the symbolism in which he is immersed are external and a matter of indifference to him. For him, as for Plato, truth is a small, contained thing.

Hugo's primary characteristic, like all Murdoch's good characters, is renunciation, and like many of them he leaves the scene completely. Renunciation and withdrawal are necessary in a world we will never get to the bottom of, as Brendan Craddock had put it. Hugo's explanation for his retreat is typically humble:

> 'Well, I don't really believe in private enterprise,' said Hugo, 'at least I *think* I don't. I'm so bad at understanding these things. And if one's in any doubt about a racket one ought to clear out, don't you think? Anyhow, while I had the factory I just couldn't help making money, and I don't want that. I want to travel light. Otherwise one can never understand anything.'
>
> (p. 251)

Hugo is an absolute, the thing itself, not a synthesis of the peculiar means and cumbersome devices human beings use to get there: thus neither Anna's theatre with her 'oriental junk' nor Jake's spurious creation from their conversations, *The Silencer*, are recognizable by Hugo. This essential difference between the absoluteness of the thing itself and the struggling products of mankind is demonstrated in an earlier part of the same conversation with Jake:

> 'No, *she* [Anna] was interested all right,' said Hugo, 'but *I* wasn't really interested. And then she would introduce all that oriental junk, heaven knows where she got it from!'
>
> 'She got it from you!' I said with as much incisiveness as I could put into a whisper.
>
> 'That's nonsense!' said Hugo. 'She may have picked up some vague notions from me, but that didn't add up to *that*.'
>
> 'Why did you act in the mimes then if you thought the whole thing was bad?' I asked.
>
> 'You're right; I oughtn't to have,' said Hugo, 'but I did it to please her – and after all she did seem to be *making* something there.'
>
> 'Yes,' I said, 'she can create things.'
>
> 'You can both create things, I mean you and Anna,' said Hugo.
>
> 'Why do you say it like that?' I asked.
>
> 'It just strikes me,' said Hugo. 'I never made a thing in my life,' he added.
>
> (p. 250)

Indeed, Hugo's frame of being resists theory and creativity: he plans to mend watches purely as a trade. When Jake, the creative theorizer, asks wildly, 'And what about the truth? . . . What about the search for God?', Hugo replies, 'What more do you want? . . . God is a task. God is detail. It all lies close to your hand. . . . You're always *expecting* something, Jake' (p. 258)

To expect nothing, to avoid theorizing, to renounce brief dazzlement and imagery, to abjure distracting magics are the stable qualities of Murdoch's character of the good. However, although Hugo is marvellously effective (and a brilliant pretype for Tallis), his power in the book is seriously challenged by the verve and development of Jake as an attractive, finally positive character who may work in the right direction. Jake is interestingly in process, testing the means whereby he can achieve the end of knowing reality, whereas Hugo despite his apparent confusion symbolizes the end itself. Much of what we learn from Hugo comes indirectly, however, and he lacks dynamism except in the minds of others who take flame from his unconscious being.

Ann Peronett in *An Unofficial Rose* is no doubt the 'unkempt . . . English unofficial rose' of the title, from the Rupert Brooke couplet used as epigraph. Although consistently handled as one of Murdoch's characters of the good, her renunciations and negatives mix curiously with her frequent muddy attempts at comprehension and her defeated struggles to assert a will she does not fully possess. After Randall's final defection, marriage to Felix Meecham would mean an access to life, but Ann's negative handling of the crucial scenes cuts her off from it:

> If she had only not for that instant tried him with the words of denial everything might have been different. Yet had she not merely and exactly done as she had decided beforehand she would do? And had he not acted as she must have known he would act? It was scarcely a matter of 'motives'. She had had no motives. Her whole life had compelled her. They had each of them their destiny. . . . She had let go of the exceedingly dear and precious Felix whom she loved and needed with all her heart, almost, it seemed to her, because of a naked meaningless incapacity to take what she wanted.                                    (pp. 333–5)

Ann mourns her painful failure, and even when she realizes how the fiendish child Miranda has orchestrated the whole scene, she retreats to a sad recognition based on Douglas Swann's unctuous earlier claim that 'being good is a state of unconsciousness':

> She was not framed for recognising, let alone for grasping, her own felicity. In the end perhaps, for her, not knowing was better than knowing. Felix would never understand either. But to be understood is not a human right. Even to understand oneself is not a human right. . . . Real compassion is agnosticism; and we must be compassionate to ourselves too. Tasks lay ahead, one after one after one, and the gradual return to an old simplicity. She would never know, and that would be her way of surviving.                                    (pp. 339–40)

There is a ring of truth about this recognition – no doubt it *is* true, and it certainly is consistent with what a clear mind like Brendan Craddock's delivers in *Henry and Cato* – but it links uncomfortably with what Randall had said about Ann early in the novel:

> She just ruins me. She – she destroys my footholds. . . . Ann has no will. She saps my energy. . . . For someone else she may be a bloody little angel. But for me she's the destroyer, and the destroyer is the devil. . . . I need a different world, a formal world. I need form. Christ, how I fade! . . . Yes, yes, form, structure, will, something to encounter, something to make me *be*. Form, as this rose has it. That's what Ann hasn't got. She's as messy and flabby and open *as a bloody dogrose*. That's what gets me down. That's what destroys all my imagination, all the bloody footholds. Ah well, you wouldn't understand. . . .      (pp. 38–9; my italics)

Later Randall pities the rejected Ann, but still sees her as 'deadeningly structureless', as 'the incarnate spirit of the Negative' (p. 77).

Tallis too lacks structure and vitality, but in Ann there is no adequate counterbalance comparable to Tallis's decisive and knowledgeable deeds. For all her manifold decency, her kindness to Penn, her courtesy to Emma, she is somehow pallid in interest (no other good character is) and faded like her once blazing hair. Like Tallis, she is poised against a demonic character, her husband Randall, whose selfish will sweeps all before him, and secondarily against Randall's 'angel of unrighteousness', the golden, meretricious Lindsay Rimmer. Frequently she feels victimized, as indeed she is, and resents the scapegoat role she is forced to play – in some obscure way she even bears the blame of others for their son Steve's death. Although a character of unconscious good without real will or self-supported structure, she does have enough will to wish for both, and there is something rather whining about her:

> Ann had never really had the conception of doing what she wanted. The idea of doing what she ought, early and deeply implanted in her soul, and sedulously ever since cultivated, had by now almost removed from her the possibility, even as something *prima facie*, of a pure self-regarding movement of will. She felt, at the moment, the lack of this strong uncomplicated machinery.      (p. 290)

Ann's characterization raises the question of how a good character is handled even more strongly than the allegorical problem of Tallis, because she is indeed deadening, and Randall is in this respect right about her. Inherent in this less than successful good character is the problem of form in general: Murdoch has chosen to take all form away from Ann, and she becomes so insubstantial that the reader justly asks why on earth she moves Felix Meecham or Douglas Swann to passion.

The structure pivots around Ann's character, and that the simple English dogrose, the unofficial rose, rather than the impressive hybrids the Peronett nursery (the world) produces, should signalize this odd-girl-out, focuses the conclusion sharply. But if the structure and machinery of the self give form to the personality, as Randall had indicated, there is an inseparable contradiction in making Ann a major character and hingeing the whole novel's organization on her. She is the only good character in Murdoch's fiction who is so much at the centre, given such dominant relationships with such a wide range of other characters, and although she can at the end renounce her own happiness and retreat to the 'old simplicity' where she is a faded, hardworking presence, holding together the idea of family for Miranda and Randall (should the latter care to return), and continuing to keep the nursery going, that old simplicity does not give her the initial complex structure required by the idea of form in a novel. Murdoch is successful in contrasting the early days of Ann's marriage to the present, but no amount of scrutiny produces any symptom or proof of attractiveness, not to mention the power fictional centrality demands.

It is symptomatic of Murdoch's characters of the good that either they are structureless themselves (Hugo, Tallis, Ann, Uncle Theo) or they renounce conventional structures or organized images (Brendan Craddock at the end, Bledyard on mimesis, Hugo again). They are also finally and permanently separated from the relationships erotic love can bestow, and in Murdoch's world this alienation is apparently one of the prices of clarity. They are not generally without power, however, except for Uncle Theo, who is peripheral to the list. Even the most impotent, Tallis, is powerless only at the ordinary, humdrum level of life. Ann is impotent throughout – even something so minor in her depiction as the mourning for her dead mother-in-law, Fanny, is enervatingly done and lowering to others. One could answer that this dreary behaviour is as it should be, especially since one of Murdoch's central points is that our sense of duration is weak – we recover too quickly from our brief glimpses of reality, which are best delivered by death: 'Ann's gentle, transparent, more reflective personality kept Fanny disconcertingly alive. Ann's consciousness of the matter seemed to leave no place for consolation, for that symbolic second slaying of the dead. But then Ann was unhappy and correspondingly unfair' (p. 59). Her gentle awareness destroys the dangerous idea of consolation, one of the evils of Murdoch's world, one of the easy devices for reducing our consciousness of the real. Why then does it not really work?

First, in this case, because the book opens with Fanny's funeral and we have no sense of her as a real character; Ann's mourning for her is as vague and structureless (and here without an objective correlative for the reader) as the rest of her activity. This example leads, of course, to the problem of vagueness in general. At crisis points like Randall's carefully planned scene,

Miranda's fit, Felix's proposal, she is not very convincing. Even shouting a bit at Randall does not classify as significant behaviour. And when her failures of energy combine with wistfully bitter resentment because she lacks the machinery of will, we have a character with no strength to call other characters or the reader to her. Compared to her rival for Felix Meecham's love, the French Marie-Laure whom we know only through letters, she lacks passion and vitality, and it is hard to pity Ann when Felix sails off to her French competitor.

The irony consists in the fact that novels are born of the inclination towards structure and form, and in order to be placed so centrally, Ann must have more to do with those qualities than she has power to enact. She represents the idea of the marriage bond, negative though it may be; the principle of work and continuity that keeps the nursery, originally the creative idea of Randall, running; the English ideal of womanhood which Felix prefers to the French sexuality of Marie-Laure, the woman in need of love and commitment. Ann's divided attention and subsequent flaccidity in these roles are indeed deadening, but that is largely because the real action is inevitably among the stylish hybrids of the world – Lindsay Rimmer and Randall, by contrast, are very formal, selfish, successful fictional products. Ann's centrality is only a chimera, and the world that thronged round her at Randall's absence and later request for a divorce (Felix, Mildred, Miranda, the Swanns, Emma Sands, Hugh) must all leave her to the lonely simplicity of the other good characters in Murdoch's fiction. Ann has tried too hard to be a participator: the plot demands that she show some will, and she does, but it is not coupled with any other quality of survival. Probably it should not be there at all. And yet she represents a reality and a good which Randall sees as opposite and alternative to his highly structured, beautiful fantasy with Lindsay and Emma:

> Then in a second it occurred to him that simply by saying 'Ann' he could make his whole palace of dreams vanish away and end the days of soft en-slavement perhaps forever. If he but spoke her name they would magically disappear, the cushions and the sherbet, the tinkling bells and the gay-plumaged birds, the golden collars and the curving blades. As if to remove a terrible temptation he slowly let the telephone fall to his side.     (p. 144)

In *The Sea, The Sea*, the retired stage director, Charles Arrowby, gives a brief analysis of the middle state in which the drama of life is played:

> Emotions really exist at the bottom of the personality or at the top. In the middle they are acted. This is why all the world is a stage, and why the theatre is always popular and indeed why it exists: why it is like life, and it is like life even though it is also the most vulgar and outrageously factitious of all the arts. Even a middling novelist can tell quite a lot of truth. His

humble medium is on the side of truth. Whereas the theatre, even at its most 'realistic', is connected with the level at which, and the methods by which, we tell our everyday lies. This is the sense in which 'ordinary' theatre resembles life, and dramatists are disgraceful liars unless they are very good. (p. 33)

Murdoch is always suspicious of drama (her own plays are ironic and peculiarly unrealistic) and of the trick-filled, actual theatrical productions of even Shakespeare whom she consistently reveres as a great truth-teller. The emotions of the top or bottom of the personality are the ones that only the few very great playwrights can produce in an attempt to tell the truth. 'Even a middling novelist' can get farther than all but the greatest dramatist because he has access to these emotions through his ability to reproduce the mind itself, to indicate the extended being of man. In general, however, the central action of a novel, like that of an ordinary play, is acted in the middle, the area of lies and role-playing; dramatically structured personalities are its chief actors. The good characters live offstage as it were, and create in themselves no drama, no scenes.

The middle range of characters who so densely and fascinatingly occupy the centre stage of Murdoch's work, however, who spin out the action through the expression of their wills and fantasies, contains many who are closely related to the idea of the good. These are spiritual strivers who manage goodness to a limited degree, who try and fail, or who are in process – characters like the touching Pattie O'Driscoll in *The Time of the Angels*, Peter Saward in *The Flight from the Enchanter*, Denis Nolan in *The Unicorn*, Edgar Demarnay in *The Sacred and Profane Love Machine*, Crystal Burde and Arthur Fisch in *A Word Child*, to name only a few. In every novel are characters who in spite of all odds point to the good, even though most characters who try fail in their quest for real vision. Besides the strivers, almost all characters, no matter how terribly blinded by their preoccupation with the self, fumble towards good: apart from three extraordinary characters – Carel Fisher in *The Time of the Angels*, Julius King in *A Fairly Honourable Defeat* and Austin Gibson Grey in *An Accidental Man* – I can think of no one whose instinctive longing is not towards a just sorting out of things.

Sometimes we see only a thumbnail sketch of a character who is evidently on the right track in the contemplation of reality: the Abbess in *The Bell*, for example, or Max Lejour, the Plato scholar in *The Unicorn*, both of them disciplined by concentration on frameworks beyond themselves. But more likely external discipline or religion produce failure, as in the example of Montague Small in *The Sacred and Profane Love Machine* (he can use the oriental devices of meditation with astonishing technical success, but it leads to no enlightenment, no alteration of his guilty self), or only partial glimmerings of success, as in the case of crazy Nigel Boase in *Bruno's Dream* or earnest

Michael Meade in *The Bell*. It rapidly becomes clear that there are no formulae for grasping the good, although disciplines like single-minded devotion to study, or religion – Christianity or Buddhism – can, if used correctly, help.

It is just to call Murdoch a religious writer in a way that past traditions of our culture would recognize, but whereas Chaucer or Spenser or Richardson or George Eliot knew that they were placing their theologically inclined characters against an accessible background, obviously none is generally available now, and the task of the religious writer is to describe what we have and to point in a certain direction. This task has led Murdoch to the creation of characters of the good, but as the middle of life must be her realistic concentration, it is useful to see how she projects religious possibilities. The loss of religious culture is what Murdoch's characters are talking about as they over and over again face the death-of-God syndrome, frequently blaming their failures and frustrations on the withdrawal of the idea of a personal God who evidently used to look after things, from the surface of behaviour to the deep level of being. Dorina Gibson Grey's brief rumination in *An Accidental Man*, when she feels lonely and freshly rejected by Ludwig just before her accidental death, illustrates the centreless longing for the functions the Christian God was supposed to have performed:

> If only there were some recourse, somewhere I could go to get out of the mess and nightmare of my failed life, somewhere where I could rest and drop the burden of my sin, as I used to imagine when I prayed when I was a child. Is there any prayer or place of gaze still left which is not a mere enchantment? There should be such, even now, even without God, some gesture which would bring automatic world-changing wisdom and peace. *Pliez les genoux, pliez les genoux, c'est impossible de trop pliez les genoux.* Who had said those beautiful words to her and what did they mean? Then suddenly she remembered. It had been her skiing instructor at Davos. Not a holy man after all. So that was all it was, another senseless fragment of ownerless memory drifting about like a dead leaf.                    (p. 309)

The secularization of a world in which one is more likely to ski than pray lays the human psyche open to the invasion of whatever substitute ideas occur to it. This problem has always been major in Murdoch's work, but is especially so since she used *The Time of the Angels* (1966) as a vehicle to point to its worst devastations.

From its opening gambit, with the black maid, Pattie O'Driscoll, stumbling over a copy of Heidegger's *Sein und Zeit*, *The Time of the Angels* explores the contemporary and final breakdown of Christianity, and exemplifies some of the subsequent ego-perverted developments. When at the beginning of Chapter 15 Pattie, a naive, disorganized repository of highlights of western culture, reads from the open translation of *Sein und Zeit* of the attempt of the

Heideggerian ego, the *Dasein*, to devour the idea of death existentially, she is filled with obscure dismay:

> She read [the words], or rather it was not reading since they meant absolutely nothing to her. The words sounded senseless and awful, like the distant boom of some great catastrophe. Was this what the world was like when people were intellectual and clever enough to see it in its reality? Was this, underneath everything that happened, what it was really like? (p. 165)

There are three theorizers in the novel – Carel and Marcus Fisher and the Anglican Bishop – three intellectuals of the sort Pattie is shudderingly thinking of. Their theories share no common ground except secularization and demythologizing, and all three ironically approach Murdoch's own serious thought to some degree.

The Bishop is a very minor character, appearing only once with Marcus and Norah Shadox-Brown, to discuss the Carel problem. His interview represents an important trend in contemporary, secularized religious thought, but carries it far out of the comfortable area of secular ideas into a devastating mysticism. For him, morality and theology serve the same initial purpose, and he believes that Marcus, who insists so strongly and proudly that he is not a Christian, directly serves the progress of a new theology which has jettisoned the old Trinitarian symbols. The Bishop claims that we live in an interregnum where the idea of a personal God must be replaced by a darker and deeper spiritual concept. The unimaginable, impersonal God gives no reward ('Obedience to God must be obedience without trimmings, an obedience, in a sense, for nothing' – a very Murdochian concept) and is at the heart of a new, non-naive longing for the transcendent. Most of his argument must be quoted:

> It [the interregnum] is a time when, as one might put it, mankind is growing up. The particular historical nature of Christianity poses intellectual problems which are also spiritual problems. Much of the symbolism of theology which was an aid to understanding in earlier and simpler times is, in this scientific age, simply a barrier to belief. It has become something positively misleading. Our symbolism must change. This after all is nothing new. It is a necessity which the Church has always understood. God lives and works in history. The outward mythology changes, the inward truth remains the same. . . . No mystic has ever thought [that the religion *is* the myth], and whom can we better believe? 'Meek darkness be thy mirror.' Those who have come nearest to God have spoken of blackness, even of emptiness. Symbolism falls away. There is a profound truth here. Obedience to God must be an obedience without trimmings, an obedience, in a sense, for nothing. . . . It is a time of trial. . . . Many are called but few are chosen. The Church will have to endure a

very painful transformation. And things will become worse yet before
they are better. We shall sorely need our faith. But the Lord will turn again
the captivity of Zion. . . . I am not speaking of course about a person . . . a
person could be dispensed with. Indeed must be dispensed with. What we
have to experience is not the destruction but the purification of our beliefs.
The human spirit has certain deep needs. Do not misunderstand me when I
say that morality is not enough. It was the mistake of the Enlightenment to
imagine that God could be characterized simply as the guarantor of the
moral order. But our need for God is something which transcends morality. The slightest acquaintance with modern psychology shows us that this
is not a slogan but a fact. We are less naive than we were about goodness.
We are less naive than we were about sanctity. What measures man as a
spiritual being is not his conventional goodness and badness but the
genuineness of his hunger for God. How does Jehovah answer Job? 'Where
wast thou when I laid the foundations of the earth?' is not an argument
which concerns morality.                                    (pp. 101–2)

Norah Shadox-Brown punctuates this discourse with vigorous, forthright
insistences on morality and Christ, which the abstract Bishop will not buy.
He not only participates in the theory of demythologizing and depersonaliz-
ing Christianity, but he is also separated from human striving, simple morality, life in a world his pastoral function should attach him to. He goes very far
indeed in giving Carel, the subject of the discussion, a kind of identification
by implication with mysticism of the *via negativa* sort, justifying his loss of
faith and eccentric, evil behaviour as part of a step forward for the soul, in
keeping with the historical rejection of such symbolic ideas as Christ. Thus a
good theory can be wrongly applied, or more precisely, theory again shows
its inadequacy.

   Marcus, a schoolmaster who has taken time off from his school to write a
book to be entitled *Morality in a World without God*, is upset and shocked at the
Bishop's theological vagaries: 'But suppose,' he said to the Bishop, 'suppose
the truth about human life were just something terrible, something appalling
which one would be destroyed by contemplating? You've taken away all the
guarantees' (p. 103). Although he is writing on 'what he proposed to call the
demythologizing of morals' (p. 77) and wishes to emphasize the 'half-
conscious realization that the era of superstition was over', he considers that
the mythological structure of Christianity believed in by others (bishops and
priests like his brother Carel, of whose priesthood he is secretly proud) has an
essential role, that of keeping the terror of meaninglessness at bay.

   Marcus represents rational man who proposes reliance on the secular order
but recognizes that there are magical, inexplicable horrors most comfortably
delegated to the mumbo-jumbo of a mythical system like Christianity. If the
Bishop is right and we do really live in an interregnum period, Marcus

illustrates all its dualities. A secular Platonist, he reasons moderately well within this mode, and like Murdoch dislikes contemporary existentialism, dreading a morality without the external claim of the good:

> Marcus' intention was to rescue the idea of an Absolute in morals by showing it to be implied in the unavoidable human activity of moral evaluation at its most unsophisticated level, and in doing this to eschew both theological metaphor and the crudities of the existentialism which was the nemesis of academic philosophy.
>
> He had completed a first chapter entitled *The Metaphysics of Metaphor* in which he argued that the idea of a spiritual world as something separate, magnetic and authoritative need not be regarded as a metaphysical concept. A rough draft of a section explaining the role of Beauty as a revelation of the spiritual had been set aside, and would probably appear as the climax of the work. (pp. 77–8)

For all his desire to be a secular man and make spiritual ideas like beauty and the good non-metaphysical, he is absolutely attached to the cultural alternative represented by myth, and as a person locked in a middle state he needs the balance that myth–ridden people like his priest–brother or the Bishop should, he feels, supply.

His secular, limited Platonism is really a modernist, watered–down substitute for religion, a comfortable reliance on the authority of the good, which is so charmingly linked with lofty words: perfection, beauty, the transcendent. Anything else, like modern philosophy's dependence on will or action, he calls 'a vulgar relativism' (p. 132). Murdoch presents Marcus's complacency as a curiously perverted intellectual state. He tends to congratulate himself privately on the advanced state of his thinking and proudly believes himself to be engaging in a real analysis of truth, but he carefully leaves out untidy or frightening concepts and is, at a basic level, shaken by his own enormous myth-making faculties. He is unable to make progress on his chapter called 'Some Fundamental Types of Value Judgment' because he can think of nothing but the magical and inaccessible Carel and Elizabeth, who very quickly take on mythical proportions for him. Both he and the Bishop use great intelligence and admirable traditions to block off what Carel Fisher perceives, but both dark-night-of-the-soul theology and the comforts of Platonism fade when they come up against the power of Carel's demonic vision.

Unlike the Bishop, who apparently thinks the world will inevitably but painfully become more spiritual as Christian imagery dies, or Marcus, who thinks one can be comfortably rationalist, substituting a secular idea of good for God and counting on priests and Christian believers to contain evil, Carel is at the very heart of the undoing of the Christian centuries. When he refutes Marcus's notion that ordinary morality can continue and is not connected with the death of God, that Platonism is another thing, Carel's reply constitutes a troubling perversion of acceptable thinking in this novel:

> If there is goodness it must be one. . . . Multiplicity is not paganism, it is the triumph of evil, or rather of what used to be called evil and is now nameless. . . . The disappearance of God does not simply leave a void into which human reason can move. The death of God has set the angels free. And they are terrible. . . . There are principalities and powers. Angels are the thoughts of God. Now he has been dissolved into his thoughts which are beyond our conception in their nature and their multiplicity and their power. God was at least the name of something which we thought was good. Now even the name has gone and the spiritual world is scattered. There is nothing any more to prevent the magnetism of many spirits.
>
> (p. 186)

Notice how embedded Carel is in the residue of Christian myth, or perhaps in its fragmented centre. The usable vocabulary western culture still retains is reminiscent of long dominant Christian imagery, and Carel is talking about our contemporary state of unknowing and somehow confident theorizing in a vocabulary both old and new. That the various ways contemporary thinkers have of explaining the universe and man's place in it can be symbolized as the angels formerly held secure in the mind of God and now, in a godless world, set free, is an apt idea. The retention of the ancient vocabulary of ideas and theories as personified in angels, each angel equivalent to an idea of God but now no longer contained in the unity God's existence implied, is a shocking, convincing way of talking about the potential horrors of our present state. With the loss of the one, the many are unacceptable and confusing to the modern mind. For Carel, Nietzsche's announcement of the death of God displayed only a momentary insight into the real horrors contained in the idea, and minor thinkers like German theologians, or men like Marcus, or 'the rationalists with their milk and water modern theism', or the comfortable atheists, have all softened the blow, have all assumed that 'Theology has been so long a queen she thinks she can now rule as a queen in disguise'. What they have been after has been 'simply a new morality. But the truth itself they did not conceive of, the concept of it alone would have killed them' (p. 183).

This 'truth' is of course the horror that Marcus has long dreaded for all his facile Platonic optimism, the kind of truth he has been able to deal with only by assuming that the Church would persist and look after its terrifying mystery. The metaphysical universe Carel describes and lives in is one in which the breaking of unity releases Chaos and Old Night, in which we face a truth which is purely horrible, evil. The image he uses is close to Marcus's long held dread, and one Murdoch will evoke again, particularly in *The Nice and the Good*, where the involvement of the human spirit with evil literally produces cages full of dead birds in a hellish underground place:

> Suppose the truth were awful, suppose it was just a black pit, or like birds huddled in the dust in a dark cupboard? Suppose only evil were real, only it was not evil since it had lost even its name? Who could face this? The philosophers have never even tried. All philosophy has taught a facile optimism, even Plato did so. Philosophers are simply the advance guard of theology. They are certain that Goodness is there in the centre of things radiating its pattern. They are certain that Good is one, single and unitary. They are sure of this, or else they deify society, which is to say the same thing in a different way. Only a few of them really feared Chaos and Old Night, and fewer still ever caught a glimpse – And if they did perhaps, through some crack, some fissure in the surface, catch sight of *that*, they ran straight back to their desks, they worked harder than ever late into the night to explain that it was not so, to prove that it could not be so. They suffered, they even died for this argument, and called it the truth. . . . Any interpretation of the world is childish. Why is this not obvious? All philosophy is the prattling of a child. The Jews understood this a little. Theirs is the only religion with any real grimness about it. The author of the Book of Job understood it. Job asks for sense and justice. Jehovah replies that there is none. There is only power and the marvel of power, there is only chance and the terror of chance. And if there is only this there is no God, and the single Good of the philosophers is an illusion and a fake.
>
> (p. 184)

The highly conscious good characters we have seen elsewhere in Murdoch's work have had no illusions at all about truth, and know that to be authentically good is to be good for nothing, with no hope of reward, and with the ego undone within them. Carel is on their side, in the peculiar perversion which constitutes his argument:

> We do not know the truth because as I told you it is something that cannot be endured. People will endlessly conceal from themselves that good is only good if one is good for nothing. The whole history of philosophy, the whole theology, is this act of concealment. The old delusion ends, but there will be others of a different kind, angelic delusions which we cannot now imagine. One must be good for nothing, without sense or reward, in the world of Jehovah and Leviathan, and that is why goodness is impossible for us human beings. It is not only impossible, it is not even imaginable, we cannot really name it, in our realm it is non-existent. The concept is empty. This has been said of the concept of God. It is even more true of the concept of Good. It would be a consolation, it would be a beatitude, to think that with the death of God the era of the true spirit begins, while all

that went before was a fake. But this too would be a lie, indeed it is the lie of modern theology. With or without the illusion of God, goodness is impossible to us. We have been made too low in the order of things. God made it impossible that there should be true saints. But now he is gone we are not set free for sanctity. We are the prey of the angels.                    (p. 187)

In this light, the Bishop's arguments about the new spirituality are exposed as another example of facile optimism. To be the prey of the angels is an idea that leads in many directions, and although Carel proclaims that the effects of their unleashing are not yet fully felt, we see them in the invasions of ideological systems – in Marcus, the Bishop, Heidegger, and *a fortiori* in Carel himself. To fill the vacuum, Carel demonically and madly steps into the role of God, and with an ironic childishness parodying the philosophers whose systems he despises, creates about him a puerile microcosm of the Christian God's large, formal cosmos. He is given to throwing paper darts as angelic messengers, winged signs of approval or disapproval, and fills his empty rooms with low-gear cosmic harmony from such balletic music as *Swan Lake*, which he obviously takes to be symbolic and to which he dances sombrely. He tells Marcus that part of his game is actually to be God when he celebrates mass, and says that for this he will be 'punished quite automatically out of the great power of the universe' (p. 187). His only pleasure, and a proof of the existence of others, is in the infliction of pain – a sharp slap administered to Marcus at the end of the scene makes his brother exist 'for just a moment'. Part of Marcus perceives this behaviour as mad, but it is so precariously close to an off-centre microcosmic version of things that he soon decides that the blow was 'designed to produce enlightenment' (p. 205). In spite of his horror at Carel's theories, Marcus's mythologizing tendency springs to the fore, and his brother becomes more important than ever as an object of love. Carel has played God quite successfully, for such a victim.

Of the three theorizers in this unusually theoretical novel, Carel is ironically closest to a kind of symbolic truth-telling. That modern man is prey to great systems which we only partially understand and the results of which we cannot face is a convincing truth for many. This is a novel devoted to preventing an easy exit from hell, and the mindless Platonism of Marcus and the ultimately enlightening mysticism of the Bishop are overpowered by Carel's relentless eloquence. If ideological routes out are blocked off, so are the social ways. Eugene Peshkov talks about the self-satisfaction of welfare workers in the refugee transit camps after the war, workers who took cheerful pleasure in an altruism which kept them from seeing the horrible reality in the crushed lives of the inmates: 'Perhaps God saw it. Only a saint could be in the truth there' (p. 63). The one thing that Eugene has learned from the camps is that they are an apt image for all human life; when Pattie says she would like to be a saint, he replies, 'All the world's a camp, Pattie, so you'll have your chance. There are good corners and bad corners, but it's just a transit camp in the end' (p. 63). Again and again in her novels, Murdoch has characters tell us that the worst image of pain imaginable is a concentration camp. For Eugene to project the experience of one as a symbol of life in the world is to argue that Carel's version is right. There is, of course, another impotent social worker as we find out in the last few pages – the psychiatric social worker Anthea Barlow – who is never let into the house and whose symbolic importance we discern only when the drama of Carel's removal is over.

A world without God, swept by powerful angels, is indeed a place where man's *Dasein*, his existential choosing self must fill in the duration. Carel's choice is to remain a priest: 'I endure in the place in which I am. I endure, my Marcus. I wait for it all to finish' (p. 187); he fills in the time with his destructive God games and perverse interpretation of ancient Christian symbolism. Like the Bishop, he is riveted by the answer of Jehovah to Job, who asks for sense and justice and is reminded of his puny insignificance: 'Where wast thou when I laid the foundations of the earth?' If we are nothing, and subject only to power and chance, then it follows inevitably for Carel that 'We have been made too low in the order of things. God made it impossible that there should be true saints. But now he is gone we are not set free for sanctity.'

The character of the good in Murdoch's fiction will direct himself towards the futile aim of good, act for nothing, acknowledge that sainthood is impossible and that we will never know much. Carel's is a demonic turning of this idea. He has slipped through one of the 'fissures or cracks', and instead of being able to go beyond the conventional imagery, as the Bishop over his claret and cheese has comfortably described as positive and necessary in the new spirituality, Carel becomes the ego-ridden human soul caught in a terrible replay of culturally defunct ideas. As he waits in the midst of the wreck, remaining a priest because there is nothing to do but wait and play and parody while chaos gathers, Carel is Heideggerian man seen as a fiendish egotist. The attraction of seizing godly power in a universe haunted by memories and icons of it is illustrated here and subsequently in Murdoch's novels. Nigel Boase plays with it in *Bruno's Dream*, Montague Small has cruel tendencies in that direction in *The Sacred and Profane Love Machine*, Matthew Gibson Grey finds it easier to manage than the blank face of Buddhism in *An Accidental Man*. But although the dark side of Hannah Crean-Smith's obsessive spirituality in *The Unicorn* is a pretype and all early power figures are related to the idea, this is the first large allegory in which a character interprets and enacts the role of God.

Both Murdoch as narrator and Carel as character work on it, so that we view it constantly from a double point of view – internal and external creativity. Trinities abound in the novel, and not only does Carel produce various symbolic images for his own delectation, but these symbols also inexorably act out their roles independently of him and finally destroy him. In a frightening way, his ironic game is reality; it is not, as he thinks, subject to his will, but relentlessly works out old patterns in culture. Hovering behind the action is Eugene Peshkov's Russian icon, representing the angelic forms of the eastern orthodox Trinity. Like many of the great cultural objects in Murdoch, it has a permanence and validity far beyond the fragile brief lives of those who lay claim to it. In the terrible hell of this book, it is repeatedly seen to exist apart as a transcendent other, on its own progress through the world. When Leo steals it and, after long lies and power games, Marcus brings it back, it independently works its way past Marcus, Leo and Muriel, so that Pattie is the restorer of the object to Eugene and part of its magic function. Almost convincing as the miraculous ruler over chance (in its history it had been reputed to have power to heal and alter lives), the icon appears magnetically to Carel's attention at the end of his long disquisition to Marcus, and its calm beauty shines beyond its surroundings, its authority and brightness a wholly other, although defeated, alternative to Carel's dark vision of very different angels:

> Under the direct light of the lamp, beside the insipid pallor of the flowers, the solid wooden rectangle glowed golden and blue. The three bronzed angels, weary with humility and failure, sat in their conclave holding their slender rods of office, graceful and remote, bowing their small heads to each other under their huge creamy haloes, floating upon their thrones in an empyrean of milky brightness.                    (p. 188)

It finally travels on with Eugene, for whom it represents the memory of a Russian past forever gone, a luminous civilization of family intimacy and love, now replaced by the refugee camp of the modern world where relationships are impossible – even his son is forever alienated from him, and Pattie is lost through Carel's and Muriel's demonic intervention and Eugene's own failure. The icon is both an art object and the powerful combination of beauty and symbolic representation a great work of art carries with it, and it stands, in its fragile beauty, in perpetual opposition to Carel's brief, created universe.

In the absence of God, Carel's need to create an ironically mimetic universe constitutes a filling-in of the void. He knows too much of the horror of reality to be able to do it without fear of both his knowledge and punishment, fear of the hell he experiences the world so absolutely to be. Pattie's 'animal communion' with him allows her to intuit his state:

> It was in this closeness that Pattie apprehended at last something like a great fear in Carel, a fear which afflicted her with terror and with a kind of nausea. It seemed to her now that, for all his curious solitary gaiety, she had always seen him as a soul in hell. Carel was becoming very frightened and

he carried fear about with him as a physical environment. His fear had some curious manifestations. He saw animals in the house, rats and mice, when Pattie was sure there were none. He complained of a black thing which kept whisking out of sight. (p. 34)

The childish gaiety that makes his paper darts, his *Swan Lake* music and his cosmic dancing alone part of his God game is no doubt a brave face put on his fear, and that he plays such a comic little scene is part of his recognition that, as he puts it, man is 'too low in the order of things' (p. 187) for greatness of any kind. His devotion to the obvious black-and-white dance symbolism of *Swan Lake* is part of the ironic universe he has created and which he keeps with him right up to his suicide – he falls into unconsciousness with the record of the 'Dance of the Cygnets' playing in the background. The elaboration of his game becomes demonic as its irony stretches into cruelty, into a real physical use of others as part of his half-idle, half-desperate creation. What he obviously has not thought of is the recalcitrance of the creative material, or the ironic fact that he is not the only creator – Murdoch is there too (standing in for the Demiurge?).

Carel smiles sarcastically and even cheerfully at the idea that the three angels of the Russian icon could be one God, but his creative instinct works towards a Trinitarian substitute. He sees himself as God, possessing both black and white: 'Lucky the man who has the sugar-plum fairy and the swan princess'. He tells Pattie, his long-time mistress, that she is his 'dark angel, I want to bind you in chains you can never break' (p. 169). Before identifying her as his sugar-plum fairy, he catechizes her on the subject of God and redemption, asking her to be crucified for him, to redeem him by bearing whatever pain he asks of her and never to leave him. Her faltering, puzzled promise is followed by his symbolic identification of her as Christ-Mary: 'I meant to deify you. I wasn't able to. I meant to make you my black goddess, my counter-virgin, my Anti-maria', and he precedes his love-making with a parodic 'Hail, Pattie, full of grace, the Lord is with thee, blessed art thou among women' (p. 169). His swan princess (Holy Ghost), we learn (with some shock) through Muriel's spying, is his niece Elizabeth, later to be identified as his daughter, whom he has carefully separated from normal, open life through the convenience of her semi-invalidism following on a back ailment. He sexually possesses her, too, as part of the perverted Trinity. Elizabeth functions for him as a kind of pure spirituality, physically present only in his sexual encounters with her. As it is, she is cut off from all society except that of her cousin Muriel whom Carel asks to help keep Elizabeth guarded and separated from the world:

She has come to live much more in her mind. Everyday reality means less to her. . . . She is trying to leave us. . . . Elizabeth is a dreamer who weaves a web. That web is her life and her happiness. It is our duty, yours and mine, to assist and protect her, to weave ourselves into the web, to be with her and to bear her company as far as we can. This is a difficult task and one which can only be achieved in an atmosphere of complete quietness and peace. . . . I want your assurance, Muriel, that you will observe this vigil with me.                                                                                    (pp. 141–3)

Muriel struggles against this abstract, symbol-making interpretation, although she has noticed Elizabeth's 'gay co-operation, in what, with another twist, might have seemed as imprisonment' (p. 105). She has also noticed Elizabeth's approximation to an abstract art object, an icon: 'her beauty . . . glowed with the soft chill of a wax effigy. There was still something dreadfully fascinating about this artificial deadened Elizabeth' (p. 103).

Carel's created Trinity, misusing two real people in the process, works gamesomely in many directions and is full of ironic resonance convenient to Carel's interpretations. He is persistently God the Father, the omnipotent creator at the centre, controlling and creating layers of symbolism both playful and anciently serious: black and white; sugar-plum fairy and swan princess; spiritualized Virgin Mary and Anti-Maria; the rich earth and luminous spirit; crucified, suffering, human Christ and the Holy Ghost, spiritual weaver of sacred, inscrutable webs. Although he tells Pattie he wished to deify her, he remains the kingpin in any combination, a heretical interpretation quite unlike the flowing, giving, receiving equality of Eugene's lofty icon. But in his creative game and its interesting ironies, Carel seems unaware of the reality of trinities elsewhere. He misses the luminous, continuous other life of the icon (he is only amazed that the angelic forms should be so tall), and he appears to have forgotten, or repressed, or not noticed the Trinity formed by himself and his two brothers, Marcus and the dead Julian.

This Trinity is framed not by his creativity, but by mere chance (or Murdoch's authorial hand, which is particularly strong in this highly patterned novel). The brothers draw together through competitive love of the same woman, after Julian and Carel are both married, and Muriel has already been born in Carel's marriage to Clara. The story which we hear first only from chance remarks by the largely ignorant Marcus, and in full late in the novel, as Pattie, driven to destructive action by grief, venomously tells it to Muriel, is very simple: Julian wins and runs off with the girl, Carel retaliates by seducing Julian's wife and begetting Elizabeth, and the girl disappears. Julian commits suicide as a result of Carel's seduction of his wife. This was a brief, doomed Trinity, held together by only one idea and quickly destroyed by its separated selfhoods, the kind of Trinity which Carel could doubtless smile over, denying that the three were ever one.

Yet it functions as an allegory of the death of a triune God, of the Trinity itself which had been united by its concentration on a symbolic woman – either the human soul, which will be so strongly the case three novels later in

*A Fairly Honourable Defeat*, or, more likely, a Sophia figure. (Hebrew Shekinah, English Wisdom. Her name in the novel turns out to be Anthea and her life-giving instinct persists in her role as social worker. She brings symbolic snowdrops with their promise of spring and renewal, to the dark, fog-surrounded, demonic and moribund house which cannot receive them, and tries to reconnect what had been.) It is a Trinity wrecked by sexuality and personality, but the identifications are clear: Carel the eldest is the God-the-Father figure as usual; Julian (a name never used idly by Murdoch, whose devotion to the gentle visionary from Norwich is everywhere made obvious by her reference in almost every novel to the central mystical statement of Julian's revelation, 'All shall be well and all shall be well and all manner of thing shall be well') represents the killed, removed Christ his namesake so purely invoked; Marcus despite his descent into hell via the coal-cellar, is a version of the Holy Ghost, a sort of Platonic world soul uncertain of his materials. The death of one figure (Julian) is not seen as redemptive, but as indicative of its spiritual defeat by another (Carel), and the three are hopelessly separated thereafter. Marcus's awkward and fuzzy attempts at reunion with Carel are violently repulsed, but his confused warmth means that he is the one left alive to meet and possibly be transformed by the Wisdom figure at the end. The psychiatric social worker, Anthea Barlow, sits and weeps alone for the death of Carel; she also tells Marcus that she is a sort of Buddhist now. The wisdom of God (or of the human soul) is left with only the shattered memory of the imagery of Christianity and has moved on to the less image-ridden ideas of oriental spirituality.

As an allegory of the death of God, this Trinitarian tale illustrates that one idea of the Trinity is ruined by a failure to give and reciprocate freely among the three members. A humanizing fall into possessiveness and selfishness intervened, and this Trinity can be said to have died of personality. Once Julian runs off with Anthea the separation occurs, and each is permanently shut off from the other. Marcus good-humouredly and rather unintelligently persists in the world, but Julian dies and Carel is utterly cut off. Unable to exist outside of his terrible consciousness, Carel is barred even from Anthea Barlow, the girl from long ago who might be the great unitive or restorative power, and remains alone in the terrible image of his mind seen here as the bizarre, dark vicarage with the roar of the Underground as an image of hell under it. Carel's active choice of evil rather than humble, hopeless obedience to the good is an image-laden illustration of the alternative demonism open to the contemporary mind. Murdoch is rather a fan of the idea of the existence of hell, and a subtle connoisseur of the broad way to destruction which is much more frequented than other paths, and Carel with his insight and creativity is one of her most effective illustrations.

There is, in *The Time of the Angels*, still another triad (the term Trinity becomes outdated) worth mentioning, that of the three young people who herald the post-Christian future, which is now without any education in or residue of the old traditional Christian imagery. Muriel, Elizabeth and Leo face lives without ideology, model or expectation. Elizabeth has been so deadened by seclusion and by the fictive shaping of Carel's interpretation of her that when we last see her through her uncle Marcus's eyes after Carel's death, she is cut off completely, and dazed and staring, carried by Muriel to a taxi and an unimaginable life. Muriel, whose mind we know much more intimately through Murdoch's narration, is caught in an irredeemably negative role – Pattie sees her as an enemy, Eugene whom she loves regards her as a demon – of permanent rejection by Carel, who leaves her no final loving communication and whom she allows to die. Her permanent responsibility is for Elizabeth:

> And now she was condemned to be divided forever from the world of simple innocent things, thoughtless affections and free happy laughter and dogs passing by in the street. . . . There would be no parting from Elizabeth now. Carel had riveted them together, each to be the damnation of the other until the end of the world.                    (p. 239)

Muriel's sudden knowledge that she had loved only her father ('Elizabeth had always intervened', p. 238) makes bondage to Elizabeth an image of hell, and in her sterility of imagination and personality she can make nothing positive for herself or for an Elizabeth now, at the end, really dazed and cut off. Leo Peshkov, accomplished liar and manipulator of the foibles of others, is apparently unable to relate to anyone and is bemused and ruined by his slender education in science. To Muriel's exclamation after his theft of Eugene's icon, 'How *could* you have deliberately hurt your father so much?', he replies, 'Quasars, Muriel, quasars,. quasars, quasars' (p. 118). Like Marcus, he suffers from being in a middle state between rationalist science and mythology, and the only thing that shakes him out of his destructiveness is the idea of 'a quest' – the possibility of an enclosed virgin which Muriel originally projected when she told him of Elizabeth's existence.

Elizabeth remains passive, but Leo and Muriel have acted – Leo negatively in stealing the icon and playing with Marcus, Muriel in sorry, misguided attempts to be positive. She works on a long, obscure, quasi-epic poem which she is forced to recognize as bad, and tries futile transformations: protecting Elizabeth from Carel's destructive symbol-mongering, or making Eugene Peshkov happy by buying him a painted Russian box with Russlan and Ludmilla on it, a gesture that backfires and causes him unspecified anguish until he remembers, in the last few lines of the novel, that it revives his deeply repressed memory of his first tragedy. Such a box had held the sugar lumps for his childhood English terrier, brutally killed by a guard-dog on the grounds of his old Russian home. Muriel's demonic agency in resurrecting this memory and her inability to connect with Eugene – or

Elizabeth, Carel, Pattie or poetry, as well as the constant defeat of her intelligence and talent, all indicate the sort of future these three young people face, with neither effective human warmth nor ideological tradition to help them. There is no pointed residual idea of Trinity here, just three characters maimed and left open to the future.

As an organizing figure, Carel has been very important indeed to the novel, and despite his palpable fear and ironic, childish games he held together in pattern the characters he so misused. He keeps Elizabeth and Pattie separate and in balance; admiration of him keeps Marcus going; Muriel's possessive love of him and Elizabeth is not intrusive until Carel as source of power comes tumbling down. Inexorably, the real world of causality and chance takes precedence over Carel's artificial godlike control, and a relentless sequence of cause-and-effect leads to his punishment and death. As he told Marcus, 'I shall be punished quite automatically out of the great power of the universe' (p. 187).

The progress of destruction is very simple and natural, with Muriel as a demonic catalyst. The sequence reveals in Muriel the same inclinations towards creative fantasy as a means of controlling the recalcitrant world that characterize Carel, and in these two destroyed and destructive characters Murdoch attacks the fantasizing of the romantic imagination. Muriel finds a peephole in the linen closet next to Elizabeth's room soon after her confrontation with Carel about Elizabeth's future separateness and holy unworldliness, a state of affairs Muriel deeply disapproves of. At the same time she has been hearing from Leo about his boredom with sexually easy modern girls, his longing for an enclosed virgin, a *princesse lointaine*, and his desire for the magic and mystic excitement of a quest. Muriel decides to plan one, to create an idea and scenario as her father has done, unknown to her, in an entirely different context. The chance timing of the world is, of course, off, so that from the closet where she and Leo plan to gaze romantically at the lovely, iconic Elizabeth, Muriel suddenly and appallingly becomes privy to the incest between her father and cousin. This discovery leads to further alienation from Elizabeth, an ordered exile from the house and some hateful scenes with Pattie. The last of these occurs after Muriel has been ordered out, and in jealousy and anger has told Eugene of Pattie's long-standing affair with Carel, thus wrecking Pattie's possibility of marriage or a happy life out of the toils of Carel's malignant influence. Wishing to pass on her pain and grief by hurting Pattie as much as possible, she tells her of Carel's incestuous relationship with Elizabeth, and Pattie retaliates by telling her the Julian–Marcus–Carel story, with its climax in Elizabeth's true identity as Carel's daughter and Muriel's half-sister. From this point, Carel's doom is sealed.

The very interesting Pattie survives the loss of Eugene, although it makes her feel 'unclean . . . unworthy . . . black', because she sees herself as absolutely connnected to Carel: 'He was the Lord God and she was the inert and silent earth which moves in perfect obedience' (p. 223). Muriel's revelation causes the dissolution of the image of power and control which Carel as God figure had planted there and nourished throughout the years: in other words, his creation wilfully separates itself from him in a firm, determined *non serviam*:

> When Carel had said 'Will you suffer for me, will you be crucified for me?' she had thought that he meant ordinary suffering of the kind she was familiar with. In all her imagination of what she might suffer for Carel she had not conceived of this. This was the one thing in the world which she could not bear. . . . Her whole body felt in tatters of wretchedness. After all there was no salvation, no one to call the lapsed soul or weep in the evening dew. The house had fallen down. . . . She would have to go, she would have to leave him at last. She loved him, but she could do nothing with her love. It was for her own torment only and not for his salvation. She did not love him enough to save him, not that much, not with that suffering. She could not stay and see him with Elizabeth. She could not love him that much. She could not make his miracle of redemption.
>
> (pp. 226–8)

Murdoch's coalescence of myth and psychology here is very convincing. When Pattie identifies herself as 'the inert and silent earth' we believe her, because her whole history has contributed to such an identification, and Carel's myth-making fecundity has assured it. Allegorically, Pattie is not only the earth but the human soul, dark and alone, 'appallingly solitary' (p. 28) before Carel steps in. Realizing that painting and poetry give access to beauty and life, she very early in her history made scrapbooks of them as an antidote to her continual misery, and throughout the novel her mind re-echoes with lines of drifting verse, particularly from Blake's *Songs of Innocence*. Carel gives her form and divinity; his mythologizing is a glorious means of life:

> She entered into Carel's presence as into the presence of God, and like the souls of the blessed, realized her felicity not through anything which she distinctly saw but by a sense of her own body as glorified. . . . Carel's divine hands created her in her turn a goddess, a dark swaying being whose body glowed with a purple sheen, glorious as Parvati at the approach of Shiva. (pp. 29–30)

At the same time she retains a longing for innocence, touches of a devout Low Church Christianity, a sense of her guilt (she smiled at Carel's wife Clara's funeral) and a non-mythical separateness which does not bend to Carel's power. Like mankind, she is alien to the tyrannous, shaping God and capable of defection. She also possesses enormous insight and ultimately resists the final excess of Carel's demonic persuasion. The story of Carel's misuse of Elizabeth breaks the bond of his power, and Pattie reverts to her own instinct, which asks for survival.

Carel had been quite right in his identifications of her, but his myth-making backfires and he is destroyed by the resistant counterforce of his infinitely precious creation. Pattie *is* mankind under God, the world soul, the good earth, and as such she is composed also of materials Carel has nothing to do with. Unlike the good Platonic Demiurge who persuaded necessity and causation into adequate form, Carel's malignity leads to his alienation from his materials. In thinking about herself and talking to Eugene about the refugee camp, Pattie had more than once indicated her longing to be a saint, to serve in a healthy, generous way, with an innocence quite unlike her diseased service to Carel; she is even willing to suffer – but healthily: 'A purely good person would do so automatically just like Jesus Christ did' (p. 70). Like all Murdoch characters who feel the charm of suffering before the awful fact, Pattie knows little about it, but in her distraught final letter to Carel, she has arrived there. She is full of pain, failure and love, and her ability to tear herself away from Carel's strangle-hold is a just representation of the real suffering of the human soul which wrenches itself from the destructive and unserviceable god. This god must die of rejection, through the removal of the subspecies he creates, loves and misuses in his frantic egotism. Pattie's defection is the real outcome of Carel's choice of personality and ironic demonism, the real result of his misapprehension and perversion of the human state (his own as well as Pattie's or Elizabeth's or Muriel's), and illustrates the ineluctable casting-off that follows from substituting and mythologizing. Pattie's instinctive strength destroys the cerebral Carel, and also demonstrates a breaking loose of the intuitive good, the permanence and survival, although in pain, of the symbolic human character itself.

From her vague, undirected hoarding of culture, Pattie picks up the notion of sainthood and, perverting Eugene's ironic tutelage, idealizes workers in a refugee camp as possible saints. The last we hear of her is that she is working in an African camp and has transformed herself into a Patricia. (Her fantasy has been to do this and perhaps even to become Saint Patricia.) Whether she can achieve sainthood (doubtful) or must fall into the rather gleeful self-satisfaction Eugene has described as endemic among social workers remains open to question. The important thing is that, like most characters of good in Murdoch, she exits from bourgeois society. This exit involves, particularly, leaving behind a cultural centre that has proven to be corrupt and destructive. The final demolition of the Wren tower in the wasteland bombsite is part of a moving forward from the images of the past, and the strongest sense at the end of the novel is of a culture sadly and destructively outgrowing and rejecting its now merely ironic traditions. Carel embodies this increase of irony as belief detaches itself from cultural object, and Pattie's escape asserts

Eugene's definition of things: 'The world was just a transit camp. The only certain thing was that one was not in it for long' (p. 251).

Many characters in Murdoch's novels long for innocence and use the term 'saint' as a talismanic device for their thinking about a perfection of self they feel to be largely impossible. Although it become fairly commonplace to identify the two central types in many of Murdoch's binary tales as saint and artist, I hope I have proven that a pure example of neither can be found. The closest we can come is in the first novel, *Under the Net*, where Hugo and Jake are at least positive possibilities, or in *The Black Prince*, where the Marsyas figure, Bradley Pearson, finally painfully achieves art under the tutelage of an Apollo figure, P. Loxias. But the religious longing for sainthood is persistently important in Murdoch's thought, a longing that exists in inverse proportion to the failures, violence and guilt the characters enact. The talismanic image of the saint tends to be historical and hallowed as a distant religious object. The holy souls of other periods – the medieval Julian of Norwich or St John of the Cross – and the saintly definiton itself are far removed from the contemporary circumstance, and indicate a tacit but categorical understanding that as contemporaries we are late-born, with only an educated apprehension of once workable connections through devices like art, myth or history.

Perhaps the clearest illustration of this historical dilemma lies in the basic separation of Murdoch's thought from Plato's, under whose banner she serves in so many ways. Whereas Plato, in spite of failure and the need to rework, alter and try new constructions, could still believe in the attainability of the absolute by the wise few, Murdoch and all the rest of us belong to the later Christian or liberal centuries where very little is possible:

> Plato spent some extremely valuable time (*Parmenides*, *Theaetetus*, *Sophist*) dismantling his earlier imagery, but then invented some more, marvellous, entirely new, mythological but still explanatory images in the *Timaeus*. . . . However, his failures do not lead him (as they might lead a later, Christian or liberal, thinker) to conclude humbly or tolerantly that the human mind is essentially limited and fallible. They lead rather to a firmer sense of hierarchy. Wisdom is *there*, but belongs to gods and very few mortals (*Timaeus*, *Laws*).                    (*The Fire and the Sun*, p. 68)

All of Murdoch's novels imply that the contemporary mind must work with materials more intransigent than those that tease the persuasive Demiurge in the *Timaeus*, even though the idea of the benevolent Demiurge casts its shadow frequently in her work. Whereas Plato's thought is a constant search for moral development and alteration in the human soul, Murdoch's *exempla* challenge the idealism involved in thinking about change, and her use of such powerful devices as circular structure (*The Black Prince*) or *déjà vu* (*The Bell*,

*A Word Child*) emphasizes our entrapment in a perpetual, flawed selfhood almost entirely incapable of moral advancement.

Although Murdoch's greatest educational thrust is towards knowing the world in its recalcitrant quotidian mode and divorcing oneself from fantasies about either the world or the ego, the great positive models presented come generally from the gorgeous forms of the past. Like Dorothea Brooke in *Middlemarch*, contemporary characters feel an unbridgeable separation from a complete religious ideal like St Theresa, but whereas the positivist nineteenth-century heroine is rendered noble by striving, Murdoch's characters invariably must recognize that their cultural identifications are merely part of their illusionary romantic inheritance and can cause them to identify with a mythology they cannot live up to. Only by jettisoning all the imagery of the culture and facing the ensuing blankness do characters begin to perceive reality, which is their religious duty. (I am not sure Murdoch would like my terminology, but it does reflect the tenor of this aspect of her novels.)

To lose the concept of God, as the adolescent generation in the novels has generally done, is not the answer. Far from filling the moral bill, this disappearance of the central idea only exacerbates their confusion, and the world of the future in their ignorant hands can only lead to even more self-centred and communally unworkable systems. For good or ill, most characters in Murdoch work through the exhausted culture and are often much enlightened by its myriad devices. Put simply, that culture is a necessary adjunct to both spiritual development and frustrated failure.

The great disunity in Murdoch's thought and its most radical paradox consist of the firmness and consistency of the point of view about reality, which is really a very serious study of death as it contrasts with the brilliant, crowding images of life and culture. On the one hand, the constant presence of self-abnegation, renunciation and withdrawal describes the route of knowledge of reality; on the other is the injunction that one accept the world and know oneself in the true context of that world as it naturally exists in a lived milieu (not in an African refugee camp, not in ameliorative work in India). Although these negative disciplines can be held together with dutiful truth by characters like Bledyard, Ann Peronett and Tallis, there is also another, experientially primary knowledge competing with it: the world as we perceive it combines powerful positive elements that delight and distract, that cause joy, feelings of transcendence, love and religious elevation. This glittering other side is probably the most enchanting repository of Murdoch's many talents, and indeed the paradox of her own joy in life in the world in the light of her knowledge of its horror throws us back once again to the problem of reader response.

# IV

# ART AND THEORY

Basic criticism, the theory of *The Fire and the Sun* and a
reading of *The Black Prince*

Murdoch works with powerful paradoxes as she strives to deal justly with
her myriad materials, and these paradoxes can be extremely puzzling to the
reader. The Platonic turning towards the blank face of the good which she
advocates must ultimately produce withdrawal from images of the world,
and is ironically aligned in effect to two negative ideas in our period – fading
cultural ideas (see the Bishop in *The Time of the Angels*) and demonic misuse
of them (Carel Fisher in the same novel is the extreme example). In one sense,
then, the novels reflect a sad interregnum period, with cultural objects and
ideas losing their power because of a civilization going wilfully and termin-
ally awry; yet they equally reflect a positive but sober moral ideal which
must rejoice in the progressive discarding of even the numinous artifacts so
useful in its development. Strictly speaking, the vast and radiant paraphernalia of culture often invoked in these novels appears at every level
to be doomed. Moreover, because the mature novels also persuade us of the
near and constant reality of death – indeed are lessons in death – the vivid life
of the world itself might ideologically and emotionally be seen as defeated,
though ultimately that is not the case.

One cannot properly estimate Murdoch's work without taking into account how her readers are compelled to respond to her full, life-giving
evocations, how every reader has a sense of a shared life in an often beautiful
and touching world full of its own natural beauty and of gorgeous and
soul-compelling human artifacts. This paradoxical other preoccupation with
the vitality and charm of life and art is extremely powerful, and its display
constitutes the major attractive element in her style – the way she can court,
tease, alienate or win the reader. Moreover, although Murdoch's frame of
complex and suggestive cultural and moral reference is enormous, much of
the pleasure conveyed to her audience is simple and visual. Her ability to
switch rapidly from detailed perception of the natural world to the extended

workings of the minds of her characters is not only a just mirror of the constant internal–external alternation of human attention, but also part of the central idea of disjunction so characteristic of her work. Her characters both live intensely in a closely perceived world and are completely separated from it by what Murdoch has described as their puzzling and extended nature and their sorry inability to pay sustained attention to very much outside of themselves. Murdoch's readers, on the other hand, receive a rich sense of the world through the aptness and fullness of her subtle descriptions which include the real, physical presence of people who live in a world of extensive mental and cultural activities.

Richness of presentation and complexity of inner and outer detail are characteristic of Murdoch's best and now most typical writing. But she has not escaped censure from her public, and it is perhaps apropos to mention some criticisms of her style. My intention in doing this stems from what I hope to be a mounting intensity in this chapter from small issues of artisanry to the largest and most profound demonstration of the function of art that Murdoch's work has been able to reach in the superb novel, *The Black Prince* (1973).

Hers is a firm and distinct style in the great novelistic tradition, replete with the eccentricity and repeated mannerisms that mark any original stylist. *Under the Net*, the first novel, although very popular is far from typical; apart from a few of Jake's ruminative passages near the end, it has a different, sharper method of commanding the reader than any of the subsequent novels. There is more of the dryness and sudden turn one would expect of Beckett and of the witty speed of Queneau, both of whom Murdoch emulated; and although she has always kept some of this, her own distinctively clever, comedic mode and subtle jokes took over almost immediately. In the second novel, *The Flight from the Enchanter*, and increasingly as she developed towards her firmest assertion of her own novel-writing method from *The Nice and the Good* (1968) onwards, a growing feeling for description and visual fullness, combined with an increasing use of a ruminative mode, made her look quite unlike the purely witty stylist she was in *Under the Net*. It took a few novels for journalists and critics to catch on to this change, and the reaction was a temporary denial of what she was doing. Some newspaper reviewers are still at it: with every new novel someone or other complains about her style or the lack of commas between adjectives. Many still stubbornly claim to prefer *Under the Net*.

Apart from *The Bell*, *The Unicorn* and *The Time of the Angels*, where the fullness and internal rhythms of the work are well sustained, the novels before *The Nice and the Good* are occasionally uneven. In the process of tracing some of the generalities of the style, I have nevertheless deliberately allowed myself a perhaps blameworthy tone which springs from my strongly positive reaction to the details and effect of Murdoch's work. In the face of what I see as unjust and too often frivolous negative journalistic criticism, I cannot apologize for my evangelism. I do hope, however, that the detailed stylistic analysis of her complex and shifting voice will become the province of other studies of her work. For it is evident that, like all good novelists, Murdoch very early established a distinctive voice which she unfalteringly retains, and which, even in the maturity and sophistication of her most recent work, causes occasional and often virulent attacks. I shall here single out as typical the case against Murdoch by two critics, one English and one American, both university professors who ought to be able to read her methods and allusions more accurately than most: Christopher Ricks in his review of *Nuns and Soldiers* in the London *Sunday Times* of 7 September 1980, and George Stade on the same book in the *New York Times Book Review*, 4 January 1981.

Ricks has a genuine foundation for his criticism, and particularly rebukes Murdoch's reiterated use of the phrases 'a sort of' or 'a kind of', claiming that these alone lead to a necessary 'distrust' of the way she writes:

> the formula is used throughout and is itself a sort of natural lying; that is, a formula for mystery and pseudo-exactness. . . . As it stands, or leans, it is merely a bland substitute for precision, pretending to furrow a scrupulous brow. If you took away the words 'a sort of' or 'a kind of', the throb would be audibly hollow.

Ricks then proceeds to compile a witty list of examples culled from various parts of the 505-page novel, forming them into a catalogue:

> let me string together the formulae – and every single one of them until the end of this review is taken verbatim from *Nuns and Soldiers*. . . . For her admirers, this novel will be a sort of sacred area, characterised by a kind of happy authority, a kind of intelligent pity, a sort of passionate anarchism, a kind of professional detachment, a kind of elated sadness, etc., etc.

It is beyond doubt that Murdoch is indeed addicted to these two phrases, and that she employs them as a deflection from the radical force of statement. Part of this is simply a stylistic tic, and one that can justly arouse the irritation of a reader like Ricks; more to the point, however, is the fact that the phrases also constitute a device of major importance given the nature of her strong and distinct statements. It is not a case of the phrases being a mode of lying on her part or a protection against the 'hollowness' of the descriptive comments she makes, but rather they serve to protect the reader from the full force of what she has to say. In many ways they can be seen as one of the useful if untruthful devices of art, about which Murdoch has so long been suspicious and negative. Their cushioning effect allows the reader to avert an eye, to imply modification of the radical statement, to make the process of the novel both in such small parts and on the whole less threatening and absolute than it would appear without such interim deflections. In their limited way they parallel her practice in forefronting the large bourgeois surface of her novels and keeping the heart of the matter partially enshrouded by antics and proceedings more amenable to the reader's immediate and necessarily superficial responses.

The case of George Stade's criticisms of Murdoch's style is quite other, in that they are prefaced by an irritable and arrogant attack on the very idea that Murdoch might be interested in allusion, ideas, or religion. Above all, he is irritated that she is not Joyce, and accuses her of imitating him without the saving grace of irony. His particular attack is on the emotional content of the prose describing characters who are in love and their private language of excess; unaware of Murdoch's attunement to the follies and charms with which twentieth-century man adorns his language of love, Stade says: 'Writing this bad cannot be faked; more likely it gushes straight from the unrelieved sincerity of an author who needs mostly to deceive herself.' Not only are context and irony dismissed, but Stade, after one reading of a book he palpably cannot understand, feels free to attack an authorial voice, whose intentions are manifold, as though it were a production of childish incompetence. There can be no question that certain passages and characters in Murdoch are irritating; the fullness of the novels and their realist intention could not be achieved without this sort of thing, but there is an essential frivolity in assuming that she is up to so little in her stylistic composition.

In general, criticisms of Murdoch's style are connected with uneasiness about the uncomfortable and extreme content of the text, or with the pronounced eccentricities which form her authorial voice. Above all, she believes to an unusual degree in unabashed eloquence and has schooled her style to its use; she applies it especially to human values, emotions and relatedness, and its effect is even greater when the feelings expressed are connected through a particular character to loving attention to other people, natural objects or high artistic achievements. She fearlessly uses an eloquent, impassioned voice for any character in her wide range, with the result that, for example, the mental articulation of the black servant, Pattie O'Driscoll, in *The Time of the Angels*, is not unlike that of the highly self-conscious, cultured Bradley Pearson in *The Black Prince*. Thus, Murdoch makes almost all characters part of the wholeness of her style, while at the same time differentiating scrupulously among them and allowing each a pointed, consistent individuation. In this she is reminiscent of Henry James, but with this difference: Murdoch's omniscient narrator often appears to be ironically and occasionally even comically aware of how private to the Murdoch style is the cohesion of the fictional world being produced. And of course it must be pointed out that in half a dozen novels she uses male first-person narrators, so that the high compulsive style is pre-eminently and narrowly the narrator's, except for the frequently impassioned conversation of others.

A few decades ago, identifying authors' worlds became a popular phenomenologist exercise. Murdoch implies an ironic use of the idea and occasionally rather puckishly pretends that her fictional world is literally enmeshed with the actual one. This leads to a comic minor overflow of detail: for example, Felix Meecham and Mildred Finch in *An Unofficial Rose* drink a bottle of Lynch Gibbon claret for lunch – a label that exists only in the make-believe of *A Severed Head*. *The Sea, The Sea* is particularly laden with such cross-references to Murdoch's other novels: Rosina Vamburgh's range of acting roles is described as omitting Honor Klein, a character from *A Severed Head* which is one of Murdoch's novels adapted for the stage. Purely fictional Adelaide and Will Boase from *Bruno's Dream* are part of the description of the 'real' theatre world in *The Sea, The Sea*, and a rising young Shakespearean actor named Erasmus Blick is talked about: he is obviously related to Calvin Blick from *The Flight from the Enchanter*. The clever irony of these evocations (sixteenth-century religious figures in the Blick family could go on for quite a while – Luther Blick, Cranmer Blick, even Zwingli or Melanchthon Blick) is a small part of Murdoch's awareness of the continuous act of private creation that must accompany any artist's progressive revelation.

At the same time, there is no pretentious sense, as occasionally in Beckett or Barth, that the reader must know all of the canon in order to understand allusions or points of view. Murdoch is, however, self-consciously aware of being the creator or selector of the world she presents; after one has read several novels, the constants are evident and we quickly become aware of her taste in populating her universe. Amulets and talismanic objects abound: stones of all sorts, old snuff-boxes, French glass or natural rock paperweights, kites, Chinese porcelain, Japanese netsuke appear again and again. Set symbols from nature recur: spiders that need rescuing, animals that create bonds, birds, fish, water, the sea, snow. Characters are all bound by set cultural objects – Peter Pan, Shakespeare, the *Iliad*, Christ – and they are very related indeed to food, and often to drink, their tastes serving as characterizing devices. Many fear vulgarity, many are pointedly unmusical, all are disturbed by their dreams. In times of crisis they tend to lie prone on the floor and madly to forget crucial actions from their near past. Tears flow and overflow. Gazing in mirrors is endemic. Central male characters are physically alike – Jake Donaghue (*Under the Net*), for example, or Austin Gibson Grey (*An Accidental Man*) and Arnold Baffin (*The Black Prince*). There are many regretted abortions and many women express general hatred of men. Jealousy, revenge and unforgivingness are recurrent emotions. The violence and excitement of falling in love abound. Obsessions lead to bizarre behaviour.

Of most significance in talking about Murdoch's work are her technical accomplishments, which tower above those of her living contemporaries in the English-speaking world. (Nabokov is dead, Beckett off both novels and English.) Early in Murdoch's career, it was possible to argue, as did many of her critics, that she was too often taken over by her own technical power, with the result that the brilliant and elaborate working-out of the plot subordinated character and verisimilitude, the two aspects of fiction that Murdoch is most serious about. When she began to turn this around, she did so very subtly, and far from abjuring the power and surprise of plot, she continued to spin and turn the action by the precise causal development her strong, bizarre and oddly convincing imagination always devises. The result has been a greater eloquence, a tighter fitting of character to event, a more consistent success in building characters, a more subtle use of myth and an extremely impressive growth in the imagery which binds together the substance of the novels.

Throughout, one of her technically most interesting areas has been closure, where her innovative devices have shown her extensive experimental tendencies. The closures consist of curt twists of the plot (the commonly used early form, never abandoned); a surprising, brief, informative visit to the future (*The Red and the Green*); the ironic and sometimes unnerving imposition of what Murdoch has called 'a Shakespearean felicity' (*The Nice and the Good, An Accidental Man, The Sacred and Profane Love Machine*); circularity (*Henry and Cato*); endgame (*The Unicorn*); point-of-view altering postscripts (*The Black Prince*); total ambiguity (*A Word Child*); meandering refusal of closure (*The Sea, The Sea*). Each novel commands its own possibility, and each closure, with very few exceptions, aims to discomfit the reader and deny expectation. Murdoch's manipulation of closure is not merely a structural trick; she uses the technically most important moment in the novel to maximum advantage. One of Murdoch's primary aims as a novelist is to convince her reader of the unpredictable, uncontrollable nature of real people in the real world, and paradoxically, her workings-out effect this aim through the violent and peculiar fecundity of her own imaginative power. (This is a good example of the paradoxical exaggeration necessary for the realist endeavour – the truthful exaggeration of the real world by the individual imagination which is one of that endeavour's most fertile contradictions.) Novel readers are skilled in expectation and predicate much of their enjoyment on the comfortable satisfaction or ingenious working-out of that expectation. In widely varying her closures and pushing to the last page against audience satisfaction, Murdoch keeps the reader where she wants him – off-balance, amazed, bereft of his expectations and open to the shock of a larger and probably more ironic or appalling idea of the world than he has bargained for. Thus in *The Sea, The Sea*, when the blessing implied by a sublime skyful of stars followed by the morning appearance of the seals to Charles Arrowby would suggest all one could ask as closure, the reader's expectation is sharply cut off and he learns how foolish, unreal and fictional his literary wishes are:

That no doubt is how the story ought to end, with the seals and the stars, explanation, resignation, reconciliation, everything picked up into some radiant bland ambiguous higher significance, in calm of mind, all passion spent. However life, unlike art, has an irritating way of bumping and limping on, undoing conversions, casting doubt on solutions, and generally illustrating the impossibility of living happily or virtuously ever after; so I thought I might continue the tale a little longer in the form once again of a diary, though I suppose that, if this is a book, it will have to end, arbitrarily enough no doubt, in quite a short while.                    (p. 477)

The arbitrary nature of any closure shows how artificial and habitual aesthetic responses are, and Murdoch is always ready to play on and confuse them, even, if necessary, to dissolve into the ironies of the artist–trickster in order to acquiesce to the demand of concluding the inconclusive.

Another of Murdoch's controlling technical decisions involves her characters. It took fewer than half a dozen novels for readers to realize that Murdoch bases her fictional world on a fairly extensive but reiterated stock of characters – recognizable types from a highly sophisticated bourgeois society. The fact of reiteration has called down some rather remarkable hostility from a few critics who find the technique merely tedious, but for most of Murdoch's readers it lends to the growing body of novels a sense of continuity, development and expansion. If Murdoch is realistic and accurate in depicting a world we recognize, then of course she must play within a limited range to maintain verisimilitude, and of course certain contemporary types have more profoundly caught Murdoch's imagination than have others.

In her third novel, *The Sandcastle*, there is a curious quasi–character, not at all fully realized, and not clearly fitted into the novel's frame: a speechless gypsy whose task seems to be the evocation of the *frisson* that comes from the hidden world of destiny, magic and the subconscious. Rain Carter and Mor come across him in the woods as he is mysteriously laying out the Tarot cards of the future which presumably these two central characters must enact. Rain and Mor do not see the details of the game, do not recognize the Tarot deck and are excluded from the secret and ominous knowledge the gypsy is absorbed in. The idea may be too picturesque, but the image of this outsider with his Tarot cards is an apt one for the game of authorial power Murdoch plays as she spreads out her plots for speculation and development. Hence we have permutations and combinations of these (and other) cards: deceiving husband, complacent middle-aged wife, troubled late-adolescent, middle-European Jew, *homme moyen sensuel*, refugee, arty mistress, scholar, would-be waif, Peter Pan boy-woman, honourable soldier, glossy civil servant, witch, demonic girl-child, outsider, secret homosexual, failed writer, dabbler in eastern religions.

From this deck, Murdoch builds, not a house of cards, but the substantial frame of each of her novels, liberally adding new and unusual characters, some of whom are marvellously eccentric: Mitzi Ricardo, the destroyed athlete in *An Accidental Man*; the Indian girl Biscuit in *A Word Child*; the versatile multi-British Fivey in *The Nice and the Good*, to name only a few. One of the great pleasures of beginning a new Murdoch novel is watching the game, for although there are many stock characters, Murdoch has a knack for differentiation. (Let me add parenthetically that comparison with the technical filmic habits of Ingmar Bergman begs to be made, although I consider Murdoch the subtler artist.) Murdoch has said that real freedom is understanding that others exist, and her novels constantly remind us of this, for although the stock characters range typically through the society she depicts, they are played to enormous advantage through their constantly surprising individuation. Thus one knows others exist because in Murdoch's novels attention is properly paid to their individual qualities. It is always wrong but usually irresistible for the reader to assume that a pattern of action can be predicted from a character's stock type; rather, the reader must constantly re-evaluate and see freshly and better the type he had idly thought he knew. Murdoch's versatility and inventiveness allow her an almost incredible amount of mileage: a writer of fecund imagination, she works the device of stock characters with stimulating originality. Although sometimes a Tarot-card character is inadequately realized (e.g. Matthew Gibson Grey in *An Accidental Man* or Gerda Marshalson in *Henry and Cato*), generally the excitement of the well-sustained variations works very well. There is a wide disparity within type, and the balance of the type with its aberrations in the same personality is effectively mixed with new characters and eccentrics. The impenetrability of response exhibited by the fact that no one acts consistently as one might predict is a great surprise to the reader, and the repeated destructions of the reader's expectations serve Murdoch's purposes well.

These characters spend a great deal of time in their own minds, and when Murdoch is playing the omniscient narrator there is usually a set piece in which that narrator enters directly into the mental workings of each of the characters. These are moments of great conviction and power in the novels, for here Murdoch gives her characters full attention and identification. Even when (as she constantly does) she allows them faulty reasoning or defensive rationalization, she does so without external authorial judgement and with a generosity that rivets the reader to the mental and emotional patterns sympathetically presented as real and believable.

When the characters are not inwardly ruminating and struggling with awesome moral energy, they engage in unremitting talk or, less often, write letters or dream elaborate dreams. Murdoch handles conversation with considerable variety and inventiveness. The perfected style of the cocktail conversation in Murdoch's novels is satiric and realistically convincing, and dramatic, very human, insulting or touching exchanges at crucial moments are perfect and beyond fiction. Often Murdoch manages marvellously funny, stylized conversations *à deux*, as Kate and Octavian Gray's gossipy, self-satisfied, bedtime pre-sex burblings in *The Nice and the Good*, which always conclude, hilariously, with Octavian's 'Ready darling?' and Kate's 'Ready'. But one of Murdoch's interesting and unanalysable successes is her curious capacity to convince even the skeptical reader that certain kinds of abstract philosophical, religious and aesthetic conversations occur almost universally. Although she risks overstepping the bounds of verisimilitude here, in fact she seldom does. Part of the explanation for what must surely be described as a *trompe l'oreille* (people do *not* generally talk this way) is in the eloquence she imposes on the consciousness of all her characters. This extraordinarily convincing verbal power is realistically broken by frequent ordinary bad temper and sharp wit, and evident throughout are notable belief in the characters and absence of condescension in the authorial voice.

I suggested earlier in this chapter that there is an anomaly in Murdoch's style in that the inner workings of the minds of all the characters, from the simplest to the most complicated, involve comparable moral complexity and similar vocabulary. Her conversations reveal the same characteristic. There are of course characters with distinctive speech patterns (e.g. Alice Lejour in *The Unicorn*, Bledyard in *The Sandcastle*, the turgidly American Ludwig LeFerrier in *An Accidental Man*), but they are relatively rare. One is dealing here with the mesmerizing capacity of Murdoch's incantatory style. It is not simply that middle-class people are bound to have the same stock of vocabulary; Murdoch's style is markedly distinctive, and some readers object to the constant intrusion into these conversations of characteristic references to magic, portent, omen and religion. Murdoch's most ardent attackers seem particularly to dislike this irrational element. Nevertheless, on the whole and for a very large audience indeed these ingenious conversations persuade, and generally meet wholehearted acceptance from the mesmerized reader.

One more technical issue is worth brief mention: the frequent presence of a male first-person narrator, and the absence of a corresponding female voice. In interviews Murdoch has said that she enters women's psyches as often as men's in her third-person narrations, and that she finally sees little barrier between men's and women's minds. In fact, Murdoch is the only writer I know who can cross the barrier so effectively and apparently so effortlessly: one thinks of Charlotte Brontë's failure in *The Professor* or Dickens's cloying Esther Summerson in *Bleak House*. It is unprofitable to conjecture *why* Murdoch does it (because all the first-person narration takes place through corrupted male psyches, is this a veiled indication that men are more likely to be debased than women?), especially since she has said she is more comfortable there, and that seems to be that, since this study does not aspire to a psychoanalysis of the author. The important thing is that male narration is a phenomenon, something that should not work and does, as happens in so many other aspects of Murdoch's startling and fascinating mode.

In reading each novel, the spectator is drawn through all these elements into a realm he has been in before, and not only by recognition of characters and conversations. There are innumerable repeated patterns: male role-model played off against adolescent boy, opposition of religious and artistic figures, good versus evil, escapes to India, Australia or America, strong mother–son relationships, men mourning the death of their wives from cancer, identifications with medieval images (questing knight, lady of the fountain). In addition, many of the climactic adventures are comparable and reflect a suffocating (sinking into a bog or mud) or drowning, redolent of the symbolically smothering, death–dealing effect of the reality–denying ego. As I mentioned earlier, some amulets and images recur from novel to novel, reminding us that this is indeed the work of a single powerful imagination whose ability to draw the reader towards her world is steady and effective.

It is most unwise to reduce that world or to assume that a few catalogues of the sort I have given convey truly the actual experience of reading a Murdoch novel. Nor is it particularly apt to use the phrase 'a Murdoch novel' as a simple means of covering the range she exhibits. There are a few novels related to the gothic style (*The Unicorn*, perhaps *The Time of the Angels*, perhaps *The Sea, The Sea*), a few early ones somewhat overpowered by their games and plots, several moderately cheerful ones, several terrifying and heart-sickening ones; but mostly each is a *sui generis* work with a social and moral inclination comparable to many of the novelistic ambitions of the nineteenth century. Although a few early ones have been recast as plays (*A Severed Head, The Italian Girl*) and one so far as a television serial (*An Unofficial Rose*), they are not, especially the late ones, very suitable for dramatization. For all the verve and energy of their action, their brilliantly exciting scenes, their sudden turns, surprises and *peripeteia*, their lasting interest and most profound life exist in issues that cannot be portrayed by means of stage or film. Every character possesses a full, ambiguous inner life, construed as a constantly audible voice which both partakes in and is differentiated from Murdoch's own strong authorial voice. When a novel is projected by an omniscient narrator, a sense of sympathy, pity and deep understanding flows from the authorial source in a way reminiscent of a humane, generous nineteenth-century style like Trollope's. When the narrator enters freely and absolutely into the consciousness of one of the characters, which happens frequently in Murdoch's version of omniscience, the reader undergoes an empathic identification even when he knows (or is not too enchanted to perceive) that the arguments can be suspect. And when Murdoch uses her riskiest style – male first-person narration through a corrupted consciousness – one is constantly won over by the breadth and perception that even a deeply flawed character regularly, even automatically, exhibits. One aspect of reader response which commonly operates is a trust in and identification with the abundant human perceptivity. Therefore when the boom is lowered, so to speak, and the grotesque, violent and destructive results of human action seize the plot, the reader experiences a very real feeling of betrayal, unfairness, frustration, even defeat, as though the defeat of good by evil which is so often Murdoch's subject has entered the very substance and texture of both the fictional action and the reader's perception. To perceive that it is in fact the defeat of fantasy and consolation by reality involves work, attention and the conscious denial of conventional reading habits.

As a realist, Murdoch is successful at portraying her wide range of character types; so accurate is her mimesis, in fact, that it can become a liability. Ironically, Murdoch's greatest problems as a writer link directly to her greatest talents: her fecundity of invention in breath-taking action, which can run away with itself, and her powerful and accurate character mimesis. She can reproduce insistently and lengthily very unpleasant characteristics in hateful characters – whining, weeping women (Priscilla in *The Black Prince*, Jessica Bird in *The Nice and the Good*, Emily McHugh in *The Sacred and Profane Love Machine*), self-pitying men (Austin Gibson Grey in *An Accidental Man*, Bradley Pearson in *The Black Prince*, Henry in *Henry and Cato*) – and let them go on and on (as indeed such people in life do; we have all undergone it too often) until one is ready to throw the book across the room. It is sadly true that some readers never get past this superficial response, or that the irritation touches them too deeply – I think it likely that those who violently dislike Murdoch's work have been accurately hit in some very tender spot. Because things are too harrowingly real and omissions of certain kinds of human foible rare, it is hard to stay comfortably in this world, hard to sustain the human sympathy that Murdoch's novels tell us it is our duty to show. This discomfort is part of her moral thrust, and instead of giving us the capacious comfort of a Trollope novel, she keeps us painfully aware of the sheer difficulty of human endeavour, reminding us that we must live through every moment without being able to select more pleasant terms.

The more one thinks of the potential faults in Murdoch's work, the greater must be the acknowledgement of her realist precision; from the nasty images that a corrupted character spawns to the often foul sophistication of clever society as a whole, her accuracy is very disturbing. Her technically flawless reproduction of social dialogue mentioned earlier (e.g. the opening of *A Fairly Honourable Defeat*, the ghastly hilarity of the parties in *An Accidental Man*) is brilliant high comedy often redolent of real evil; her use of letters to reveal the lying, silly and corrupt reaches of the human psyche is almost enough to make one renounce pen and paper entirely and question whether any one of us has ever managed a letter devoid of doublethink. Murdoch catches with terrible accuracy social behaviour as we all enact it; I can think of no other writer so clever and so relentless. The only possible contemporary analogue is Saul Bellow, whose hammer blows at American self-centred folly lack the concomitant compassion and real generosity that Murdoch shows her characters. Although so many of the themes in his work compare to hers, Bellow is always on the attack, tending to see only the ugly or meretricious, and never goes beyond a condescending pity.

Basically Murdoch does work to avoid a complete takeover by her imagination of the world we all share. Putting aside her reiterated talismans and natural symbols, as well as her ideological grasp of the nature of human failure, we are drawn forward in many of her novels by the quality of attention she concentrates on the physical presence of person and place. Whether she is describing faces, features, bodies, or rooms, houses, gardens, artifacts, her eye is extraordinary, as indeed it is in landscape or skyscape or seascape. Settings are full of detail and the visual impression unusually striking for a contemporary writer. Her botanical knowledge is as complete as her architectural range, and her subtle colour sense and ability to convey light change are equalled in our time only by Nabokov. This concentration of attention on the milieu carries the impression of joy and illumination which is so powerful a part of reader response. Murdoch has said that one of the tasks of fiction is to renew our attention, and this is certainly one of her ways of doing so. When Murdoch is at her best, terms from older literature have a pointed application to her work – perhaps because her thinking is so immersed in the texts and concerns of the Greeks and Shakespeare. Certainly the old idea of invention, as a finding and revealing of what the psyche dimly knows combined with a relentless, persistent urge to make us see the manifold forms – actual and intellectual – of the perceivable world, is an apt way of describing this visual focusing with its deep psychic roots.

The physical, visual world with its myriad attractions includes the actual physical being of characters whose connection with their real setting varies from intense symbolism – what Ruskin implied and mildly underestimated in the term 'pathetic fallacy' – to total disjunction. In Murdoch's depiction, characters are given an almost too extended physical awareness: just as she lends them her voice on frequent occasions, so too she surrounds them with her vast and precise descriptions of the potentially perceivable, partly to endow them with the munificent gifts of a bounteous universe, partly to show the delicacy of the attention so many of them are capable of, mostly and sadly to show how discontinuous that attention is and how limited human character is by the nature of its private obsessions. In *A Fairly Honourable Defeat*, Morgan, in a rare moment of insight which is part of a mystical, literal panic, suddenly sees the radical, dazzling wonder of flowers by an old, disused railway line:

> The flowers were beginning to quiver in front of her eyes. How extraordinary flowers are, she thought. Out of these dry cardboardy rods these complex fragile heads come out, skin-thin and moist, like nothing else in

the world. People from a planet without flowers would think we must be
mad with joy the whole time to have such things about us. She now saw
that what she had taken for flowering nettle was white comfrey, a plant
which she had not seen since she had found it long ago in rivery meadows
in Oxfordshire on holidays in childhood. She leaned forward to caress the
drooping flower heads and touch the strong slightly hairy stems.

The next moment she was lying full length in the long grass and there
was a great deal too much light. Light was vibrating inside her eyes and she
could see nothing but dazzling and pale shadows as if the whole scene had
been bleached and then half blotted out by a deluge of light. . . . The great
ray from afar was pinning her between the shoulder blades and trying to
force her down again. Was it giddiness she was feeling now, a dazzled
sensation of spinning drunkenness, or was it something else, disgust, fear,
horror as at some dreadfulness, some unspeakable filth of the universe?
Saliva was dripping from her mouth. The loathsomeness at the centre of it
all.								(pp. 164–5)

Through the horror of the sudden turn in the experience Morgan is led to an
affirmation of beauty, an utter conviction that it is there, in both nature and
the glories won by art through the very horror of existence: her example for
her nephew Peter is Shakespeare's beautiful, flawless song of death and
transformation from *The Tempest*: 'Full fathom five thy father lies.' This kind
of vision of the heart of things hovers behind Murdoch's natural descriptions
with a vivid sense of life that invokes a reaction beyond the bland, reasoned
quotidian. One could say that nature lies in wait for the attentive mind and
that its purpose is not only to delight, but often also to inflict pain and cause
instruction. As well as nature, other personalities also infringe, dwelling
behind mobile and precise faces, eyes, bodies, dressed in clothes and colours
that pull out certain half-unconscious responses.

All of this projects us into the complex and disturbing area of magic or
enchantment which is possibly the most important single characteristic,
device and enemy in Murdoch's thought and style. She has heeded Plato's
warnings against the use of art as magic, and is very aware of the rationalist
conviction that mankind has graduated from the era of magic into one of
reasonable clarity. She obviously believes Plato, in a limited way, and disbe-
lieves the rationalists, whom she satirizes gently in a character like Marcus
Fisher in *The Time of the Angels*. To begin with, her own central disjunctions
have to do with her power to play the magician as artists are wont to do, and
our unsettled response to her dualities can be traced to her frequent, determined withdrawal of the instruments of enchantment. Hence her unrelieved limning of the barren, difficult path of the good, her removal of image
and consolation when reality is approached, her early decision to use death as
a means of the most profound instruction.

The vital beauty of the world and Murdoch's ability to convey its joys are countered by her knowledge of its illusionary and magical qualities. For a writer so committed to many of Plato's arguments, it makes sense that enchantment and reality should remain so separate, yet that magic should be so significant and constant a device for the groping psyche which longs for truth. Murdoch's revered model here is Shakespeare, especially the Shakespeare of *The Tempest*, the creative artist behind the humbled Prospero figure who knows what it means to abjure 'this rough magic'. Equally important is the ability of the highly developed soul to allow the magical consolations of religious imagery to disappear as Brendan Craddock does in *Henry and Cato*.

★

But this is starting too much at the top. Against all the rationalist theorizing of modern man and our brave belief in our ability to act freely and reasonably, Murdoch would interpose a sharp, realistic criticism: we are much more subject to our obsessions and neuroses than we care to admit, and really free action (as opposed to self-pleasing, permissive solipsism) is no more easily possible than clear-sightedness. In order to create an illusion of freedom, Murdoch's characters translate reality into a series of subjective magical devices. Murdoch is at great pains to illustrate that the world lies fully, in plenitude, before her characters, but they can perceive it only patchily, briefly. That they can see even this much is a sort of miracle, a positive achievement, given that they are so blinded by their concentration on the infinite interests of their own being. Following her Platonic bent, one can describe the majority of her characters as living mediocre illusionary lives in the state of *eikasia* (laden by images); they see only the shadows of the cave, not the fire, certainly not the sun. Murdoch's perception of the progression from the shadows to the sun is a progression from self-protective magic to reality.

To pull this conception further into ideology, we perceive Murdoch's characters as utterly dominated by their own vision and consciousness. In this respect, and radically in many ways throughout the novels, Murdoch shows her allegiance to the basic tenets of Freud's thought, and indeed some major Freudian ideas – obsessional neurosis, the attachment of the personality to infantile modes, the psychic power of dreams – inform Murdoch's fictions to a remarkable degree. After Freud, no writer can persist under the sole aegis of nineteenth-century fictional taste; subconscious peculiarities as well as the sources of these mental processes have become part of the data in creating and transmitting character. Murdoch avails herself openly of Freudianism, and often allows the Freudian materials to heighten the fun of the game or, on occasion, illuminate – as in *The Unicorn* and *The Sea, The Sea*. Her characters are endlessly given over to psychoanalysis and ingenious at using their analyses, as they use everything in the world that swims into their ken, as adjuncts to the points of view they have established or wish to establish. Occasionally a character will seize Freudianism wholeheartedly as a way of exonerating himself (Effingham Cooper at the end of *The Unicorn*) or crazily and comically (Francis Marloe in *The Black Prince*), but in general a discriminating interpretation of limited parts of Freud's thought is central to Murdoch's method. He is useful in many ways, and like her he argues against the rationalist illusion that human beings are free.

In concentrating her considerable talents on describing the things that bind people, Murdoch purposively builds up a fascinating situation – a vision of the world as it can be said objectively to exist, and an illustration of how ordinary illusionist creatures compulsively must or can use it. Nature, with its unlimited and transcendent power of beauty, can not only contribute to intense emotion (Bradley and Julian at the seashore in *The Black Prince*), but can also by its perpetual change and peculiar constancy show its alienation from the wandering human mind. That this view of nature easily tosses us back into the quagmire of the Lockean subject-object question of Romanticism is obvious, but also ultimately irrelevant to a just estimate of Murdoch's work. For her, reality spawns real objects, external to and independent of the perceiving mind, which function as images of a middle stage but point towards the absolute good if we are able to read them accurately. As we can see from her essay, 'The Sublime and the Good', the human mind is constantly defeated by its attempts to build patterns of harmonic unity: the sheer intractability of the natural world, its multiplicity, its sudden achievements of the sublime, are part of what Murdoch has termed 'the mysterious transcendence of reality'. But human life in nature nevertheless implants automatically a series of symbols (the basis of imagery and art in all cultures) that give the materials for identifying or failing to identify the human place in this milieu. To put it another way, people *think* via nature; it is essential for articulation and a means forward for the questing soul.

The reality of the transcendent other of nature and our necessary humility before it extend through the changing face of landscape to what Murdoch sees as nature's greatest product – human beings, to whom we owe an attention more profound than that which we turn in any other direction. In considering people, we come closer than with anything else the natural world can present to an understanding of the real nature of our middle state. In *The Sandcastle*, Bledyard describes this necessay apprehension of human beings:

What is the first and most fundamental truth which an incarnate being must realize? That he is related on the one hand to God, who is not a thing, and on the other hand to other things which surround him. Now these other things [*sic*] . . . are some of them mere things, and others of

them are God-related things like himself. . . . when we are in the presence
of another human being, we are not confronted simply by an object. . . .
We are confronted by God. . . . Who is worthy to understand another
person? . . . Vices and peculiarities are easy to portray. But who can look
reverently enough upon another human face? (pp. 77–8)

Murdoch thinks it is important to perceive ourselves as literally incarnate,
existing in flesh which is an object in nature, and yearning towards the
unthingness of God (or good, or reality, or beauty, or even Christ – our term
for the absolute, as so many of Murdoch's characters point out, depends on
the local mythology we are attached to). In describing this yearning, she pulls
herself out of the subjective socio-philosophy of our period and hearkens
back to certain thought patterns that characterized western comprehension
before its cohesiveness spun out of control during the late Renaissance. She
cannot be locked glibly into the Great Chain of Being, however, because of
her resistance to pattern and insistence on the random and thus holy nature of
the particular. It is this stress on the particular that creates the extended detail
of every landscape, and that above all causes the careful differentiation of
characters, even those who could easily be grouped together because they are
so predominantly the types and products of their socio-economic background. Thus Murdoch's painter's eye rests carefully on every face and mood
and costume of her characters. Her descriptions are invigoratingly rigorous
and scrupulous, combining duty and joy in a way that reinforces our powerful sense of her as a religious writer.

It is rather odd for a contemporary novelist who is not a servant to
orthodoxy to have as a fundamental part of her style such a presentation of
religious attention and love, especially when the main underlying ideas
acknowledge contemporary society's loss of the workable religious concepts
that once united it. The withdrawal of traditional consoling images of God is
accompanied in Murdoch's fiction by a sense that even the most advanced
soul goes forward into darkness, that all human forms are deceptive chimeras
that lead to destruction, that the metamorphoses people attempt to formulate
and enforce in themselves are defeated, so that they crawl painfully rather
than leap forward. Murdoch would have us see that human tasks and progressions are small (again, she is close to late Plato); for all the ruins and defeats
that large human dreams and myths – like happiness or heroic triumph –
unconsciously induce, there is a continuous, distinct counter-current where
people are continuously tested minute by minute and where they very
occasionally triumph over their inherently selfish nature. They also fail here,
and fail crucially, so that the laws of causality which govern the universe can
move in terribly. As Bradley Pearson puts it in *The Black Prince*:

the young . . . cannot see how all things have consequences . . . there are
no spare unrecorded encapsulated moments in which we can behave

'anyhow' and then expect to assume life where we left off. The wicked regard time as discontinuous, the wicked dull their sense of external causality. The good feel being as a total dense mesh of tiny interconnections. My lightest whim can affect the whole future. Because I smoke a cigarette and smile over an unworthy thought another man may die in torment.                                                                 (p. 95)

The continuous and unending nature of the moral task and its presence in the smallest, most apparently insignificant action inform all Murdoch's novels, and what real human progress is made occurs through enactments of the task. As Hugo Belfounder told Jake in the first novel, *Under the Net*: 'God is detail. It all lies close to your hand' (p. 258).

As Murdoch depicts it, neglect of detail occurs because characters are blinded by the pursuit of the large and glorious, utterly false ideal, and this neglect leads ineluctably to defeats and the misuse of others. Devastation comes from the inability to see, to distinguish minutely, to pay attention. In Murdoch's world, we come to expect and even accept this devastation and betrayal, these lies and mistakes, but the spontaneous response to her novels is nevertheless one of deep psychic shock. That she can cause it in novel after novel attests to the degree of truth she is telling, and proves that the issue is an awakening of a horror and fear which reflect all too accurately the world we live in.

And yet this sturdy counter-current built into the novels – attention to detail, the full differentiation and particularization in all descriptions of people and places, and the small, good actions of almost all characters, even the corrupt – displays a less pessimistic power persistently at work. The fascination of the novels has much to do with this generosity: so buoyed is the reader by the beauty of detail and the frequent insights of the characters that the final overwhelming and triumphant pull of death and defeat is so much the stronger. The idea of contrast in this context takes on great force; Murdoch's sudden juxtapositions of good and evil, and of a full world beside the blank reality of death, wring the psyche intensely. Her reasons for such juxtapositions and their intended effect are surely concerned with radical moral intention. In *A Fairly Honourable Defeat*, Morgan's literal panic (experience of Pan, quoted above) forces her to see the coincidence of beauty and horror in nature, and leads her to perceive a sudden new *Gestalt* of the unity and real structure of things. This *Gestalt* involves a new apprehension of how pain and horror participate in the beautiful, as they do in nature, in human experience, in art. Murdoch's work attempts to illustrate this perception with a force that keeps it far removed from either simple brutality or the lulling effect of cliché.

Such visions as Morgan's are rare, and Murdoch's characters who believe themselves on a quest for truth or moral victory generally perceive that they have certain materials to work with, materials which will forward the aims they project. Although these aims vary enormously from book to book, a relationship to virtue ostensibly stands behind them all. Sometimes the desire is only for the justification and survival of the ego, which for all its window-dressing merely wants to get away with things (*The Sacred and Profane Love Machine, An Accidental Man*); but often what is sought is one of the loftiest human ideals: to be a just judge (*The Nice and the Good*), to learn to die (*Bruno's Dream*), to create great art (*The Black Prince*). The distance between the character (finally *any* character, no matter how minor, since they are all totally absorbed in their particularized quests, all *en route*) and the end he or she longs for is enormous and always in danger of becoming an uncrossable void. The subject of Murdoch's fiction is the methods devised by various kinds of consciousnesses to traverse that distance. The novels describe the cunning of the human mind in gathering useful tools for the crossing, and illustrate how the distance alters as the end invariably recedes and demands redefinition. Those who find the best answers and surest route (the few characters of good) decline to define the end at all; they concentrate on the route itself, the humble details of the means whereby we advance to the unimaginable. Unlike Plato's version of the possibility of perceptible progress for the virtuous soul, Murdoch's formula (if such a term can be used for immersion in and perception of the moral duties of the moment) suggests that the light of the sun exists, but that it is not our job to presume to see it. Concentration on the particulars of nature and man will automatically produce temporary breakthroughs to reality, the perception of which must not be interpreted as a permanent experience but as a rare and occasional gift, a sort of grace partially controlled by the quirks of causality.

In *The Fire and the Sun*, Murdoch sums up the limited human state by identifying mankind with two wistful, comic, allegorical figures in Shakespeare's *Henry IV, Part II*:

> however much we idolize each other, we are limited specialized animals. . . . We are creatures of a day, nothing much. We do not understand ourselves, we lack reality, what we have and know is not ὄντως ὄ'ν, but merely ὄν πῶς. We are cast in the roles of Shallow and Silence, and must not, in favour of art or philosophy, protest too much. (pp. 84–5)

Murdoch agrees with Shakespeare in thinking that each human being functions exactly like a figure in a work of art, subject to a design he cannot perceive. Our brief lives and limited perception should keep our plans small, but of course they do not. Murdoch's characters are mimetic of us in a society we are not yet historically separated from, and this proximity gives us the advantages and disadvantages of responding without an intermediate lapse of time. The devices these characters use in moving towards their ill-conceived goals are therefore also the ones available to us as readers. Because of our highly-developed but now faltering culture, the objects of that culture and the analysis we bestow on them become major tools, and one of the most permanently sustained elements in these novels is a loving brooding on and examination of these objects and an encouragement that we follow the example set.

The specialization characteristic of our culture has kept it divided basically into religion (theology), art and philosophy, and indeed we are losing our grip on these, taken either together or separately. Murdoch's characters, with their generally fairly high educational level, perceive themselves as part of a tradition that long ago began to disintegrate and is now in its final stages. The middle-aged are futilely patient with the young, who are often described as aimless and detached from the cultural preoccupations of their elders. We are told several times that this is the first generation to grow up entirely without God, and it demonstrates the results stemming from the lack of this cultural binding power. Hence the barrenness of the world for the young Muriel, Elizabeth and Leo at the end of *The Time of the Angels*, or the waywardness of Peter Foster in *A Fairly Honourable Defeat*.

Another contributing factor to the now nearly complete loss of tradition is the bourgeois use of cultural artifacts as mere decoration or proof of a proper education – a use that involves a refusal to pay the sort of attention to them that these spiritually oriented devices require. Young Peter in *A Fairly Honourable Defeat*, who is busily occupied in throwing away his chance of a Cambridge degree and is described justly by Axel as 'a symptom of corruption', accurately puts his finger on this bourgeois failure of seriousness:

> People read a lot of old authors without understanding them or even liking them, they learn a lot of facts without feeling anything about them or connecting them with anything that's present and real, and they call that training their minds. . . . You stopped *experiencing things* long ago. When did you ever really compare Shakespeare and Swinburne? When did you last read a play by Shakespeare, if it comes to that? (pp. 113–4)

Murdoch pits her considerable energy against such indifference and complacency, and her habitual method is to cause the reader to re-examine and rethink the ideas and artifacts he so much and so glibly takes for granted. Within this novel, Morgan's panic experience, by its awful forcing of her attention, can serve to convince Peter that human creative activity exists, that Ariel's song from *The Tempest* is indeed a marvel, whereas his father's self-satisfied clichés and comfortable distance from Shakespeare are merely impediments of the sort that govern the typically mediocre life.

If middle-class complacent unconsciousness is symptomatic of the receding of a vividly felt culture, Murdoch's novels are vehicles for its revival. Most of her characters are attached at least to one and often to many art objects, ranging from fairy tales and medieval romance to Titian,

Shakespeare, or Plato, and reading a Murdoch novel involves an enormous cultural evocation – one indeed that many readers are barely up to. But Murdoch (unlike many contemporary experimentalists) avoids condescending to her clientele, and her reader's response to the novels is unlikely to be impaired by failures to recognize mythical structures or resonant references. Again, her resemblance to a much earlier period must be pointed out; Shakespeare's huge, allusive frame of reference echoes through the plays, but popular audiences have never been dismayed. Even mandarin, highly allusive Renaissance writers like Spenser and Milton understood the pleasures of a slow, progressive entrance into the fully extended frame of a work whose initial charm is unimpaired by a dread of the work still required of the reader. In spite of the speed of her action, Murdoch demands time and frequent rereading, and she asks us to stop and reconsider, to give a new real attention to the particular cultural objects she places before us – Peter Pan or Bronzino, Christianity or Max Beckmann. But even as she does so, her central focus is on the human being, her instructional aim is still to have us see how characters' minds gain fuller articulation from the presence of these things, how richly they serve as *exempla* to the groping psyche, how their palpability focuses the drifting fantasy.

The problem Murdoch perceives so clearly is that, as Plato had warned, art (all of culture that has to do with image-spawning) can too easily be used as magic, and as such can encourage our dreams and fantasies rather than aid in the perception of reality. For this reason, Brendan Craddock in *Henry and Cato*, the most spiritually developed character so far in the Murdoch canon, goes off with nothing, neither artifact nor the imagery of the personality of godhead built into Christianity – without even the speculation of theology and philosophy that had so fascinated him. For him spirituality will not degenerate into magic as it does for James Arrowby in *The Sea, The Sea*, another highly-developed character, whose clear-minded knowledge of where he has gone wrong cannot prevent him from inexorably playing out the game. Once the imagination succumbs to the infinite enchantments of magic in any of its forms, its rescue is doubtful. James's mistake involves what he calls 'a less than perfect meddling in the spiritual world' which 'can breed monsters for other people':

> Demons used for good can hang around and make mischief afterwards. The last achievement is the absolute surrender of magic itself, the end of what you call superstition. Yet how does it happen? Goodness is giving up power and acting on the world negatively. The good are unimaginable.
>
> (p. 445)

His cousin Charles, who understands nothing of what James is talking about, counters by claiming that surely goodness has to do with loving people, an old Christian argument that Murdoch doubtless would agree with. This discipline too requires perfect action and a divorce from the magical interpretations which so endlessly absorb us and interfere with the quality of action possible. Although Murdoch can so fruitfully use art as a positive device for her characters' enlightenment, it too is easily misused and seen as magic by the cunning ego, as her characters amply illustrate in the novels. Like us, they attempt to use the structures of art to mythologize themselves and others, to control the world by imposing a referential frame on things. It is easier to love this mythic form than to allow the real existence of others to carry on freely; hence human beings in Murdoch's novels are constantly trying to control their fellows, to exert power, to create imaginary dream worlds, rather than looking clearly at the reality the world and the best art spread out before us. Of course, good art and bad art coexist in the breadth of most people's cultural experience, and Murdoch makes it clear that characters define themselves by choosing their artistic models. In *Henry and Cato*, the distance from Beautiful Joe's projected image of himself in a tawdry filmic mafia (bad art) to Henry's brooding over Titian's *The Death of Actaeon* (good art) is a mighty step, but the fate of the characters is subject to both, and the laws of causality extending from the characters' apprehension of these cultural objects are inexorable.

Murdoch's characters, for all their sophistication, have also fed, as Freud says we all do, very richly on the diet of primitive superstition which underpins our culture. Hence the presence of certain kinds of magical ritual: the rites of the Mor children in *The Sandcastle*, the central image of *The Unicorn*, the propitiatory gifts to Willy Kost in *The Nice and the Good*, the frequency of characters who fancy themselves witches, the habit so many characters have of interpreting the existence and behaviour of others as portents. The difference between our would-be rationalist world and this primitive superstitious one is swept away by sheer psychic pressure, and it is with real relief and pleasure that so many of Murdoch's characters unleash their primordial inner demons. Indeed, Charles Arrowby, in the last sentence of *The Sea, The Sea*, hits a deep chord when he describes human life as a 'demon-ridden pilgrimage'.

The shifting line between the rational belief that primitive superstitions are defunct and the mind's recurrent inclination to dig them up and put them to use is confusing, as is that between superstition and religion. Murdoch suggests the probability that anyone involved in religion must also be involved in superstition, a category consisting of a bottomless need to use various advanced magics for peculiar and often specious ends. So untrustworthy is the dreaming, fantasizing ego that it can twist into instruments of power even the most subtle and positive materials available to it. Thus the clarifying devices that theology has used to try to get at the real, especially the arts that have served the proliferation of the images of Christianity, can become powerful ends in themselves, obscuring through the seductive haze of beauty the real they were intended to transmit. The images of art thus can convey specious, mythic, superstitious power; as Murdoch says in *The Fire and the Sun*: 'the bad side of human nature is secretly, precariously at work in art' (p. 82). Her characters, if they are trying to move towards reality or the good must take on the task of attentive discrimination, must carefully *see* the cultural object with precision and learn its profound reality, as Charles Arrowby learned to distinguish between his egotistical, stagy image of *The Tempest* and Shakespeare's real idea.

We see in the novels a need to fix attention on cultural devices that will help us towards reality, that will assist our pilgrimage by the transcendent breakthroughs they allow. In a profound way, serious religion and, especially in our secular age, great art can call human attention to the remote, external other (God, Plato's forms); that attention must be properly directed and perfect, without the distraction of the myriad forms of self-concentration or – its main component – the need for power. Versions of magic interfere in this process and are the ego's instrument for allowing fantasy and consolation rather than the hard, pure forms of reality. But of course the magic is also essential and here again Plato and Murdoch part company.

Whereas Plato in the *Laws* considers that lower, simple arts and the bright images of simplified religion can be used only to beguile and guide a mentally and spiritually limited populace, Murdoch argues for the great power of transcendent art to illustrate truth and beauty and lead to the good (reality) in a more effective way than philosophical dialectic can manage. That even the greatest art spins from the dangerous unconscious and spawns images, that it, like religion, can all too easily be misused, that its primary success involves magic and enchantment are all tacitly accepted by Murdoch in the course of the novels. The serious artist nevertheless presents reality because he has soberly and truthfully looked for it through a full examination of the entire range of his materials – the detail of the natural and human world, the work of his fellow artists and the moral discipline required in turning his clear vision lovingly on both the divine and the necessary or random. In conclusion, although the paradox and radical disjunction have already been put another way above, here is this version: images and magic are dangerous, yet they are nevertheless central tools for leading the discriminating mind forward. The human psyche must learn to use the various magics and be led forward by them before it can abjure them – and what a painful and treacherous trip it is, to what an unknowable end, Murdoch's novels richly teach us. As in the case of attention to all the details of the physical world of things or the middle world of our love and duty to people, we must concentrate on the process, the means whereby we can slowly discipline ourselves to see at least a little.

★

Murdoch's devotion to works of art is a constant in her novels and shows her commitment to their sustained usefulness. As her characters stumble or rush on obsessed by the often spurious ends they have set for themselves, art is both marshalled to the aid of their quests by their cunning egos and exhibited in the purity of its commitment to and portrayal of reality. Although the reader will often be too enslaved to see accurately, the great work of art stands as an object to be justly perceived by the disciplined mind, and is capable by its sheer beauty of attracting and altering even the most muddled and ordinary person. Murdoch puts it eloquently in *The Fire and the Sun*:

> Good art, thought of as symbolic force rather than statement, provides a stirring image of a pure transcendent value, a steady visible enduring higher good, and perhaps provides for many people, in an unreligious age without prayer or sacraments, their clearest *experience* of something grasped as separate and precious and beneficial and held quietly and unpossessively in the attention. Good art which we love can seem holy and attending to it can be like praying. Our relation to such art though 'probably never' entirely pure is markedly unselfish. The calm joy in the picture gallery is quite unlike the pleasurable flutter felt in the sale room. Beauty is, as Plato says, visibly transcendent; hence indeed the metaphor of vision so indispensable in discussions of aesthetics and morality. The *spectacle* of good in other forms, as when we admire good men and heroes, is often, as experience, more mixed and less efficacious. As Kierkegaard said, we admire and relax. Good art, on the other hand, provides work for the spirit.                                                                (pp. 76–7)

Murdoch first put this far-reaching idea of the essentially religious function of good art in our period to work in her early novel, *The Bell* (1958). Here Dora Greenfield, the girlish, worldly, straying wife, much out of place in the quarrelsome piety of the religious community at Imber, goes to the National Gallery with the unconscious intention of temporarily escaping her two possible wretched lives – unhappy marriage to the neurotic Paul or unsatisfying continuation of an affair with the hedonist journalist, Noel. Instantly she is taken over by an attention to the paintings which functions as a religious act, overflowing into the basic nature of her life and auguring change:

> Dora was always moved by the pictures. Today she was moved, but in a new way. She marvelled, with a kind of gratitude, that they were all still there, and her heart was filled with love for the pictures, their authority, their marvellous generosity, their splendour. It occurred to her that here at last was something real and something perfect. Who had said that, about perfection and reality being in the same place? Here was something which her consciousness could not wretchedly devour, and by making it part of her fantasy make it worthless. . . . But the pictures were something real outside herself, which spoke to her kindly and yet in sovereign tones, something superior and good whose presence destroyed the dreary trance-

like solipsism of her earlier mood. When the world had seemed to be
subjective it had seemed to be without interest or value. But now there was
something else in it after all . . . she felt that she had had a revelation. She
looked at the radiant, sombre, tender, powerful canvas of Gainsborough
and felt a sudden desire to go down on her knees before it, embracing it,
shedding tears. . . . Her real life, her real problems, were at Imber; and
since, somewhere, something good existed, it might be that her problems
would be solved after all.                                    (pp. 191–2)

She is also momentarily moved to the same profound but temporary insights
before the medieval bell, 'a thing from another world' (p. 222), whose
castwork represented a vision of reality for the artist of long ago, and which is
engraved with the name Gabriel and the words: 'Vox ego sum amoris' (I am
the voice of love): 'The squat figures faced her from the sloping surface of
the bronze, solid, simple, beautiful, absurd, full to the brim with something which was to the artist not an object of speculation or imagination'
(p. 270).
    Dora is a naive and in many ways primitive character whose capacity for
analysis is slight, and whose ability to transfer even the knowledge imparted
by the paintings to her life is almost non-existent. Her understanding of the
bell is characterized by fantasy: she wants to use it to perform a miracle over
which she would officiate as priestess. Not truly seeing it as the *vox amoris*,
she succumbs to hatred, envisioning herself as a witch and opposing the
otherworldly magic of the medieval bell to what she interprets as the
hypocritical and imprisoning piety of Imber. Unwilling to talk to Mother
Clare, whom she fears as a mere instrument of the disapproving morality
about her, she is forced into fantasy by her desire for revenge against her
enemies: by causing a miracle she will become powerful. The destructive
results of this misuse touch every character in the book. She slowly begins to
learn, but the reality of the bell exists beyond Dora, as does the real spiritual
life of Mother Clare, the Abbess, and the other cloistered sisters. Dora
nevertheless is seen in the novel as slowly moving forward, very slowly
being transformed by the painful interaction of art, religion and life. Her
moral ordinariness makes her an excellent illustration of human duality: on
the one hand, she displays a humble capacity to see the transcendence of art at
work in the moral life (her apprehension of the paintings in the National
Gallery); on the other, her blind obsessional behaviour misapprehends the
bell as a work of art and uses it in a personal arsenal of magic, witchcraft,
hatred and revenge.
    Both responses haunt Murdoch's characters, and when she says in *The Fire
and the Sun* that art provides work for the spirit Murdoch is indicating the
fundamental moral responsibility we all undertake in setting out to perceive
accurately what the work of art is about ('the metaphor of vision so indis-

pensable in discussions of aesthetics and morality'). Earlier in the same essay, she points out that

> the relation of art to truth and goodness must be the fundamental concern of any serious criticism of it. 'Beauty' cannot be discussed 'by itself'. There is in this sense no 'pure aesthetic' viewpoint. Philosophy and theology have to reject evil in the course of explaining it, but art is essentially more free and enjoys the ambiguity of the whole man; hence the doubleness which of course it shares with Plato's Eros.                    (p. 72)

In Plato's myth of the demon Eros in the *Symposium*, as in the image of the soul as charioteer in the *Phaedrus*, the constant pull of the opposites of good and evil describes the moral doubleness which it is art's task to illustrate.

That good and evil are easily distinguished is one of the illusions of the simple-minded, as pointed out so bluntly by Carel Fisher in *The Time of the Angels* and illustrated by the harmful naivety of James Tayper Pace in *The Bell*. Two of the novels, *The Time of the Angels* and *A Fairly Honourable Defeat*, are dedicated to allegorical proofs of the existence of evil, which Murdoch urges contemporary man to remember, to reintroduce into the permissive anti-evil consciousness of present liberal western society. But even apart from these two pointed studies of the truly demonic, Murdoch's work persistently takes on the task of showing how evil, in its deceptive guises of fantasy, ego-concentration, inattention, thirst for power, easy consolation, comfort and well-meaning, rules our morally sloppy world. Much contemporary art too easily follows the psychological and philosophical fashions of our time, not only in allowing this moral inattention but even encouraging it. Indeed, current fashions in literary criticism, off-shoots of structuralism, which see all works of art as without objective reality and governed only by private semiotic indications, tend towards an assertion that the critic's own semiotics are an end in themselves.

Thus the fashionable idea that every reader or perceiver of the work of art is engaged in a permissively private critical act where nothing external or real is to be learned leads directly to increased concentration on the already overactive ego, which needs not discern 'the relation of art to truth and goodness' since the art object has no objective reality anyhow. The ensuing frivolity and ego satisfaction need no comment here, but in Murdoch's world false criticism – like Dora's of the bell – leads to terrible results. If art does not function as a powerful means of drawing the self out of the self, of alerting the soul to a reality infinitely beyond its solipsism, much damage ensues. A criticism that does not aim at discovering the relationship between art and reality is not only not serious, it is dangerous, since art as a tool for the reality-seeking spirit is not merely an aesthetic addendum to life's pleasures but one of the many objects of perception (like the moral discipline of personal relations or the excitement of being in love) that form the core of our moral development.

Thus proper criticism in Murdoch's view is the product of a training in moral discrimination as well as a reflection of aesthetic taste and knowledge of the formal materials the critic must master. These qualities depend on discipline and insist on attention paid fully to the object in question. Similarly and much more importantly, the artist's crucial task is to purify his own egotism by intelligent use of the imagination. As Murdoch's central manifesto, the last twenty-four pages of *The Fire and the Sun*, densely written as an explanation of her radical deviations from Plato's fruitful and, for her, infinitely useful ideas, are an eloquent statement of the responsibility and possibilities of art for all involved in it.

In spite of her strong adherence to the basic Platonic outlook, Murdoch justly quarrels with attempts to identify her as a wholehearted Platonist. She is indeed an interpreter of Plato, but they part company frequently, and nowhere so strongly and originally as in her explanation of the ultimate superiority of art to philosophy. As she sees it, 'learning to detect the false in art and enjoy the true is part of a life-long education in moral discernment' (p. 83). This bravely unfashionable point of view not only opposes the egotism of the critic, it is critical of the retrieval of an easy good which characterizes so much art and so much flabby criticism. Art that deals with reality is rare and difficult; I will allow Murdoch to talk *in propria persona* in an eloquent passage which employs and builds on Platonic imagery:

> The high-temperature fusing power of the creative imagination, so often and eloquently described by the Romantics, is the reward of the sober truthful mind which, as it reflects and searches, constantly says no and no to the prompt easy visions of self-protective self-promoting fantasy. (Like the daemon of Socrates which said only 'No'.) The artist's 'freedom' is hard won, and is a function of his grasp of reality. . . . The imagination fuses, but in order to do so it must tease apart in thought what is apart in reality, resisting the facile merging tendencies of the obsessive ego. The prescription for art is then the same as for dialectic: overcome personal fantasy and egoistic anxiety and self-indulgent day-dream. Order and separate and distinguish the world justly. Magic in its unregenerate form as the fantastic doctoring of the real for consumption by the private ego is the bane of art as it is of philosophy. Obsession shrinks reality to a single pattern. The artist's worst enemy is his eternal companion, the cosy dreaming ego, the dweller in the vaults of *eikasia*. Of course the highest art is powered by the force of an individual unconscious mind, but then so is the highest philosophy; and in both cases technique is useless without divine fury.
>
> What is hard and necessary and unavoidable in human fate is the subject-matter of great art. . . . Art is about the pilgrimage from appearance to reality (the subject of every good play and novel) and exemplifies in spite of

Plato what his philosophy teaches concerning the therapy of the soul. . . .
The divine (intelligent) cause persuades the necessary cause so as to bring
about the best possible. It is the task of mortals (as artists and as men) to
understand the necessary for the sake of the intelligible, to see in a pure just
light the hardness of the real properties of the world, the effects of the
wandering causes, why good purposes are checked and where the mystery
of the random has to be accepted. It is not easy to do justice to this hardness
and this randomness without either smoothing them over with fantasy or
exaggerating them into (cynical) absurdity. Indeed 'the absurd' in art,
often emerging as an attempt to defeat easy fantasy, may merely provide it
with a sophisticated disguise. The great artist, while showing us what
is not saved, implicitly shows us what salvation means. Of course the
Demiurge is attempting against insuperable difficulties to create a harmonious and just world. The (good) human artist, whom Plato regards as such a
base caricature, is trying to portray the partially failed world as it is, and in
doing so to produce something pleasing and beautiful. This involves an
intelligent disciplined understanding of what may be called the structural
problems of the Demiurge.                                    (pp. 79–80)

The Demiurge in the *Timaeus*, the builder of the world and archetype of the
'good' artist, was forced as he created to recognize the intractability of certain
of his materials (necessity) which he persuaded into some kind of acquiescence. Our major problem in the world is dealing with this contingent stuff,
the necessary (as opposed to the divine or intelligible and formal) which
makes our world irreversibly imperfect and our life in it resistant to pattern
and meaning. The task of the artist is to use the necessary as well as the divine,
to distinguish reality from illusion, to clarify our vision so that we can discern
the operation of evil. For this task Murdoch claims that realism is best:

> Strong agile realism, which is of course not photographic naturalism, the
> non–sentimental, non–meanly-personal imaginative grasp of the subject-
> matter is something which can be recognized as value in all the arts, and it is
> this which gives that special unillusioned pleasure which is the liberating
> whiff of reality; when in high free play the clarified imaginative attention of
> the creative mind is fixed upon its object. Of course art is playful, but its
> play is serious. . . . Freud says that the opposite of play is not work but
> reality. This may be true of fantasy play but not of the playfulness of good
> art which delightedly seeks and reveals the real. Thus in practice we
> increasingly relate one concept to another, and see beauty as the artful use
> of form to illuminate truth, and celebrate reality; and we can then experi-
> ence what Plato spoke of but wished to separate from art: the way in which
> to desire the beautiful is to desire the real and the good.          (p. 84)

Murdoch is perfectly, even devastatingly, aware of the imperfection of even the greatest work of art; she never overestimates or completely glorifies the artist, who in fact will, like the Demiurge, 'never entirely understand' (p. 85). But although acknowledging that 'even at its most exquisite art is incomplete' and 'pierced' (pp. 85, 86), she points to the operation of the artist's 'sober truthful mind', which can play with the materials of reality and make it into 'the great general universal informant' (p. 85). Art's availability to all, as opposed to Plato's ideal of the specialized few trained in philosophical dialectic, is its greatest virtue, but of course is also its bane in our period of egocentric criticism and dwindling cultural awareness. Murdoch's proselytizing spirit would put us all back to work on the great art universally available, not only by her evocation of the art objects she wishes us to see anew, but also by her own serious novels – all good stories, well-spun yarns – whose close mimesis of our world calls out an alert moral intensity:

> Art can rarely, but with authority, show how we learn from pain, swept by the violence of divine grace toward an unwilling wisdom, as described in the first chorus of the *Agamemnon* in words which somehow remind us of Plato, who remained (it appears) so scandalously indifferent to the merits of Aeschylus. (p. 82)

Murdoch's novels at their best – and so great has her authority become since *The Nice and the Good* that each succeeding book manages this best to some degree – can locate this painful knowledge for us with an immediacy we cringe under. Her repeated claim is that tragedy is difficult to write (for her probably only Shakespeare and Aeschylus have succeeded) and non-existent in the real world, where so much is governed by the dark comedy of causality put into motion by our misuse of ourselves, others, the world, art – the whole range of things our ego operates upon. If tragedy does not enlighten our lives, pain certainly does push the unwilling psyche forward, force it on to a better path – or a worse one. The unattainable quest for goodness constitutes the most important idea in Murdoch's art, a quest too obscure for human beings to see clearly, and about which we usually deceive ourselves when we think we are on it. The pain of Murdoch's art aims to pull us out of ourselves, just as her characters are pulled, so that something of the real good can be perceived.

The *locus classicus* of this phenomenon of pulling the self from the self is the Apollo–Marsyas myth, which has hung in the background of western art for centuries and which I mentioned briefly in the previous chapter. Its connections to the moral-spiritual aspirations of mankind are strong and its application to our experience of life profound. As we have seen, in the myth Marsyas, a mortal of uncommon musical abilities, hubristically challenges the god of music Apollo to a contest, which Marsyas of course loses. His penalty is flaying – a horrible and painful death. In Ovid's version, he cries out in agony, 'Quid me mihi detrahis?' (Why do you draw me out of myself)

According to Edgar Wind in *Pagan Mysteries in the Renaissance* (1968), to whom this paragraph is indebted, the Neo-Platonists interpreted this pulling of the self from the self as a Bacchic pain leading to the clarity of Apollo, and Lorenzo de Medici declared that the way to perfection was by this road. The ordinary human who aspires to the transcendent is overwhelmed and shrieks with pain under the disproportionate strength of the god: to aim so high involves tearing off the earth to achieve the divine ecstasy. The longed-for confrontation with the god involves pain to the death, and the achievement of art surprises by the disproportion of this awful demand to our human, quotidian frame. The Christian centuries perceived the myth as a poetic theology, a perfect fusion of art and reality (the divine), and as such, Dante used the myth to open the first Canto of the *Paradiso*.

In *A Fairly Honourable Defeat*, Murdoch applies the Apollo–Marsyas myth to the homosexual couple, Simon and Axel, very briefly but powerfully. Simon as usual is in a state of love wrung by anxiety as he tries to make Axel promise to love him forever. Axel, who tries to live safely by limiting the lies he believes inherent in absolute statement, dodges the issue, saying that he has not the faintest idea whether he will. Simon's reference to the myth is frivolous at first:

'You're Apollo and I'm Marsyas. You'll end by flaying me.'
    'That's an image of love, actually, Apollo and Marsyas.'
    'How do you mean?'
    'The agony of Marsyas is the inevitable agony of the human soul in its desire to achieve God.'
    'The things you know.'
    'The things you failed to learn at the Courtauld.'
    'I don't believe it though. Someone is flayed really. And there's only blood and pain and no love.'
    'You think our planet is like that?'
    'I think our planet is like that.'
    'No redeeming grace?'
    'None at all.'
    'None, Simon?'
    'Well, only this kind.'                                        (p. 31)

Axel's interpretation of the myth as 'the inevitable agony of the human soul in its desire to achieve God' is historically correct but rather academic, and Simon's statement of the horrible reality – 'blood and pain and no love' – takes it away from its too formal definition. The most interesting thing in their conversation is the usefulness of the myth and the commitment of the human spirit to both interpretations. Pain is in waiting for mortals, and whether it can be transformed by ecstacy or seen only blankly, as pain without redeeming grace, depends entirely on the psyche experiencing the flaying. One is reminded of Henry in *Henry and Cato* looking at Titian's *Death of Actaeon* and remarking that these goddesses are killers, and in *The Unicorn* Hannah Crean-Smith uses the image of the leaping salmon returning to their spawning pools in the same way, with the same idea of human bravery in entering another element: 'It's a most moving sight. They spring right out of the water and struggle up the rocks. Such fantastic bravery, to enter another element like that. Like souls approaching God' (p. 51).

In Murdoch's working proof, however, the pain and bravery are not really thought out in advance by the participant, and the soul leaps as Marsyas did, with egotistic hubris and no grasp of the consequences or of the powerful side issues and apparently random elements which accompany any step forward to *exstasis* (a standing outside of, a result of separating the self from the self). The pain that drives one forward has not been bargained for, and is terrible and bitter. To this pain and death Murdoch's characters are frequently subjected, and, occasionally, through a forced knowledge of them, they achieve a partial redemption.

Her most extended use of the Marsyas myth and its consequences occurs, as I mentioned earlier, in what I consider her best novel so far, *The Black Prince* (1973). The last twenty-four pages of *The Fire and the Sun* set out firmly and eloquently Murdoch's view of the uses of art, and prove again even more powerfully than her well-reasoned earlier essays had done what an extraordinarily clear and radical theoretical literary critic she is. But *The Black Prince* embodies the doctrine she preaches and shows broadly and deeply the manifold operations of art in a particular man's use and pursuit of it. As a novel, it illustrates the profound and essential practice of irony, which Murdoch claims the artist must use and which is more natural in describing the real lives of human beings than the peculiar grand abstractions of tragedy. In recounting Plato's point of view in *The Fire and the Sun*, Murdoch tells us that he disallows the existence of the good artist, who in Murdoch's definition should 'imitate the calm unenvious Demiurge who sees the recalcitrant jumble of his material with just eyes, and with a commanding sense of proportion' (p. 76). What Plato does describe is the bad and mediocre artists, and Murdoch agrees with him. The bad artist is 'a naive fantasist . . . and construes the world in accordance with the easy unresisted mechanical "causality" of his personal dream life (the bad thriller or facile romance and its client)' (p. 76), and the mediocre artist

thinks he 'knows himself but too well', parades his mockery and spleen as a despairing dramatic rejection of any serious or just attempt to discern real order at all. This figure (a fairly familiar one in the pages of Plato's dialogue, where he is criticized, and of modern literature, where he is indulged) is on the road toward the 'all is permitted' and 'man is the measure of all things' of the cynical sophist. Neither of these, as artist or as man, possesses true self-knowledge or a just grasp of the hardness of the material which resists him, the necessity, the ἀνάγπη of the world. Confronted with semi-chaos the Demiurge is steadied (if he needs it) by the presence of the Forms. But must the mortal artist, condemned to some variety of self-indulgence, be either a dreamer or a cynic; and can he not attempt to see the created world in the pure light of the Forms?          (p. 76)

In achieving good art and this view of Platonic reality, as Murdoch argues through the shifting progress of *The Black Prince*, the artist finds irony his most accurate tool. This is not the ironical self-flattering delusion of the mediocre artist, but irony induced by the duality of our experience, our highly-developed sense of the comic on the one hand and the inevitable pain of our existence on the other, both exacerbated and driven often to absurdity by our obsessional prejudices and need to belittle others.

Irony is certainly the primary operative method in the framed, integumental structure of *The Black Prince*. The enclosure of a realist tale (which is simultaneously a love story, an adventure story and a dramatization of a theory of art) by an elaborate system of qualifying forewords and postscripts, as well as by intrusions into the narrative of what profess to be highly self-conscious truth-telling addresses to the editor, forces the reader into a world of multiple points of view. In this world where the human consciousness of the artist-protagonist strives towards clarity and just account, contradiction abounds and characters lose no opportunity to gainsay or diminish the most passionately expressed and convincing truths. The device of forewords and postscripts shatters the security of a highly-structured tale whose crafted design, even without these ironic addenda, is itself broken by intrusive apostrophes and the shifting nature of the narrative voice or persona. The pun on Pearson-person-persona is surely intentional. (Because Murdoch is obviously playing with Bradley Pearson's name, not only in this pun, but in the BP initials which equate him with the Black Prince of the title, I have decided to use the initials as an acronym in referring to him. I also suspect that the name Bradley may be intended playfully to evoke F. H. Bradley, the English idealist philosopher whose famous book, *Appearance and Reality*, was really a study of the Absolute. And of course the shadow of the Shakespearean critic, A. C. Bradley, casts its pall, as Richard Todd has pointed out in *Iris Murdoch: The Shakespearian Interest*, 1979.) The density of the tale constantly works against its clarity, and Bradley Pearson as both self-conscious artist and literary critic is at once achieving art and illustrating its pain and impossibility: Marsyas always loses, and yet the losing provides the *extasis*, the human achievement and the ultimate contact with divine 'other' reality.

BP, as narrator and central character of *The Black Prince*, is both a good and bad aesthetician and moral thinker, constantly reflecting on the autobiographical work of art he is in process of unravelling for us. In one of his elevated moments, his first direct address to his 'dear friend' and great teacher – the editor whose identity is at first obscure to the reader – he discusses art's difficulty in finding a method of telling the truth. Both simplicity and complexity can be used, but because truth is so slippery and multiform and the human artist automatically limited by his own personality, irony exists both positively, as a just device in presenting our duality, and negatively, in our use of it to misuse others:

> Of course, as you have so often pointed out, we may attempt to attain truth through irony. (An angel might make of this a concise definition of the limits of human understanding.) Almost any tale of our doings is comic. We are bottomlessly comic to each other. Even the most adored and beloved person is comic to his lover. The novel is a comic form. Language is a comic form, and makes jokes in its sleep. God, if He existed, would laugh at His creation. Yet it is also the case that life is horrible, without metaphysical sense, wrecked by chance, pain and the close prospect of death. Out of this is born irony, our dangerous and necessary tool.
>
> Irony is a form of 'tact' (witty word). It is our tactful sense of proportion in the selection of forms for the embodying of beauty. Beauty is present when truth has found an apt form. It is impossible finally to separate these ideas. Yet there are points at which by a sort of momentary artificiality we can offer a diagnosis. . . . How can one describe a human being 'justly'? How can one describe oneself? With what an air of false coy humility, with what an assumed confiding simplicity one sets about it. . . . How the angels must laugh and sigh. Yet what can one do but try to lodge one's vision somehow inside this layered stuff of ironic sensibility, which, if I were a fictitious character, would be that much deeper and denser? How prejudiced is this image of Arnold, how superficial this picture of Priscilla! Emotions cloud the view, and so far from isolating the particular, draw generality and even theory in their train.                                    (p. 55)

Murdoch is quite aware of the further irony of her own falsely subjective method, since BP is indeed a character in a work of fiction whose book is about him and his friends. Murdoch's technique nevertheless brings off successfully an illustration of the problems involved in presenting the world as it is, in practising realism.

*The Black Prince* is a tale of the process of potential human development; its centre is the reality of the leap into another element as opposed to fantasizing or theorizing about it. The Marsyas who would create art is not praised and lionized as BP wishes to be, but metaphorically flayed, and his final, genuine relatedness to Apollo, the divine reality of good art, is gained only at this immeasurably painful price. Murdoch's decision to translate this mythic idea into fiction is extraordinarily adventuresome and very risky indeed, especially as it is necessarily woven into the fabric of her persistent moral and realist concerns. Not only must the artist have himself pulled from himself; all experience of the world and the whole of human moral life demand the same transformation. Hence the artist cannot be seen (as BP originally saw him) as a solitary chosen being separated from participation by the holiness of his gift, nor can he safely think that the dark creative Eros functions simply or will choose the route of his mere talent.

The naive BP of the plot had believed in an easy and sacred-romantic definition of the artist. But as we begin reading this elaborate book, we come first to a peculiar Editor's Foreword by P. Loxias, who is anxious to give himself a vast role as BP's impresario, clown, harlequin and judge, and who reserves the last word for himself; we are thrust into an obscure world where a heavily disguised Apollo figure claims to be the *alter ego* of the writer of the love story we are now embarking upon. The identification probably has its source in Aeschylus, where in the *Agamemnon* Cassandra addresses her god Apollo as Loxias as she strips herself of her prophetic garment and prepares to die. We first meet the narrator, Bradley Pearson, after this editor has presented him and the novel to us. BP instantly explains his method of proceeding, saying he will 'adopt the modern technique of narration, allowing the narrating consciousness to pass like a light along its series of present moments, aware of the past, unaware of what is to come' (p. xi). This past point of view is opposed to some new knowledge that he has achieved since the events of his story, some secret which is at the base of his new personality:

> The virtues have secret names: they are, so difficult of access, secret things. Everything that is worthy is secret. I will not attempt to describe or name that which I have learnt within the disciplined simplicity of my life as it has latterly been lived. I hope that I am a wiser and more charitable man now than I was then – I am certainly a happier man – and that the light of wisdom falling upon a fool can reveal, together with folly, the austere outline of truth.                                                        (p. xi)

Putting these things together produces no immediate sum for the reader, and although we know the authorial voice has a double persona – that of the past as opposed to the wiser one of the present – we are still in a considerable state of confusion as the one voice begins and the other intercepts. The primary voice, that of the artificial narrating persona of the past, is given to precious statements about the sanctity of the artist and his role as a saint who has 'kept his gift pure' and reached 'only a perceptive few':

> 'A writer' is indeed the simplest and also the most accurate general description of me. In so far as I am also a psychologist, an amateur philosopher, a student of human affairs, I am so because these things are a part of being the kind of writer that I am. I have always been a seeker. And my seeking has

taken the form of that attempt to tell the truth of which I have just spoken. I have, I hope and believe, kept my gift pure. This means, among other things, that I have never been a successful writer. I have never tried to please at the expense of truth. I have known, for long periods, the torture of life without self-expression. The most potent and sacred command which can be laid upon any artist is the command: wait. Art has its martyrs, not least those who have preserved their silence. There are, I hazard, saints of art who have simply waited mutely all their lives rather than profane the purity of a single page with anything less than what is perfectly appropriate and beautiful, that is to say, with anything less than what is true.     (p. xii)

This is obviously and irritatingly the kind of desperate, lying rationalization that characterizes failure, but when the other voice of the wiser present breaks in it yet retains some aesthetic view of art's separation from real life, and needs the modification of the Apollo figure who had claimed instantly that the tale to be presented is art in its truest form – a realistic description of human pain and transformation. This Apollonian truth makes Bradley's original and precious ideas about purity and silence simply frivolous:

Man's creative struggle, his search for wisdom and truth, is a love story. What follows is ambiguous and sometimes tortuously told. Man's searchings and his strugglings are ambiguous and vowed to hidden ways. Those who live by that dark light will understand. And yet: what can be simpler than a tale of love and more charming? That art gives charm to terrible things is perhaps its glory, perhaps its curse. Art is a doom. It has been the doom of Bradley Pearson. And in a quite different way it is my own.
(Loxias, p. ix)

The original BP persona, at the point where his 'novel' begins, thought he was a servant of a real, vaguely supernal truth which demanded removal from life (i.e. London) to a seaside solitude uncontaminated by all too mortal and ordinary others, and perhaps demanded also a saintly martyrdom, should his attempt to create fail and he achieve only continued silence. He also perceives art as a talent which is his doom, but as he describes this doom he sounds precious rather than convincing, pretentious rather than genuinely truth-telling. The foreword of his Apollonian editor, reread after the novel has played out its elaborate structure, changes and gives a hard reality to a vocabulary that BP begins by using frivolously. If I may for clarity's sake speak of the unflayed (i.e. the pre-trial) BP as the primary narrating voice and the flayed (i.e. imprisoned with P. Loxias as teacher and companion) BP as the secondary voice, this Apollonian personification is aligned to the secondary voice, and like it can present words, terms, phrases with hard reality, whereas the naive primary voice misuses them out of ignorance and hubris.

It is the secondary, educated voice of BP who presents the novel (without forewords and postscripts) entitled *The Black Prince: A Celebration of Love.*

The blind and hubristic primary voice of BP is the basic narrator, however, and knows nothing at first of either celebration or love. From the first two prefatory pages we have the Apollo figure obscurely telling us what the process of the novel will finally bring home – a precise knowledge of what the hackneyed term 'love story' means; not the romance of an elderly man, but 'man's creative struggle . . . for wisdom and truth', which can be told only 'ambiguously' and 'tortuously', which is 'secret', which is 'a doom'. These words are signals for our reading of the novel, and ways of talking about the density of human experience connected by a firm causality which emerges in this work of art devoted to presenting that experience as form.

That life is automatically opposed to form poses the first irony of the novel, an irony expressed by the need of both 'author' and 'editor' to tamper through prefatory and postscript material, to modify and extend the tight form of the finished art work itself, a product which Murdoch herself paradoxically speaks through and is invisible from. Just as Shakespeare projected the nervous and contradictory structure of *Hamlet* which will become so important in this work, Murdoch presents the Chinese box structure of this integumental and difficult novel. The story itself has a very pure form, and one that BP as an artist is anxious to retain. Scrupulously considering his structure on page one, he points out that there are from the beginning several ways of seeing the thing. Nervous about and inimical to conventional art forms, he explains that beginnings are entirely arbitrary. The 'dramatically effective' one would use Arnold's phone-call stating that he thinks he has just killed his wife Rachel (with a poker), and end in neat circularity with Rachel's phone-call summoning BP as a witness to her having indeed killed her husband (with a poker). This neat structure would suggest that the story is the drama of Arnold Baffin's murder, which in a way it is. BP, however, chooses 'a deeper pattern' of causality or consequence and begins with Francis Marloe's arrival to announce that BP's ex-wife Christian has returned to London from America. This return begins the long and complex action which leads BP to his murder trial, and focuses thus on him and hence 'man's creative struggle' rather than on Arnold and Rachel. In other words, BP's self-consciously iterated choice means that the murder and revenge theme which makes this novel in a sense a general thriller is encapsulated by more serious concerns. The artist-narrator chooses so that structure can enlarge rather than reduce the subject matter.

As Murdoch presents BP in his primary voice he is an extremely precious, hellenistic perfectionist – a Rimbaud character filled with theories about art, and hence fussily enslaved to form, which he cannot produce. Given the right experiential circumstances, the early BP could, at best, force pen to paper and produce a neatly constructed, bloodlessly contrived adventure story, thriller, love story, tale of error and consequence. But in the terms controlled by the Niagara force of the present narrative, the fastidious BP is rendered, at one level, in simple and gross terms as a naive and barren follower of Rimbaud who can be seen as plunged into the loosening experience of a love adventure which, as his own postscript warns, can be simplistically interpreted as driving away his writer's block and forcing him to write, at another level entirely new to him, a good, racy, autobiographical quasi-work of art. But this novel is pre-eminently about transformation and metamorphosis, and we must therefore from the beginning deal with the secondary, transformed, educated voice who, together with the Loxias figure, conspires against form and undercuts it wherever possible.

The paradoxical conjunction of form and formlessness is very important in Murdoch's thinking about art. She described it in an interview with Michael Bellamy (1977) as the 'conflict between the form–maker and the truthful formless figure', and certainly it is the basis of the contrast in her work between the would-be artist and the would-be saint, even perhaps in such a novel as *A Fairly Honourable Defeat* between evil and good, as the struggle of Tallis versus Julius will illustrate. In BP Murdoch has constructed a character who, after his education, combines qualities of both and shows through his experience the subtle linking of art and ethics when they perform their proper truth-telling function.

The primary artist BP forms the artwork, while the secondary, ethical, experienced, clear-sighted BP tampers and interrupts, destroying the neatness of the form by deliberately interjecting a contradictory impulse toward disunity. This anti-formal impulse, however, is exactly the factor that removes BP's novel from the domain of the mediocre, and because of it a vulgar estimation of the book as merely the story of an elderly man in love with a young girl or of a violent murder is entirely incorrect. Not only is Murdoch fusing the artist with the ethical thinker, but she is showing also how the painful winning of knowledge and in some measure a perception of reality enlarge the scope and texture of art. The secondary voice frequently breaks the form, as does Apollo-Loxias himself in his forewords and post-scripts, because formlessness delivers truth even while it here coexists at first so confusingly and finally so fruitfully with form.

Although the primary BP tries to depict himself and his feelings at the pre-educational time of the action, the secondary voice several times interrupts the 'story' to address his dear friend in a 'direct speaking' (p. 54), a device the two have discussed and decided is legitimate. These interruptions are devoted to ruminations on the function and nature of art, as well as of its task in the human struggle towards reality:

Art . . . is the telling of truth, and is the only available method for the telling of certain truths. Yet how almost impossibly difficult it is not to let the marvels of the instrument itself interfere with the task to which it is dedicated.

(p. 55)

One of the functions of these interruptions is to restrain the slickness of the instrument or form, to slow down and deepen a plot which is whirling quickly by, and above all to concentrate on 'the task to which it is dedicated'. 'My book is about art', BP has said immediately before this quotation, and since a definition and description of art constitute the task at hand, it is crucial that we discern the process and instruments of that definition.

*The Black Prince* is Murdoch's fictional manifesto, her pouring into fiction of her best thinking about art itself and its relationship to human behaviour and development. The process of defining resides in the progress of the novel, and by hanging the plot on the character of BP she allows his journey from ignorance to knowledge to become the image of her definition. The task of the reader is to perceive the Pearson persona clearly, to know what BP understands at any given point, to estimate justly. The complexities imposed on the plot by interruptions and denials of unity in structure or point of view are part of the unfolding and hold the reader when the irritating and flawed primary BP in his confusion wanders wide of our sympathy. Above all, the fact of a plot gives Murdoch the basic material for her central claim that experience is better than the 'demons of abstraction' (p. 268), and that art and morality are interwoven in substance: 'all art is the struggle to be, in a particular way, virtuous' (p. 154).

Implicit throughout this novel is a demand that this state of equivalence between art and morality be recognized. Just as Dora in *The Bell* under-estimated the medieval bell, perceiving it inadequately and applying it de-structively to her own ego, the primary voice of BP and the four writers of the postscripts who fail to engage in a just and moral estimation of his story are involved in a double failure: a failure to recognize the truth of the art object and a failure to make an adequate moral judgement. Although Murdoch's subject is the description and definition of art, one important corollary is thoroughly examined: the nature of literary criticism and the responsibility of the critic. In this Murdoch is very unfashionable, for, as she argues in *The Fire and the Sun*, 'learning to detect the false in art and enjoy the true is part of a life-long education in moral discernment' (p. 83), and *The Black Prince* shows the result of the lack of such discernment. Bad criticism, rendered inaccurate through the ego-interference of the critic, is severely attacked in this novel, and the contempt of Loxias for the self-serving postscript writers can also be directed against all critics whose cowardice and failure in moral engagement cause them to belittle the object.

In *The Fire and the Sun*, Murdoch says that 'the final best instrument' in criticism is 'the calm open judging mind of the intelligent experienced critic, unmisted, as far as possible, by theory' (p. 78). The primary voice of BP is not only misted but clogged with theory, some of it good, most of it bad. The theories he holds refer to his own artistic career and offer consolation for his purity and meagre output; they also give him ample material for attacking

Arnold Baffin, with whom he quarrels manically and compulsively on the subject at every chance. The fairly long excerpt BP quotes of his review of Arnold's new book typifies bad, self-serving, theory-ridden criticism, a criticism which reflects on itself (and the critic's self) rather than on the object at hand. The reader has really no doubt (given the plot summary of it) that Arnold's book is bad, but naive Julian is the better and more reliable critic when she comically addresses her father's work directly and objectively: 'He lives in a sort of rosy haze with Jesus and Mary and Buddha and Shiva and the Fisher King all chasing round and round dressed up as people in Chelsea' (p. 107).

Murdoch is of course using Arnold's prolificacy and BP's contempt of it as an ironic echo of the journalistic attacks she herself has received. A self-critical writer constantly refining her style, Murdoch herself could be speaking Arnold's words:

> You, and you aren't the only one, every critic tends to do this, speak as if you were addressing a person of invincible complacency, you speak as if the artist had never realized his faults at all. In fact most artists understand their own weaknesses far better than the critics do. Only naturally there is no place for the public parade of this knowledge. If one is prepared to publish a work one must let it speak for itself. It would be unthinkable to run along beside it whispering 'I know it's no good'. One keeps one's mouth shut.
> (pp. 138–9)

Tongue in cheek, she presents Arnold possibly as a parody of Anthony Powell, but also of what some critics have accused her of being because of her mysterious allusive frame and awesome prolificacy. In BP's self-justifying attacks on Arnold, however, Murdoch is exploring a serious failure of insight and moral discrimination, a failure of calmness which inhibits the development of the coolly judging mind and leads to a violent act of jealousy when BP rips up in ten wild minutes every volume of Arnold's entire huge *oeuvre*. This symbolic murder of Arnold is a foreshadowing in the world of art of what Rachel performs in the world of experience. BP's trial, as he himself feels, is partly an exorcism of a very real guilt.

He manages good criticism only when his transformation has begun and he is talking about *Hamlet* to Julian, immediately before recognizing that he is in love with her. In his extraordinary monologue on the peculiar nature of Shakespeare's achievement in projecting both experienced feeling and spiritual energy into the play, BP suddenly transcends his typical jealous grumbling and perceives a work of art radically and originally. His eloquent insight allows a fusion of the various elements in his usual vocabulary about art and the artist, and this central moment with its dense, allusive perception articulates many of the issues about the role of the artist which, up to this point in the novel, have been so puzzling. This is, in short, good criticism, because BP is concentrating his considerable intelligence and originality on something outside himself, on an artist so good that his own mean-spirited competitiveness and personal neuroses are simply swept away.

The most important point about this eloquence in the midst of the novel's fast, almost Dionysian process is that it is prompted by the rapid approach of a metamorphosis in BP's character and life prompted by, indeed entirely coinciding with, his falling in love with young Julian. In the progress of BP's adventures, he had previously shown an inclination to believe that perhaps the sudden, unnerving crowding-in of experience that he had been undergoing, and particularly the growing affair with Rachel Baffin, Julian's mother, might be instrumental in his writing his great book. 'Was I upon the brink of some balls-up of catastrophic dimensions, some real disaster? Or was this perhaps in an unexpected form the opening itself of my long-awaited "break through", my passage into the presence of the god?' (p. 112). That the two – disaster and contact with the god – might coincide did not occur to him, but he had perceived that a metamorphosis associated with personal destiny and somehow controlled by a divine power was in store for him:

> And yet, so complex are minds and so deeply intermingled are their faculties that one kind of change often images or prefigures another of, as it seems, a quite different sort. One perceives a subterranean current, one feels the grip of destiny, striking coincidences occur and the world is full of signs: such things are not necessarily senseless or symptoms of incipient paranoia. They can indeed be the shadows of a real and not yet apprehended metamorphosis. Coming events do cast shadows.          (p. 113)

Instantly on perceiving that he incongruously but absolutely loves Julian, he assumes that this is the final step, the real metamorphosis, and that the affair's break-up will constitute the disaster. Only by extended painful astonishment is he pulled beyond anything he had imagined, and with real amazement the reader learns much later in the conclusion of the basic plot and in the Editor's Postscript that the real end is death – Arnold's and, more significantly in terms of this book's study of the nature of the artist, BP's own.

The complex aesthetic ideology of the novel must be absorbed step by step as Murdoch, her Apollo impresario and the two voices of BP present it. Let us begin by looking at BP and his vocabulary. The primary voice – the BP undergoing the experiences that lead to knowledge – is one of Murdoch's most highly-polished comic figures. For all the grimness of the secondary persona's cogitations, he steadily reasserts that human beings are endlessly comic to each other. Defining what comedy is and how it can be played out in the middle of action which can also be seen as full of pain and horror is one of the many tasks of this novel.

The BP of the process of the book enacts a grim comedy at every turn because the person he then was, as his knowledgeable later persona puts it, was 'captive and blind' (p. 156). The failure to coalesce intelligence and real perception, to see himself and his relations with those about him clearly, to distinguish between his compulsive neuroses and the real state of things, all contribute to the long process of enlightenment necessary. We have therefore a character who, despite his carefully attained cultural expertise, his sophistication, his narrow but real ability as a writer, his years of experience in the routine of the tax office, and his fifty-eight years of complex human relationships, can be thrown easily into situation after situation in which his neurotic compulsions rule and his actions comically fail to coincide with the self-knowledge he wrongly believes himself to have. Captive to his neuroses and mesmerized by a false image of himself, he is badly in need of metamorphosis, of a pulling of the self from the self so that he can reach the divine end in which he sees art (and Murdoch sees life) as participating. But the comic genius of his presentation consists in the risible contrast between the wisdom he believes he has and the tyranny of his compulsions. It is clear from the novel that Murdoch sees this gap as the central idea of comedy and, embellished by a wit which serves to heighten the distance between personal ideas of the self and its reality, the novel only slowly unfolds the horror that the comedic circumstance leads to. 'How the angels must laugh and sigh' (p. 55), as the secondary BP puts it. For Murdoch, comedy is a servant to seriousness and a necessary part of mimetic descriptions of real people.

BP's comic-tragic drama opens with a situation which is realistic, unfunny and rather dull. Its swirling into comedy and the speed of its causality occur against his will: he himself persistently believes that he is all ready to perform the great act of his life in writing a good book. Recently retired from years of tedium in the tax office in order to write, BP finds himself with an unexpected writer's block and decides to try for privacy and silence at a secretly rented cottage by the sea. Already packed and ready to leave, he fussily decides to check if he has packed his sleeping pills, his belladonna, his proper notebooks. This delaying tactic obviously reflects an unconscious knowledge that he is not at all ready and does not want to be in silence with himself, and in fact the unpacking completely smashes his plans for retreat. By casual chance, he is swept out of dullness into hectic action as Murdoch, in one of her typically manoeuvred *coups*, coalesces three crises in the lives of her main characters. Had BP not been nervous over his retreat, he would have escaped this dramatic juncture, but suddenly Francis Marloe descends on him to announce that Bradley's long-divorced wife Christian is back after her American marriage, Arnold phones to say he thinks he has murdered Rachel, and BP's sister Priscilla arrives on his doorstep to announce that she has left her husband and must be looked after. Each of these crises is played out to its irreversible end, all three intermingling with each other and all clawing at BP, who does in fact try to escape by turning to Julian, who at first had looked like only a side issue.

The speed of the action and BP's reaction to everyone and everything that swims into his ken constitute the novel's plot. The authorial control that causes the multiple crises of the other characters is perceived by BP as somehow connected to some cosmic intention. (This plot control can indeed be seen as reflective of the random condition of the universe: the issue is an interesting one in that those who wish to claim – and I do not – that Murdoch's plots are mere contrivances would deny that she could, in creating such circumstances, be in any way reflecting odd occurrences and concurrences in any human life.) As the plot overthickens, a frantic BP feels that he must get out of London or 'something would reach out and grab me'. His whole frame of reference centres on psychic projections of gods and powers whose metaphorical images serve as definitions of the ideas that obsess him. Until he is reluctantly caught up in the affairs of others and his relations with them (he is caught up *because* of his relations with them, but he fails to see this) these metaphorical ideas concern the abstract nature of great art and his potentiality in producing it. Murdoch, however, believes with Plato that truth must live in present consciousness, and for her this consciousness is related not to abstract theories but to the details of the necessary moment. BP is, therefore, generally wrong in his theories, but his vocabulary, as he will later find out, may be occasionally correct, although wrongly understood. The experience from which he so ardently wishes to escape is the necessary tool for purifying his knowledge of what art is.

In an earlier novel, *Bruno's Dream* (1969), Murdoch presents a pretype of BP, Miles Greensleave, who is also an avoider of life's intensities and whose talent and vocabulary are reminiscent of the early BP's. Both men are essentially seen as silly as they work preciously and long on the purifying of their talent; both are incapable of production. Miles spends endless hours with his commonplace book, describing the delicacy of a flower or a wet leaf on the windowpane; BP writes and writes his way through notebooks to no avail. When BP speaks of his recognition of himself as an artist, he speaks, with Miles's sort of self-aggrandizement, of a radiant experience of seeing a fox: 'the child wept and knew himself an artist' (p. 87). Like BP, Miles has an egotistical conviction, not sustained by achievement, that his personality is conducive to the production of art, which he too refers to as the visitation of a god. And like BP, Miles is jogged through the experience of pain and deprivation into writing. But Miles is in all respects such a negative character, and the nature of his final turning to poetry so unexplored, that the reader is not at all convinced of his competence. The point that this earlier character contributes to, however, is the tendency in Murdoch's fictions about art to depict the artist as initially flawed and egocentric – and as waiting for a god.

The whole metaphor is, of course, very Greek. It suggests the relationship of Apollo and the Muses and opens the way for our identification of the Loxias figure. (It is significant that Arnold, the professional and popular writer, claims to have no muse.) As the primary voice of BP sees it, however, the external other which joins itself to the talented creator, the god whom BP and Miles await, is the mythic Eros of the *Symposium* and *Phaedrus*. BP interprets this figure narrowly as a certain kind of creative energy, and hence as the power controlling the idea of art and its production. He feels obscurely that at the right moment for composition he will be profoundly shaken by this god, and he knows that '[his] development as an artist was [his] development as a man' (p. 113). Yet his desperate need for silence and detachment, his urge to get out of London and his repugnance at the messy involvements he finds himself in the middle of all indicate that he misunderstands the nature of his relationship to this external god who rules not only the creation of art, but also the erotic centre of all human beings.

Murdoch, who argues so firmly for 'strong agile realism', sees BP's fastidious recoil from the necessary present as an illustration of his inadequacy and blindness. Plunged into the untidy, generally depressing middle-aged erotic affairs of others – Rachel's and Arnold's violence, Priscilla's sad protracted failures, Francis Marloe's pitiable failed homosexuality, Christian's sleek flirtations, Roger and Marigold's uneven and cruel match – BP cannot perceive that these are where the real Eros resides. Self-consumed, he identifies this tumult with some alien power destructive of his creativity and becomes increasingly frantic to escape into solitude. It is only after he has been well taught through the process of the tale that he recognizes that the symbolic Eros extends his activity not mythically and abstractly, but in the real world with these messy characters whom BP must suffer and learn from. The compulsive, Dionysian speed of the action and of BP's mode of narrating it produce the present work of art – a work utterly unlike anything the primary fastidious persona of BP could have envisioned. Finally Apollo teaches Dionysian energy, but his major lesson is that the lived details of the present moment give the artist his material.

BP is wrong not only about the nature of artistic inspiration and what is required of the artist in terms of participation and observations, but also about the composition of his own erotic self. His youthful divorce from Christian was followed by some affairs which he declines to talk about, and certainly Francis is partially right in his postscript when he says that BP's relationship to Arnold has homoerotic elements. Comically obsessed by the phallic Post Office Tower, he takes unanalysed steps to resume the connection with Christian, and becomes really interested in his now crazily complex milieu only when Rachel makes sexual overtures to him. Suddenly he remembers that his dark veiled god, Eros, is sexual in most manifestations, and adds the image of Aphrodite to his arsenal of symbols. It occurs to him that 'Rachel might indeed be the messenger of the god' (p. 113). Having an affair with her would take a new sort of courage: 'It had often, when I thought most profoundly about it, occurred to me that *I was a bad artist because I was a coward.* Would now courage in life prefigure and even perhaps induce courage in art?' (p. 114; my italics). This dawning realization of art's dependence on life certainly is a first step forward for BP, and one that is both easy and pleasant: having an affair with Rachel which she will look after and keep from getting awkward would not significantly interfere with what he images as a visitation of Eros. His impotence when he actually finds himself in bed with her comically announces his failure in both areas of eroticism, and it is clear that he is far from ready for the creation of art. The secondary voice, in commenting on BP's muddle and inadequacy with Rachel (and with Priscilla, Francis, Arnold, Christian, *et al.*) indicates how removed that past self had been from any kind of insight:

> There is so much grit in the bottom of the container, almost all our natural preoccupations are low ones, and in most cases the rag-bag of consciousness is only unified by the experience of great art or of intense love. Neither of these was relevant to my messy and absentminded goings-on. (p. 155)

Still BP continues, as he enacts his tale, to feel that the new frenetic pace of his life is connected to the 'hand of destiny' (p. 158), a destiny divided between a negative sense that some power is causing all this muddle and is out to get him and his positive belief that the visitation of the creative Eros ('a great dark wonderful something', p. 156) is imminent. So convinced is he that he can protect his ego from suffering and keep some kind of power over things that he is utterly taken by surprise when the process begins and he suddenly experiences an intense love which sets him on the path towards real art. Having fooled around with Rachel, BP now falls absolutely in love with young Julian, who has been unimpressively in the background from the beginning, ripping up love letters, childishly asking for BP's little bronze water buffalo lady, demanding that he tutor her, flying a balloon which he chases. After tumbling ignominiously out of bed with Rachel, he had stumbled into Julian and bought her an erection-producing pair of purple boots. So untuned to his erotic being is BP that none of these incidents registers, and it is only after Julian irritatingly appears to study *Hamlet* with him and he launches into the impassioned lecture–interpretation of Shakespeare's relationship to his masterpiece that he recognizes himself to be in the grip of a power he has no preparation for.

Falling in love with Julian affects BP in two ways. First he loves her as a real woman in the real world, and in this respect he acknowledges the inappropriateness of the situation. This novel is constructed carefully so that mirrored actions occur frequently, and here the January-May affair which earlier he had so brutally attacked in Roger and Marigold becomes his own dilemma. And just as he sees falling in love with Julian as a moment of revolution in his art, he receives a letter (the fatal letter which leads Rachel to murder her husband) from Arnold saying that he too has fallen in love, with

Christian, and that this event will create a revolution in his art. These ironic doublings and repetitions help the novel's strong sense of the erratic and impenetrable, and therefore unjudgeable, nature of the world. Nevertheless, the sexual, erotic love for Julian is real, and BP experiences what he calls 'a sort of incarnate history of human love' (p. 271). Certainly Murdoch's masterly eloquence through BP in describing the nature of being in love day by day is one of the most penetrating and exciting achievements of the novel.

But what is even more interesting in a theoretical way is the second level of BP's love for Julian. Here Murdoch shapes her central symbols into a tight coalescence which allows a subtle enactment of Eros's many creative energies. Julian's presence forces BP to think hard about *Hamlet* and Shakespeare, and his as yet unrecognized sexual response to her drives him to the intense and radical re-evaluation he makes of that play. This erotic energy is then suddenly and fiercely focused on Julian, when she identifies herself with the artwork by saying, 'I played Hamlet once' (p. 164). BP instantly feels that 'she had filled me with a previously unimaginable power which I knew that I would and could use in my art' (p. 172). He feels that he has 'become some sort of god' (p. 170) and at the same time recognizes the primary issue: 'There was an overwhelming sense of reality, of being at last real and seeing the real. The tables, the chairs, the sherry glasses, the curls on the rug, the dust: real' (p. 173). Included in this complex experience is an evocation of the god. As BP renders Hamlet, he refers to the Marsyas-Apollo myth by identifying Hamlet with speech: 'He is the tormented empty sinful consciousness of man seared by the bright light of art, the god's flayed victim dancing the dance of creation' (p. 164). Shakespeare in writing *Hamlet* is

> speaking as few artists can speak, in the first person and yet at the pinnacle of artifice. How veiled that deity, how dangerous to approach, how almost impossible with impunity to address, Shakespeare knew better than any man. . . . But because his god is a real god and not an *eidolon* of private fantasy, and because love has here invented language as if for the first time, he can change pain into poetry and orgasms into pure thought –   (p. 164)

Shakespeare's real god is not merely Eros but Apollo, and for the first time BP understands the pain Shakespeare through Hamlet is speaking about, the flaying, metamorphosis and wild energy of the whole enterprise. He knows that Shakespeare's god is a 'real god and not an *eidolon* of private fantasy' as his own version of the dark Eros has been. Oddly enough, much of what BP says appears to come from his subconscious and not to be wholly retained. He does not replace the image of Eros with that of Apollo (and beyond) until his trial and education, after which he returns to this central insight: 'And the black Eros whom I loved and feared was but an insubstantial shadow of a greater and more terrible godhead' (p. 337).

Nevertheless knowing at least some reality and anticipating pain take BP very far forward. Later, also in his postscript, he will describe Julian not as an end but as his gateway: 'Human love is the gateway to all knowledge, as Plato understood. And through the door that Julian opened my being passed into another world' (p. 337). During the process of his love affair with her, however, his knowledge continues to be imperfect. The pain he inadequately envisages is first his own silence (which, as Francis points out, he breaks almost immediately), then the impracticality of the whole thing because of the age difference, then Arnold's fury and Rachel's burning jealousy and anger. He is completely unprophetic about the real results and still blind to the subtleties of causality: another large leap into the appalling unknown will be demanded.

The passage in which he envisions the confluence of all major elements enacts the life and intention of Murdoch's title: *Hamlet* points to Shakespeare, Hamlet to Julian, and all three to BP and Apollo and the creative Eros. Who, indeed, many readers have asked, is the Black Prince? Obviously and traditionally Hamlet, of course. But also Julian, who in dressing up as Hamlet enacts in flesh the Eros of BP's apprehension of art. Julian as Hamlet is what BP loves. (He is impotent in bed with her as he had been with Rachel until she costumes herself as the literary black prince. Through this prodding, BP's remembrance of Hamlet's pain gives substance – and violence – to his own horror at Priscilla's death, and rape results.) But there can be little doubt that the black Eros as dark god so often addressed must be considered the real black prince: the subtitle, *A Celebration of Love*, gives the clue to the mythological identity. There is more to come, however, and Francis Marloe in his not altogether mad postscript also rightly points out that BP's initials give him the right to the title. Finally there is Loxias-Apollo himself, whom BP will in conclusion address as 'the crown of my quest':

> I was seeking you, I was seeking him, and the knowledge beyond all persons which has no name at all. So I sought you long and in sorrow, and in the end you consoled me for life-long deprivation of you by suffering with me. And the suffering became joy.                    (p. 338)

What are we to do with all of these identifications of the title? 'My book is about art', BP told us at the beginning of the novel, and P. Loxias had said that 'Man's creative struggle, his search for wisdom and truth, is a love story.' Eros as love at its highest, but including even its lowest reaches, commands the title, but the others participate in that title, as art at its most intense and serious toils to project an adequate definition. *Hamlet*, mythology, an ordinary girl, human brutality and vengeance, a talented but spiritually blinded man, all combine to define the erotic connecting energy between art and love and their power to point still further, beyond themselves.

Like BP, the reader could at this point falter, forgetting that Julian is only the gateway to the other world that BP enters. This qualification in no way diminishes her importance, and indeed BP links his capacity to write with her, using her as poets immemorially have done with their loves, celebrating her and conferring immortality on her: 'She somehow was and is the book, the story of herself. This is her deification and incidentally her immortality. It is my gift to her and my final possession of her. From this embrace she can never now escape' (p. 336). BP's loss of Julian through his own subterfuge (not telling her instantly about Priscilla's death or the quasi–affair with Rachel) and lying (he says he is only forty–six), drives him backwards again to distraction and fantasy, but it is not at all the flaying of the Marsyas artist by the real god. BP much later points out that 'the false god punishes, the true god slays' (p. 300). Julian's flight from him and her disappearance impose punishment, but he is in for much more.

The causality of BP's punishment in losing Julian is part of the larger pattern of inexorable cause and effect which governs this book. Given Murdoch's spiritual inclination towards the infinite and veiled idea of the good, it is natural that she uses it to fight against human failure by evoking it in relationship to causality: 'The wicked regard time as discontinuous, the wicked dull their sense of natural causality. The good feel being as a total dense mesh of tiny interconnections. My lightest whim can affect the whole future' (p. 95). BP's secondary voice recognizes and comments on these tiny interconnections throughout. He also opposes form or art to the good, thus remaining within Murdoch's paradox of celebrating art and yet fighting it:

> One of the many respects, dear friend, in which life is unlike art is this: characters in art can have unassailable dignity, whereas characters in life have none. Yet of course life, in this respect as in others, pathetically and continually aspires to the conditions of art. A sheer concern for one's dignity, a sense of form, a sense of style, inspires more of our baser actions than any conventional analysis of possible sins is likely to bring to light. A good man often appears *gauche* simply because he does not take advantage of the myriad mean little chances of making himself look stylish. Prefer–ring truth to form, he is not constantly at work upon the facade of his appearance.
>
> (p. 95)

Although art may admire, it cannot easily proclaim the good, which is too undramatic and unglamorous. Plots of fascinating but devastating causality such as this one are produced by the activities of the infinitely punishable, guilty, average person:

> The natural tendency of the human soul is towards the protection of the ego. The Niagara-force of this tendency can be readily recognized by introspection, and its results are everywhere on public show. We desire to be richer, handsomer, cleverer, stronger, more adored and more appa–rently good than anyone else. I say 'apparently' because the average man

while he covets real wealth, normally covets only apparent good. The burden of genuine goodness is instinctively appreciated as intolerable, and a desire for it would put out of focus the other and ordinary wishes by which one lives. Of course very occasionally and for an instant even the worst of men may wish for goodness. Anyone who is an artist can feel its magnetism. I use the word 'good' here as a veil. What it veils can be known, but not further named.                                  (p. 149)

The main characters who act the plot through to its end – Bradley Pearson, Arnold and Rachel Baffin – are average people who do not particularly think about the good and indeed would find its blank face intolerable. Although their egos lead them to evil deeds, their intentions are no more than merely muddled.

It is extremely interesting that of all the characters, only the secondary, educated persona of BP in his 'monastery' prison ponders what good might be, and in his wide-ranging use of religious vocabulary, connects it with sainthood. Wretched Francis Marloe comes closer than the other characters to fumbling thought on the subject as he tries incompetently to show his love for all others, but BP's ruminations are central and comprise Murdoch's device to illustrate how far, through his experiences and education, he has travelled. In the first place, he knows what a saint would be like and that, as Loxias has told him, none exists because the absolute relationship to the good implied imposes an intolerable burden on the personality: 'A saint would identify himself with everything. Only there are, so my wise friend tells me, no saints' (p. 81). He also knows the right (or real) questions and their ultimate unanswerability: 'What is it to love God?' (p. 80); 'What does the artist fear?' (p. 55); 'How can one change the quality of consciousness?'; 'Can there be a *natural*, as it were Shakespearean felicity in the moral life? Or are the Eastern sages right to set as their task in their disciples the gradual total destruction of the dreaming ego?'; 'Could constant prayer avail?' (p. 155); etc.

A barren complete listing of these questions would fail to convey their contextual strength, and the strong sense Murdoch manages to get across is that reaching the questions belongs not to the quotidian but to another 'world' or state of advancement into which BP has finally passed. But for all the emphasis on his passage, the quotidian or ordinary world is not forgotten, and Murdoch throughout the novel keeps it in focus with strong image patterns ranging from the absurdly funny (the phallic Post Office Tower, the mad recurrence of milk chocolate) to the very serious amulets which attach themselves to personality as possessive love objects (the water buffalo lady bronze, the snuff box inscribed 'A Friend's Gift', statues of Aphrodite). In one most beautiful nexus of symbols from the real world, Murdoch evokes drifting, air-borne objects – a balloon, kites, faces as radiant moons, huge pale globes, pigeons (being shot down) – and in talking of the kites, gives a touching description of part of their imagistic power: 'What an image of our condition, the distant high thing, the sensitive pull, the feel of the cord, its invisibility, its length, the fear of loss' (p. 79).

Meanwhile, BP's love for Julian, his 'gateway', imposes an interim metamorphosis on him. Like Marsyas, he enters the game blindly and perhaps hubristically, but it takes only a few days for him to realize how desperate his situation is, how inevitable his failures will be, and how in his 'chess game with the dark lord' he may make 'perhaps a fatally wrong move' (p. 212). Nevertheless, although consciousness may be unified (as BP tells us on p. 155) only 'by the experience of great art or of intense love', this love requires a mode of description, and the one chosen is, typically enough, that of religion. This is partly because BP's whole story has a religious idea as its end, but more because in contemporary western experience religion is seen as a source of metaphor rather than as a lived belief. As M. H. Abrams pointed out in *Natural Supernaturalism* (1971), this secularization of inherited theological ideas and ways of thinking dates from the great romantics, and it is in a way artistically natural that BP's transformation be given particularity and intensity when a religious mode of discourse once central to our culture is enlisted to its aid. Filled with his still secret love for Julian, BP talks to Christian (the women's names are not accidental!), who sees him thus: 'Brad, what is it, you look extraordinary, something's happened to you, you're beautiful, you look like a saint or something, you look like some goddam picture, you look all young again' (p. 189). And later (p. 192), she describes him again as a saint and identifies the change with Christ's mystical temporary transfiguration. Julian's name, as usual in Murdoch's many evocations of the saint of Norwich, gains even more pointed significance as BP associates her with the famous words, 'All shall be well and all shall be well' (p. 183). He returns to his flat, now made divine by her visit to it: 'So holy men return to temples and crusading knights feed upon the blest sacrament' (p. 181).

The love affair takes a firm step forward, comically in the restaurant on the Post Office Tower, seriously through the intensity of art, as BP and Julian attend a performance of Richard Strauss's *Der Rosenkavalier* at Covent Garden. Here BP, who previously disliked music and was irritated by Arnold's passion for it, is pushed by Julian's presence not merely to listen to the soaring opening duet, but to 'undergo it' (p. 218). The focusing caused by love's interaction with art here, as in the lecture on *Hamlet,* leads to a crisis, as this fastidious man rushes from the intensity of the music and vomits violently. His vomiting involves an acknowledgement of his body, of the messiness of human physical being, which BP has hitherto associated only with Rachel and the vomiting and suicidal Priscilla. This reminder of himself allows his confession to Julian and the launching of their affair. Pursued by Arnold's outrage and Rachel's hatred, the two soon begin their retreats, in which meeting in churches (even at Patara, their seaside haven, they explore the church) plays a large part. There can be no doubt that the inscription of the Christian incarnation on the roodscreen in St Cuthbert's Philbeach Gardens, 'Verbum caro factum est et habitavit in nobis' (The Word was made flesh and dwelt among us), is a powerful metaphor for the literal translation of the power of Eros (or of Aphrodite or of other ancient sacred powers) into their flesh and being.

When they finally reach Patara the sense of the sacred persists, and again art (Julian as Hamlet again) is called forth to reinforce it. After the frenzied rape which contains so much motivational content (Julian herself, Priscilla's recent but concealed death, Hamlet, an unshakeable sense of doom, the fury of Eros's image), the two are overwhelmed by a sense of being in a sacred space, surrounded by bad spirits (p. 282). Julian, as BP had done earlier, goes through a metamorphosis and becomes for him a holy object:

> She looked so much, and beautifully, older, not the child I had known at all, but some wonderful holy woman, a prophetess, a temple prostitute. She had combed her hair down smoothly and pressed it back and her face had the nakedness, the solitude, the ambiguous staring eloquence of a mask. She had the dazed empty look of a great statue.          (p. 282)

From their powerful experience for which religion serves so well as a metaphor, they both assume that they will write great books. The persistence of this idea and the belief that it is intense human love (Eros) that produces art are broken fairly quickly by BP's all too human lies and moral inadequacy, by his imperfection as an instrument.

In a very different context in *The Fire and the Sun*, Murdoch, in talking about Plato's long path to enlightenment, points to his fears that art is 'a sham, a false transcendence, a false imitation of another world . . . where the veiled something which is sought and found is no more than a shadow out of the private store-room of the personal unconscious' (p. 67). In this novel, where BP's moral progress somehow equals the progress towards good art, this is unfortunately the stage he has reached. Having achieved the intensity of love, he is imperfect in other dimensions, and so the far-reaching stories of Priscilla and of the Baffin-Christian enclave must take over. Because virtue and art are aligned in Murdoch's mind, the final developments take place as means to the knowledge of virtue, and the characters' progress is through guilt and punishment.

Priscilla's death, long in building and harrowingly well-prepared for, is inevitable as is Nina's in the early novel, *The Flight from the Enchanter*. In both cases, cries for help go unheard by a central character, so self-absorbed that, as BP puts it, 'I had not got a grain of spirit to offer to any other person' (p. 209). When Priscilla is dead, BP in conversation with Francis realizes that the truth of the matter, 'Priscilla died because nobody loved her', results from a fatal problem in BP's love for Julian. His perception of that love as divine and absolute, even when she is apparently lost to him, does not at all jibe with his failure to help Priscilla or to tell Julian about her death when he would rather put his false sexual 'ordeal' first. Blindly he thinks his enlightenment has taken place, and that through Julian he has gone as far as he can:

> Her love for me was an absolute word spoken. It belongs to the eternal. I cannot doubt that word, it is the logos of all being, and if she loves me not chaos is come again. Love is knowledge, you see, like the philosophers always told us. I know her by intuition as if she were here inside my head. . . . Because I love Julian I ought to be able to love everybody. I will be able to one day.
> (p. 315)

To have been so wrong and to be in such agony over Priscilla's death and Julian's absence puzzles him, but it also sets him up for the real crisis: Rachel's murder of Arnold because of the letter the latter had written Christian. How Murdochian and clever this plot turn is, and yet how absolutely and ingeniously dependent upon causality!

BP's trial for Arnold's murder arouses the reader against the perfidy of Rachel, but it also provides the final irony of the novel. In his magnificent postscript, BP says that this unexpected, dreadful and objectively unjust public humiliation and the myriad guilt feelings it arouses in him are the real point of his life, whereas all his other ideas of transformation, new being, ordeal, etc. had been chimerical:

> I had been confronted (at last) with a sizeable *ordeal* labelled with my name. This was not something to be wasted. I had never felt more alert and alive in my life, and from the vantage point of my new consciousness I looked back upon what I had been: a timid incomplete resentful man.
> (p. 331)

and

> I also felt something like this, that the emergence of my life out of quietness into public drama and horror was a necessary and in some deep sense natural outcome of the visitation with which I had been honoured. Sometimes I thought of it as a punishment for the failure of my vow of silence. Sometimes, shifting the same idea only very slightly, it seemed more like a reward.
> (p. 336)

The trial comprehends the real flaying and leads BP to the 'writing' of the present book, to his education by P. Loxias, to his real metamorphosis. Because of this trial the primary persona of BP is replaced by a new man whose existence modifies and improves the narrowly structured artwork that his autobiography would have been.

No longer lost in ignorance and darkness, BP now knows what the silence is which he had, in his blindness, identified as some calm of mind at the writing-desk with the creative Eros hovering over him. In one of the most subtle paragraphs of the novel, Murdoch, through BP's final address to Loxias, gives us the full substance of the novel she has written:

> So we live on together here in our quiet monastery, as we are pleased to call it. And so I come to the end of this book. I do not know if I shall write another. You have taught me to live in the present and to forswear the fruitless anxious pain which binds to past and to future our miserable local arc of the great wheel of desire. Art is a vain and hollow show, a toy of gross illusion, unless it points beyond itself and moves ever whither it points. You who are a musician have shown me this, in the wordless ultimate regions of your art, where form and substance hover upon the brink of silence, and where articulate forms negate themselves and vanish into ecstasy. Whether words can travel that path through truth, absurdity, simplicity, to silence I do not know, nor what the path can be like. I may write again. Or may at last abjure what you have made me see to be but a rough magic.
>                                                                    (pp. 338–9)

Art's pointing beyond itself, its hovering of form and substance (finally united in Apollo's music) upon the brink of silence, its negating and vanishing into ecstasy, are all part of Murdoch's stringent concept of the good which can be perceived only as unknown, wholly other, silent. The high claim for art that she makes is that at its best, when not blinded by illusion, this is the end to which it points. BP is Murdoch's metaphor for the stages of art, and he has here reached the final step in the human knowledge that can be conveyed by art functioning at its purest.

What remains for BP is the question of whether he will write again or, like Prospero, 'abjure this rough magic'. Because in this paradoxical book he has gradually, progressively and finally become, for all his realism as a character, the symbol for the farthest reaches of art, Murdoch chooses the path of abjuration, and he passes on to silence. After the betraying, amusing, point-of-view obscuring postscripts of the other characters, P. Loxias chastises them, and then settles in to a description of BP's death. 'The false god punishes, the true god slays' (p. 300). Murdoch's concentration on death as the real subject to be studied (see Socrates, of course) is brought into serious, ironic play here. Art points beyond itself to the void, to death, and thence her symbol BP travels. The last few sentences of the book and of P. Loxias's postscript are fraught with understatement even as they comprehend the novel's whole thought pattern of progress from bad art to real art to the 'nothing' which human beings, with their flawed sense of duration in seeing the reality that death reveals, so ardently turn aside from: 'Art is not cosy and it is not mocked. Art tells the only truth that ultimately matters. It is the light by which human things can be mended. And after art there is, let me assure you all, nothing' (p. 364).

And yet, the paradoxes remain. The reader's uncertain sense of BP from the other characters' postscripts makes him somehow still a figure of fun and absurdity, and according to P. Loxias, art celebrates this and because of it can be seen as made up of adventure stories. The idea is tied up with Murdoch's sense of fiction as a reflection of mankind's activity in the world, where novel plots at their best are spun from the tragi-comic doings of characters who live and love their adventures. The artist's job at its highest includes the transmission of those adventures with as much energy and excitement as possible to an audience eager to be absorbed by the pleasures of the tale; hence BP dies wishing he had written not *Hamlet* but *Treasure Island*. As Loxias says of art, 'At an austere philosophy it can only mock' (p. 363). Although it points to death, this novel does not break its comedic frame to wallow in tragedy and, even more pointedly, it does not lose its feeling of realism. In one of his last tricks, Loxias–Apollo claims that he has the real amulets – the water buffalo lady bronze and the Victorian snuff box inscribed 'A Friend's Gift' – on his desk; they do indeed exist as did Bradley Pearson, as does he. This final sleight of hand joins the fictional to the real in an oddly convincing way; even though, as he points out, some may claim that both BP and Loxias are 'simply fictions, the inventions of a minor novelist' (tongue-in-cheek Murdoch), their triumphant life in the high realm of reality exists. BP himself, in his postscript, expresses the central paradox in Murdoch's work. Torn out of himself by the hands of the terrible transforming godhead of reality, he remembers Plato's injunction against the artist, and observes that Socrates and Christ wrote nothing:

> And yet: I am writing these words and others whom I do not know will read them. With and by this paradox I have lived, dear friend, in our sequestered peace. Perhaps it will always be for some an unavoidable paradox, but one which is only truly lived when it is also a martyrdom.
>
> (pp. 337–8)

The martyrdom (another concept the early BP misunderstood) coexists with life and creativity, silence with words.

And with what Dionysian energy Murdoch has spun her web of words. Every technique in her considerable arsenal is displayed: false beginnings, false and real endings, *peripeteia*, strong and often amusing image patterns, mythological interweaving, precise, causally worked out ideology, brilliant conversations, ironic letters, profound ruminations and high comedy all coalesce in this most difficult and fruitful of novels. In no other book has she taken a character so far, from irritating inadequacy to the absolute of art and thence to death, and never is she as positive and generous in that journey as she is with Bradley Pearson. The result is an affirmation which one must feel even on a first, superficial reading. Although the supercilious, self-absorbed

Julian may remark on reading the manuscript of the story, 'A literary failure' (p. 360), the detached reader of this whole and subtle novel surely cannot agree.

# V

## ESTABLISHING THE STYLE

From *Under the Net* to *The Nice and the Good*

The distance from the early Murdoch novels to the subtle images and hard-won modified spiritual optimism of *The Black Prince* is great, and at times on the journey it certainly looked as though the great Murdoch talents might fold back into their own potential hazards. In spite of the success of *Under the Net* and the technical excellences of *The Bell* and *The Unicorn* a general sense of unease progressively settled in among her readers, who grumbled about tricks and prolificacy. But there was a turning-point after which such complaints lost their validity, a point I have arbitrarily identified with the publication of *The Nice and the Good*. Since that novel, Murdoch's mastery of her genre and clarity of presentation have allowed her to write with a consistency and strength which will, I think, establish the greatness of her reputation in the twentieth century.

I do not suggest anything so bizarre as that with *The Nice and the Good* Murdoch suddenly at last found her own voice. Yet this novel does mark her liberation from a certain obscurity of meaning and tight formulaic patterning that hindered the reader's grasp of much of what she was doing in the earlier novels. With the exception of *Under the Net* and *The Bell*, these first ten books can make the reader who has not caught on to the system feel very much in the dark, or that he is merely following ingenious plots and the inventiveness of Murdoch's always skilful but puzzling comedy. It is not surprising that A. S. Byatt explained her motivation for writing a book on the first seven novels as an attempt to understand. Indeed, the three major studies of early Murdoch (listed in order of merit), A. S. Byatt's *Degrees of Freedom* (1965), Peter Wolfe's *The Disciplined Heart* (1966) and Rubin Rabinovitz's 'Iris Murdoch' (1968, roughly updated 1976), combine philosophical sources and summaries of ideas in order to steer the reader towards meaning. These critical works tend to over-emphasize existentialism by concentrating on Murdoch's early study of Sartre, and to use almost exclusively the language of Murdoch's philosophical and literary critical essays. They are also largely responsible for tagging her erroneously and simplistically as a philosophical novelist.

The result is that serious criticism of Murdoch early became very stale, and did so, I believe, also because the novels themselves were not always working as they might have done. It is unfortunately true that Murdoch lost much popular support and even many of her serious readers in the period of *An Unofficial Rose*, *The Unicorn*, *The Italian Girl*, *The Red and the Green* and *The Time of the Angels*: that is from 1962 to 1966. This is apparently her most uncertain period, although one must also see, as always, her extraordinary strengths and the gradual focusing of direction. *The Unicorn* and *The Time of the Angels*, in spite of their heavy gothic tone, are important books, but they require of the reader work of a new sort which will become central to Murdoch's mature style, and for many readers their stylized mode and claustrophobic tone are simply not acceptable. Admirably, however, Murdoch has never courted her popular audience to the extent of refusing to take unusual and difficult directions in her development.

What caused the uncertainty and dissatisfaction of so many readers during the 1960s, and how did Murdoch's fictions change so that she has now become the best serious realist in our language? The question as posed is flawed, redolent of points of view having to do with decisions of taste and arrogant implications that the early novels were simply not succeeding. But it is nevertheless just to say that the first ten novels are puzzlingly dissimilar and ultimately of unequal interest. This situation is especially curious when one realizes that, as Murdoch herself confesses in interviews, all her major themes are to some degree already present in her first novel, *Under the Net*. In spite of changes, one of the distinctions of Murdoch's work is its essential consistency: she appears to have thought out most of her central ideas before she published anything. But although the ideas were there, much of the method of transmitting themes and making them effective was still to be worked on. Most significantly, a central preoccupation with the relation of the good to death was not very early as clear as it was later to become. In considering the early works, the most surprising and absorbing thing is the speed in which so much was clarified; as one looks back at these first ten novels, the artistic experimentation with modes and vehicles is of enormous interest.

*Under the Net* (1954) was a great start. It was not her first novel (A. S. Byatt, among others, mentions that there are five earlier unpublished ones), but the first Murdoch saw fit for publication. She had published her book on Sartre the year before, so that her career was launched with a double reputation as existentialist (anti-existentialist actually) and extremely talented novelist. The immediate popularity of *Under the Net* was connected to many factors: its literary relationship to Beckett and Queneau, which Murdoch has always readily acknowledged, the concurrence of English novels in a kind of post-World War II renascence by very clever novelists such as Kingsley Amis and John Wain, and extraordinary narrative pacing. The basis for her serious concerns is set by the success of her first-person male narrator and by his opposition to Hugo Belfounder. Jake Donaghue as narrator, creative articulator and would-be philosopher is balanced by Hugo, the monolithic silencer whose honest inclinations keep him from seeing the perverse philosophical uses to which Jake puts his ideas. This is also a very stylish, hyper-sophisticated, fashionable book. Murdoch boldly introduced large swatches of ironic philosophical dialogue – an unabashed philosophic content which is not central to the novel, but which helped to set up her binary code of art and anti-art. The title itself, as many critics have told us, in a way refers to Wittgenstein's image of the net of language or form or theory which the human mind puts over the chaos of reality (as Jake wishes to do) and then operates as if this artificial ordering were reliable. One of the strengths of the novel, however, is that it is absolutely unnecessary to know the philosophical reference (indeed, Murdoch, who loathes and denies the tag 'philosophical novelist', is swift to point out that the idea of a net of language is a fairly general and abiding one), or to be at all philosophically oriented in order to get to the heart of this fast and hilarious book. Murdoch justly succeeded instantly in making a reputation.

Yet this first novel, although directly related in theme and idea to all that follow it, is somehow atypical. It is not the way Murdoch will sound, and indeed when she later reverts to some of its stylistic characteristics, as in *A Severed Head* and *The Italian Girl*, many of the potential faults latent in the style emerge: the substitution of speed for realism, the overbalancing of plot to the detriment of quieter strengths and an inclination to perceive many of the characters as limited by their all too glossy surfaces. Nevertheless, *Under the Net* conveys a feeling of successful wholeness, with all parts connected and controlled. The question of where to go from here (one cannot wish to be a breakaway version of Beckett for long) is answered by a surprising array of experimentation over the next few novels.

*The Flight from the Enchanter* (1955), *The Sandcastle* (1957) and *The Bell* (1958) are very different in texture from each other and from *Under the Net*. Of these three *The Bell* is the best novel and the clearest foreshadowing of Murdoch's real style, the one she was to choose from her several possibilities. It is useful to look at those possibilities by setting all the early novels in array and extrapolating the directions and turnabouts, although in doing so it is difficult to avoid simple-mindedness and reduction. As Murdoch went ahead she tested herself constantly and frequently backtracked: having succeeded in so many ways in *The Bell*, she reverted to artifice, pattern, speed and surfaces in *A Severed Head* (1961), then returned to the more ruminative mode again in the next novel, *An Unofficial Rose* (1962), which yet missed the power and success she had managed in *The Bell*. After that she tried something new entirely: the imitative gothic combined with religious symbolism of *The Unicorn* (1963). *The Italian Girl* (1964) is again a throwback to *A Severed Head*, but without its successful comic devices. *The Red and the Green* (1965) is another try, combining the historical novel with the trickery of her most dangerous plotting. *The Time of the Angels* (1966) has the gothic overtones of *The Unicorn* and a newly conceived, pointedly demonic inclination: it is also a serious preparation for *The Nice and the Good* (1968).

As Murdoch moved back and forth, three dominant inclinations can be discerned; (1) the novel of tricks where plotting dominates: *Under the Net*, *The Flight from the Enchanter*, *A Severed Head*, *The Italian Girl*, *The Red and the Green*; (2) the ruminative novel characterized by deepening of character: *The Bell*, *An Unofficial Rose*; and (3), which is closely connected to (2), the increasingly religious novel which is concerned with definitions and enactments of good and evil: *The Sandcastle*, *The Bell*, *The Unicorn*, *The Time of the Angels*. For Murdoch the gothic is not just a literary exercise but a device for the transmission of serious religious ideas. She reluctantly but finally turned from or greatly reduced her inclination towards too heavy reliance on the glittering surface of plot, a shift which allowed her to work more realistically on character. At the same time, her interest in the discipline of the good and her careful discriminations on the nature of various religions as paths to the good became more marked, as did her preoccupation with death, but these changes towards religion and death did not come simply and clearly as single developments.

*

She had given over at least part of her talent to them, however, by the time of her second thoroughly successful novel, *The Bell*, and the two interim books, *The Flight from the Enchanter* and *The Sandcastle*, make a useful bridge from the *éclat* of *Under the Net* to its quieter successor. *The Flight from the Enchanter* is a strong but not entirely successful novel, and *The Sandcastle* must in literary terms be counted a failure. (In my opinion only it and *The Italian Girl* can be judged so harshly.) The second novel, *The Flight from the Enchanter*, sounds very different indeed from *Under the Net*. An omniscient and generous narrator, a sort of abbreviated Henry James, has taken over; the false subjective mode which had allowed the extraordinary comic verbal turns of the first novel is gone. Beckett, and to a large extent Queneau, are gone. The specific introduction of philosophical material is gone. Instead, much of what one now thinks of in terms of Murdoch's style emerges – complexity, interrelatedness, strength of imagery, even indirect didacticism – and for this reason I will explore it rather more fully than the other novels of this early period.

The struggle to compose this novel shows in its occasional awkwardness, and in place of gaiety a dark, miasmic demonism makes its bow. The characters fall into two dramatically opposed categories: complicated often mysterious ones and those whose narrow dimensions hinder the novel.

Social concerns are more in the forefront than anywhere else in Murdoch's fiction; it looks as though she experimented here with placing them in the foreground and subsequently retreated from the experiment, even though these concerns remain quietly in the corpus. Inherited as an idea from *Under the Net*, where the apocalyptic communist Lefty is kept so well in balance, the social viewpoint is here part of the content of every character, but is not genuinely as central as it appears to be. Murdoch is finally more interested in the larger moral issues of power than in politics which is only a subdivision.

The two central characters, Mischa Fox and Rosa Keepe, are kept in a sharply adversary position, signalling the fundamental sexual conflict which is a more central concern of this novel than its political internationalism. Mischa Fox is the enchanter of the title, Rosa the character in flight, although her conflicting approach to and avoidance of Mischa constitute a major idea. With both major and minor characters, there are serious problems: Mischa as a power figure is too alien from the reader and perhaps too exotic, and Rosa's characterization lacks profundity and motivation. Murdoch's rather frenetic minor creations like Calvin Blick and Annette Cockeyne work nicely in the ideology of the novel, but irritatingly distract from the reader's engagement. All in all, the novel is more peculiar than *Under the Net*, and the clever and fantastic elements often impede attention to character development.

It is not in the glossy world of the London upper middle classes that Murdoch really succeeds in this novel, but in demonic and mysterious evocations which had not existed in *Under the Net*. The real demonism flows not primarily from Mischa Fox, the power figure, but from the outsiders, the Polish brothers, Jan and Stefan Lusiewicz, who live in a room in Pimlico with their infinitely aged, silent and immobile mother, around whom they dance wildly, calling her the earth. In a novel which strongly opposes men and women, as well as eastern and western Europe, Murdoch uses these two brothers with their mysterious cultural otherness as true and alien representatives of the primitive, earthy Poland of their childhood, a middle-European world which also produced Mischa Fox and the trapped, pitiable dressmaker, Nina. Power, revenge and a threatening upward mobility characterize these brothers as they use their major weapons – sex, intelligence, work, greed, bullying – against the society they intend to conquer. They are geniuses with machines, and their use of Rosa almost as an extension of her factory machine is part of one of the most interesting imagistic devices in the novel.

From the beginning it is hard to understand the power that Mischa Fox so calmly and with such threatening charm wields over Rosa. The two had evidently been in love and near marriage in the past, but Rosa had escaped from Mischa's enslavement, and is still escaping. Her escape and his real nature are, however, obscurely conceived, for Mischa's qualities are only vaguely reported and often attached to other characters whose being and activity illuminate him. The atavistic Polish brothers are particularly effective in that they complement our knowledge of Mischa, whose childhood cruelties, such as killing animals because he loves them so much he cannot bear their sufferings, were based in a middle European village and are as inexplicable as the primitive logic of Stefan and Jan. In English society they are in the process of establishing themselves, whereas Mischa is the now perfectly assimilated product. All three in various ways represent the mysterious powers which western society has excised and at the same time is so vulnerable to. The excision of these primitive, uncontrollable powers has led to artificial substitutes which Murdoch symbolizes through the machines which the western mind has invented and uses, but does not understand and cannot control. Rosa literally has a machine: when her residual and admittedly phoney bolshevism, combined with bored despair, causes her to go to work in the factory where the brothers are employed, her labour is machine-minding. Her machine, with its plangent, personal chant (Kitty Kitty bang click), is an incomprehensible object to her, even though it represents by analogy her own mechanical personality and activity, which Stefan or Jan can so easily control. This carefully worked out analogy introduces to Murdoch's work the characteristic theme of mechanical and machine-like human behaviour, a theme which she will develop as her career advances.

Rosa strives, but not very ardently, to understand her world. She finds it easier to remain locked in slavery to various machines, to compartmentalize and fulfil a limited function, to be encaged by the Polish brothers' empty bed-frame, to be trapped by her brother Hunter's need for her, to perceive characters narrowly as she does Nina, who seeks her out as a life-saver but is ignored because of the greater mechanisms that crowd Rosa's mind. The Polish brothers find it easy to invade hers as well as other constrained, machine-like minds – Annette's and Hunter's – with their threatening and mysterious power, and the aimless western characters have no resources with which to answer this invasion.

Mischa, as finished product, as accomplished power figure, no longer uses such naked devices as do the brothers, and is an almost toally ambiguous character. Murdoch gives him one blue and one brown eye to indicate this quality, and through his absolute and strangely sourceless wealth and subtle connections with all the major characters (except the Polish brothers who are his avatars) implies a mysterious universal magnetism as the source of his power. It is also clear that he is a source of great fantasy for all of his London victims except Peter Saward, a too faintly achieved would-be-good. They all pursue him, are proud to know him, listen to his gnomic utterances as to an oracle, obey him, fall in love with him. Like Richard III to Macbeth, he is a pretype of the power demon so fully developed and so much better handled later in the character of Julius King in *A Fairly Honourable Defeat*. Mischa's active instrument is Calvin Blick, perverted and cruel, but like Mischa, with frequent flashes of real truth and comprehension. At the end of the novel Blick tells Rosa that Mischa killed him years ago, and indeed Mischa's power appears to involve making his victims into clones of himself, as Calvin has become, breaking down personality and destroying selfhood. The selves he is dealing with are a confused lot, but Murdoch makes clear that they deserve their own devices, solutions and limited freedoms rather than his demonic redemption.

I am generally playing down the idea of freedom in this discussion of the early novels, partly because A. S. Byatt has commented on it so well and fully, partly because my own view of the novels sees them as functioning even more powerfully outside this strong thematic compulsion on Murdoch's part. Mischa Fox's real power lies in his ability to charm and churn the imagination of others. He himself is relatively quiescent and certainly calm, while the characters on whom his magnetism works flounder about, like the rare fish in his party drawing-room in their frantic desire to live after their aquarium has been broken by Rosa's glass paperweight. Like the fish , the characters are doomed, not to immediate death (this will come later in Murdoch's work) but to the horrors of life outside the secure world of a really adequate social and emotional environment. Mischa's persona is at least partially a creation of his friends' imaginations, and realizing that, he enjoys his mystery and his ability to manoeuvre and observe their struggles.

The plot-workings of the novel, as well as the fish–like flounderings of the characters, evoke the archetype of the labyrinth and the temple. The novel opens with silly Annette Cockeyne's rejection of Dante's image of the Minotaur from Canto XII of the *Inferno*. This creature of the labyrinth 'bounded to and fro in pain and frustration, Dante was saying, like a bull that has received the death blow' (p. 7). Annette naively sees the whole thing as God's fault and as very cruel and unpleasant, then dashes forward into the maze which she calls the School of Life. Her unconsciousness and ignorance are not very interesting, nor do they ever become so, but the allusion to the Minotaur with its suggestion of labyrinth and its present, hellish, physical fury serves as a good introduction to the characters who thread their way through tortured lives and the peculiar physical brutalities of civilized London. What they seek is elusive and in its various expressions pointless. The sheer aimlessness of the characters is occasionally and temporarily focused on something like the feminist periodical, *Artemis*, once the powerful instrument of the suffragette movement and now edited by poor spineless Hunter Keepe. Rosa is the modern inheritor of the wonderful, now old ladies who founded *Artemis* and whose cause seems very old and far removed from Rosa's fractured life. Yet because Mischa in his endless hunger wants everything, including *Artemis*, Rosa takes a combative stand, going to beg rescue for the journal from one of its founders, the grand old suffragette, Camilla

Wingfield, who happens to live just across the square. Help in this book is always near; the characters are simply too trapped and compartmentalized in the machine to be able to see it. Camilla Wingfield, dying, eccentric and in touch with the real, is able to galvanize the old suffragettes and defeat Mischa's takeover bid in a splendidly comic scene; she then dies and leaves Rosa one valuable external and social way of redeeming herself: the majority of shares of the *Artemis*. *Artemis*, which represents the struggle, power and certainty of women in the past, can potentially save modern Rosa from the entrapment of men that has characterized her wandering in the maze of her life, and this undeveloped idea is as close as Murdoch ever gets to an extended feminist statement.

This novel, as I said before, is most convincingly about the warring opposition of men and women. It does not end with marriage ceremonies (brothers and sisters are closer here than sexual lovers) or with harmonious solutions; it rather asserts the reality of the labyrinth and the falseness of the temple. Although Rosa fears Mischa and his former power over her, she still regards him as a source of salvation, and in the course of the novel she narrowly misses falling under his enchantment again. Rosa and all the characters wrongly anticipate Mischa's big party in his mysterious, almost sacrosanct temple (two interconnected houses in Kensington) as a redemptive and sublime moment. The troops assemble, glowing with excitement, for a splendid and somehow meaningful affair. The confused nature of their hopes, their breathless expectations and their pride in being present are all unwarranted. They assemble as for a holy moment, something in their secular minds like a theophany, and perform instead a nasty drama of the violence of reality, in which human destructiveness and the impotence of the god are central.

The account of Mischa Fox's party is given entirely from the point of view of John Rainborough, who, rather than Mischa, is the most carefully elaborated male character. Like Rosa, he is very lost and in uncertain flight from Miss Casement, his lower-class, uneducated, but ambitious secretary in the vaguely international organization SELIB. Her insidious steps forward, including intimidating him through her machine, a red Triumph, into an engagement, are comic parodies of Mischa's successes, and underline the vulnerability of the main characters to any focused source of power. Needless to say, Miss Casement is at the party.

So also is Murdoch's failed good character, Peter Saward, who leaves before the going gets rough. Unlike the other characters, he pierces Mischa Fox's reality, sees his nostalgia and weakness, preserves photographs of his middle-European past for him and above all does not mythologize him. A classical scholar working hopelessly on hieroglyphics, he loves both Rosa and Mischa with an impotent love, and he provides the truest evaluations of Mischa's cruel-kind behaviour. His constant withdrawal, together with his terminal illness, leaves him powerless, and his effect as a wholesome outsider or agent of the good is weak.

The major issue of Mischa's party is the revelation of a deadly enmity between Rosa and Annette, whose cat-fight is appallingly destructive. Young Annette, dressed like a sea-green mermaid in a cocktail costume devised by the absent Nina, is full of the power of youth. Rich and flirtatious, she is one of a series of Murdoch's uninteresting caricatures of the still adolescent girl (Felicity in *The Sandcastle*, Miranda in *An Unofficial Rose*, Flora in *The Italian Girl*, Barbara in *The Nice and the Good*), who always and destructively loves the most powerful male. She also represents the myth of the unicorn virgin which Mischa Fox expounds to John Rainborough in an earlier comic scene where Mischa combines his most typical forces: his secret knowledge that Annette is locked half-undressed in the china closet listening, his exploitation of John's nervousness and his godlike categorizing. As he explained it, there are three types of women divided by age – the unicorn girl, the siren and, most importantly, the wise woman:

> 'There is a kind of wise woman,' said Mischa; 'one in whom a destruction, a cataclysm has at some time taken place. All structures have been broken down and there is nothing left but the husk, the earth, the widsom of the flesh. One can create such a woman sometimes by breaking her.' (p. 144)

The novel is patterned so that the wise woman not broken by men (the route Mischa has planned for Rosa) is Camilla Wingfield, and perhaps even, bizarrely, the Lusiewicz mother. Rosa is the siren who may become the wise woman, and Annette the unicorn virgin in process of becoming the siren. This state of becoming puts her into an adversary position to Rosa; they fight savagely over Mischa at the party after the fish-bowl has been broken, and somehow the frantic writhing and death of the fish open them to their own violence and confusion.

At the party, the struggles of the dying fish and the ugly, sex-centred brawling of the two women destroy any image of the holy or godlike. In this respect Mischa's intention is broken, but his destructive power is still satisfied as he displays his *alter ego*, the god who loves all creatures and weeps to see them destroyed and moribund. Annette's subsequent misery and comic failure at suicide balance Rosa's near submission to the Mischa she thought she had escaped. She is saved from this willed bondage only by Calvin Blick's indication of her guilt in the death of Nina, one of the novel's most touching characters. Ironically, as it turns out, the real saviours are not the obvious power figures, but negative and minor characters like Calvin Blick and the falsely glamorous Marcia Cockeyne, who redeems John Rainborough from the meretricious enchantment of the predatory bird-secretary, Miss Casement. These minor saviours release the entrapped, not into easy redemption, but back into the maze where life is lived and reality faced.

Nina, the dressmaker, is an interesting and significant device in the novel. Like Mischa and the Lusiewicz brothers, she is from eastern Europe, and tries to acclimatize or metamorphose herself by bleaching the exposed black hair on her body. Like the Polish brothers, she is in a middle state between two cultures, but she lacks their power and ruthlessness. In spite of her will to break away, she is caught in Mischa's cage and is devastated by the new, prohibitive immigration laws revived through Mischa's destructive attempts at power over Rosa. Nina kills herself in despair, having tried repeatedly to get help from Rosa, who is also encaged and unable to pay proper attention to those suffering around her. Halfway through the book Nina has a dream in which her sewing machine is metamorphosed into a devouring dragon, its steel jaws ripping apart and destroying the fabric of the world. This devouring dragon machine, projected from the subconscious of a character who does not understand the real situation, has the same destructive power Mischa refers to in his myth of the three types of women. Nina's psychological machine of terror which would destroy her world is like any subjective projection which contains frightening objective correlatives; although Mischa's myth looks more positive, its subjectivity leads to the same dragon:

> Every young girl dreams of dominating the forces of evil. She thinks she has that virtue in her that can conquer anything. Such a girl may be virgin in soul even after much experience and still believe in the legend of virginity. This is what leads her to the dragon, imagining that she will be protected. (p. 142)

That there is no protection, that each person is imprisoned and fights the dragon of the enchanter or of the self-projected image of terror, is the lonely and serious message of this novel. That human beings in the contemporary west have no ammunition is its great pathos.

★

From the bizarre and always interesting energy of *The Flight from the Enchanter*, Murdoch next turned, surprisingly, to a quiet, even small novel, *The Sandcastle* (1957). Unlike *The Flight from the Enchanter*, this novel has no power figure who delights in making people play roles, no real puppetmaster. And although Bill Mor hopes to run for a safe Labour seat, has a political friendship with the jeweller Tim Burke and makes public party speeches on the nature of freedom, the novel does not aspire to significant political statement. Compared to its two predecessors the plot is quite simple and the number of characters limited. At its centre is an adulterous but unconsummated love affair between the schoolmaster, Bill Mor, and the painter, Rain Carter, with Bill's wife, Nan, playing the villain. The character of Rain, on the make and recalcitrantly childish, constitutes the novel's central failure, although the depiction of the demon child, Felicity, comes in a close second.

The name Rain, obviously symbolic in relationship to the dryness of Mor's life, comes straight out of women's fiction, as indeed does her whole character. Although she is the practising artist, it is the art master, Bledyard, who has thought about and knows art's powers and functions; Rain is too confused by sex to be able to turn proper loving attention to her serious work. Essentially retarded by her love for and dependence on her recently dead painter father, she treats both her subject, Demoyte, and her painting of him wrongly. It is not her authority as a painter but her childish appeal which causes the scratchy, vulnerable old Demoyte to fall in love with her. Knowing his own is a hopeless cause, he encourages the burgeoning love affair between Mor and Rain, making Mor into an *alter ego* to live out his life for him vicariously. Mor, trapped in a loveless marriage with unhappy, indifferent and decidedly destructive Nan, succumbs quickly, even though he recognizes and is offended by Rain's emotionally retarded childishness and her tendency to put him into lying situations which he finds hateful and wicked. As the liaison progresses he feels, for all his new happiness, like a soul in hell: 'an unpleasant odour lingered in his nostrils, as if he could literally smell the sulphur of the pit; and he had from time to time the curious illusion that his flesh was turning black' (p. 233).

Mor's suffering and defeat are well handled, but the strength and interest of the characters around him elevate the issues to something larger than a hackneyed sexual triangle. Whereas Rain undoes Mor and makes him participate in her childishness, characters like his wife Nan, his friend Tim Burke, his children Don and Felicity and his several colleagues provide him an adequately real setting which ultimately defeats the false fantasy, symbolized by the sandcastle, of a dry Mediterranean life with Rain:

> 'Yes,' said Miss Carter, 'but a melancholy sea as I remember it. A tideless sea. I can recall, as a child, seeing pictures in English children's books of boys and girls playing on the sand and making sandcastles – and I tried to play on my sand. But a Mediterranean beach is not a place for playing on. It is dirty and very dry. The tides never wash the sand or make it firm. When I tried to make a sandcastle, the sand would just run away between my fingers. It was too dry to hold together. And even if I poured sea water over it, the sun would dry it up at once.' (p. 73)

Mor's own child Felicity plays by an English sea in Devon, not building fantasy sandcastles but indulging in black magical rites hoping to destroy Rain's power over her father. Rain and Felicity stand in a peculiar parallel relationship. Both afflicted by childhood, they play their arts of enchantment: Rain through sex, Felicity through magical enactments which she partially shares with her maturing brother, Don. The object of both is possession of

Mor, and the final sentences of the novel herald Felicity's triumph: 'It was all right. It was all right' (p. 318).

If the basic character of Rain is an irritating cliché, the problem of Felicity is very peculiar. It appears that Murdoch was experimenting with the basic stuff of a traditional romantic novel – an unexpected surprise for her readers – and then chose to embellish it with hints of the supernatural. Felicity's parents, who are not happily married, soothe their frequent quarrels with the memory of their dead golden retriever, but for Felicity the dog's ghost exists as her perpetual, 'real' companion. She also projects a spirit of various manifestations whom she calls Angus. Moreover, she and her brother have a magic pact game, 'tears of blood', which they play on finding out the secret connection between their father and Rain. Felicity's determined voodoo on the seashore might perhaps be touching, but somehow the demonism is all too serious, too powerfully designed. Like Miranda in *An Unofficial Rose*, there is something unreal, overly adult and vicious about her, and again like Miranda, she has much more power than the woman she wishes to defeat. As demon child, she could simply be put down as a local, internalized disaster as a character, but Murdoch has gone very far in giving fictional flesh to Felicity's imaginary Angus. The wordless gypsy of the novel who appears to Felicity as, she believes, a manifestation of Angus, also appears with his Tarot deck to Rain and Mor in the woods, and he leans eerily and terrifyingly on Mor's doorbell during the one night Rain stays over, chastely, in Felicity's empty bed. His physical presence makes the issue stranger and more important than just the projection of a childish psyche and raises the unanswered and not entirely interesting question of demonic, mysterious forces in the real world, beyond the mind's always fecund imaginative productivity.

The link between this kind of superstition and the real substance of the book is not easily seen, for this novel, in spite of its failures and irritations, also contains Murdoch's first serious religious examination of the moral life of the good. I have in Chapter II discussed Bledyard's character and the effect his interference in her affair with Mor has in leading Rain towards a career as a serious mimetic painter instead of a mere decorative designer. His discussion of art is Christianized Plato; his long luncheon monologue on the nature of representation, its sanctity and its impossibility (pp. 76 ff.) sounds like Socrates in the *Phaedo* saying that only a god could tell the long tale of the nature of the soul. He seems to feel that only in the early Christian period did the right sort of reverence exist, exemplified in the Ravenna mosaics. To have the necessary quality of attention, Rain or any other artist must not be distracted, as she so clearly is, by romantic fantasies. But indeed Bledyard is questioning the very possibility of art outside an intense moral and religious frame, and implying that the artist must even be a god, an idea whose paradoxes will deepen for Murdoch as her work progresses.

Bledyard is not alone in his advocacy of the discipline and self-abnegation of the good. The Reverend Giles Everard, the present headmaster, is an in-effective, courteous, self-denying character, capable of the conscious attention Bledyard almost absent-mindedly directs to things and people. Although not convincingly a follower of the good himself, Everard preaches a sermon which is doubtless to be seen as an unheeded antidote to Mor's problem:

> God is to be thought of as a distant point of unification: that point where all conflicts are reconciled and all that is partial and, to our finite eyes, contradictory, is integrated and bound up. There is no situation of which we as Christians can truly say it is insoluble. There is always a solution, and love knows that solution. *Love knows!* There is always, if we ponder deeply enough and are ready in the end to crucify our selfish desires, some one thing which we can do which is truly for the best and truly for the good of all concerned.
>
> (p. 209)

Needless to say, this crucifixion of selfish desires has nothing to do with Mor's secularity or desperation. His romantic fantasy loses not to theological or moral argument but to the concerns of real people in the real world, himself included.

His wife Nan is an impressively realized character. Recovering from her shock on recognizing that her marriage may be in trouble, she sacrifices just enough to destroy the relationship between the lovers. It is, however, not her formal announcement that Mor will run for Parliament (which she had previously resisted) that breaks the romance, but a simple piece of causality: Mor had not mentioned this important ambition to Rain. He had withheld a major fact about himself in order to enact his fantasy of being in love and 'free'. And of course he is defeated by his children, not only Felicity but also Don, whose near fatal tower climb and subsequent determination to become a jeweller like his idol, Tim Burke, break Mor's dreams about his son's career. Although the demonic Demoyte pushes him to break free, Mor's infrangible connections combine with his basic flaws to keep him in an unromantic world where Nan, although changed slightly, will nag as before, and Don and Felicity will remain alien. The life of an MP will replace his schoolmastering, but it will be an unglamorous quotidian business, a life in the real world.

The three elements of *The Sandcastle* – popular romance, a partial religious examination of the good and the fey introduction of the supernatural – do not meld particularly well. My impression is that the first two have ironic connections, but that the third is too flimsily tricky. Surely Murdoch's readers in 1957 must have been amazed at this book, which apart from the intrusion of Bledyard's theology appears geared for a popular audience at a fairly low level. I, for one, am glad she dropped the genre.

Nevertheless, its moments of religious seriousness, if not its simplicity, formed an important bridge to *The Bell* (1958), where Murdoch's two principal inclinations – towards the religiously moral and the highly-plotted secular – coalesced very successfully. Of the ten early novels, this one, much more than *The Flight from the Enchanter*, predicts her mature style. Although I shall discuss it at greater length in Chapter VIII, let me survey just a few points here. In this fourth novel there is an increased and pointed emphasis on the past and its ability to poison and pervert the present, a major Murdoch theme which will provide a constant in the later novels. Michael Meade, the would-be hero of *The Bell*, has tried through intelligent self-analysis and religious discipline to expiate a fourteen-year-old homosexual scandal, minor in itself but major in effect, which involved the then schoolboy, Nick Fawley. Nick has worrisomely re-entered Michael's life by appearing on the scene of the experimental religious community of Imber to spend the last few weeks before his sister Catherine enters the nearby convent. Things at first appear to be going dully and uneventfully, a factor which signals trouble in Murdoch's fictions. Although Michael badly wants to act well, he fails for a subtle complex of reasons, some almost accidental, some connected to the pernicious hold his past guilt has on him: he carelessly drinks too much strong cider and thoughtlessly kisses young Toby, constantly ignores Nick's unspoken cries for help and is indirectly responsible for his death.

Trapped in his own character, as Murdoch always emphasizes her people are, Michael feels that his failure in making a sexual advance to the innocent Toby constitutes a cyclic *déjà vu*. His inability to change and enact a proper religious ideal of love, in spite of prayer and discipline, and his subsequent dangerous if unintentional concentration on himself are preparations for one of Murdoch's powerful later characters, Hilary Burde in *A Word Child*. Michael's guilt lies constantly in some back chamber of his mind, haunting his dreams even before the frenzied dance of the complex plot really begins.

One of Murdoch's successes in this novel is her knitting of this guilt to the strong, organizing image of the bell. This image is presented precognitively in Michael's recurrent dream, which is always accompanied by 'an overwhelming sense of evil' (p. 80) and a nauseating odour. It begins with a 'hollow booming sound' (p. 79) which appears to waken him and draw him to the window where he sees nuns pulling a corpse out of the lake. The booming sound will occur literally later in the novel, when Dora and Toby, having succeeded in pulling the huge medieval bell from the bottom of the lake, fall inside its rim in an embrace. The nuns of the dream prepare the scene for Mother Clare who will pull Catherine and Dora from the water, and the body is an augury of Nick's death. These parallels illustrate the enactment in the real world of certain kinds of subconscious data, including both prediction and what Michael later will see as the 'demons within himself which his action [will] set loose' (p. 167). That the bell does indeed lie at the bottom of the lake, and that in its mythical history its strange flight into the water had sprung from the sexual guilt of a nun unites the dream sound to the mystery of the lake, making both the bell and the water into symbolic forces much stronger and more complex than any authorial statement could be. The medieval bell, a symbol connected to the past and to sexual guilt, reflects the guilt in Michael's own past, its retrieval in the present and in various degrees the guilty sexuality of Dora, Toby and Catherine.

This wonderful old bell images most completely the perversion of what had once been a great and positive thing. *Vox ego sum Amoris. Gabriel vocor* reads its rim. The religious love that drew its maker to a beautiful piece of craftsmanship, and the love that it evokes as an artifact are loves that even in its own early history sexuality had interfered with and confounded. Michael's guilt over his sexual misdemeanours means that the perpetual practice of *agape* is overlooked, and his religious concentration and observances are inadequate to make love clarify the confusions of sex. The image of the bell unites the two loves, showing the confusion between sex and *agape* and yet separating itself from that confusion. Its detached beauty and separate reality as an object reflecting the faith of its maker allow a brooding, melancholy contrast between the muddle of human characters enslaved by their sexual being and the concentrated clarity of the love they seek without finding or understanding it.

In keeping with the reflective qualities of *The Bell*, there are many sermons in this book, which try to approximate a definition of that elusive *agape* – James Tayper Pace and Michael Meade both deliver formal sermons, Nick punishes Toby with a sermon, the Abbess's elegant and impassioned discourses to Michael must be classified as such. After her most eloquent delivery, Michael ponders: 'He was too tarnished an instrument to do the work that needed doing. Love. He shook his head. Perhaps only those who had given up the world had the right to use that word' (p. 238). When Michael falls through the crack that leads to the abyss (p. 163), as will Carel Fisher in *The Time of the Angels*, he slowly recognizes the futility of his dreams of the priesthood or of a religious community. The world he goes forward to is the real world for Murdoch, the world that will be so clearly characterized in her mature novels – real, muddled, unprotected, without the consoling image of God, without the consolation of redemption of the self.

So searing and yet somehow gentle is Murdoch's treatment of her main ideas, and so well-integrated her form and images, that this novel lucidly reveals her own voice and the breadth of her technical strengths when functioning at their best. The increasingly religious content, the open inexorable destruction of false idealism and the attack on guilty dependence on the past give this novel a clarity of intention its predecessors did not quite have. Its generous ruminative mode as the authorial voice explores Michael's and Dora's psyches works well, and reduces and balances the sense of hyperactive plotting which permeates the three earlier novels.

★

After the ruminative mode of *The Bell*, it is extremely surprising that the next novel, *A Severed Head* (1961) plays entirely to fast high comedy, evocative of *Under the Net* but lacking its texture. The three-year gap, from 1958 to 1961, is the longest so far in Murdoch's prolific career, and it precedes a new period of fast, clever novels, all sharing a high degree of technical mastery, and many of them whittling away her clientele. *A Severed Head* presents in thirty hectic chapters a stunning attack on the egocentricity and folly of fashionable psychoanalysis. Georgie Hands's reference to Martin Lynch-Gibbon as a double-dealer makes plain the connection to Restoration comedy, and indeed the novel has been rewritten as an amusing and fast-moving play by Murdoch and J. B. Priestley.

In interviews, Murdoch has talked about her desire to write open novels and her early tendency to write closed ones. The tight design of *A Severed Head* and its commitment to satire automatically limit this novel, and even though it was a great popular success, admiration of it sprang, as often in popularity, from its worst features. The male first-person narrator, Martin Lynch-Gibbon, rushes his story along with a minimum of introspection, and speed of activity and comic turns of action are the techniques used. Ideas that had a serious base in the earlier novels are comically deployed here; characters gabble about freedom, and mythology and art are tossed about with abandon. Symbolic interiors are dismantled, tousled, redesigned, as relationships permutate and recombine so that every character falls in love with every other possible and impossible character. Technically, of course, this show is all rather dazzling, but it makes Murdoch look like quite another sort of writer than she had seemed to be in her earlier novels.

The comic flow and harshness of the satire make certain important points, indicate a more pessimistic attitude towards her characters than the first four books suggest. She estimates society as deceitful, lying, given to vanities, shamelessly determined to do what it wants in the name of a callow freedom which falsely pretends that, as the psychoanalyst Palmer Anderson puts it, ' "do what you want" costs others less than "do what you ought" ' (p. 205). The permissiveness is largely sexual, but includes decadently heavy drinking and the misuse of social courtesies as mere forms which mask raw and primitive will. Murdoch savagely undercuts her own typical generosity here, and this novel can be seen as giving a definition to the society which constitutes her subject matter generally. Although she has only seven significant characters, they are people who by taste, education and privilege ought to reflect the highest level of middle-class civilization: a Cambridge don, a university lecturer, a psychoanalyst, a sculptor, a cultivated wine merchant with a more than amateur interest in history. The two others, Rosemary and Antonia, are rapacious and idle women, the latter the first in what will become a long parade of self-satisfied, emotionally greedy and superficial, wealthy, middle-class, middle-aged women.

The comic goings-on of this group not only reveal the follies of psychoanalysis and its hand-maiden, existentialism, but also point to a basic artificiality in the use of civilized devices. These characters are much too self-conscious to allow the naked exposure of their permissive wills, and they therefore adorn their activities with the products of their education. Palmer Anderson's Freudianism is very much a part of the texture of the book, as is Honor Klein's titular image of the severed head. Freud on Medusa is bantered about to elevate the action; the Psyche myth is evoked; Martin on discovering the incest of Palmer and Honor takes to reading *The Golden Bough*; Dionysus, alchemy and primitive tribes are called on; the tale of Ares, Aphrodite and Hephaistos is brought into play; Dante's Love is pressed into service; and the book ends with Herodotus' story of Gyges and Candaules. The addition of Honor Klein's *Samurai* sword, with its spiritual power, and her use of it to define herself as a power figure balance Martin Lynch-Gibbon's historical interest in warfare.

Because this study of Murdoch's work is at every other point so positive about her allusive frame, I must emphasize that in this novel pessimism and satire reduce all the materials of civilization, perceiving them as sheltering devices behind which the primitive ego hides. Just as Carel Fisher in *The Time of the Angels* seizes and perverts so much of Murdoch's most significant thought, the characters in this novel use serious myths as well as artistic and religious products to dress up their moral failures. The severance of the head from the body which the title points to emphasizes the peculiar duality of this book in which the intellectual materials sort so poorly with the physical or sexual.

References to the head abound, from evocations of the *Samurai* sword and Medusa to Georgie's symbolic cutting of her hair, Alexander's tendency to touch and want to sculpt everyone's head, Martin's habitual despairing gesture of covering his face with his hands and the tendency of lovers in servitude to put their heads at the feet of the beloved. Most gestures and actions in the novel involve warfare and power, and although Martin studies warfare in history, it is Honor Klein who is the power figure and magician, described as possessing a black-demon splendour. Her Jewishness and knowledge of Japanese spiritual culture make her an outsider and suggest depths of being which are not explored and which probably the reader is expected to assume Martin Lynch-Gibbon will take on now that, at the end of the book with all the couples as bizarrely sorted out as possible, he takes on Honor Klein in a lover relationship which supposedly has 'nothing to do with happiness'.

Perhaps. But Martin, with his long history of parent-surrogates and longing for power figures, does not seem very far advanced in his substitution of one rapacious woman for another. Under no circumstance is *A Severed Head* a novel of moral amelioration. In a way it marks a turning-point in Murdoch's fiction, inasmuch as the reader now knows certain things about Murdoch's position very clearly indeed: talk about freedom indicates essential frivolity, and the reader is prone to dislike rather than sympathize with characters who go on about it – an attitude not openly expressed in the first four novels; and innocence is an illusion, in that when characters think themselves in a state of innocence, they are so corrupt and surrounded by such corruption that the ideal is ludicrous. Murdoch is far from being an advocate of the sophisticated society she is so conversant with; indeed, there is more than a touch of the judging puritan in her.

Although *A Severed Head* must be seen as a comic masterpiece, it is redolent of real evil and is uncommonly easy to dislike. It ushers in that difficult period I mentioned at the beginning of this chapter, where the novels, despite their individual excellences, began to pall on Murdoch's public. The closed form of satire here presents the first in a series of closed forms and structures. But again, as in the case of the first four novels, Murdoch will move radically from novel to novel with no repetitions and very few carry–overs, except in character type – that basic deck of cards with which she plays.

*An Unofficial Rose* (1962) is an unsatisfactory book which frequently hovers on the brink of excellence but is defeated by its ultimately over–extended formal contrast between the demonic and angelic, evil and good, would–be artist and saint, amorality and morality, form and formlessness. These analogous contrasts will become central to and successful in Murdoch's mature art, where instead of being simple opposites their coexistence and paradoxes will form much of the substantial irony of the style. Here, how–ever, they are represented quite simply by the married pair, Randall and Ann Peronett. This novel presents the first clear example of a fairly honourable defeat, where Ann's hopes are beaten down by her husband's, and especially her daughter's, in combination with her own errors. The defeat here of good by evil is not as interesting as it might be because, as I pointed out in Chapter III, Ann is too pallid to carry her central role. Her ruminations are too insubstantial and too self–pitying, and her formlessness resists the attractive–ness she must have in order to make the motivations of other characters like Felix Meecham and Douglas Swann convincing. Randall, on the other hand, is too weak to be demonic; compared to Julius King in *A Fairly Honourable Defeat* or even to the Polish brothers in *The Flight from the Enchanter*, he is merely selfish and unable to distinguish values. Both Ann and Randall are well–drawn characters – but somehow tedious. Indeed the whole book is rather drawn out, but for reasons less good than in the later case of *The Sea, The Sea.*

As a tale of the burdens and disciplines of family life, *An Unofficial Rose* has an interminability and gentle dullness that reflect the reality of that situation. There are no peculiarities, nothing exotic. The power figure on whom the imaginations of most of the characters play is, this time, elderly Emma

Sands, a successful mystery writer and the former mistress of Hugh Peronett. A profaner of all relationships who passes on her suffering to others in a Weilian way as she operates on complex human relationships, her mythology is suppressed by Murdoch and the more puzzling and dangerous for being so. Nevertheless, her mysteries partake more of the ordinary world than those of Mischa Fox or Honor Klein. Similarly, the dominating symbolism of the formal hybrid rose opposed to the simple, formless dogrose comes easily out of the ordinary life of the characters, since Randall and Ann Peronett own and run a large rose nursery. Even Hugh's Tintoretto is natural enough: for all its splendid beauty, it is his only treasure. The one joker in this unexceptional pack is young Miranda Peronett, one of the most fiendish of Murdoch's demon children. Balanced by her appealing Australian cousin Penn, she outstrips her father in the craft of destruction; she is so out of key that she breaks the tone and becomes unbelievable. Although Penn suggests a possible world of innocence among the very young, Miranda's unchildish, pointedly spiteful knowledge works against such an idea.

Following the secularism of *A Severed Head*, this novel returns to a limited theological frame, comparable to that of *A Sandcastle*. As in that novel, it is partly a means of talking about the good and partly an illustration of an accessible but now meaningless power. In these early novels Murdoch places several false sermons on the good, reduced in impact and believability by the limitations of their preachers: Everard's sermon in *The Sandcastle*, James Tayper Pace's in *The Bell*, the Bishop's speech in *The Time of the Angels*. Here we have the vacuous Anglican priest, Douglas Swann, delivering speeches on the good and on Christian marriage which cannot begin to penetrate the misery of Ann's situation. The inadequacies of such speeches and sermons are important in Murdoch's representations, where the good is seen as bound not to theory but to experience and pain. Ann muddles along more intelligently, if negatively, by feeling her way and being defeated than by subscribing to bland Christian tenets. Nevertheless, the novel drags its feet for anyone who expected a repetition of the speed and satire of *Under the Net* or *A Severed Head*.

The next novel, *The Unicorn* (1963), again presented a new (for Murdoch) form – the gothic. But as in the other novels of this period, there is a limitation in tone if not entirely in structure. *The Unicorn*'s relation to such works as *Wuthering Heights* and the decidedly decadent novels of Sheridan Le Fanu closes it in on itself, and the oppressive echoes from the tradition, combined with the claustrophobic atmosphere of the alien landscape, the two houses and the room of Hannah Crean-Smith's imprisonment, cloy and sicken the spirit – as indeed they are meant to do. It is, however, one of Murdoch's major achievements among the early novels – a novel of serious religious dimension, and the best and most profound analysis of some of her most compelling ideas. Its obscurity sorts well with the gothic mode, which

embraces the ideas of violence and death so easily and naturally. Since
Murdoch was so inexorably going in this direction, her vehicle was perfectly
chosen. I shall discuss this novel more fully in Chapter IX in relation to *The
Sea, The Sea*.

★

Given the matching of tone, ideology and direction in *The Unicorn*, it is hard
to fit in *The Italian Girl* (1964) at all. For anyone wanting to attack the excesses
of Murdoch's style, this shortest of her novels is an easy target. Its shortness
may be its greatest liability, inasmuch as Murdoch's strength lies in amplification and extension, not in contraction. But even more problematical is its
function as an unintentional parody of its author's usual amusement and
expertise in plot turns. Some other critic will soon, I hope, explore in detail
Murdoch's use of Freud, but in *The Italian Girl* the dominant Oedipal pattern
is almost tediously evident. By this time in Murdoch's career, the male
first-person narrator can be taken as a signal of an established kind of narrow,
fast-moving novel where introspection is limited and self-perception questionable. In the previous novels of this sort, *Under the Net* and *A Severed Head*,
the fast plot-turns maintained a certain fantastical interest; here they are
reduced to unmotivated hysteria and formulaic devices. For such a short
novel, much too much is thrown in: not only do we have a few well-defined
versions of Oedipal hatred, but also mad comic dreams, Russian sorcerers
and outsiders, Medusa hair imagery, Freudian hatreds and loves, abortion,
bizarre matings. One can work the whole overly complex thing into a
debased Murdochian formula, as many critics have done, but this book is not
to be taken seriously as a novel, and it is strange that it should appear this late
in the *oeuvre*. No doubt it shows quite dramatically that Murdoch's style was
far from established – and perhaps it shows a few other things too.

In 1967, Murdoch collaborated with James Saunders to turn *The Italian
Girl* into a play, as she had done with J. B. Priestley to its nearest relative in
her work, *A Severed Head*. In 1970 and 1972, she was to fit into her heavy
writing schedule two other plays, *The Servants and the Snow* and *The Three
Arrows*. These two plays were not originally written as novels, but show a
marked resemblance to the quality of action in the two early dramatized
novels. I conjecture that the impulse to write the sort of novel that became
parodic in *The Italian Girl* was siphoned off by actually writing plays directly,
by separating her novelistic talent from her narrower, dramatic writing so
that they could take their own directions. Certainly Murdoch never wrote
this sort of novel again, and it is unfortunate that so many readers identify her
with this style. I myself have often felt that *The Italian Girl* is not only out of
place in Murdoch's development, but may have been written earlier as a
novella and resurrected to be published out of sequence.

It is with real relief that one enters the somewhat more convincing and expansive world of *The Red and the Green*, Murdoch's one historical novel. Taking as its crisis the 1916 Irish Easter rebellion, it has an immediate charm or problem, depending on one's point of view. Those excessively famous few days in Irish history apparently cannot be written about without the infection of Yeatsian romanticism, and although all Murdoch's skill in structuring, combined with some interesting historical special effects, is in play, one still feels that the novel is part of a questionable tradition. In an epilogue ironically dated just before World War II, an older version of the character Frances says of the Irish and English characters she knew and loved as a young woman: 'They were inconceivably brave men' (p. 318). Given the progress of the novel, these words ring false in terms of Murdoch's realism. Particularly troublesome is the occluded nature of the young Irish hero, Pat Dumay, who although not unscathed by Murdoch's pen is essentially a romantic character whose fascination for the other characters is utterly bewildering to the reader. The evidences of patterning in the novel are, however, well handled. Its structure, which projects Ireland as a demanding woman, a negative 'Cathleen ni Houlihan', and divides response between her two manifestations, is very much in the forefront. The contrast between the formless drudge, Kathleen Drumm, with her Catholic charities and smart, stylish, form-ridden Millie Kinnard with her pistols presents not only a choice of Irelands but also an embodiment of Murdoch's binary code of formlessness versus form, would-be saint versus would-be artist, possible good versus inevitable evil. Marvellous Millie is everyone's choice and poor Kathleen is seen only as a pitiable negative by the characters, as Murdoch plays out the Irish smash-up among men who are, typically, dazzled by form and drama and not by a humble character pointing towards an unromantic good and longing for survival.

The fictional problem of the good is present in this novel, although artificially, almost as an absent-minded habit. It exists not only through Kathleen's symbolic role – more symbolic than real, I am afraid – but also through one of its more touching characters, Kathleen's alcoholic husband, Barney. A failed priest, failed husband, failed stepfather, he vents his quiet resentment against Kathleen and his life on a lying, egocentric autobiography, which he gives up after a Good Friday apprehension of God and love. His bumbling failures and impotent intentions cannot begin to gainsay the machinery of his own and Ireland's destructiveness, but his engaging attempts and Irish alcoholism (although he is English) make him a more useful character than Kathleen, and a sturdy if failing counter-current to the full tide of defeat. Yet this whole thematic issue stumbles before the automatic romanticizing date of the 1916 uprising, and one is left with simply another version of that famous event, ingeniously fitted to the larger Murdochian mode. Again, the ingenuity is rather too much in the forefront, and one feels the aggression of the design too strongly. The failures of realization in character and event here are not as complete as in *The Italian Girl*, but the book belongs to the same period of aggressive design at the expense of realization – the period which began with *A Severed Head*, and during which, as I have said, Murdoch lost many of her serious readers.

It is interesting, of course, that a book as good as *The Unicorn* should be part of that period, and that another dark, at least semi-gothic novel, *The Time of the Angels*, should end it. One can argue strongly for Murdoch's skill in the gothic mode, but in a very real way this entire six-novel sequence (1961-6) is characterized too much by technical skill, as though Murdoch had largely forgotten that other more subtle talent of transmitting perception which she managed to do so often in the first four novels of her career. *The Unicorn* is a very good book, but for all its sustaining of tone, it does not have a great deal of the feeling of relatedness to characters that her best work has. In significant ways, it is too ideological, and so, indeed, is *The Time of the Angels*, as I pointed out in Chapter III. Nevertheless, there is a real change from the earlier to the later quasi-gothic novel. Both depend on an examination of the perils of the spiritual life, and both produce flawless mythological frames – indeed, Murdoch, when operating at her best in this rigid form, appears to pour her ideology into something close to allegory in order to subdue it.

The real difference between the two is that in *The Time of the Angels* the realization of key characters becomes overwhelming, and the reader therefore cannot feel that he is reading a secret conundrum. This novel exudes the dreadful presence of evil; there is no sense whatever that evil is merely sitting for a portrait, or that good is a theory to be talked about, as Max Lejour did in *The Unicorn*. The devouring of Carel Fisher's spirit by darkness, the cold eeriness of his fear, the chilling cogency of his theories all spring from Murdoch's conception of his character as real and her flawless ability to transmit that reality with no distancing from the reader by either gamesmanship or multi-directed energy. In comparison with, for example, *The Italian Girl*, with its devices and formulae marring every other page, *The Time of the Angels* is transparently integrated.

*The Time of the Angels* also works on the imagination at something close to the anagogical level. The proximity of the fissure of evil into which Carel Fisher (the pun is too obvious, but good nevertheless) has slipped is countered by the surprising ability of Pattie O'Driscoll finally to say no to it, and the relationship between these two characters becomes an allegorical description of the eternal war between good and evil. Whereas in simple allegory, Marlowe can in *Doctor Faustus,* for example, project this kind of psychomachia as a straightforward contest between the Good Angel and the Bad Angel, Murdoch fits it to the contemporary existential psyche where the presence of evil is unwillingly if at all acknowledged, and good is seen as a dark, primitive, poetic idea, outside the borders of educated bourgeois society. Hence Pattie, with her aspirations to sainthood and her loving simplicity, is merely a black servant, an extra-societal being, infinitely seduced by the evil Carel, whom she sees as a god. Pattie's seduction indicates the basic defeat of the yearning towards good in the contemporary mind; her love of evil shows good's helplessness and confusion; but her ability to deny the final demands asserts absolutely that the core of longing in goodness can survive as a psychic idea. Pattie, like Carel, is felt as an extended and developed character, and the ideology she carries is absolutely subservient to the fine detail of her real being, constituted in all the minutiae of her tasks, her boots and coat, and her shifting consciousness as the lines of Blake run through her memory, a touching illustration of the uses of art.

*The Time of the Angels* is a novel in process of breaking away from the aggressively stylized patterns that Murdoch gave full rein to for some time after her fourth novel, *The Bell*. Although it still participates in some of those patterns, as does all of her subsequent work, *The Time of the Angels* illustrates a stronger grasp of techniques which, although they determine the action of the novel, are subservient to its ability to convince the reader of its independent life. Despite the power of *Under the Net*, *The Flight from the Enchanter*, *The Bell* and *The Unicorn*, this is the first novel where atmosphere and the author's relationship to character project a consistent, believable, thoroughly inhabited and specialized space, compelling the reader to follow into an area of response where he is taken over by the power of the novel, where he abandons the disbelief that always accompanies the critical act and where Murdoch's difficult lessons must, willy nilly, be heeded at some level. From this point on, Murdoch as a writer is no longer controlled by the fecundity and charm of her devices, and cannot henceforth be faulted as a trickster. The ability, always there even when unexploited, to project the essential nature of both ordinary and eccentric personality without openly depending on ideology or pattern, is here shown most convincingly. In this novel, one of Murdoch's basic contradictions or dualities – her instinct towards determinism and control and her loving brooding on the vagaries and puzzling realities of human personality – proves its strength.

★

*The Time of the Angels* is, however, rather too specialized a case, bound as it is by its mythological frame and by the claustrophobia of its genre. The closed world of the near-gothic, its limitations in space and atmosphere, make its effect strong but its task narrow, and it is therefore necessary to look to the next novel, which I see as the pivotal one, for the shifts in fictional perspective which take place in the establishment of Murdoch's mature style. *The Nice and the Good* (1968) brings together the manifold talents always

present in early Murdoch, plus an open range of characters whose activity
and thoughts unobtrusively reveal the vast and ambiguous area which Murdoch has set out to explore. Although this novel fairly bristles with ideas,
they occur at the human, experiential level rather than being conveyed
through authorial control or allegorical power. The result is a translucent
realism, where realization of person and place carry the novelistic task.
Murdoch is successfully absent here: the reader feels authorial power only
ironically at the end, when a kind of false Shakespearean felicity (as she was to
call it in *The Black Prince*) takes over to tie character and event to form and
closure.

The subtraction of the personality of this very strong author from her text
is, as we know from her criticism, one of Murdoch's major aims. The
triumph of this negative capability demanded both ideological and technical
achievements, and one can claim that Murdoch at her weakest, during her
second early period, was partially writing her excesses out of her system.
What remains after this period of purgation are the devices of plot without
formula, an increasingly clarified point of view and a strong sense of the task of
the serious novelist – a task that includes entertainment and hence a degree of
popularity. In a recent interview with Bryan Magee on the BBC, Murdoch
claimed that some of the vital functions of a serious novel 'seep away' into the
texture of the life of the reader, and the implication is that for Murdoch the
function of art lies subtly in the intuition of the reader rather than in his
ratiocination or analytical response. Murdoch's mature novels exude a greater aura of clarity than the early ones, but are harder to perceive adequately.
They defy analysis to a certain degree, and cannot be approached, as could
the earlier ones, through a knowledge of her intellectual sources. In other
words, character and action have found a free technical medium in which
simplicity and pattern are generally elusive for most readers.

In Murdoch's view, this is as it should be. If the mystery of human life
which is the real subject for all serious realist artists is to be transmitted
faithfully, the reader should not feel the manoeuvring power of the authorial
mind. Indeed, one of the impossible demands of realism is that the realism of
description, bland and true, should replace the realism of assessment where
the novel becomes a forum for airing moral ideas. No realist writer can quite
manage this feat, but Murdoch goes quirkily far along in this direction, at
least in terms of reader response, and her strong moral achievements are well
submerged in the natural realistic body of her major novels.

From the beginning, Murdoch kept her biographical presence from the
novels, except in such questions of taste as her predilection for certain objects,
animals and activities like swimming. The great intrusion was the shaping
power of her imagination and her commitment to certain ideas. In looking at
the *oeuvre* as a whole, one must quite objectively say that the major influences
on Murdoch's thought, as opposed to her style, were Plato, Simone Weil,

Shakespeare and Christianity, with Buddhism, Wittgenstein, Kant and Freud maintaining a strong secondary position. Her allusive frame covers a much wider field of culture, art and thought, but it was possible in the early novels to follow her tracks fairly accurately through these influences, as so many critics – most notably and admirably A. S. Byatt in *Degrees of Freedom* (1965) – have rather destructively done. The consequent narrowing of the achievement and the sense of seeing the plot as a vehicle on which to hang the ideas limited the critical act and made it largely mechanical. I have tried to avoid influence studies in my brief discussions of the early novels not only because they have already been well done, but also because they reduce the energy and originality of the fresh fictional powers of Murdoch's imagination.

*The Nice and the Good* ushers in a new style in the sense that, although they remain, the influences no longer dictate as much (or even very much) of the educated critical response they had done before, and certainly there is no feeling of the overload seen so extremely in *The Italian Girl*. Plato and Buddhism form allusive points to help define the good, which in fact a few of the characters work out in the real world without bookish help. Shakespeare is evoked in a discussion among the characters about why he ignored Merlin and Arthurian material (he abjured magic, as Murdoch believes the real artist must) and as a model for closure. Simone Weil's definitions of evil and good are in play, and her theories in the *Cahiers* about *amor fati* are given to the questing religious figure, Willy Kost. Kant's moral imperatives are ironically present, as are Freud's theories of human sexuality. But none of these is central, intrusive or really very useful to a good reading of this rich and ambiguous novel.

Murdoch has learned to give her characters a natural primacy and to concentrate on cause and effect at the local level of action, so that plot-turns grow directly out of the quality of action of convincingly real characters. Credibility is not strained, yet none of the page-turning impetus the reader has learned to expect is lost. Most significantly, the juggling of elements in a really crowded novel looks like an easy game – something done without strain, with every mechanism quietly humming in the background rather than seizing the foreground. Even the eccentric characters – Fivey and Judy McGrath – share in the naturalistic surface, so that the act of acquiescence so central to the novel reader is smoothly and unobtrusively elicited.

This novel is not for the lover of experimental fiction: Murdoch is very much concerned with keeping the formal successes behind the scenes, even as they carry the book's central tasks. Yet she handles astounding technical games with flawless expertise. The omniscient narrator moves from character to character and scene to scene, linking and moving the plot through shifting perspective, so that often the same scene is presented from different viewpoints. The inward ruminations of two carefully chosen characters,

John Ducane and Mary Clothier, are central, and in the comedic Shakespearean pairing-off of the characters at the end, it makes sense that these two,
whom we know best and perceive as morally similar, marry. Even more
important is the nature of their ruminations: Ducane's theme is justice, Mary
Clothier's is death, and both learn through pain something about the absolute
of love. Murdoch is not using rumination for the first time, but here she
achieves a particular triumph – and not only technically. In both *The Time of
the Angels* and here, the clarity and originality of Murdoch's own point of
view are evident, and the ruminations participate in a thought complex both
original and compelling.

> I think [freedom] might have been [my main subject] in the past. No, I
> think love is my subject. I have very mixed feelings about the concept of
> freedom now. This is partly a philosophical development. I once was a
> kind of existentialist and now I am a kind of platonist. What I am concerned
> about really is love, but this sounds very grandiose. One is always telling a
> story, making jokes, and so on. I think the novel is a comic form.
>
> (interview with W. K. Rose, 1968)

Murdoch, talking thus in 1968, the year of publication of *The Nice and the
Good*, gives us a significant key to the change in her work. Whereas in the past
her characters by their very nature were arguing against easy existential
definitions of freedom, something previously partially submerged in Murdoch's ideology has come to the fore and focused the talent. This focusing
leads to an overall strength and conviction of authority, something that had
been present in the necessarily narrow form of *The Time of the Angels* and is
here exploited. When the characters go through their ruminative exercises,
then, as many had done in the early novels, these no longer project the quality
of mere exercises, but are part of a felt and total sense of the characters as
personalities living through cogitations rather than having them thrust upon
them by an external world of ideology and device. In other words, Murdoch's thought and her identification with her personalities have melded, and
technical form brilliantly and almost automatically emerges.

As her comment in the interview indicates, the technical difficulty is the
joining of the large, even grandiose theme of love as she conceives it to the
particular limitations of the novelistic form. As Murdoch argues so strongly
in *The Black Prince*, the novel, no matter how serious its intentions, cannot
masquerade as tragedy, cannot make too large claims. The genre is humble,
involved in telling stories and making jokes, but since it ought to be transmitting a sense of the real and to be dedicated to pursuing accurately the
workings and pain of the psyche, it is automatically characterized by irony –
that immeasurable and puzzling gap between the fictional, with its attendant
flimsiness and falseness, and the true, characterized by starkness and almost

unendurable spiritual discipline. To put it more simply, the coexistence of fun and pain constitutes the novel as an ironic form.

In *The Nice and the Good*, Murdoch exploits this coexistence, balancing the pleasures of the novel with its serious examination of the good and its connection to love. Formally, she falls back on the fascinating Victorian device of presenting a murder mystery complete with a strongly conceived sleuth. John Ducane's unravelling of the puzzle of Radeechy's hidden life and suicide forms a baseline along which the novel travels, but the solution and Ducane's handling of it join the serious concerns of the novel and are altered by them. In *An Unofficial Rose* and later in *The Sacred and Profane Love Machine* Murdoch gives her opinion of mystery writers – Emma Sands and Montague Small are both grimly aware of the limitations and tawdriness of their work and its distance from real art. Even Bradley Pearson in *The Black Prince*, autoreflexively pouring out his complex tale, indicates a kind of humility in the face of his achievement, a sense that the artist must in honesty be uneasy about the quality of his product and treat it with the sort of ordinariness that objects in the real world have. In *The Nice and the Good* Murdoch joins the charming but limited mystery form to some of her most precise and serious thought. The resultant product is very much at home in the real world, and entertainment and wisdom balance as the ironies of Shakespearean felicity are enacted in the last few pages.

That the balances work so well accounts for the novel's success, and it is obvious that Murdoch has mastered a method of building up the humble mystery genre to a point where it is no longer limited and superficial. By giving it texture, by adding to it, she shows quietly how fiction, the mere telling of stories, can propel the idea or genre of the novel into earnest achievement and moral operation. In *The Fire and the Sun,* Murdoch argues eloquently for art's function against the scorn of Plato, who advocated dialectic as the best and only genuine mode of thought. In an important way, a humble book like *The Nice and the Good* unobtrusively speaks to this argument and teaches a high level of moral awareness and the drawing of distinctions.

Unobtrusiveness is the key word in this novel's favour, for although it is the first time Murdoch is really precise about the good, there is no false sermonizing on the subject as in the early novels. John Ducane, the central character, is the focus for ideas of the good, for his passionate desire and failure to be a good man and consequently a just judge carry much of the plot. But, as I explained in Chapter II, the real definition of the good comes to us through Uncle Theo, whose stripped and even dreary personality keeps him in the background. His ruminations are infrequent but profound, and his past and present failures indicate the stringent demands of the real good. Hovering in the background, Theo appears most powerful when he talks to Willy Kost, another guilt-haunted character on his own painful quest towards reality, who, although trapped by the horrors of his concentration camp past, argues for the discipline of a hopeless Weilian waiting, accepting chance and loving fate, while spending time on small, ungrandiose exercises in love: working on the Propertius text, teaching languages.

For John Ducane, Theo's knowledge does not exist, and he argues with Willy against *amor fati* which he sees as pure wickedness. He prefers logic and action to chance and waiting, and is in this respect very much a man of the ordinary, quotidian world. Willy and Theo are basically involved in the contemplative life, however, and Murdoch, in drawing her distinctions, concentrates on a more regular, workaday, bourgeois life. The key distinction, between the nice and the good, is not easily made – indeed not made at all – by the central cast of bourgeois characters. Kate and Octavian Gray, who own the Dorset house inhabited by the major characters of the novel, apply the two terms indiscriminately to nice Ducane, and this inability to discriminate typifies the general attitude. One of Murdoch's most precise points is that the average or mediocre mind shears away from a real definition of the good and describes it carelessly. She is also carefully illustrating that even a fair degree of discrimination is inadequate to the terrible, blank absoluteness of the term. Hence Theo in his years in the Buddhist monastery was frightened by it and fell by the wayside, and Ducane limits his pursuit of the good to a narrow, logical framework focused on the possibility of just judgement. His interest in the *specificatio* of Roman law and his inner conviction, which he tries to stifle because he knows its hubristic danger, that he alone is the upright man capable of being a judge, stress his logical inclination and his dangerous desire to shape and command the world. His conviction that he is powerful, ought to be in charge, is capable of perceiving and helping others, leads to his estimation of the naturalness of his role as sleuth in the Radeechy affair, and to his feeling of control over and responsibility towards the other characters in the Gray household. His intelligence and concern add up, at their best, to niceness, and in a serious sense – although he doesn't understand Theo's and Willy's knowledge – he knows that even at this best he is somehow lacking, that he remains in the realm of the mediocre and is merely nice.

There is, of course, a major impediment to his acting and being at his best: the existence of his clinging ex-mistress, Jessica. This guilty aspect of his past (and it is important to see how moral and spiritual striving for the questing characters in this book is impeded by guilt) at first keeps him from seeing himself accurately and later helps him towards certain revelations. Willy and Theo have been through the fires of knowledge well before the action begins; they therefore recede and we focus on Ducane's progress. By nature a Scottish puritan for whom moral struggle is a basic characteristic, Ducane expends his considerable powers of rumination on examining his own moral potentialities. Far from being one of Murdoch's naive characters, he is able to perceive both faults and methods by which he could change in order to align himself with love and justice. Apart from the messy and secret Jessica problem, he and the other characters think of him as a wise, clear-headed person. But Jessica resists being cleared away, and the calm, innocent, tidy love he had envisioned sharing with Kate Gray cannot survive the strains placed on it by his imperfection and deceit. The steps forward Ducane actually takes are limited, and achieved not through his skilful power and logical manoeuvring, which quickly collapse in the face of intractible circumstances, but through the terrors of chance which lead him almost to his death with young Pierce in Gunnar's Cave, and by his gradual recognition, through his investigation of the Radeechy affair, of the dreary smallness of evil and the wickedness of his own lust for power.

In spite of its mystery frame and felicitous conclusion, *The Nice and the Good* makes its points more negatively and subtly than the solutions and comedic pairings–off would indicate. Murdoch's allusions have always been extensive, but here she employs a successful device which will characterize her mature style – the use of a major work of art as a background against whose qualities much of the action is set. The work she chooses is Bronzino's cool and elegant painting in the National Gallery in London entitled 'An Allegory', but referred to by Biranne, the character to whom it is centrally linked, as Venus, Cupid, Folly and Time. Its smooth sexual surface is modified by the curtain of malevolent Time, by the howling image of Jealousy, and by the enamelled, twisted figure of Deceit, and its very design presents the reader with the underlying pattern of the novel: the charming folly of sexuality and the fragility of human sexual love are foregrounded, while the forces of destruction which modify and limit that love hover in the background. All that is necessary for the triumph of the destructive forces is the movement of Time's arm to sweep away the lovely blissful moment of Cupid's kiss of Venus.

This is indeed how the novel moves, replete with Venusian images, until it becomes evident that sexuality and ordinary romantic human love affairs are not real, lasting, useful or accurate. Theo tends to rail to Willy about the other characters, whom he regards as sex maniacs, even though he himself is hopelessly and silently trapped by his love for young Pierce. Theo, however, has gone far enough on the path towards reality to know that it is part of moral discipline to keep the blackness of sexual misery inside himself – and so he advises Pierce to do with his adolescent unrequited love for Barbara. But Pierce and the other characters are very much driven and controlled by their confusion of sexuality and sexual power with a more spiritual love and with the good. The novel is at pains to point out this confusion and to describe the mediocrity of the direction in which sex, despite all its positive charm, drives.

The most potent image of this Venusian sexuality is Judy McGrath, an Aphrodite-Circe-Helen of Troy figure of seduction, who appeals to

Biranne's sexual peculiarities, and who had worked for Radeechy during his black magical rites: '"After all," said Octavian, "spiritualism and magic and all that are connected with sex, always have been. Sex comes to most of us with a twist"' (p. 36). It is Ducane's task, as it is the reader's in a very different way, to investigate that twist. Judy provides the link between the investigation of suicide and the black magic which is part of a larger sexual game at the heart of the business. In the final unravelling, Ducane discovers that Biranne has not only been involved with Judy but also had an affair with Radeechy's wife, Claudia. This affair led to Claudia's violent death and was directly responsible for Radeechy's suicide, and it is clear that Radeechy's black magic is equivalent to Biranne's promiscuous sexuality, and ultimately to the power games that abound in this book, as they do in Ducane's personality.

With real finesse, Murdoch nudges the reader towards a nexus of equivalences through organically implanted images. The whip that signals Biranne's sexual practices is repeated as one of the objects in Radeechy's underground black magic games, and occurs again as an instrument of Ducane's desire for power and dominance when he strikes the offending Pierce with Barbara's riding whip. Similarly, the well-sustained pattern of bird images – the cuckoo of lust, the seagull with the broken wing which symbolizes the maimed intentions of the all too human characters who must come to terms with death, and the dead caged pigeons in Radeechy's den – progressively illustrate the dragging down towards death and evil of certain activities that at first seem merely bourgeois and frivolous. Thus a morally striving character like Ducane begins by believing in his superiority and his separation from guilt and evil. He feels free to throw off Jessica and condescends to the sneaking deceit of McGrath, whom he sees as far removed from himself. But again Murdoch will employ a subtle image – the eating of a half walnut, with its ancient sympathetic-magical identification as one of the lobes of the brain – to cement the final equivalence between the morally degraded McGrath and the hubristic, self-satisfied, 'good' Ducane.

In the course of his investigation, and through his relationship with Jessica and flirtation with Kate, Ducane is gradually forced to recognize himself as a hypocrite, a 'whited sepulchre'. As his ruminations express it:

> It is in me, thought Ducane, as he continued to look through the empty blue staring eyes of McGrath. The evil is in me. There are demons and powers outside us, Radeechy played with them, but they are pygmy things. The great evil, the real evil, is inside myself. It is I who am Lucifer. (p. 214)

An interesting and ironic feature of this apparently quite positive novel is that it is much more profoundly related to evil and to the mode of _The Time of the Angels_ than is immediately apparent. Murdoch is deeply concerned with absolutes – the nature of absolute good at its most stringent and alien, and the insidious terror of absolute evil which invades the very being of every person who is involved in lying or deceit and who pursues any power role whatever. Ducane's recognition of himself as Lucifer reveals how dreadfully unattainable goodness and its correlative, justice, are, and how near to hand are the elements not of mere failure but of real evil.

Murdoch is very interested in the lack of quality and duration of this kind of recognition in her characters, and it is significant that Ducane's moment of truth is instantly defeated by the simple passage of time. He persists in his judgmental investigative job, routing Biranne as he gathers all the cards of power over him, and to a lesser degree, McGrath. It takes a desperate encounter with his own death to jell the lesson, to make him realize that he (indeed, human beings in general) can judge no man and that all power must be abjured. The unravelling of the tale of Radeechy forms an interesting analogue for Ducane between demonic black magic and the magic game of power – a part of the structure of equivalences which Murdoch has very carefully set up in this novel. Poor crazed Radeechy, carried away by his magic and fantastical demonism, had written a cryptogram on the wall of the underground air-raid-shelter room where he had kept his gadgets and enacted his black masses. Ducane copies it down and finally decodes it, working out as part of the mystery structure of the book that it is the ancient, secret Christian device involving the first two words of the Lord's prayer arranged in the form of a cross. Its mystical truth is wrecked by Radeechy's egomania which identifies himself as God: Radeechy Pater Dominus.

Ducane instantly sees this extended magic as childish, disappointing and pathetic – but he also sees its extension into his own life, and now, having survived his brush with death, he can perceive more clearly and is more convinced than he had been earlier:

> Perhaps there were spirits, perhaps there were evil spirits, but they were little things. The great evil, the dreadful evil, that which made war and slavery and *all man's inhumanity to man lay in the cool self-justifying ruthless selfishness of quite ordinary people, such as Biranne, and himself.*
>
> (p. 320; my italics)

This time he resigns from his Whitehall position where the magic of power was so tempting, but Murdoch does not intend that he be seen as an achiever of the good. He has learned, and genuinely learned, something significant about evil and hence about the way ordinary people must be perceived – but that is all.

When he was trapped with Pierce in the black cave, Ducane's confrontation with death was softened by the floating image of a woman's face, a saving Venus figure who turns out in the denouement to be Mary Clothier. Although Murdoch is working seriously on the tough terminology of good and evil, she focuses the main action of the novel on the middle range of the quotidian – that range which, she claims in *The Fire and the Sun*, Plato ignored at his peril. Certainly this area is where she serves literary realism most thoroughly, and in *The Nice and the Good* much important contributory action occurs here. An important strand of the plot involves the emotionally voracious Kate Gray presiding as a glowing Aphrodite Pandemos over Trescombe House, aided by Mary Clothier and Paula Biranne. Octavian sees them as his harem, Willy as the three Graces, and they appear to inhabit a sunny world sustained by Kate's enormous self-confidence. But Paula is haunted by sexual guilt, Mary by the fact that she has been unable to come to terms with the long distant death of her husband Alistair. The power of the past over them is extreme, as it is in the case of most of the other characters, and Murdoch makes it clear, as a major theme in the book, that the past must be accepted and worked through before any steps forward can take place.

In the slick working-out of things, Paula is reunited with Biranne, her divorced husband, and Kate is gently reprimanded by the withdrawal of her admirers from her power. But the character and ruminative mode of Mary Clothier complement Ducane's spiritual developments. The final marriage of the two is really an external seal on the mental growth whose total dimension requires the experience and inward questing of both. Mary feels that she has 'shirked the past' (p. 138) and is haunted by the accidental nature of Alistair's death, as well as her tendency to belittle him in her memory. Murdoch is pointed in her descriptions of how the human mind is plagued by its own products, and by images or *eidola* that uncannily bind people to each other in devastating ways:

> There are mysterious agencies of the human mind which, like roving gases, travel the world, causing pain and mutilation, without their owners having any full awareness, or even any awareness at all, of the strength and the whereabouts of these exhalations. Possibly a saint might be known by the utter absence of such gaseous tentacles, but the ordinary person is naturally endowed with them, just as he is endowed with the ghostly power of appearing in other people's dreams. So it is that we can be terrors to each other, and people in lonely rooms suffer humiliations and even damage because of others in whose consciousness perhaps they scarcely figure at all. *Eidola* projected from the mind take on a life of their own, wandering to find their victims and maddening them with miseries and fears which the original source of these wanderers could not be justly charged with inflicting and might indeed be very puzzled to hear of.
>
> (p. 144)

For Mary, the *eidolon* of Alistair travels with her until it is expelled by what appears to be a re-enactment of death and loss, as she sits through the night waiting for low tide so that she can see whether her son Pierce (and Ducane) have survived the night in Gunnar's Cave. Again, as she had done in *The*

*Sandcastle* and *The Unicorn*, Murdoch stages a cliff-hanging physical dilemma, but there is a new dimension to it here, inasmuch as it occasions Mary's most powerful rumination, and indeed eloquently presents the connection between death and human love that Murdoch would have the reader see. It is beyond the Venusian surface of sexual love, beyond niceness and human happiness, but it represents the real seriousness of this novel, even though time remains as a limiting factor on both change and duration. Mary begins by experiencing 'a sort of sad impersonal love' for the dead Alistair, and then continues:

> Death happens, love happens, and all human life is compact of accident and chance. If one loves what is so frail and mortal, if one loves and holds on, like a terrier holding on, must not one's love become changed? There is only one absolute imperative, the imperative to love: yet how can one endure to go on loving what must die, what indeed is dead? *O death, rock me asleep, bring me quiet rest. Let pass my weary guilty ghost out of my careful breast.* One is oneself this piece of earth, this concoction of frailty, a momentary shadow upon the chaos of the accidental world. Since death and chance are the material of all there is, if love is to be love of something it must be love of death and chance. This changed love moves upon the ocean of accident, over the forms of the dead, a love so impersonal and so cold it can scarcely be recognized, a love devoid of beauty, of which one knows no more than the name, so little is it like an experience. This love Mary felt now for her dead husband and for the faceless wraith of her perhaps drowned son.

> (pp. 307–8)

This expression of *amor fati* wrenches the book from its surface adherence to the muddle of human love and aligns it to the absolutes the novel so subtly and secretly, yet so clearly is working on. Recognition of this love comes only *in extremis*, and underlying the seriousness of the idea is the grim question posed by Theo very near the end of the book: 'How does one change?' (p. 348). The implied answer is that in the life lived by the average and therefore mediocre person there can be no change. It is too difficult, too terrible, too absolutely associated with death to be sustained in the quotidian under the aegis of time, where all the characters ultimately take their chances and continue to live.

It was also Theo who saw most clearly the untraversable distance between the nice and the good. Mary Clothier and John Ducane are not as far along as he is, but they have perceived something of the nature of the real and of the demanding task of change. This change is not possible in the hell of suffering, as Willy had explained to Mary, because there one has no energy for it and escape to the daily world inhibits the task. As this task is described, magic must metamorphose into spirit; the magics of power, self-esteem, sexuality and tricks like Radeechy's must undergo a spiritual alteration which only death can deliver.

This radical statement constitutes the heart of the novel, and its dry impossibility certainly lives in the fiction. Murdoch opts for a brittle gaiety, however, and ends with reconciliation, marriage and a flying saucer for the luminous and innocent twins. The ironies persist in the conclusion, but are somehow overshadowed, and the reader leaves this important novel puzzled and partially reassured by the serenities of its basic balance. Murdoch will allow this felicitous conclusion once more, in *Bruno's Dream*, but thereafter the darkness of man's squalid limitations will give a resounding 'no' to Bradley Pearson's first question in this quotation from *The Black Prince*: 'Can there be a *natural*, as it were a Shakespearean felicity in the moral life? Or are the Eastern sages right to set as a task to their disciples the gradual total destruction of the dreaming ego?' (p. 155). *The Nice and the Good* launches Murdoch on a serious examination of death and of Buddhist stringencies to which she will return again and again. For the time being the comedic frame dominates, but although this novel ushers in her mature style and formulates the now developed viewpoint, it is not at all, in any way, the last word.

# VI

# PILGRIM'S PROGRESS

*From change to defeat in Bruno's Dream and A Fairly
Honourable Defeat*

*The Nice and the Good* takes as its task the drawing of the distinctions and the
assertion of equivalences. Its mode is governed by precision, as character and
event play out a definition of approaches to the good against which the
tawdry evils of human beings stand crowded and in contrast. The exact
nature of the barren face of the good can, however, be only partially inferred,
given Murdoch's stringent interpretation of it, and it is known primarily by
its unreachable distance from the all too flawed characters. Apprehension of
that good comes only when the seeker is *in extremis*: at the point of total
religious failure for Uncle Theo, or when the near proximity of death forces a
depth of attention alien to the quotidian working of the moral faculty, as in
the cases of Willy Kost in the past and John Ducane in the present. The real
subject of the novel is imperfection, inasmuch as apprehending the good
merely causes the characters to turn aside in partial defeat, overwhelmed by
the evil of their own lies and futile bondage to the past.

Although Murdoch is causing her characters to confront the absolutes, the
very form – if one takes it literally – of *The Nice and the Good* deflects the
reader from the grimness of those absolutes, almost hiding the theme by
knitting our interest to standard novelistic felicities. The resultant irony is
deliberately too slick, and in the next two novels Murdoch will turn her
attention again to some of the directions in which *The Nice and the Good*
points. One of her lessons involves the near impossibility of change, so that
moral knowledge with its brief span of endurance tends to leave the
characters only slightly touched. Because the good is so terrifying, ordinary
mortals are put into a strange adversary position to it, and dodge into
convenient outlets like immediate and welcome happiness as a means of
lulling the mind. To put it another way, the healthy psyche chooses the hope
of life rather than dwelling in the absolute of death. Because death is where
Murdoch's characters find the true and real to lie, however, it is obvious that

she is using the novel to show how ironic the human condition must of necessity be.

The resounding negatives of such a basic viewpoint lead to a natural conclusion about Murdoch's pessimism, especially as this view is central to all the subsequent novels. Realism is notoriously connected to pessimism, and Murdoch's ideological development gives such a tradition double applicability. One of the most interesting preoccupations for the reader of later Murdoch is observing the extensions of that pessimism and its occasional carefully timed withdrawal. The illustration of the good in *The Nice and the Good* establishes an absolute against which the subsequent novels must all be set. Henceforth the major question is whether the ironies of this moral setting will indicate any significant moral developments in the characters.

*Bruno's Dream* (1969) presents an anatomy of death in which the dying Bruno does indeed learn something, and the entire novel studies his death as an image of an ordinary human mind slowly and reluctantly apprehending what life and death are. Like *The Nice and the Good*, this is a strangely cheerful book; Bruno's death is an achievement, and most of the other characters are projected again into a felicitous world. It is important to question Murdoch's allegiance to that artfully constructed world, because many of her definitions of the comic and ironic – and hence of the core of her art – relate to it. When Lisa Watkin turns from a life of self-denial and discipline to a happy secular-sexual relationship with Danby Odell, she enrages Miles Greensleave, the artist figure in this novel. The implications are significant, for Miles as a character is Murdoch's device for ironic teaching about the nature of art. Using artist figures for self-reflective, negative brooding on the art she so vividly practises is one of Murdoch's most assertive peculiarities, and although clearly connected to her central paradoxes, a character like Miles Greensleave goes far in the belittling of the artistic enterprise.

Miles is one of Murdoch's most dislikable, damnable characters; nothing in his actions does him credit, although in the past he had at least managed to love his Indian wife, Parvati, and his sister, Gwen. Overwhelmed by Parvati's death, the young Miles had written a long, bad poem; when he loses Lisa the middle-aged Miles, devastated by what he regards as her shoddy behaviour, begins to write the inspired poetry he has been waiting so long to be able to do. His selfishness and insensitivity combine to persuade that, despite his smugness, he could not produce great art – although that is not what the novel literally tells us. Death and loss spur him to production and indeed seem to be his subject, but he cannot pay much attention to his dying father or suffering wife, because to do so would be too devastating. His limitations are personal, but they affect the reader's feeling about the work of the artist in general. Murdoch appears to be making through him a statement on creativity: Miles is less than mediocre as a human being and a poor agent of truth; evidently he represents the contemporary artist whose concentration is on barren image-making and on his egotism as creator, and who in his moral selfishness perceives very little of the externally real.

This sourness about the artist and tendency to see him as possessing demonic qualities are fairly general in Murdoch's fiction, except when she is talking about the great artists of the past. The artists in her novels participate in the self-concentration of the quotidian and usually come off very badly, partly because of the sorry nature of everyday life, but more because Murdoch finds the contemporary artistic type unacceptable. The positive creative acts in this novel occur in the minds of characters who break through into the hard reality which lies at the centre of the moral impulse. Significant change, the possibility of which constitutes the starting point of Murdoch's major novels, can occur only when this reality is sought or glimpsed, and consistently in Murdoch's work artists neither understand change nor seek it humbly. 'Artistic' virtues like perceptivity and the projection of life-giving images appear in less pretentious characters as part of their insight into human experience; for Murdoch these qualities help to constitute realistic creative acts that can reflect moral development if and when it occurs. That the self-professed poet, Miles, lacks the moral component means that neither his perceptions (always presented as overwrought and precious) nor his image-building is tied to the moral base that is so major in Murdoch's thinking. Indeed, he refuses to participate very deeply in the suffering of others – Bruno, Diana, Lisa – because seeing it clearly would make him vulnerable to that suffering and to the reality of death itself in a non-fantastic, non-imagistic way which he tries at all costs to avoid. Through Bradley Pearson in *The Black Prince*, Murdoch will later allow the artist to take slow, unwilling steps towards his proper moral and spiritual identification, but in *Bruno's Dream* something very different is going on.

Lisa Watkin, the sister-in-law with whom Miles falls in love, begins the novel as a character very close to aspiring sainthood, and her relationship to Miles at moments looks like an expression of the binary contrast – would-be artist, would-be saint – that Murdoch so often depicts. Lisa's life of discipline, religious questing and service to others is disrupted by the love affairs that develop, but she nevertheless persists in self-denial, giving up Miles and planning to go to India to work for the Save the Children Fund. Her sudden reversal at the end, when she chooses to seek ordinary secular happiness with Danby, is a deliberate attempt to destroy the image of herself as saint and enter a world of self-interest. Encaged by a devotion to moral duty, she had begun a variety of essentially unnatural life-denying roles – as a nun, and as a potential worker with Indian children – and was for years a teacher in a tough East London school. At one point, her discipline led to a serious physical breakdown. Dropping this inclination towards role-playing allows her to become a pleasure-loving sexual being. She is transformed by her subsequent happiness, and nothing in the novel implies that this metamorphosis is other than positive: she laughs again, looks years younger and is filled with vitality. Meanwhile, her prettier, more worldly older sister moves in the opposite direction, and as Diana sits with the dying, almost comatose Bruno, her face takes on the kind, self-denying lines that had for years been Lisa's. This chiasmus of the two sisters does not belittle Lisa's new pleasures at all, and the non-judgemental straightness with which Murdoch describes the changes in their moral structure presents the reader with a curious double frame of reference.

It would be altogether too easy to align Murdoch with the rigours of the good at the expense of human pleasure and to perceive the powerful negative impulse as characteristic, but here she appears to be indicating something about the rhythms of human lives and about their progressive unravelling in the human time span. Far from imprisoning these lives in pattern, she allows them to enact their personalities wholly, to break out of the system which Murdoch both asserts and denies. Lisa's disinclination to continue her quest for sainthood – her eschewing the very image of it – connects to Murdoch's distrust of all such images; for her they belong to fantasy, not reality. Those qualities in Lisa's character – selfless love, understanding, generosity – which are offspring of her discipline are also convertible to the open capacity for free change: they are the qualities Danby falls in love with, allowing her to exit from her closed world into erotic happiness. Murdoch is completely generous about this new felicity; the abjuring of images is important here, not the following of a difficult moral pattern controlled by the authorial source.

Yet we never enter Lisa's mind as we do Miles's, so we do not see her very extensively as an image-maker as we do him. As he romantically awaits his inspiring god, he lives placidly in a false world created by his limited imagination and by the will of his wife, Diana. Diana, a considerable fantasist herself, sees their relationship in archetypal fairy-tale terms in which she is the sustaining 'mysterious lady of the fountain who heals the wound of the wandering knight, the wound which has defied all other touches' (p. 87). Her aesthetic creation of their house and milieu, where for years she has governed and looked after the mourning Miles and the bird-with-a-broken-wing Lisa, cannot withstand disruption from external reality in the persons of Danby and Bruno. Her work of art shatters, as do all her charming fantasies about Miles, herself, Lisa, Danby and Bruno, and only afterwards can her education proceed: from this household as an artificially created image to blank, real love for a Bruno too ill to respond very much. The process is painful, and is characterized by the displacement of every false image; as Murdoch traces that process, Diana's spiritual nature enlarges while her secular expectations and creativity diminish, and she becomes a major vehicle of the novel's deepest positive intention. At the end, sitting by Bruno, Diana wryly estimates the present:

A Lisa in India would have become a divinity. A Lisa sitting in Danby's car with an arm outstretched along the back of the seat, as Diana had last seen her, was fallen indeed. Miles said venomously, 'Well, she had chosen the world and the flesh. Let's hope for her sake she doesn't find she's got the devil as well!' Naturally it did not occur to Miles that Diana would be other than pleased. In fact, he was not concerned with Diana's feelings, being so absorbingly interested in his own. He will manage, she thought, he will manage. We've all paired off really, in the end. Miles has got his muse, Lisa has got Danby. And I've got Bruno. Who would have thought it would work out like that?

(pp. 290–1)

Diana's ability to travel far in the domain of hard reality is a considerable surprise; she begins as one of Murdoch's narrow types – the attractive, middle-aged woman, trapped by complacency and emotional greed – and the choice of her as a vehicle of knowledge shows Murdoch's perpetual capacity to mould her materials freely and unexpectedly. It also reminds the complacent reader of the generosity she directs without discrimination to every character type in her unpretentiously bourgeois collection. Yet Diana, like her sister Lisa, is not ultimately as fully realized as many of the male characters, and one feels that Murdoch's struggle against aggressive design is not quite triumphant in the surprising reversal of both sisters.

Miles, a tight, narrow person and a limited image-maker, is contrasted not only to Lisa and Diana, the women he loves, but to his ex-brother-in-law, Danby, and his dying father, Bruno. Indeed, each of the latter two directs his own energy to proper ends – love and death – in stark opposition to the artist Miles, whose interpretation of both major themes is superficial and self-protective. In a novel full of strongly conceived characters, Danby and Bruno are extraordinary productions. Their humility before the substance of the unpredictable real world, present and past, is a quality they share in different degrees, but Murdoch's conception of them goes beyond their moral qualities. Although Miles's awfulness is also extremely well done, in Danby and Bruno Murdoch takes a major stride forward in character projection. The stale critical commonplace that Murdoch's characters tend to flow into one another certainly does not fit the strong characters of her mature style. *Bruno's Dream* has arresting characters at every level, but Murdoch's brooding attention to Danby, and particularly Bruno, illustrates a free realism she had not totally been able to project before. One problem was and is the pallid uniformity of the late twentieth-century bourgeois personality, but the more interesting one has to do with Murdoch's increasing bravery and closer identification with the essential, as opposed to the authorially contrived, nature of her characters.

Whereas Lisa's progress and reversal may be seen as contrived, Danby's curious blend of qualities surprises and delights the reader. In many ways this marvellous character resists the formal frame of the novel and belies the experienced Murdoch reader's attempt to categorize his mysteries. At first glance he is one of Murdoch's types – the *homme moyen sensuel* – and his easy, honest recognition of himself as such and no more would appear to reveal his social, moral and spiritual limitations. His easy-going ways place him at the centre of a very ordinary life for his type: he is a skilful businessman and printer, he sleeps routinely and passionlessly with Adelaide the maid, he likes chasing women, he drinks too much, he sings a lot. Yet two things distinguish him, and set him in a line of development which his undemanding sensuality would not indicate. First is his absolute and reliable responsibility for the dying Bruno, whose pretentious son, Miles, is hostile and indifferent; second is the fact that the almost mythical Gwen had loved and married him.

In the background of this novel is a minor but firmly used Shakespearean allusion, a quotation from *Othello*, which plays at the fringes of both structure and denouement in *Bruno's Dream*. It is Brabantio's statement of dismay and disbelief on hearing of his daughter Desdemona's unlikely marriage to Othello: 'For nature so prepost'rously to err'. The phrase is used to report Parvati's family's reaction (and indeed, Bruno's) to her marriage to Miles, as well as Miles's reaction to both Gwen's and Lisa's taking up with Danby. Brabantio's rigidity and formulaic definition of life is reflected by characters in Murdoch's novel who see not reality (nature), but only their narrow and constrained definition of it. Although Miles saw his marriage to Parvati as serious and utterly justified, he was horrified when his intellectual, morally serious sister, Gwen, married the haphazard, sensual Danby. The saint-like Gwen, long dead, is described as having had physical and moral characteristics much like Lisa's, and Danby's turning to Lisa is partly a circular re-enactment of the past. It is also, of course, Danby's re-entrance into the intense and real world of the present, his shaking-off of the dead hand of the fabulous Gwen. Not only was Miles amazed at the unnatural Gwen/Danby marriage, but Danby himself was overwhelmed by it:

> Danby's relationship with Gwen had seemed to him, even at the time, something that was not quite himself, but more like a visitation from outside. He had perfectly understood Miles's looks of incomprehension and amazement. Such a conjunction was so improbable. Gwen was not his type and he was not hers. Gwen had had a kind of authority over him which seemed more an attribute of her sheer alienness than the result of any rational effect of persuasion. Perhaps it had simply been the authority of a terrifying degree of love. And in retrospect Danby saw his marriage as a pure celebration of the god of love, something almost arbitrary and yet entirely necessary, invented and conducted at the whim of that deity without the help of any mundane basis in nature. Of course Danby, though he had never opened a textbook of psychology in his life, knew that the working of nature is very often hidden and that what had so powerfully

brought him and Gwen together could well be, after all, something natural, but he did not want to know. He preferred to believe in the action of the god in his life, an action which he took to be entirely *sui generis* and unique. (p. 134)

The creative Eros awaited by the artist Miles automatically entered Danby's life years ago and will enter again with Lisa, and there is no doubt that Murdoch has chosen Danby as the fit receptacle for such a visitation. This whole idea of the artistic versus the sexual Eros will be played out again in *The Black Prince* when Bradley Pearson goes from being a despicable artist character like Miles through a painful metamorphosis at the hands of sexuality, reality and death. In *Bruno's Dream*, however, Murdoch splits the erotic energy of artistic creativity from that of sexuality, and opts tonally for the latter. Of course, it is not sexual eroticism simply perceived, because Danby's easy-going nature extends far beyond his ability to attract women. He knows very well that his love for Adelaide and flirtation with Diana are mediocre commitments, while his marriage to Gwen, and, we infer, his relationship with Lisa as well, can bring him out of the dream of ordinary life into reality: 'Danby held it for gospel that Gwen had been reality and his subsequent life had been a dream' (p. 135). His ordinary world produces 'a very much easier and more natural and Danby-like mode of existence', but he never swerves from his belief that

> Gwen had been a sort of miracle in his life the nature of which he would never entirely understand. . . . But had he ever really existed in the world of which his love for Gwen had given him intimations? . . . on the whole he felt that the god must have found him, for all the frenzy of his enthusiasm, something of a disappointment. He had loved wholeheartedly but with too ordinary a heart. (pp. 135–6)

His humility and sense of himself as nothing much are in fact his strongest attractions. He does not accept the former visitation of the god Eros as though he expected or deserved it, and he expects no repetition. When Lisa appears on the scene he is once again obsessed, though he distinguishes her scrupulously from Gwen despite their similarities. He sees clearly and assumes no desert, intelligently perceiving precisely what is and what is not; and he understands that he must not be trapped by memories of his past life with Gwen:

> He was an older fatter more drunken man than the one whom Gwen had so unaccountably loved. But he was also perhaps, and this intimation somehow entered into the deepest part of Danby's pain, a wiser man. The years had brought him something which, potentially at least, was good. That obscure small good seemed to suffer and ache inside him as he thought vaguely but intensely about all the might-have-beens of a quite other life

with Lisa. It seemed to him that in spite of his casual mode of being and his bad behaviour to Adelaide and his general willingness to play the fool, he had found something in the world, some little grain of understanding which that glimpse of Lisa had made suddenly luminous and alive. He felt obscurely the dividedness of his being, the extent of what was gross, the littleness and value of what was not.                                    (p. 231)

Danby's just, simple estimate of himself goes far in defining where Murdoch sees value to lie. His limited but genuine goodness and wisdom far outweigh Miles's blindness and arrogance; and surely Danby's god is more real than Miles's muse.

Danby is a very fully fleshed out character. Not only are serious, intellectual, almost saintly women in this fiction charmed by him; he interests the reader on several levels, most significantly in the blending of his comic dimension into a larger, largely unconscious identification of him as morally valuable. Murdoch's view of her most serious characters as quintessentially comic is shaping itself very firmly here: his vitality and high spirits lead to his flirtation with Diana and his terribly funny drunken entrance into the Greensleave garden, but such actions are genuinely amusing rather than degrading. Murdoch's Danby comedy has no dark shadows. Years ago, when Miles had asked Gwen what she saw in Danby, she had replied, 'Oh well, Danby is such *fun*' (p. 57), and Danby had habitually identified himself as her 'comic relief'. Indeed, he *is* fun, and this is the major key to his importance as a character. Beset by easy-going foibles, he does not take himself very seriously – a great relief after the affected seriousness of Miles. The result of his humble, careless self-image involves a release into a world of generosity, and because he does not think incessantly about himself he can act well towards Bruno, studying the old man's slow progress towards death. He is not, of course, idealized; he commits many standard errors of inattention: he is insensitive to Adelaide, indifferent to Nigel, hurtful to Diana, occasionally impatient with Bruno and suddenly self-absorbed when Lisa appears on the scene as another Gwen. He submits to the pistol duel with Will Boase as a punishment for his bad behaviour to Diana and Adelaide, and he sees the potentially fatal duel and the loss of Lisa as necessary chastisements for his inadequacy: 'He thought I am dying for a girl I didn't love, I am dying because I failed to love, I am dying just upon the brink of love. I was not worthy' (pp. 238–9).

He does not die and he gets the girl, and the reader feels that this is true and not contrived Shakespearean felicity. His unworthiness is genuine, but his clear knowledge of it indicates his status as a morally advanced person for whom and in whom the comedy of the world is enacted. When Gwen died by jumping into the Thames to save a child who could swim, Danby for all his grief thought it was funny; as Bruno's death approaches, Danby cuts the comedy and concentrates with kindness and sympathetic vision on that event. That he is finally distracted by Lisa's arrival and that the real burden of enduring Bruno's death falls on Diana do not reflect negatively on him; Murdoch wishes the reader to enter the realm of death with an unconsoled character who can participate wholly in it without outside distraction.

If Danby illustrates the positive erotic experience of a life lived decently and realistically in the world of the present, Bruno's life and death function as an opposite learning process, to be undergone when vitality ebbs and all hope of worldly felicity is gone. Early in the novel, Bruno thinks sadly to himself, 'If only he could be loved by somebody new. But it was impossible. Who would love him now when he had become a monster?' (p. 14). The gentleness of Nigel the Nurse and the generosity of Danby are not enough, as, fuelled by his guilty memories, he longs for the vitality that love can infuse. Lisa helps him, but ironically, it is finally Diana who learns to love him absolutely, when he can no longer identify her rationally. Like Danby, however, he *is* rewarded, in this warm and compassionate book.

Love and creativity are very close in Bruno as in Miles and Danby, and although we have a strong sense of the two middle-aged men, it is Bruno's reconstruction of his past and relationship to his present which really dominate the novel. Murdoch is didactic here, but that didacticism is restrained by the strength and success of Bruno as a character. Murdoch shows herself to be dedicated to the Socratic injunction that we should study dying, and her minute observation of it through successive stages in Bruno's last few months is one of the most accurately observed pieces of thanatology in our literature. The didacticism is implied, not pressed, and Bruno himself, the characters around him and the reader undergo the lessons of death merely by following through to the last page.

As Bruno lies on his death-bed, images of an entire lifetime crowd his memory, and through a subtle reportage of that memory, in conjunction with the experiences and acute feelings of the present, Murdoch projects a complete thanatopsis. The stages of Bruno's progress towards death are curiously universal, yet the detailed richness of the data evokes an elaborate picture of this particular old man's past and his endurance of a desperate present. Moment after moment illustrates Murdoch's bravery in undertaking a subject which could quickly fall into artificiality or sentimentality. On the thin edge of credibility, she never breaks tone or causes disbelief. From the opening pages when Bruno can still get out of bed to use the lavatory until his last moment of consciousness, the reader participates in a progressive study which never falters or averts an eye.

Bruno's contemplation of last things is obscured by his guilty memory of bad behaviour and failed relationships. His two great sorrows – that his affair with Maureen may have led to his wife Janie's death and his estrangement from his son Miles, about whose first wife, Parvati, he had made a racist joke – obsess him, and, he feels, keep him from absolute truths, some harmonious state of reconciliation that he feels could save him. Fearing that she would curse him, he refused to go to Janie when she called out to him in her last moments, and so his entire memory of the relationship is scarred with guilt and fear. Irredeemable as that is, he still feels that reconciliation with Miles may be possible, and he directs his very considerable will towards it. Astute Danby fears that Miles cannot handle it, and Bruno's pain following the meeting jolts him further downwards.

The Miles attempt does, however, bring the listening Lisa – a piece of marvellous luck, as it turns out, for Bruno needs a sympathetic, loving audience – as he had fantasized Miles might be. Lisa's transforming power in Bruno's and Danby's lives is puzzling and mysterious, but she presents to Bruno a vocabulary about the past and the whole of life as a dream which is central to his painful progress. Miles and Bruno are eventually reconciled on Miles's limited terms, in a slipshod, superficial way with great courtesy on both sides, but the miracles Bruno had hoped from him come from other directions entirely. The collapse of Bruno's fantasy about Miles is necessary to Murdoch's didactic scheme: it is not the past but the lived present which offers illumination. His great illumination occurs only in his last moments, when in the awful presence of death he realizes that Janie had called out to offer him love and forgiveness. This final knowledge crowns his life and is his gift to the reader.

Bruno's lived life, the subject of the novel, is, finally, a completed whole, the tale that is told, a fiction whose hero or actor also appears to be its author. Bruno's consciousness forms the tale while the authorial presence lies in hiding, dodging anonymously from his consciousness to Danby's to Miles's to Diana's to Adelaide's to Nigel's. Bruno's story is presented as his lived reality but its structure is perceived as a work of art. This is of course a trick, and participates in Murdoch's variously repeated attempt to use the medium of the novel to create the firm illusion of actuality. The ironies arising from such a paradoxical undertaking are imbedded in the text where the imagistic controls very quietly speak against the naturalistic simplicity of a structure which begins in the middle of Bruno's dying and works forward with frequent flashbacks to the inevitable end. Murdoch projects the image-making power into Bruno's consciousness, where it seems to grow naturally from his present milieu and the preoccupations of his past life.

The tale of his dying is framed by his old red dressing-gown

> hanging on the door, a big shrouded thing in the dim light. It was the only garment now which he put on, it represented his only travelling, his wardrobe was shrunk to this. Why had it somehow become the symbol of his death? Danby offered to buy him a new one, and Bruno had refused, saying 'It's not worth it now.' Danby accepted the remark. The old dress-

ing gown would still be there when they returned from the funeral.
(p. 14)

As he becomes permanently bed-ridden, this symbol of his death hardens into folds which he has memorized but keeps studying, and as he drifts into death the dressing-gown moves to the bottom of the bed to claim him. The restrained controlling elegance of this and other naturally projected symbols binds Bruno's life together as his tale is spun, as though the spiders he loves and has spent his life studying are participating in the web of his cogitations. Bruno dying looks like a spider, as do his hands, and the spiders give him his best vocabulary for talking about what God might be. His memories dodge in and out, through dreams and conscious re-enactments of the past, until gradually, with his advancing illness, waking and dreaming become equivalent, as Lisa had said they were. The fate of his stamp collection is dramatically and structurally extended, and the scene of its loss functions as a symbolic marking-off of the moment when he can turn from his past and its concentration on self and possessions. A legacy from a feared father who thought Bruno inadequate to such a grand philatelic treasure, the stamp collection is in fact more loved and studied by the son than by the father. When the flooding Thames threatens it, Bruno, long bed-ridden, vainly tries to save the great and valuable object which binds him to the past. His fall aggravates his illness, but the break with the obsessions of the thing-centred world is accomplished. In this half natural, half artistically contrived structure, Bruno's dressing-gown, his stamp collection, his spiders, his body as a thing, his old hands on the counterpane, his champagne all contribute to the cage he lives in until he receives the knowledge that comes with death.

The novel opens with Bruno in a state of guilt about the past and bewilderment about the end of his life. His imperfect contemplation of his dying is very natural, and he frequently asks himself what it means to be dying. Its actual, present, non-abstract quality is its primary characteristic, and as Murdoch protracts that death for the reader, it is seen step by step to be tied to the very ordinary quotidian. Two people urge against abstract speculations and help Bruno's dying to extend itself into useful images. In both cases, the significant conversations are about the great and abstract subject of God. With Nigel the Nurse after a bad dream, Bruno talks of the presence and withdrawal in his life of various ideas of God from childhood on. One of his early perceptions of God was as a spider:

Later it was different, it was when I first started to look at spiders. Do you know, Nigel, that there is a spider called *amaurobius*, which lives in a burrow and has its young in the late summer, and then it dies when the frosts begin, and the young spiders live through the cold by eating their

mother's dead body. One can't believe that's an accident. I don't know that
I imagined God as having thought it all out, but somehow He was
connected with the pattern, He was the pattern, He *was* those spiders
which I watched in the light of my electric torch on summer nights. There
was a wonderfulness, a separateness, it was divine to see those spiders
living their extraordinary lives.                                    (p. 95)

Bruno then describes the continual diminution of the image of God – to a
petty official, to a small, crazed, pitiable being in country churches, finally to
'nothing but an intellectual fiction, an old hypothesis, a piece of literature'
(p. 96).
     The long conversation leads Bruno to the knowledge that the divine lives,
if at all, in the quotidian. Absorbed in the task of dying, he knows his
childhood identification of God with the beauty of the spiders was good, and
ponders his current state when, no longer able to use that spider image, he
sees God as the details of the present – the experience of his dying which is
again imaged by the homely old dressing-gown:

'You understand almost everything, Nigel.'
     'I love everything.'
     'But you don't understand about death. Do you know what I think?'
said Bruno, staring hard at the dressing gown in the dim light.
     'I think God is death. That's it. God is death.'              (p. 97)

The sense of the holiness of present experience is nowhere better expressed
than in this scene with Nigel, but with Lisa Bruno goes even further. Again
the conversation is about the lack of a god who could forgive the past, and
without whom the flagellation of the guilty self goes on endlessly and
fruitlessly. Lisa's luminous analysis denies the value of Bruno's wallowing in
guilt by employing what has rapidly become a fixed term in Murdoch's work
– the idea of the accidental nature of most human activity. As Lisa explains it,
Bruno really consoles himself by calling himself a demon in his wife Janie's
life: 'Human beings are not demons. They are much too muddy' (p. 166). She
tells him that he lives too much in these memories:

'Where else can I live, child?'
     'Outside. Leave yourself. It's just an agitating puppet. Think about
other things, think about anything that's good.'
     'An agitating puppet. Yes, I feel so tired out with waving my arms
about.'
     'Brooding about the past is so often fantasy of how one might have won
and resentment that one didn't. It is that resentment which one so often
mistakes for repentance.'                                          (p. 167)

As in the conversation with Nigel, the thrust is towards other and external things, and indeed Bruno progressively learns to quiet the voices of the past and live absolutely but briefly in the muddied, demanding present, remaining loving and courteous to the end with his new love, the essentially anonymous Diana, whom he does not even recognize and therefore cannot associate with a past time that had so plagued and interfered with him.

Involved also in Bruno's dying is another remarkable group of characters: the Boase brothers, Nigel and Will, their mad old Russian 'Auntie' and Adelaide the Maid. These characters – except Auntie – are linked to the central action, but serve it rather than participate in it. Adelaide and Nigel are actually servants, and Will's only contact with Danby before the duel involves servant-like activity, when he is hired to paint the railings. He instantly enters into the banter of Shakespearean quotation with Diana, and plays the fool very wittily. The Shakespearean connection is sustained not only as a parody of the great comic frames – twins, fools, a duel, reversals – but also in the hilariously tearful marriage of Will and Adelaide with all its attendant ironies, and the projection of twins-to-be-born, Mercutio and Benedick, one tragic and one comic, non-identical, absurd. Will's life as an actor combines a professional realistic reference with Shakespeare's idea of life as a dream. The whole Will-Nigel-Adelaide-Auntie group functions as an elegant play-within-a-play, having its own boundaries, its own conclusion in comedic, ironic marriage, its own completeness and wholeness. The insights they earn are essentially tangential to the central plot-line, but contribute to it in the manner of comic relief through the marvellous immediacy of earthy, vile-tempered Will and ordinary Adelaide, and through the not altogether successful peculiarity of Nigel – surely an updating of the Shakespearean fey fool.

Each of these characters is comic and eccentric to a degree, but the really puzzling one is the crazy Nigel, in so many ways a failure as a character and yet so useful to the fiction. He is like the small, crazed God of Bruno's middle period, with its dwindling apprehension of the divine. Obviously unhinged in some radical way, Nigel parodies contemplative religious rituals as he wanders through Danby's house and the streets of London peering, eavesdropping and vainly imagining himself as an all-seeing God. He carries tales and interferes, causing the duel between Will and Danby, and generally knows altogether too much. His power madness is potentially destructive, and so oddly is he handled that the reader is often hard put to assess him adequately. Crazy though he is, he is extremely kind to Bruno before he disappears, and he saves Diana's life by almost hypnotizing her with his knowledge of and solutions to a situation which has driven her to the brink of desperation and loss. He reminds her that she is caught in a machine which is 'just a fantasm of our pain' (p. 227), and that she must forgive Miles and Lisa

and Danby, who appear to have so misused her. All this action is pure
Murdoch, with its concentration on selflessness and insistence on images of
machines, cages and the accidental, but it is strangely put into the mouth of
this fey fellow:

> I am God. Maybe this is how God appears now in the world, a little
> unregarded crazy person whom everyone pushes aside and knocks down
> and steps upon. Or it can be that I am the false god, or one of the million
> million false gods there are. It matters very little. The false god is the true
> God. Up any religion a man may climb.                          (p. 224)

In this novel which denies gods, Nigel, far from being a character of the
good, nevertheless enacts it in certain ways – in talking Diana out of suicide
and in withdrawing from Danby rather than intruding his hopeless
homosexual love. It is extremely interesting to see how Murdoch bestows
elements of the good on a cast of imperfect characters – Danby, Bruno, Lisa,
Diana and even Nigel, who goes off to the self-sacrificing life in India that
Lisa had contemplated. Access to that good in this novel is not easy, but a
variety of human types bend towards it and find it not impossible; in fact,
much of the movement and real progress of *Bruno's Dream* concentrates on
the moral progress of these characters.

During the best of Nigel's persecutions of his twin brother Will, he
explains their relationship by saying 'Any juxtaposition of brutish material
and spirit involves suffering' (p. 199). The brutish material of the body is, in
the study of Bruno's death, endured with great grace as his mind wards off
fear and gropes for illumination. Halfway through the novel, Lisa describes
their father's death to Diana, thus presenting an early version of the study of
dying:

> 'Was he – frightened?'
> 'Yes.'
> 'That must have been terrible for you.'
> 'It's like no other fear. It's so *deep*. It almost becomes something im-
> personal. Philosophers say we own our deaths. I don't think so. Death
> contradicts ownership and self. If only one knew that all along.'
> 'I suppose one is just an animal then.'
> 'One is with an animal then. It isn't quite the same thing.'
> . . . .
> 'What was awful was that he didn't want to know. We're so used to the
> idea that love consoles. But here one felt that even love was – nothing.'
> 'That can't be true.'
> 'I know what you mean. It can't be true. Perhaps one just suddenly saw
> the dimensions of what love would have to be – like a huge vault suddenly
> opening out overhead –'
> 'Was it – hard for him to go?'

'Yes. Like a physical struggle. Well, it was a physical struggle, trying to do something.'

'I suppose death is a kind of act. But I expect he was really unconscious at the end.'

'I don't know. Who knows what it is like at the end?'     (pp. 130–1)

For all its positive achievement, this novel does not pretend to go beyond the point of pain. The suffering that comes from the juxtaposition of brutish material and spirit remains to the end for Bruno as he passes mildly away. Murdoch's tact is flawless, giving him illumination but not pushing it to positive extended statement. Bruno is an image on which the reader broods: one studies his death without presuming to understand completely, as Lisa put it, 'what it is like at the end,' but convinced that this pilgrim has made progress.

★

'Human beings are not demons,' argued Lisa Watkin in *Bruno's Dream*, and in the context of that novel she is shown to be right. Even Miles Greensleave, its most negative character, is not demonic but operates out of a self-protectiveness which is simply an unconscious knowledge that attention to others would open him to versions of suffering and death he cannot begin to face. Murdoch's next two novels, *A Fairly Honourable Defeat* (1970) and *An Accidental Man* (1971), will explore Lisa's assertion that people are too muddled to be demons by very different paths, the one acknowledging a kind of formal demonism, the other analysing the evil of selfish mediocrity. The positive thrust of *Bruno's Dream*, with its bestowal of partial good on many characters, depends on Bruno's death and on the idea that his death studies dying to some degree for all the other characters. Danby, Miles, Lisa and Diana are initially in much the same straits as Bruno – so attached to the past or to fantasies about their lives that it is impossible to live in the present – and the extensions of Bruno's death reach out to the ironic but felicitous pairings-off in the present as Bruno reaches his final illumination. But with her commitment to grim realism, Murdoch's gifts of happiness to her characters are limited. Diana in *Bruno's Dream* can set herself into a pattern of change and be directed towards reality; but Hilda Foster, a comparable character in *A Fairly Honourable Defeat*, is systematically undone by a clever manipulator and by the caprice of circumstances. Never can one assume, on the basis of one or two novels, that Murdoch has made a set of assumptions about her subject matter or adopted a positive or negative formula.

As she depicts it in these two novels, the problem is structural: most human beings, luckily or unluckily, are controlled by the activity of a central character, and their own actions must relate to that control. In *Bruno's Dream*,

Bruno's dying provides a background against which the other characters are set, and the positive learning present in that death effects a measure of change and happiness. In *A Fairly Honourable Defeat*, on the other hand, the central character is Julius King, a glamorous demon whose cynicism enacts Murdoch's definition of evil, and who manages a stunning amount of destruction. The contrast in the direction of the two novels stems from circumstance, the luck of the draw, so to speak: the characters of *A Fairly Honourable Defeat* are no more or less flawed or incapable of positive change than those of *Bruno's Dream*, whose centre is more conducive to amelioration, but they are ruthlessly victimized from outside until their flaws become fatal.

One obvious antecedent for the much admired 'honest' Julius King is Shakespeare's Iago, and like him Julius acts out of bottomless cynicism and with limited motivation. Unlike him, however, Julius is opposed to a good that is less luminous and sympathetically conceived than Othello and Desdemona. The awkward Christ character, Tallis Browne, attempts a redemptive solution at the last moment, but his defeat, through Hilda's small vanity in conjunction with a broken telephone, a rain storm and car trouble, is part of the necessary and capricious structure of the universe. Thus the defeat of good by evil can from Tallis's point of view be described as 'fairly honourable', inasmuch as his methods were just and correct. More pointedly, however, Julius sees himself as inflicting a fairly honourable defeat on Rupert, Hilda and Morgan in that, as he argues, they are justly destroyed by their own vanity. Julius's manipulation is not unlike Iago's with his use of talismanic evidence, but the characters on which he operates are flawed by solipsism, and, as he implies, deserve their defeat. This viewpoint allows him to go off remorselessly to Paris to enjoy its pleasures and think happily, in the concluding sentence of the novel, that life is good.

His destructive demonism is so effective, however, that the novel's audience declines absolutely to acquiesce to the idea that his defeat of the others was even fairly honourable; one of the most interesting aspects of this novel is the rage it elicits from readers. Murdoch reports with some pain that the very fact that she made Julius a Jew resulted in accusations of anti-semitism, whereas it seems clear that she was merely identifying the Old Testament source of the Satan legend and indicating that the idea of the Prince of Darkness is the product of the Jewish imagination. (Another possible Jewish reference which has not been caught by those who suggest anti-semitism lies in the name of Julius's adversary, Tallis. Whereas Julius is the king and Roman conqueror, Tallis's name evokes the positive harmonic connection of the sixteenth-century British composer, Thomas Tallis. More to the point in the allegorical and Jewish substructure of the novel, however, is the reference to the Jewish tallis or tallith, the prayer-shawl symbolizing the spiritual life of the Jew, which was commanded by God in *Numbers* 15: 38–40:

38   Speak unto the children of Israel, and bid them that they make them fringes in the borders of their garments throughout their generations, and that they put upon the fringe of the borders a ribband of blue:

39   And it shall be unto you for a fringe, that ye may look upon it, and remember all the commandments of the Lord, and do them; and that ye seek not after your own heart and your own eyes, after which ye use to go a whoring:

40   That ye may remember, and do all my commandments, and be holy unto your God.

Tallis Browne, with his adherence to selflessness and the good embodies the Jewish symbolism here expressed. His wife's name, Morgan, contrasts with this austerity and discipline through its connections with magic and demonism as indicated in the Arthurian character, Morgan-le-Fay.)

In impact Julius is satanic indeed, and his tampering in successful human relationships is unforgivable. The enraging success of the character comes not only from the reader's complete sense of his evil, but also from his charm and glamour: one begins the book beguiled and convinced by comments from the whole range of characters that he is important, admirable, interesting and exciting; the shock of his monstrous subsequent activity constitutes an ironic betrayal of the reader's expectations – an old fictional device over which Murdoch has extraordinary mastery.

In his final conversation with his adversary Tallis, Julius comments: 'Do try to get yourself a decent job. As things are, what does your life amount to? I suppose it's always like that, but it does pain me. After all, I'm an artist. This is just a mess' (p. 386). Obviously we are dealing with the saint-artist contrast which has come out so often in Murdoch's work, but here the symbolic stakes are higher than usual. In the same conversation, Julius remarks, 'I suppose in the nature of things we shall meet again' (p. 387), and he has mentioned that he 'may take on another big assignment quite soon. This was just an interim' (p. 386). Hovering behind the Tallis-Julius relationship is a curious, entirely non-realist suggestion that the competition of Christ versus Satan is merely being played out again in another version. Murdoch's presentation of this allegorical frame suggests a moribund Trinity (see Chapter II of this study) through Tallis's dying father, Leonard, and the holy but ambiguous ghost of his raped and murdered twin sister. But the allegory is far from absolute, and the situation is certainly not an eternal return in which the staleness of an endlessly re-enacted drama ineluctably calls out an ancient arsenal of symbolic activity. The important point is that Tallis and Julius, as the High Incarnation and the Prince of Darkness, are both spiritual beings and as such are necessarily drawn irresistibly to each other.

The general implication is that Julius and Tallis *sub specie aeternitatis* are shape-shifters, and especially that Tallis as Christ is a surprise this time around to the brilliant and sartorially elegant demon. Julius says on an earlier visit to Tallis: 'I didn't quite take you in when I first saw you. However I feel bound to say – you're a disappointment to me' (p. 302). The disappointment is built in very carefully by Murdoch and is felt as much by the reader as by Julius. The Christ figure as good cannot appear in the post-Christian world Murdoch insists on in the light of any sentimental or romantic radiance, and as Julius points out in an argument with Rupert, the role of the good man is, as a role, impossible:

> Good is dull. What novelist ever succeeded in making a good man interesting? It is characteristic of this planet that the path of virtue is so unutterably depressing that it can be guaranteed to break the spirit and quench the vision of anybody who consistently attempts to tread it. . . . What passes for human goodness is in reality a tiny phenomenon, messy, limited, truncated, and as I say dull. (p. 199)

Nevertheless, by a freakish inversion of sympathy, Murdoch, against all odds, manages to make Tallis very interesting indeed. Although he lives very much in the dreary reality Julius describes, his power has ways of showing itself – and he very nearly wins.

'If there were a perfectly just judge I would kiss his feet and accept his punishments upon my knees', says Julius to Rupert (p. 201), cynically certain that no such judge exists. Yet he acknowledges a peculiar subservience to Tallis, who is the principle agent for eliciting true information from and about him, and who finally very tactfully orders him out of the wrecked London scene. If there is a just judge in Murdoch's world it is Tallis, who, like some of Milton's angels or the idea of the good from Simone Weil's notebooks, can do nothing but stand waiting. Tallis does in fact perform two forceful actions, aimed not at accusation and judgement but at the cessation of cruelty: the first in a Chinese restaurant where he violently slaps a punkish racist youth who is torturing a black man, the second when he leads Julius to the telephone to confess his perfidious games to Hilda. But basically, he simply waits. He waits for two years for his wife Morgan to end her affair with Julius, he waits for her when she comes back to London, he waits for young Peter to recover, he waits for Julius to come to him with his confessions, and at the end of the novel he is waiting for both the next step, if any, in his relationship with Morgan and Hilda and the soon expected death of Leonard. This generous but passive waiting which refuses to interfere is, for Murdoch, the only route for the expression of good.

The interfering Julius is surprised not only at Tallis's unimpressive demeanour, but at his embarrassed courtesy towards him, his humility and his messiness, and the result of this surprise is a new version of the Christ-Satan conflict which alters the traditional allegory completely. Christ declines to fight or judge, so Satan has to go to him with his confession, whereas in the old tale, the two mighty forces were in combat. Murdoch, who denies expectations of many sorts in this novel, alters both the Christ figure and the Satan, and it is questionable whether the reader can follow her entirely in either case. Tallis's interest comes largely from his sheer peculiarity – his hypnagogic visions of his sister, his hearing voices and seeing forms and beings beyond the ordinary world and his astoundingly odoriferous house; but he combines all of this with unimpressive humility and absolute charity to his community – his foreign lodgers, Peter, Morgan and all he comes in touch with. His filthy house is a symbol of the confusions of the contemporary world with which he can do nothing until Morgan's possible but unlikely return. Morgan's allegorical role as the human soul – married to Christ, seduced and defeated by Satan and finally off on its own to a new land (America) with its guardian angel Hilda – completes the artificial structure.

Because Tallis simply waits in a state of negative power, the Satan figure as Murdoch perceives him must inevitably come to him – first to report Morgan and Rupert's putative affair, and subsequently to indicate that things have unfortunately got out of hand. Tallis's response to the news of the Rupert/Morgan affair is that it 'simply cannot be true' and he consigns Julius to hell (p. 302), where he so obviously belongs. Tallis's refusal to believe him brings a sigh from Julius: 'I won't say I'm misunderstood: I'm sure you understand me very well. But I am, as I say, disappointed, in more ways than one' (p. 303). Julius's recognition of and even subservience to Tallis, however, indicate something rather undemonic – a less than whole-hearted pleasure in evil, as well as a desire for punishment and judgement. As it turns out, Tallis is more absorbed in the terminal cancer and imminent death of his father than in Julius's demonic shenanigans, and as he discusses his father's death during both visits it is obvious that Julius too is upset by the news. The crumbling of the system, with the death of the God the father figure, who complains about things going wrong from the start and criticizes the incompetence of his son, diminishes Julius's expectations, takes away the bite and tension that the powerful adversary idea of good had assured in the far past. Although Tallis refuses to judge and punish (he only smiles silently at the end as Julius unsuccessfully justifies himself), he does pay full attention to Julius. He discovers the Belsen concentration camp number tattooed on Julius's arm, something Morgan had missed during their long affair; the others know only what Julius had reported, that he had a 'cosy war'. The concentration camp mark is a significant discovery: it records that Julius has suffered and may in his vile games be passing on that suffering according to the Weilian formula. It is not, however, seen as an excuse or a psychological dodge, and Tallis rightly orders him out of London.

Murdoch's alteration of the Christian myth is also her undoing of it, her readjusting it to fit what she sees as more true if less traditional terms. The dismantling of the Trinity – something she also did earlier in *The Time of the Angels* (1966) – emphasizes the terminal confusion of a culture that no longer works except through the energy of destruction. Tallis, with his powerful eyes and terrible grief over the past death of his sister and the imminent death of his father, becomes not only a revised symbol of the suffering Christ in the new chaos but also a definition of the good man, humble and powerless, in a society where only the mammoth selfishness of Morgan (mankind) and the ingenious idea of evil are energetically forging ahead. The Christ that Satan meets is diminished, but still there, like the tiny kernel of good that Danby Odell perceives in himself in *Bruno's Dream*: for Murdoch this is the true balance, and she opposes it to the traditional Christian idea of Christ's power in people's lives. In this novel realism struggles against allegory and mythology by using them ironically as a basic device for identifying the main characters. Thus although Julius is Satan, Tallis Christ, Leonard God the father and Morgan the human soul, these allegorical identifications are subservient to the transmitted sense of real personality in the characters. The resulting redefinitions nevertheless carry the points Murdoch wishes to make: evil is not absolute but desires to be stopped and judged by good; good is there but small, messy and impotent; mankind is hopelessly involved in selfishness; God is moribund; the life-giving power of the Holy Spirit is dead; Christianity is finished.

It is worth insisting again that the ideas listed above come after both the realism and the planted mythology in *A Fairly Honourable Defeat*, and as always in mature Murdoch, are less important to the reader (although not to the critic) than the other two. In her interview with Bellamy (1977), Murdoch admitted surprise that her newspaper critics had not picked up the Trinitarian allegory, and it is a credit to her tact that it is not compulsively handled or absolutely central to a reading of the novel. The reader perceives this novel as, again, a bourgeois product, a realistic representational tale; Julius's demonic character need not be read allegorically in our secular or post-Christian society. Similarly Tallis, who does not suffer for himself, can be seen as a weary, crazed little eccentric, rather as Nigel in *Bruno's Dream* had said God might be perceived in the contemporary world, and the splendid verbal comedy of the sick and complaining Leonard is more believable as human and natural than as mythological.

Julius, however, contrary to the realist inclination of the novel, is essentially interested in enactments of magic and mythology, and all his practices depend on them. When Tallis ignores him and refuses to play the expected mythological role of judge, Julius is terribly disappointed: he is the artist as magician who vainly and rather naively seeks applause for a nicely designed bit of action. In Murdoch's now common practice, the central idea of the novel is placed against a major cultural document or work, and it is the artist-magician-puppeteer Julius who projects the operative text: the sections

(644–5) in Plato's *Laws* in which the Athenian describes mankind as puppets dangling from cords of pleasure and pain:

> Athenian: Let us look at the whole matter in some such light as this. We may imagine that each of us living creatures is a puppet made by the gods, possibly as a plaything, or possibly with some more serious purpose. That, indeed, is more than we can tell, but one thing is certain. These interior states are, so to say, the cords, or strings, by which we are worked; they are opposed to one another, and pull us with opposite tensions in the direction of opposite actions, and therein lies the division of virtue from vice. In fact, so says our argument, a man must always yield to one of these tensions without resistance, but pull against all the other strings – must yield, that is, to the golden and hallowed drawing of judgment which goes by the name of the public law of the city. The others are hard and ironlike, it soft, as befits gold, whereas they resemble very various substances. So a man must always co-operate with the noble drawing of law, for judgment, though a noble thing, is as gentle and free from violence as noble, whence its drawing needs supporters, if the gold within us is to prevail over the other stuff. In this wise our moral fable of the human puppets will find its fulfillment. It will also become somewhat clearer, first, what is meant by self-conquest and self-defeat, and next that the individual's duty is to understand the true doctrine of these tensions and live in obedience to it. (translation by A. E. Taylor, Bollingen Series LXXI)

Julius sets himself up as a godlike puppeteer, pulling the iron cords of the emotions, exploiting the confused foibles of the characters and viciously using the Platonic image to describe their vulnerability. In conversation with Rupert, he repudiates ideas of the good, of sainthood and of God, and when Rupert objects that Julius makes people sound like puppets, he replies:

> But they *are* puppets, Rupert. And we didn't need modern psychology to tell us that. Your friend Plato knew all about it in his old age, when he wrote *The Laws*, after he had given up those dreams of the high places which so captivate you.
> (p. 200)

Similarly, as he pulls Simon into the closet in the Prince Regent Museum to watch Rupert and Morgan enact the first stage of their folly, which he has arranged and controls, Julius says, 'Come, come. I promised you a puppet show. You will be immensely diverted' (p. 232). And finally, as he unravels the whole story of his contrived puppet theatre to Tallis, he rages against his too easy victims: 'I must say, they have behaved predictably to an extent which is quite staggering. Indeed if any of them had been less than predictable the whole enterprise would have collapsed at an early stage. They really are puppets, *puppets*' (p. 366).

Julius's major characteristic is his ability to pervert the perception of anything or anyone he comes in contact with. Murdoch's depiction of him indicates a high degree of elegance, but he is also frequently described as having a coy aspect as he plays on his victims, and he has a nasty inclination to giggle demonically as his so predictable results speed well. The giggling is irritating and deliberately degrading to the dignity of his victims – he uses it, for example, to condescend to Simon, and when the too serious Axel unwraps the pink teddy-bear Julius bought to humiliate him – and indeed one of his aims is to destroy any self-image other characters may have. He is even more interested in obliterating anyone's respect or idealistic regard for anyone else: he constantly derides Morgan to others, he teases Simon with Axel's future decline in physical attraction, he cannot stand the happy Foster marriage and sets out to destroy it, and of course he is particularly out to get what he calls the great fat Rupert image.

Devastating though he is to people where he really concentrates his attention, Julius can also destroy external valued things and easily alter the received perceptions of cultural works. The best example occurs in the Tate Gallery, where Morgan remarks on the marvellous beauty of the Turners; his response is typically destructive: 'A hopelessly derivative painter. Always copycatting somebody. Poussin, Rembrandt, Claude. Never finished a picture without ruining it. And he had far too high an opinion of himself. He should have remained a minor genre painter, that's about his level' (pp. 203–4). He so enchants Morgan that leaving the gallery, 'she looked round upon the Turners. She could see now how limited and amateurish they really were' (p. 209).

And so with the Plato text. The central puppet image from the *Laws* opens the whole novel to a discussion of Platonic influence, something never far from Murdoch's mind, and in its most obvious structure (rather than the deep structure which opposes Julius and Tallis) this novel sets Julius's cynicism and deliberate narrowness of vision against Rupert's Platonic idealism. To Julius there is no golden cord whose gentle pull it is mankind's task to nurture and forward; therefore he interprets the puppet image entirely negatively. As in his many arguments against value in anything, Julius sees the human puppet as responsive only to the cords of egotistic passion, which he in his intelligence as puppeteer can pull at will to show how irremediably lost mankind is. This perversion of the Plato text is countered by Rupert Foster's questionable but sincere devotion to the good he sees can be enacted in the moral life of the disciplined man.

Rupert is a successful civil servant, like so many of Murdoch's middle-aged men; his bourgeois life and happy marriage are marred only a little by a bit too much self-indulgence, a bit too much drinking and problems with his drop-out undergraduate son, Peter – but he freely acknowledges these flaws. His successes far exceed his failures, and he sees himself as a man fairly humbly striving towards the good. With great discipline, he has compiled many notebooks which comprise a nearly complete book on the nature of the moral life, and he proudly acknowledges his debt to Plato as his source. In several ways *A Fairly Honourable Defeat* is related to its pretype in Murdoch's *oeuvre*, *The Time of the Angels*: both feature a consideration of Christianity in its Trinitarian aspect, a demonic character at its centre and a rather self-satisfied person working on Plato's ethical ideas. Marcus Fisher in the earlier novel misestimated Plato in precisely the way that Rupert does in the present text, but Rupert's case is considerably more ambiguous than Marcus's had been.

The characters align themselves fairly neatly for and against Rupert and his moral stance: Hilda, Morgan and Simon are on his side, and love and admire him; Julius is sarcastically opposed to the project, Axel is scornful of it and Peter has rejected such moral ideas together with everything else in a society he hates as father-dominated. Naturally Julius is kindled to rage by any treatise on the good, and of course Peter, a disillusioned late adolescent in revolt, would not like it, but the telling argument is Axel's. The most austere character in the novel, Axel insists on truth-telling in human relationships and refuses any emotional statement of absolute love or permanence. Indeed, his principle criticism of Rupert's project is that it will be an undisciplined 'farrago of emotion' (p. 26), and herein lies one of the most interesting illustrations of Murdoch's central disjunctions. Rupert exudes a warmth and love which is genuine if somewhat smug; the deeply anxious Axel practises emotional and intellectual discipline to keep himself from the pain that commitment to life in the world automatically causes. Murdoch's inclination is to warn her readers subliminally at most points that the austere discipline is the only real path, but with Axel she also indicates its dangers. He nearly causes his relationship with Simon to break down by holding back an essential part of himself, by trying to evade pain by abjuring commitment, but still his is a path along which any one heeding Murdoch's signals might choose to travel.

Axel is quite right about Rupert's work on Plato and the moral life. Rupert believes deeply in his own wisdom and in the ease of the path towards a worthy good, and because his belief stresses ease he does not pay attention to the fact that his vanity is tickled by what he believes to be Morgan's sudden grand passion for him; he finds a few lies to Hilda and some *suppressio veri* about the business not very culpable, and he is easily pulled about by Julius, the master puppeteer. His error lies in thinking that the golden cord is the main one and the others minor; in overestimating the pull of the good he misreads the discipline of Plato, which Murdoch is always urging us to consider at its root level. But it would be inaccurate to dismiss Rupert simply as someone who got his Plato wrong. Although flawed and wrong in the Morgan business, Rupert is nevertheless engaging, kinder and more gener-ous than the rebarbative Axel. The pull of the golden cord in him is real if not strong enough to counter the pull of egotistic passion, and his defeat is appalling.

At the beginning of the novel while the Fosters celebrate their twentieth wedding anniversary, Simon picks up the resident hedgehog, an organically planted symbol whose existence raises a tremor in the smug bourgeois life of the Fosters. What if the stupid but charming animal were to fall into the swimming pool and drown? It does do so at an apt time, when Julius's string-pulling has almost reached its expected end: Hilda has just discovered that Rupert's love-letters to her, which she kept in her desk, are missing, and is about to find a planted passionate letter from Morgan in Rupert's hidden drawer, when she sees the hedgehog floating dead. Symbolizing the love, wholeness and happiness of the Foster marriage, the drowned hedgehog anticipates Rupert's drowning after the one thing he cannot live without – a conviction of the good – has been lost (p. 343). Like the hedgehog, Rupert cannot manage the alien element which forms such a basic image in this novel.

Morgan, in describing her feelings about her marriage to Tallis, uses the image of the sea which is also the place of the compounding of the amber in the necklace which is a symbolic bond between them:

> I think I wanted to sink down into some deep deep sea with you. When I married you I felt I was killing myself. It seemed somehow wonderful at the time. But I couldn't kill myself. I couldn't even love in the end, down in that deep sea. I have to be outside, in the open, in the clear air, on the high places, free, free, free. It's only out in that clear fresh air that I can really love people. (p. 190)

Morgan's inability to destroy any part of her ego is absolute. Later, in *The Sea, The Sea*, Murdoch will once again contrast the sea and the high places with a rather different emphasis, but it is clear that the ability to handle the potential destructiveness of water and to see this element as life-giving is major, and in a way reflects Joseph Conrad's use of the same image. It is important that the satanic Julius cannot swim, and when Simon (who swims frequently), in a frenzy of trapped rage pushes him into the pool, his monumental panic presents the only picture of his broken facade in the novel. Morgan's definition of freedom in the clear high air is part of her folly and passionate selfishness, and Rupert's death by drowning represents the degree to which Murdoch judges his alienation from the truth on which he so piously discoursed.

One of Julius's greatest talents as puppeteer has to do with the sense of reality he projects. His reputation for honesty rests on this quality, and significantly, his reality is a demonic version of what Tallis's hypnagogic visions reflect. Again Morgan gives us the key, as she thinks about her affair with Julius:

What she did not tell [Julius] was that she had despaired. Morgan had seen something in those later days with Julius which had seemed like a deep truth. It had been like a mystical vision into the heart of reality, as if one were to be promised the secret of the universe and then, with all the sense of significance and finality fully preserved, to be shown a few mouldering chicken bones lying in a dark corner covered with dust and filth.

(pp. 131–2)

The horror of the dead bird bones is reminiscent of images from *The Time of the Angels* and *The Nice and the Good*, and is part of the larger image patterns from nature which so forcefully dominate this book. Murdoch has long had a penchant for bird imagery, and it is very powerful here. The desolate picture of the dead birds at the centre of Julius's illustration of reality as perceived by Morgan is caught up again in the exciting sequence of action in which Morgan tries and fails to rescue a pigeon from the Underground and runs panic-stricken to Tallis as a source of life. Significantly she also loses her purse during the Underground chase; Morgan's character is split between crass money-seeking and the spirituality that birds represent in this book. The dying Leonard too concentrates his positive activity on feeding pigeons, and Julius refers to more glamorous birds (hawks and eagles) to pull Morgan's ego into his snares.

Julius can succeed so well as puppeteer largely because his victims lack an adequate theory of personality. From her earliest essays, Murdoch has challenged existentialism's as well as British empiricism's stress on sincerity, and argued that in the contemporary world accurate and humble knowledge of the self has been obscured by these grand theories. The result is the inability of contemporary people to think outside themselves or to effect desired real change or amelioration. Early in *A Fairly Honourable Defeat* Morgan, who admires Rupert's moral authority, wishes (as does Julius with Tallis) to be scolded, judged, told how to act. Her analysis of the problems of perceiving one's own psyche is a pure reflection of Murdoch's thought:

'You're quite right to reproach me but I'm afraid I simply enjoy your reproaches. They comfort me. They don't connect with any real possibility of change at all. How very peculiar one's mind is. There's no foothold in it, no leverage, no way of changing oneself into a responsible just being. One's lost in one's own psyche. It stretches away and away to the ends of the world and it's soft and sticky and warm. There's nothing real, no hard parts, no centre. The only reality is just – immediate things – like – oh like what – like this.' Morgan stretched out her hand. She picked up a green oblong paperweight off the desk and laid it against her brow.     (pp. 82–3)

Picking up something real like the paperweight carries us back to the small objects of Hugo Belfounder's reality in *Under the Net*, but it fails to satisfy

Morgan's urge for punishment and the obsessive desire to find a definition for human personality.

Morgan eagerly seizes Julius's definition in all of its cynicism when she meets him in the Tate Gallery. It is a limited and evil definition, but both qualities appeal to Morgan in her role as the muddled and falsely sophisticated human soul. She eagerly goes along with his damnable experiment in breaking up a successful relationship (as she believes), the one she disapproves of between Simon and Axel. That she will be a major instrument and victim in the real game and that such an experiment will cause terrible pain and death do not occur to her as she is kindled by the cynical simplicity of what Julius has to say:

> You want some sort of drama now, you want an ordeal of some kind, you don't want to suffer in a dull way, and you want me to help you. But these are merely superficial agitations. Human beings are roughly constructed entities full of indeterminacies and vaguenesses and empty spaces. Driven along by their own private needs they latch blindly onto each other, then pull away, then clutch again. Their little sadisms and their little masochisms are surface phenomena. Anyone will do to play the roles. They never really see each other at all. There is no relationship, dear Morgan, which cannot quite easily be broken and there is none the breaking of which is a matter of any genuine seriousness. Human beings are essentially finders of substitutes. . . . All human beings have staggeringly great faults which can easily be exploited by a clever observer. . . . I could divide anybody from anybody. Even you could. Play sufficiently on a person's vanity, sow a little mistrust, hint at the contempt which every human being deeply, secretly feels for every other one. Every man loves himself so astronomically more than he loves his neighbour. Anyone can be made to drop anyone.                                                      (pp. 207–8)

Julius's subsequent success attests to his appalling accuracy, but the real strength of this novel rests in the human recoil from the enactment of the theory. Julius's one error is in assuming that the breaking of relationships is not a matter of great seriousness.

Julius takes on the Simon-Axel relationship as a side-line according to promise, and is nearly successful at destroying it. In the process, however, Murdoch puts the reader sympathetically into the mind and insecurities of Simon, who from the beginning has had major reservations about Julius, and who almost by intuition perceives his real nature. Simon's objections spring originally from his nervous insecurity, his inclination towards the seedier side of homosexuality and his sad knowledge of himself as, to use Axel's vocabulary, a lightweight. Feminine and childish, Simon yet possesses a real core of strength, and though constantly victimized by both Julius and Morgan (by the latter in the very funny scene in Julius's flat and in her teasing reference to Axel about the Athenian *kouros*), he finally, belatedly, fights back. It is extremely interesting that Julius not only tells Tallis about the Rupert–Morgan game early on, but also that he has Simon witness its first scene. Whereas Tallis refuses to believe what he has not seen, Simon is too intimidated by Julius's threats regarding Axel to be able to pick up the telephone and do something about it. Julius is on the one hand acting demonically and on the other trying to be stopped; he is a real but rather ambiguous demon. When Simon finally does act, he chooses the one route Murdoch sees as available and ameliorative: he tells the truth. Pushing Julius into the pool constitutes a *non serviam*, but it is only when he tells Axel to stop the car and starkly recounts every bizarre detail that the relationship is salvaged, and indeed by this ordeal clarified and strengthened, so that there is, at the end of the book, one happy couple.

Rupert, on the other hand, exudes self-confidence, and is stupidly vain about Morgan's sudden apparent love of and reliance on him. Throughout this book Murdoch appears to be questioning the roots of human confidence and allowing the action to undermine them. Nevertheless, Rupert's inclination towards a moral mode of being and his previous success as an authority figure and husband indicate that he has a genuine hold on ordinary life which can be shaken only by the peculiarly tempting intervention that Julius causes. In the opening long conversation with Hilda, Rupert had said with ominous insight: 'Cynicism is real vice. It's the vice of the age and it could be the end of us all' (p. 11). In *The Fire and the Sun*, Murdoch defines evil as the way good degenerates into egotism, and this is indeed the process which Julius imposes on a too weak Rupert. But evil is much more than this in the action of the novel – it is both cynicism and the creation of a mammoth confusion which impedes honest reaction. As Julius near the end purrs over a devastated Rupert, whom he cynically treats as having had an understandable actual affair with Morgan, Rupert's mind returns to his original knowledge. He says he is guilty of vanity and lying, but argues doggedly with Julius about the principles of human action:

'You're deliberately confusing things – I couldn't *live* like that.'
  'Like what? Without a false picture of yourself?'
  'No. In cynicism.'
  'Why use that nasty word? Let us say a sensible acceptance of the second-rate.'
  'I won't accept the second-rate.'
  'If you stay in the same house as yourself you may have to. Come, there will be a few smiles at your expense, but why worry? The smilers merely demonstrate their own tawdriness. But human life *is* tawdry, my dear Rupert. There are no perfect marriages. There is no glittering summit. All right, Hilda will stop admiring you. But when have you really merited her

admiration? Haven't you deceived yourself, just as Morgan has deceived herself? All right, Hilda won't love you quite as she did before. She may feel sorry for you, she may even despise you a little. And you won't forget what you've learnt either, how to pretend, how to lead a double life. It's natural to you, Rupert, you all do it. There will be those late nights at the office, and Hilda will sort of know and sort of not know, and it won't matter anything like as much as it seems to do at the moment.'

'Stop', said Rupert. 'There's something I can't live without –'  (p. 343)

Despite his failures, Rupert returns frantically to a core of goodness, an anti-cynical centre which is essential to life and belies Julius's convincing, all too worldly wisdom, but he dies feeling that this centre has been removed. It is not the destruction of his egotistic image that obsesses him, nor the ripping-up of all his idealist Platonic notebooks, but the withdrawal from life of the good and the implanting of deceit and cynicism in its place:

> Tomorrow he would talk to Hilda. He would persuade her not to go away. But of something he knew that he would never persuade her and never persuade himself again. There was something which had vanished away out of the world forever.  (p. 344)

This is Julius's real devastation: the removal from an upright, intelligent, bourgeois man of a central positive mode of being. While Murdoch makes it plain that Rupert and the other characters are haunted by various false and easy theories of virtue and the good, their destruction and replacement by utter cynicism constitute real evil.

Rupert's final suffering and death are dreadful indeed and are described with relentless power. Where he might actually have gone mentally after this experience is in doubt, because Murdoch chooses his death as an inevitable lesson. It focuses the attention of the reader as well as the other characters, teaches in a way ordinary, egocentric suffering does not. In *The Sovereignty of Good* Murdoch talks about the conflict between the good self and the bad self:

> In reality the good self is very small indeed, and most of what appears good is not. The truly good is not a friendly tyrant to the bad, it is its deadly foe. Even suffering itself can play a demonic role here, and the ideas of guilt and punishment can be the most subtle tool of the ingenious self. The idea of suffering confuses the mind and in certain contexts (the context of 'sincere self-examination' for instance) can masquerade as purification. It is rarely this, for unless it is very intense indeed it is far too interesting. Plato does not say that philosophy is the study of suffering, he says it is the study of death (*Phaedo* 64A), and these ideas are totally dissimilar. That moral improvement involves suffering is usually true; but the suffering is the by-product of a new orientation and not in any sense an end in itself. (p. 68)

Rupert's death causes this new orientation in a way that his suffering could not, and the horrible fact of that death casts light on the greatly suffering but still basically unsympathetic Morgan.

Morgan is a curious problem in the novel – she comes on stage weeping and is constantly demanding love and pity. Her misery after the Julius affair is convincing, but her negative counter-currents spoil her for the reader: her cynicism about the abortion until Julius points out that there may be a moral issue and that the child might have salvaged the relationship, her great love towards Hilda which she lessens by claiming it cannot survive a financial or emotional transaction with Rupert, her lying to Tallis about money, her arrogant lying power over Peter, all contribute to the sense that she is demonic in her suffering and better matched to Julius than to Tallis. Her self-examinations interest her terrifically, and she is well armed against Tallis, as well as against Rupert at the end, by lessons she has learned during her time with Julius:

> She . . . realized what it was that could save her: contempt. That which was at the opposite extreme from love: the cynicism of a deliberate contemptuous diminution of another person. As she profited by it she thought, I am seeing him as Julius sees him.                               (p. 136)

In working on Morgan's character, Murdoch allows her an extended ruminative development, but never permits her to be seen as other than absolutely concentrated on her own being and suffering, a factor which diminishes her, especially in contrast to Tallis who, although exhausted by his perception of human misery, persistently looks beyond the dazzlement of his own being. Morgan's depiction is a firm denial of the idea that suffering is genuinely interesting, and Morgan's interest as a character fades and diminishes on Rupert's death.

The possibility of her reunion with Tallis is dim at the conclusion of the novel, and every moment of *rapprochement* during the action is broken by young Peter's bounding in to interrupt the two. Many of the characters in this novel confront sad moments of recognition when they must see the world as utterly changed – Hilda when she begins to suspect Rupert, Morgan and Rupert when they begin their 'affair', Tallis when he learns his father Leonard is dying. This powerful theme of a changed and revised world is major in both process and conclusion, and Peter, who represents the next generation of humanity, makes sure that nothing positive can happen. Whatever power Tallis has over Morgan is vitiated by Peter's repeated intrusions, and his destruction of his father's notebooks helps to speed Rupert's death. Morgan and Hilda, caught in a strong sisterly affection, do what they can for him in America, but Murdoch is not projecting a positive future world. All the changes in this novel have to do with loss and diminution; the only happy note comes from the hard-earned joy of Axel and Simon. This happiness combines with Julius's statement that he is content in Paris because 'he was not closely involved with human beings' (p. 402) to show that evil in Murdoch's world resides in the failure of human relationship, whereas good exists in its narrow and infrequent success.

Meanwhile Tallis waits, a permanent countering force to Julius's anti-social power, an image of quiet, undemanding love directed towards whoever needs it. In the puppet image which dominates *A Fairly Honourable Defeat*, Tallis steadily pulls the pliable golden cord, but the devastation has been so great that the reader justifiably questions any hope for humankind in a world where the golden cord is so humble and powerless. Murdoch would, I think, answer that the didacticism of the novel tends towards the lessons of human limitation and clear acknowledgement of the overwhelming difficulty of any moral step forward. Simon's painful submission to truth is the only positive way, but that submission occurs only when the pain becomes too great; he is also lucky in being in a good situation for the proper working of the truth-telling technique, in that Axel's disciplined following of hard reality gives his account fertile ground. The sheer difficulty of the moral task is uppermost in *A Fairly Honourable Defeat*, as it will be in all the subsequent novels: there are serious lessons in the reading of any Murdoch novel, but she will never again allow herself the cakes and ale of *Bruno's Dream*.

# VII

# THE MEDIOCRE LIFE

Readings of *An Accidental Man, A Word Child* and *The Sacred and Profane Love Machine*

*Bruno's Dream* and *A Fairly Honourable Defeat* serve as vehicles for what henceforth will be Murdoch's primary themes, and although much material will be discarded from these themes as enunciated in the two novels, the reader of mature Murdoch must, as Socrates enjoined, become a student of death. Studying dying will no longer be a positive exercise as in *Bruno's Dream*, but henceforth involves a concurrent study of defeat, to which Murdoch sees death linked. *A Fairly Honourable Defeat* is arguably her most significantly entitled novel; its human failures involve a repeated pattern of defeat of good by evil in spite of the enormous moral and spiritual energy her characters expend in their attempts to become better or to push themselves towards a wished-for, shared categorical imperative in the social order. As a saving grace for the other characters, *A Fairly Honourable Defeat* features a demonic character, Julius King, as an outside agent of evil invading an apparently secure milieu and spreading destruction on to those who lack an inner core of adherence to the truth and thus cannot effectively resist his manipulation. This use of an outside agent somewhat contradicts Murdoch's mature practice, for as she had illustrated through the character of John Ducane in *The Nice and the Good*, a central necessary recognition must be that evil lies within the self. It is nevertheless true that the idea of the outsider had haunted her early work, and Julius King is the extreme development of that idea. He is a real demon, but realized successfully as an ordinary human being, and hence his instinct towards evil is not so pure that he does not wish the impossible good to exist and his evil practices to be stopped. The allegorical substructure of that novel avoids interfering with its realistic surface, but I am not entirely convinced that Murdoch quite communicated the sense she evidently wished to convey, that of a break with the tradition of Christian ideals like the communion of the Trinity and the redemptive power of good. As in *Paradise Lost*, the Satan character obscures the structure by his brilliant demonic will.

In ensuing novels Murdoch works on a much less symbolic plane, and indeed in the next work, *An Accidental Man* (1971), skilfully imposes the idea of the accidental on a largely concealed but insistent structure of pattern and ideas. As the opening novel in a series dedicated to the varieties of human failures and defeats, *An Accidental Man* is utterly without amelioration, and even its most positive characters fail to achieve any ideal they might set for themselves. Mediocrity, in the sense used by Plato to describe the ordinary person in the vaults of *eikasia* or image-making fantasy, is the key term, and Murdoch's novels illustrate that mediocrity with characters whose obsessive behaviour blocks them off from steps towards the light. In *An Accidental Man* the demon role is filled by Austin Gibson Grey, one of whose minor functions is to counter, for the dedicated Murdoch reader, the coolly formulated organization of Julius King in the preceding novel. Not at all a master puppeteer operating on his milieu by observation, power and cynicism, Austin is hopelessly muddled, without plans or schemes, entirely accidental. Although thoroughly destructive and even rather frightening, as his wife Dorina attests, he is not at all like Julius, the artist type who can organize and play on others; his acts of destruction are random, geared by his mood or the neurotic whim of the moment. Raging through a bourgeois world crowded with characters, Austin assumes that others will pick up the appallingly broken pieces he leaves in his wake, and indeed he is right.

*An Accidental Man* is an ambitious novel in every respect, and not the least of its ambitions is technical. In both *A Fairly Honourable Defeat* and this novel, Murdoch gives us long stretches of conversation in which dramaturgy plays a big part. It was during this period that she was writing her two plays, *The Three Arrows* and *The Servants and the Snow*, and the conversational mode of these dramas carried over very successfully to the novels, mixing well with her other devices. In *An Accidental Man* she extends her dramaturgical capabilities to include cocktail parties with huge casts, engaged in fast, witty conversation which shifts from group to group around the room, plunging the reader into absurd and decadent hilarity. This device is strongly joined by another one that Murdoch has always been good at: the use of letters or sequences of letters to develop the characters. Here she again extends her cast of characters, and instead of having occasional letters, she regularly punctuates the novel with great batches of them written simultaneously: one typically mad batch, for example, is made up of letters to Ludwig from his father, to Karen from Gracie, to Sebastian from Karen, to Gracie from Patrick, to Dorina from Clara, to Gracie from Sebastian, to 'Louis' from Dorina, to Ludwig from Andrew Hilton, to Austin from Matthew, to Ludwig from Garth, to Dorina from Austin, to Patrick from Gracie, to Clara from Hester, to Charlotte from Mavis, to his father from Ludwig, to Austin from Dorina, from 'Louis' to Dorina. The sheer quantity of letters has the same effect as the extended cocktail party conversations: it shows the complexity within frivolity of the characters, and it attaches the reader's attention to the extended world Murdoch is so interested in depicting.

This ambitious novel includes more characters than any other Murdoch novel, so many in fact that even within its 377 pages there is no room for many of them to act except through the gossip of social gatherings and letters. Whole plots are carried on peripherally, love affairs shifted about and enacted, boutiques and pig farms begun and ended, fatal accidents bleakly reported. Not just the parties but the whole of society here feel very crowded, and the plot itself keeps touching an almost endlessly extended world. This large, real world, because of the very nature of the novel as a literary genre requiring limitation and containment, must somehow be debarred and its encroachments kept at bay, even though Murdoch's instinct for realism cannot avoid indicating its presence. Again and in new terms Murdoch is touching on the problems of the artist, and *An Accidental Man* is in this respect a worthy predecessor to *The Black Prince* where the ambiguities of form so fruitfully battle against the apprehension of the real world.

The centre provided by the titular character, the accidental man Austin Gibson Grey, is dominated by the vagaries of his selfishness and fantasies, and therefore can scarcely serve as an organizing factor. It was Murdoch's aim rather to free him and his actions from the restrictions of carefully plotted, apparent authorial control so that he can look convincingly accidental – can, in fact, trick the reader into believing in the absolute and free realism of his being. The ironic tricks involved in such a task indicate that Austin can be freed only by Murdoch concentrating her obvious formal attention elsewhere, by deflecting the reader from the centre to the peripheries and by boldly over–using formal devices. The artist as magician is Murdoch herself as a technician, as earlier demonstrated in the questionable felicities of *The Nice and the Good* and *Bruno's Dream*. Here, in an even more subtle virtuosity, the author appears to withdraw from the real substance of the work, which for her is the depiction of real characters in the real world, while the technical display continues and even burgeons.

Two major characters in *An Accidental Man*, Dorina and Matthew Gibson Grey, articulate a formula for reaching an ideal each desires deeply. Their contexts are very different, but the generalized formula for both of them is to 'change magic into spirit', which Murdoch certainly holds as a major task for the artist as well. In her view, the magic of the artist's devices is an impediment to the proper functioning of genuine art which also, paradoxically, depends on them; thus the real spiritual end sought for in art may be lost if the magical tricks of structure and literary process dominate. Throughout her career, Murdoch has been seriously concerned with spiritual issues, which she connects directly to the Platonic idea of the real; at the same time her deflecting technique has always involved realist attention to contemporary bourgeois society, even in its superficial trivialities. Her most advanced characters and most earnest seekers nevertheless come out of that mediocre society, and her determined pursuit of realism has bound her to the ingenious use of devices to describe that society wryly, comically, but accurately as it is. The test of her work is whether she can manage the transformation and achieve her version of spirituality by binding the magic of devices to accurate realism while describing the human quest for spirituality – a spirituality which turns out generally to be a confused or debased substitution for the real rigours of the spiritual life. The purpose of her novels can thus be seen as the transmission of a description of the spiritual life of contemporary man.

Dorina and Matthew Gibson Grey on the fictional plane long for what Murdoch sees to be central in both art and the spiritual life, and their longing is, in extended terms, extremely symbolic. Dorina desires a spiritual haven, 'some recourse, somewhere I could go to out of the mess and burden of my failed life, somewhere I could rest and drop the burden of my sin, as I used to imagine when I prayed when I was a child' (p. 309). The traditional images of God cannot help her, however, and the trick of transformation that used to work for her in Christianity no longer operates. As a character Dorina is weakly reminiscent of Tallis Browne in *A Fairly Honourable Defeat*, but she lacks his strength and adult resignation. Like him she is plagued by visions, demonic beings and supernatural horrors which separate her from a normal life. Childlike and somehow retarded by these aspects of supernatural intervention, she must constantly be supervised and looked after in a subtle but definite way, and can be seen as representing some more spiritual aspect of her hopelessly childish and selfish husband, Austin. The horrors of her demonic visions and her terrified apprehension of the world as a place of infinite cruelty constitute an overwhelming black magic which she knows she must transform in order to survive in the world. Austin and her peculiarly happy yet wretched marriage to him are part of this magic:

> Her only way back to the world was through her husband. Only here could magic be changed into spirit in the end. And now she had run away from him. Or was that what had happened? . . . He surrounded her with anxious possessive jealous tenderness, but in obedience to what he professed to think were her wishes he did not come to see her. He wandered about outside her prison like a fierce protective wolf. She heard him baying in the night.
>
> Thus they remained utterly obsessed with themselves and each other, and some natural healing process of which Dorina felt she ought to know the secret could not take place.                    (p. 84)

Her fear of Austin is also connected to her horrors, and as a character she can fruitfully be read as an extension of his own image-projecting, mythographic being. Her spirituality is unfocused because there is nothing to focus it on, nowhere to go, and certainly the marriage to Austin does not constitute the refuge she desires. If it could, and she feels it must be the only route, then both of them – she as spiritual being and he as social creature — would be perfectly united in an image of totality.

Dorina's death is well prepared for and inevitable as a symbol of her defeat; as so often in Murdoch it involves water. In her demon-ridden dreams, Dorina often feels the electric waters closing over her head, an image of drowning in the terrifying absoluteness of the real which carries such symbolic weight in Murdoch's typical image patterns. Moreover, Austin's first wife, Betty, had drowned, perhaps murdered by Austin, and Dorina's hyper-sensitive nature easily and fearfully picks that up. Her actual death follows her sad, frightened time on her own in a grim little hotel room and a meeting with Ludwig on the street during which he, enveloped by his own misery, does not talk to her; the result is a feeling of final alienation, a despair of ever being able to transform the black magical misery of her being into any meaningful spirituality. Thus her accidental death is, ironically, a piece of logical causality. The result of it is an even more limited and demonic Austin – but more of that later.

Matthew Gibson Grey's magic is of a quite different order, and has three distinct aspects. In the first, his own practice as a magician and charmer enjoys enormous success; no one except the neurotic Austin can resist his mesmeric power to draw others to him, and as Murdoch depicts him he is a man who counts very much on such successes. So certain of himself is he that he securely believes his return to England from the Orient will supply a substitute quest for the one he had longed for as a potential Buddhist monk in Kyoto. He now counts on his ability to charm his brother Austin and win an amicable, even loving relationship with him. In both old and new quests, the magical transformations he seeks fail, and he heads off inconclusively and fairly defeated with the interesting young Ludwig to Vietnamized America, where his primary magic or charm, such as it is, can probably function.

His real dream, however, had to do with the transformations of the spiritual life, something he had seen as a wonderful magical source of peace and a resting place where a spiritual success would automatically occur; like Dorina, he sought a haven:

> In matters of the spirit the difference between false and true can be as narrow as a needle, but only for the very great does it disappear altogether. Matthew had so long dreamed of the *place* which awaited him at that tiny monastery, a seat kept there for him, not quite so glorious as the empty thrones which Giotto imagined in paradise, but just as certainly reserved. Almost like an economist he had reckoned it out, how his future would pay for his present. He had advanced the day of his retirement with the impatience of a man awaiting his beloved. The anticipated savour of that

time was as honey to him. Then he would be at peace and his life would begin.

But, as in almost every human life, something had gone wrong some-where and the *malin génie* had got in and twisted something, ever so slightly, with huge huge results. . . . It was no good. A human being has only one life. And Matthew had had his.                    (pp. 102–3)

Like Uncle Theo in *The Nice and the Good*, Matthew was enchanted by Buddhism but underestimated its rigours; unlike Theo, however, he can fall back on secondary and tertiary magics which distract his attention from his failure. The process of the novel is, at one level of meaning, the process of Matthew's defeat in his secondary attempt at transformation and his entrance into a tertiary quest with Ludwig in America.

The task of curing his younger brother 'of a crippling hatred' (p. 105) replaces his Buddhist aspirations and takes over his mind. It becomes a centre for his attention, a focus, even a place of being of the sort that everyone in this novel is seeking. When Austin comes to him for money, Matthew correctly identifies their hysterical relationship as one in which they are merely 'slaves to this sort of black magic' (p. 142), understanding that Austin's hatred of him stems from a subjective and fictionalized account of the childhood accident in a stone quarry which had injured Austin's hand. The boy Matthew may or may not have helped cause the accident, but the whole incident is lost in the obscurity of Austin's perverted memory. For Austin this is merely the first in an endless series of events, including his first wife's drowning and his second wife's separation from him, which he mythologizes according to his manifold neuroses, creating subjective fictions which he can then use to cripple his life as the first accident had crippled his hand.

Matthew, then, if he is to save his brother by changing their relationship, must fight Austin's fictionalizing; he must strip Austin's perceptions of their fanciful accoutrements and focus his brother's attention on the reality of what has actually happened in many areas. The magic to be transformed in this case stems from Austin's fecund and paranoid imagination; the potential result is a reintegrated Austin, at peace in the world. Matthew's problem is essentially that of the mediocre artist who tries to subdue his material to his own preconceived design, instead of following the example of the persuasive, creative Demiurge from the *Timaeus* which Murdoch advocates in *The Fire and the Sun*. Matthew's design is, on the surface, full of high moral intent, even though it does not accept with adequate patience the real problems of Austin's personality. And as things work out, of course, Austin *is* reintegrated into society and goes off happily into the future, not through Matthew's agency, but through a congeries of events, including the death of Dorina, Gracie's marriage to Garth and especially Mavis's idealistically taking him on as a duty and a heritage from Dorina, whom she begins to resemble even to the extent of producing a *poltergeist*. Matthew, in disappointment, recognizes that he has failed in another quest, and again because his conception of that quest was inadequate:

> When a man has reflected much he is tempted to imagine himself as the prime author of change. Perhaps in such a mood God actually succeeded in creating the world. But for man such moods are times of illusion. What we have deeply imagined we feign to control, often with what seem to be the best of motives. But the reality is huge and dark which lies beyond the lighted area of our intentions.
>
> I came to set him free, thought Matthew. I came to change magic into spirit. It was all to be brought about by me. Now when it appears that somehow or other, by means which I do not even understand, he has got out, I ought to be glad. Did I really want to be his mentor and to set up as his judge? No. He has his desolation as I have mine, and let him be free of it. I wanted that bond to be cut, but I did want to cut it myself. And now I am sad as if I had lost a beloved.
>
> (p. 352)

Undeterred, and indeed enslaved by his own nature, Matthew sets off for America with Ludwig, who is caught in the snares of his charm; he remains a determined, eternal taker-on of quests involving power, manipulation and the playing of God roles. Transformations are impossible for Matthew because he cannot relinquish the tools and images of the various magics which beset him. He is not, however, ignorant of alternative possibilities, and he and Garth are spokesmen of a much tougher route to the spiritual life than any he has attempted and failed at. His experience as a diplomat gave him one memory that he retains and perceives as an example of a higher sort of activity:

> He had seen decisive moments in men's lives. He had witnessed a scene in the Red Square when demonstrators were arrested, and when an ordinary citizen, an accidental passerby, had suddenly gone across to join them and had been arrested too. Matthew knew about some of the men involved. They were still in labour camps. Some were in 'hospitals'. Their lives were ruined. . . . He had never truly lived in places where duties were terrible and their consequences life-destroying and long.
>
> (p. 103)

In his first long, serious conversation with Ludwig, in the course of which he so easily wins the young man's heart, Matthew reverts to this story, giving heroic acts proper credit, even as he places them in a serious, unromantic context:

> These are our real heroes. These are the people whose courage and devotion to goodness goes beyond any dream of one's own possibility.

> Courage is after all, when sufficiently refined, the virtue of the age. It is
> always perhaps the only name of love which can mean anything to us. . . .
> Where is the end? Where those men stood? I'm not even sure of that any
> more. One wants things to be better, things ought to be better. There
> shouldn't be starvation and fear. That's obvious. It's when you try to go
> deeper than the obvious, when you try to go where God used to be – . . .
> There are absolutes where calculation about causality comes up against a
> brick wall. But these are not moral absolutes. Perhaps indeed they make
> moral absolutes impossible. When you can't calculate perhaps it doesn't
> matter so much how you act . . . there are no categorical imperatives. . . .
> Very few people ever come here. Here language breaks down.  (pp. 231–3)

This is the realm of Murdoch's idea of the good, the blank face which so
harrowed Theo's soul in *The Nice and the Good* and which Brendan Craddock
in *Henry and Cato* will so eloquently describe and submit to. But in *An
Accidental Man* it is ultimately dismissed by the characters, including
Matthew himself, who prefer more romanticized and accessible routes to
mediocrity.

Matthew is in process of remaining mediocre, and the universality of such
a process constitutes the major theme in this novel. Through him Murdoch
points out why such mediocrity is endemic and defines the central problem as
perceived, probably erroneously, by the other characters:

> A sense almost of ennui came to him out of the trees which seemed now to
> be drooping and darkening before his eyes. London seemed a city not even
> wicked, but devoid of spirit, dusty, broken. God had died there since
> Matthew was young and Jesus Christ, who might have been waiting for
> him in England, was gone too, faded utterly, his old Friend and Master,
> gone. How abhorrent to him now was the image of the Crucified One, the
> personal local Godhead of Christianity. . . . And here in England, where it
> might have been forgiven, have been the bearer to him of something
> ancient and holy, he found it offensive too and shuddered away from its
> message of anxiety, suffering, personality and guilt. He thought, the west
> studies suffering the east studies death. How utterly different these things
> are, as indeed the Greeks had always known, that deeply secretly oriental
> people.  (pp. 105–6)

As the characters look for a place where they can be at peace, an internal-
external space of repose, they reiterate again and again the absence of God,
the yearning towards something in the past that played an enormous and
consoling parental role. As they contemplate that past time, Murdoch makes
it perfectly clear that they are often really mourning for their childhood, a lost
past enriched by doubtful memories. Their problem is that they decline adult
life, or perceive it through the veils of suffering and guilt. The idea of

suffering in western tradition is perfectly imaged by the Crucifixion, and again, as in *A Fairly Honourable Defeat*, Murdoch stresses the inherent failures of the Christian tradition which sees suffering as having a primary value. Weary contemporary London reflects the residue of personal suffering after the withdrawal of Christ, and in Murdoch's analysis of the diseased contemporary mind, 'anxiety, suffering, personality and guilt' automatically and irremediably remain. *An Accidental Man* mimetically, in character after character, studies this suffering, now rendered meaningless by the withdrawal of its primary religious vitality.

For Murdoch, however, the death–of–God syndrome is a neurotic chimera by which the characters console themselves for larger failures. It is easier for Matthew to talk about the absence of Christ than to enter the realm of real knowledge, and he uses this absence as he uses his quests, to obscure a terrifying spiritual potentiality. When, at the Peter Pan statue in Kensington Gardens, Gracie asks if he believes in fairies, his answer is ' "Yes". There were no more gods, but all the minor magic remained, beautiful, terrible, cruel and small' (p. 108). These minor magics preoccupy him and all the characters when the major magics fail and the real quest is too difficult; and the progress of any given character in this novel involves jumping from one minor magic to another. Thus Matthew at one point feels that the resurrection of his old affair with Mavis will effect the yearned-for peace. Later still, when he suddenly has Dorina captivated and immured for three days, she becomes a piece of magic which will transform his spiritual life even while he controls her and is her only saviour. When she dies, he returns to Ludwig as a substitute.

But Matthew is no hero, and merely sets the pattern for this pursuit of minor magics in the absence of major ones; in doing so, he is one of the most intelligent expositors of the whole potential range of thought on the subject. His nephew Garth Gibson Grey is equally eloquent, and more than Matthew full of good deeds and acute ameliorative judgements. Like Matthew, he has seen something which becomes a pattern of truth for him, something against which his fancy existential theories crashed and were destroyed. In his case, it was the murder of one man by two others – a typical but ghastly phenomenon of New York street life – and the awful reality of it changes him from a romantic to a realist, in the root sense of those terms as Murdoch so frequently uses them. Garth had sublimated the experience into a novel which was lost in a baggage muddle typical of any flight from America to England, and he tells a confused and bewildered Ludwig that he is actually glad of its loss, because it would have been a temptation. Indeed it *is* a temptation, to which he succumbs all too easily when the manuscript novel is finally restored to him, but throughout most of the book he earnestly attempts to participate in the pure reality which lies at the base of Murdoch's religiousness:

One should do simple separated things. Don't imagine you *are* that big complicated psychological buzz that travels around with you. Step outside it. Above all don't feel guilt or worry about doing right. That's all flummery. Guilt is the invention of a personal God, now happily defunct. There is no Alpha and no Omega, and nothing could be more important than that. Remember I once quoted to you that thing of Kierkegaard's about metaphysics, that in order to sew you must knot the thread? Well, that's wrong. You don't have to knot the thread, you can't knot it, you mustn't knot it. You just keep pulling it through. . . . Oh there are temptations, there are trials, there are even goals. . . . To give up the world. To have nothing, not even hopes. To make life holy. You remember in the *Iliad* when Achilles' immortal horses weep over the death of Patroclus, and Zeus deplores the sight of deathless beings involved in the pointless horrors of mortality? . . . Gods can't really grieve. Men can't understand. But animals which are godlike can shed pure tears. I would like to shed pure tears. Zeus sheds none.                                           (pp. 92–3)

This is a compact but rather difficult statement of Murdoch's view of the ultimate spiritual quest: to have no theories (not to knot the thread), to denounce the obsessive control of personality, to have an apprehension of the purity of the nothing for which one should act, to see the limitations of both gods and men.

Such apprehension translated into action makes Garth a rather alien chum for poor Ludwig, but it also leads him to clear insights about the needs and problems of the people around. He is not so foolish as to believe that he can change people, but he retains a small 'magical' belief that he can help them, and this plus the temptations of his novel ultimately drag him down to the mediocrity of all the other characters. His sympathy for the suffering Gracie after the breaking of her engagement to Ludwig (a sympathy the reader cannot give) traps him in marriage to a frivolous rich girl, and the success of his novel launches him on a worldly career as a mediocre writer. From someone who had wished for the purity of the real, for the ability to see the nothingness at the true centre of things, he has become completely absorbed in these deflecting minor magics which close the doors of spiritual quest to him. Again Murdoch is warning against the charms of art when not practised at its highest level, and Garth's substitution of facile literary success for a deeper task is far from felicitous.

Matthew and Garth are the central truth-bearing characters in *An Accidental Man*, but all the others equally share the idea of a quest to find the redemptive magical solution to their confusion. All of them fail. The atmosphere here is as heavy and miasmic as that of any novel in the twentieth century; in this world with no particular way of being virtuous, where self-congratulation over virtuous deeds only increases one's flaws, the entire cast of characters, central and peripheral, intensify the sense of social frenzy and spiritual failure which produce the novel's ambience. Again and again Murdoch will raise some hope of happiness: the burgeoning affair between Mitzi and Charlotte, or Gracie's sudden wealth or Ludwig's anguished but sensible decision to take Oxford and reject an unjust war in Vietnam. But as each one turns to dust and bitter ashes, is destroyed by personality or selfishness or suffering, it is exposed as precisely one of those minor magics by which characters live but by which they also lie to themselves and impede the spiritual development they so yearn for.

In Murdoch's world, the concentration of contemporary people on external devices of the ego rather than internal spiritual development creates a situation in which the spiritual self is alienated in a way totally unlike the theories of alienation which have characterized twentieth-century personality theories. As Murdoch depicts it, the inner quest persists as a moral struggle perpetually trying to attach itself to spiritual attainment. But since these sophisticated persons are unlikely to believe comforting views of God, they must themselves create religious symbols or magics which will not only lead to an acceptably happy life in society, but more importantly will satisfy their endemic spiritual thirst. Murdoch often shows that people are essentially finders of substitutes, and in this novel she explores the tremendously varied methods by which people seek to quench a spiritual thirst deeper and conducive to more pain than they can face. The objective tone of *An Accidental Man* gives it the almost documentary aspect of a report on how the human imagination tries, and fails, to sort out its confusion.

The vocabulary of the quest is an interesting one in this novel, for Murdoch uses it to show how the cultural past of western civilization can be an adjunct to the contemporary imagination. Freudian terminology for the operation of the psyche is very important here, for Murdoch indicates that the most troubled characters in this novel are trapped by the traumas of childhood, which they mistake for an historical longing for the period when God existed and functioned. Hence Mitzi looks back to her girlhood as an Amazonian athlete; Dorina to the world of prayer; Mavis to her childhood Catholicism; Matthew to his period of belief in Jesus and then his Buddhist aspirations; Austin to the golden time before his hand was crippled and his hatred of Matthew born. Freudian theories of emotional retardation illuminate their inability to transform the essentially magic period of childhood and youth into an adequate adult spirituality, though Freud would of course have scorned the religious vocabulary prevalent here. The traumas which produce this retardation are fairly normal and not at all dramatic – even Austin's accident is not a grandiose thing except in his own obsessive neurosis – and essentially the characters' longing looks backward are simply a naive expression of the classical archetype of the lost golden age.

These characters' imaginations are interestingly representative of contemporary western culture, however, as they cast their creative attention on what can be seen as the golden age of operative Christianity and art – the middle ages in its aspect of knight, maiden, castle, the Grail and quest. Whatever the medieval period may have been in itself, the characters borrow only its most romantic and mythic elements, hoping to aggrandize and make holy their all too barren lives. Thus the potty Welsh photographer, Mr Secombe-Hughes, writes a Welsh bardic poem to Mitzi, dresses her in his mother's silk shawl and photographs her before the backdrop of a castle so that he can stage an affecting proposal. The sharp juxtaposition of his absurd romanticism and her realistic discomfort at his repulsiveness is a model for the whole process, and shows how childishly inflated are the characters' desires for the past, for the security of childhood, for the fairy-tale world of romanticism.

Austin Gibson Grey, the accidental man himself, is the most extensive myth-maker and user of medieval formulaic fairy-tales, ideas of quests and the consecration of the princess (Dorina) – and of course he is by far the most childish of the characters in question. There is a sustained hilarity in his frequent evocations of castles, sleeping princesses, magic kisses, the Grail and fairy-tale islands, and although much troubling material is included – his misapprehension of Dorina, his probable murder of Betty, his unjustified hatred of Matthew – many of his little fairy-tales are wildly comic and full of Kafkaesque energy. The import of his fairy-tales cannot be obscured, however, by our amusement at them; many of the most negative of them occur in dreams, and indicate the subconscious depths of his guilt and hatred, but generally they are part of a frenzied, ironic attempt to transform the bitter reality of the world into a prelapsarian place. His psyche cannot traverse the hopeless distance between the middle ages and the late twentieth century until the maternal Mavis steps in, massages his hand and gradually, by returning him again to a secure dream of childhood, draws him out of his obsessive misery.

The cure is not seen as radical, however, since it preserves him in the state of retardation which this novel so glumly sets forth through Austin as an extreme model of much contemporary behaviour. Austin as a character is an absolute triumph for Murdoch; the reader experiences a wonderfully pure hatred of him, equivalent to but different from that directed towards Julius King in *A Fairly Honourable Defeat*. Austin is too disorganized to be a pure demon, but his utter separation from human decency, his madly obsessive perversion of everything and his total lack of moral faculty create a demonic effect. Even more than Julius King he projects a nasty aura, through his self-pitying weakness, unpredictability and the accumulating details of his foul behaviour: stealing and selling Ludwig's books, stealing Dorina's ring and brooch, killing the child Rosalind, smashing Norman Monkley's skull, smashing Matthew's beautiful Chinese porcelain collection, stealing five pounds from the impoverished Mitzi, etc. Murdoch makes no attempt to justify him; she enters his perverse, suffering mind with cool objectivity. Nor does she make any specific symbolic effort to align him with demonism; her descriptions of his activity are almost clinical, and she is very close to identifying him with Everyman. When he triumphs in his wife Dorina's death, Murdoch coolly avoids that beckoning trap of literary realism, the use of character as an arena for moral assessment, and allows Austin's mind a selfish statement of relief: 'Now she was shut up forever in the most final of all prisons. Now at last she was absolutely safe, and could never hurt him any more' (p. 316). Murdoch's backdrop to this objectivity is, however, alive with the moral struggles of many, especially Ludwig, Matthew and Garth, and the reader has been nudged throughout the novel towards a thorough arousal of the moral faculties. The result is an inevitably powerful moral reaction against Austin, and against the entire society which defends and protects such a product. At the same time, a careful reader must realize that these judgements are part of a defunct and mechanical traditional system of thought, and that Austin's functioning as an accidental man – i.e. a man unmotivated by system or theory and entirely in the grip of his own uncontrolled psyche – is part of the necessary material of the contemporary world, with which we must make our peace.

The childish Austin survives everything, including Dorina's death which proves so profitable to him by putting him in Mavis's care, but two real children die – one, the Monkley child, Rosalind, killed by him in the crash in Matthew's car; the other, Henrietta Sayce, a fugitive but charming peripheral figure from the huge cast of characters. The other innocent deaths – of Dorina and of an owl – relate directly to Austin and to the forlorn sense of destruction which weighs so heavily in this novel. The loss of the children indicates some sort of lost innocence, the pointless force of an indifferent world which does not function by causality, reward or punishment. Austin, however, wilfully smashes in the breast of the owl which has swooped down on him and which had earlier attacked Mitzi. The act is seen realistically as self-defence, but the whole episode has a lingering nastiness about it – the death of the beautiful, domesticated owl attacking people because of its nesting time reflects the partly casual, partly malicious destructiveness that automatically follows Austin, and the owl may also be, as birds so often are in Murdoch, the symbol of a spirituality which cannot survive. The death of Dorina, however, is much more significant, since she represents not the fairy-tale ideal that Austin keeps playing with but a deeper tie with the oceanic and terrifying aspects of the spiritual life. Unable herself to organize or combat the supernatural apparitions haunting her, she is doomed as the fey representative of something that cannot succeed in a society which demands quotidian practicality. I am not convinced that she succeeds as a character: she is too childish as she sits reading *The Lord of the Rings* and broods over her apparitions, and to the degree that she represents spirituality, it is of an external superstitious sort, unconvincing beside the hard religious apprehensions of Matthew and Garth at their most realistic.

Let me conclude this discussion by pointing out that *An Accidental Man* is a Vietnam novel, set against a foul world of political muddle, cruelty and moral chaos. Ludwig Leferrier is not terribly interesting or even very bright, but his earnest American aspect is tediously well done. The dilemma he faces shows the political dead-ends of contemporary morality, and his decision after his broken engagement to go back to America to face prison is pointedly typical of all ameliorative steps in this novel. That decision is capricious, without real moral basis or logical causality, and no amount of conversation with Matthew can aggrandize it. Its caprice is part of all of the concluding action: Garth's marriage to Gracie, who in sheer nastiness is bettered only by Austin, Mavis's settling into her role as a substitute Dorina, Charlotte's reluctant decision to stay with Mitzi. Although the novel is full of moral turmoil, the denouement is marked by the accidental, by caprice, by an indifferent working-out of things. Murdoch essentially denies meaningful closure, and by doing so frees herself from the burden of statement. In the general category of realism, two modes predominate: the realism of moral assessment which so tempts a much resisting Murdoch, and the realism of mere description which this conclusion manages very purely to convey.

'Our revels now are ended', a cocktail-party person quotes from *The Tempest* at the end of the book, and indeed the game of social life in a spiritually deprived society has been played to a formal denouement which vanishes noisily into thin air and has solved nothing. The novelistic feeling of continuation is cut off simply because a phase is over for these characters, and the tight formal controls of drama, in which the manipulator imposes an ending, take over. Murdoch as Prospero-magician stages her last gossip-laden cocktail party, and the savagely ironic tying-up of ends parodies closure. Murdoch's presentation of the mediocre is so convincingly embedded in objective realism that the reversion to technical devices and the drama of form (or the form of drama) causes a whiplash effect on the reader. The open prolixity of the realist novel as a genre is suddenly wrenched about by the most artificial devices of the most artificial form – the masque-drama as written by Shakespeare and controlled by the art of Prospero. But this ending does not remind us of the satiric or touching but gamesome round-ups of *Bruno's Dream* or *The Nice and the Good*; here the capricious savagery of meaningless action, the foul perversion of the cocktail gossip and the reader's inevitable and persistent sense that every character has failed or compromised, convince that there is no possibility of any character even approaching the disciplines of the good. And instead of perceiving the technically brilliant but obtrusive finale as a wizardly return to form after the accidental and free nature of so much of the action, the reader is somehow dismayed by it, jolted by its savagery, intruded upon by the form itself.

This, obviously, is what Murdoch is after in a novel which damns the creation of fictions and relentlessly exposes the illusions the characters so untiringly spawn. *An Accidental Man* is deeply related to certain previous novels, not only in its Shakespearean closure but in its use of so many images from earlier works – the quest, magic, the accidental, the loss of God – but its miasmic darkness, seemingly an automatic accompaniment to allowing the characters an apparent freedom from authorial control, fights with particular venom against the necessary intrusions of form. As noted earlier, Murdoch can allow a character like Austin, or indeed the entire cast, a genuine quality of accidentalness only by distracting the reader from the real problems of authorial control in the process of character creation. This she effects by ingeniously overdoing certain other strong formal devices of which the ending is a notable example, so that the reader, even while acknowledging the excellence of their execution, half rebels against them. The rebellion cannot be complete, however, for these strong devices both absorb and express much of the comedic irony which this grim fiction produces; and by contrast to these pyrotechnic virtuoso displays, the apparent 'reality' of the characters' usual activity gains remarkable credence.

Not only are the high moments of form strangely intrusive, distracting and often comically irritating in spite of their evident usefulness, but they also suggest an analogy between the negative ironies of form as an authorial 'magical' device and the characters' own inclination to impose form and control as they tell tales and mythical medieval stories. The intrusiveness and use of Murdoch's ironically overwrought pyrotechnics are part of the substance of fictionalizing – a negative activity which the novel's primary moral energy works against. Thus Garth fictionalizes a personal trauma so that it becomes a semi-autobiographical novel and he a success, thereby failing to follow the good he had in the past so unfalteringly perceived; he succumbs to the temptation that art automatically posits and accepts an easy but final mediocrity. His ability to write a saleable novel is a transformation of the wrong thing into the wrong thing, and in this extremely black, heart-sickening novel not even the death he had witnessed on a New York street is sufficient to change magic into spirit.

Dorina's death is equally inadequate to halt the fictionalizing tendency. Although transformations occur after it for most of the characters, they are negative as in Garth's case, and the real spiritual potentiality her death could have evoked is vitiated by the characters' decisions to substitute new quests and new fictional fantasies. They dodge spirituality and reality and choose instead the ease of the frenetic, bitchy, but comfortable bourgeois world – and this choice is Murdoch's greatest indictment of them. Their world is rendered possible for them by their misreading of it, and by the frantic energy through which they create fictional versions of its qualities and activities. The final cocktail party, with its wild conjectures about Matthew and utter forgetfulness of Ludwig, typifies the misuse of reality which is so necessary to ordinary people. Always suspicious of any except the greatest art as a positive human activity, Murdoch here uses it to devastate her characters and readers alike. One cannot help being in awe of *An Accidental Man*, but there is no exit from its darkness except through the games of form which artificially produce closure. The recognition that this highly-stylized closure accurately echoes the daily lies by which convincingly realistic characters live forces a harsh picture of spiritual and moral incompetence. The elegance of the closure as it effects its impact reflects Murdoch's complementary concern with the duplicity of art, an issue that *The Black Prince*, with all its ironies and its subtle tracing of potential steps towards truth, will pull into a more compromising, but even more serious focus.

★

Austin Gibson Grey is a forerunner in violence to Hilary Burde of *A Word Child* (1975), another of Murdoch's depictions of a man egomaniacally choosing mediocrity and retardation instead of looking humbly at the truth. *A Word Child* is separated from *An Accidental Man* by two other novels, *The Black Prince*, in which Murdoch's central and, for her fiction, definitive examination of art takes place, and *The Sacred and Profane Love Machine*, a complex and savage novel with which I shall conclude this chapter. *A Word Child* is much simpler than either of these or than *An Accidental Man*: compared to the latter it is contained, controlled, uncluttered, its cast of characters limited, its structure coherent and fast-moving.

That structure is dominated by the powerful will of the first-person male narrator, Hilary Burde himself, whose personality is reflected in the relentless and controlled march of days which drives the narrative to its fatal conclusion. Murdoch is by now a masterly projector of first-person narration, and as in *The Black Prince* all the perceptions are uniquely attached to the character who projects them. Again, Murdoch absents herself from the immediate sensibility of the novel; every device focuses on enlarging the reader's comprehension of Hilary Burde, the word child spinning out his tale according to the tightly controlled laws of his falsely disciplined being.

Like Bradley Pearson in *The Black Prince* or Charles Arrowby in *The Sea, The Sea*, Hilary Burde is, for many if not all readers, a maddening and negative character on whom Murdoch so riskily projects her fiction and to whom she gives over the entire substance of her text. He is painfully dislikable, but has a Byronic, grim self-perception, an almost romantic aura which can draw some readers and which certainly has significant power over all the women in his story. What aids him chiefly in gaining any sympathy whatever from the skeptical reader is the rapid pacing of the novel as day after day is given its space during the brief four and a half weeks which comprise the action. A tight and narrow product of a grim, orphaned childhood, Hilary shot into that peculiar examination-taking success which Oxford (and Cambridge) can, with a condescension shocking to North Americans, bestow on the brighter members of the lower classes. His election to a fellowship was a great triumph promising a golden future, but his appalling guilt in the Gunnar-Anne fiasco shut him out forever from the bright career he had dreamed of, and subsequently his study of languages continued in its narrow boundaries, relentlessly going forward but perpetually without value, meaning or direction.

His narrow interest in words parallels a similar restriction in the organization of his life, where every day has a special pattern and social occasion allotted to it. His day of agony is Sunday, when he does not go to his lowly job at Whitehall and has no set social engagement for the evening; opened to time and with no routine to fill it, Hilary enters the underground regions of his own mind which he prefers to keep pressed down beneath the surface. Apart from the rigidly kept routine of his work and set 'days' for seeing various people, he perceives no real life and nothing of value:

> By what after all does a man live? Art meant little to me, I carried a few odd pieces of literature like lucky charms. Someone once said of me, and it was not entirely unjust, that I read poetry for the grammar. As I have said, I never wanted to be a writer. I loved words, but I was not a word-user, rather a word-watcher, in the way that some people are bird-watchers. I loved languages but I knew by now that I would never speak the languages that I read. I was one for whom the spoken and the written words are themselves different languages. I had no religion and no substitute for it. My 'days' gave me identity, a sort of ecto-skeleton, a phantasmagoria. Religion, and indeed art too, I conceived of as human activities, but not for me. Art must invent new beauty, not play with what has already been made, religion must invent God and never rest. Only I was not inventive. I did not want to play this play or dance this dance, and apart from the activity of playing or dancing there was nothing at all. I early saw that the nature of words and their relationship to reality made metaphysical systems impossible. History was a slaughterhouse. Mortality itself was my philosophical robe. Even the stars are not ageless and our breaths are numbered.
>
> (p. 28)

Hilary's love for his sister Crystal at first appears to be, but is not, a humanizing fissure in the dense facade of his highly structured life. He refers to himself as 'oned in love' (p. 14) to Crystal, and the permanence of his attachment somewhat softens the brutally realistic descriptions he gives of this plain, podgy, uneducated, naive and generous lower-class woman who lives in a lonely bed-sitter with her sewing machine. Nothing in Crystal's timid, gentle behaviour belies Hilary's image of her simple homeliness until he compares her, fairly late in the book, with Lady Kitty, with whom he is by then completely in love. He makes the comparison before Arthur Fisch, who wishes to marry Crystal; the difference between Hilary's estimation and Arthur's offers not only a new way of seeing her, through Arthur's eyes, but also suggests an important contrast in the moral nature of the two men:

> 'I don't like that sort of vain upper class woman, she's spoilt and silly and I wouldn't trust her –'
>
> 'How much do you know about women, my dear Arthur? Well, I suppose Crystal's rather blunter simpler charms are more up your street.'
>
> 'Please don't speak like that about Crystal.'
>
> 'Well, she is my sister and I wouldn't at all mind seeing her in mink, some decent clothes might do something for her appearance. I suppose I'm allowed to be realistic enough to see that she dresses like a guy and has a face like the back of a cab. If I realize she's ugly that doesn't mean I don't love her.'
>
> 'She isn't ugly!'
>
> 'Your illusion is touching. Now Kitty –'
>
> 'I won't have you talking here about Kitty this and Kitty that – I won't have you speaking of that woman in the same sentence as Crystal –'
>
> (pp. 292–3)

Arthur subsequently kicking Hilary out takes them both by surprise, but it is the sort of realistic, rapid, truthful assessment of a situation that Tallis could manage in *A Fairly Honourable Defeat*.

Crystal and especially Arthur point to a world from which Hilary is totally cut off, that he indeed treats with contempt – a world which has the humble moral savour of striving towards reality – and both these minor characters are in process towards the good. Arthur, to whom I shall return later, is far along the road, and serves as Murdoch's major spokesman in the novel, but Crystal has been retarded by her generous love for Hilary which has in fact enslaved her and prevented the progress of which she is capable. At the end of the novel, Hilary acknowledges to himself how this slavery has limited her life, and how he has stifled her with a terrible love:

> *Then* (i.e. after Anne's death) I had someone, a passive spectator who was also a fellow sufferer, to enact it all to. I suffered before Crystal as believers suffer before God; only doubtless the latter derived more benefit from their suffering than I did. And she, innocent loving darling, connived, out of her sheer goodness and her identification with me, at an establishment of pure desolation. I was determined that our lives should be wrecked and she, poor sparrow, had so readily made her little nest in the wreckage. How profitless it had all been I could now very clearly see. Repentance, penance,

redemptive suffering? Nothing of the sort. I had destroyed my chances in life and destroyed Crystal's happiness out of sheer pique, out of the spiteful envious violence which was still in me. . . . And I perpetuated my suffering out of resentment. If I had been the only recipient of this violence the incident might have been, in some recording angel's book, regarded as closed. But I deliberately made Crystal suffer with me. Could her pure suffering have redeemed me? In some ideal theory, yes, in reality, no.

(p. 381)

Crystal has been condemned to share Hilary's guilt and resentment, and she remains imprisoned by her continued slavish devotion to him. Although she wants very much to marry Arthur, she breaks off the engagement which would let her break free from the cage of the past. This she does partly because of Hilary's power over her, and especially because of her feelings of guilt over a brief affair, years before, with a desolate Gunnar. When Gunnar now comes to her to be helped a second time, she feeds him lower-class fish fingers and a major quotation from the Bible, neither of which had ever before entered the ken of this sophisticated, wealthy, much psychoanalysed man. Her quotation, 'Whatsoever things are true, whatsoever things are honest, whatsoever things are just, whatsoever things are pure, whatsoever things are lovely, whatsoever things are of good report – if there be any virtue, and if there be any praise, think of these things' from *Philippians* 4:8, cuts to the heart of both Gunnar's and Hilary's perceptual errors, and points to a way that might lead out of the maze which dominates both their lives.

Filled with anguish over the death, almost twenty years before, of Gunnar's first wife Anne, both men mythologized her, themselves and each other, and in doing so kept themselves from perceiving the honest and true things that lie about them. As Gunnar puts it in his first interview with Hilary: 'I have got to get rid of her, not of *her*, but of this filthy ghost thing – and let her alone and let her be alone as the dead should be – at last – and doing that means getting rid of *you*' (p. 265). Later, in a second warmer, more deceptively open interview, he says that this ghost 'wasn't really her at all. And I've felt – just in these last days – as if the ghost was crumbling – and there she was, the real Anne, very very far away – and somehow safe, out of it –' (p. 326). As Anne's false mythology fades for Gunnar, Kitty's intensifies for unredeemable Hilary; as Gunnar talks, Hilary reflects that 'the image of Kitty burnt me, as if a red-hot burnished plate had been put in front of my face' (p. 326). Cursed by an inveterate inclination to create images and myths, the two ineluctably play out a desperate *déjà vu* in which Kitty with her own complicity becomes a surrogate Anne.

As Kitty describes it, Gunnar has long been psychologically mired in an obsession about Anne's guilt and Hilary's mythologized being, but the more interesting issues in the novel involve the curious workings of Hilary's mind.

As in the case of most mature Murdoch novels, *A Word Child* is set against a work of art, and in this case the work, J. M. Barrie's *Peter Pan*, serves as a mirror reflecting the essential character of Hilary Burde. A staging of *Peter Pan* is planned as the office Christmas pantomime, so there is much talk about both the casting and the symbolic meaning of the play. Many characters in other Murdoch novels are interested in this play, and the Peter Pan statue in Kensington Gardens is often, as here, a focus. Murdoch generally refers to *Peter Pan* to indicate minor magic and sinister childishness, but in *A Word Child* its centrality enlarges the referential frame. Because of the imminent pantomime everybody is busily interpreting *Peter Pan*, and interestingly everyone makes the play into a spiritual allegory. Gunnar claims, fairly simply, that the play is 'about parents and being unwilling to grow up, but what made it sinister was that the childishness had been invested with spirituality . . . "The fragmentation of spirit is the problem of our age"' (p. 227). Another major commentator is Arthur, who argues sturdily against Hilary's inclination to make the play, and Peter, romantic. Whereas Hilary says Peter Pan is 'reality breaking in', Arthur points out that he is really 'spirit gone wrong, just turning up as an unnerving visitor who can't really help and can't get in either . . . the spiritual urge is mad unless it's embodied in some ordinary way of life. It's destructive, it's just a crazy sprite' (pp. 87–8).

Hilary's interpretation of the fey boy as reality, as opposed to Arthur's view of him as crazy and destructive, offers an interesting clue to Hilary's views of many things. Himself a 'bad boy' from the beginning, given to violence and constantly feeling lonely and excluded from ordinary society, Hilary's energy, like Peter Pan's, grows into a misplaced spirituality which remains destructive because it cannot be embodied in or absorbed by ordinary life. Arthur argues not for Peter Pan or Smee as hero, but for the dog Nana, who is bound to conventional ideas of duty and who instantly recognizes the threat Peter Pan imposes. In arguing for family life as opposed to magic, Arthur posits a centre which ultimately he and Crystal will produce through their marriage – a centre where the ordinariness of family life lived simply and realistically can produce the happier possibility of a real childhood for their children.

Hilary's cynicism scorns such humble solutions, but this novel is much dominated by ideas about childhood – its literature, Hilary's inability to break out of the basic patterns of his lonely, unloved boyhood, the significant coincidence of the desire of the three major women in the book, Crystal, Kitty and Tommy, to become pregnant. Moreover, the pregnancy of the dead Anne had caused the frenzied anger and car crash which began Hilary's pursuit of defeat and the annihilation of his talents and hopes for the present and future. The reference to the past suicide of the Jopling child, Tristram, adds another sorry entry in the catalogue of the frustrations of bearing and being children which so dominate this tale, and it is important that the one positive note Murdoch sounds is from Arthur and Crystal's marriage which will, we are assured, produce children – by adoption should nature fail.

The connection with *Peter Pan* persists not only through Hilary's personality, but also by Crystal's possible role as a Wendy who plays the mother to the various lost and abandoned boys of this Peter Pan-ish tale. She is a wonderful and magical image to four men, each of whom defines her nature for himself according to his needs. For Hilary, she is part of himself, oned by love to him; for embittered Clifford Larr she is the image of the virgin and chaste woman in a world of whoredom; for Gunnar she is a simple, generous, loving woman who supplied his need when Anne died and now gives him comfort of a sort that no psychoanalyst could manage; and most significantly, for Arthur she is the symbol of family life. Like Wendy in Barrie's novel, she grows up and marries, and is thereby forever alienated from the Never-Never Land of the Peter Pan fantasy. Inasmuch as Hilary is a version of Peter Pan, her marriage and entrance into the ordinary world of family life causes her essentially to lose him. Arthur suggests Crystal's dilemma in describing the Wendy of the play: 'Wendy is the human soul seeking the truth. She ends up with a compromise [living half in an unreal world] like most of us do. It's a defeat but a fairly honourable one. That's the best we can hope for, I suppose' (p. 88). Crystal's life between Hilary and Arthur, between an unnatural world and a natural one, reflects this defeat, but her marriage finally removes her entirely from the world produced by Hilary's circular reversions, his recurrent childishness and his unnatural commitment to unacknowledged fantasies.

In describing himself early in the novel, Hilary claims that religion and art, although real activities, have nothing to do with him. The action of the novel proves him quite wrong. He acknowledges that he carries certain pieces of literature in his mind, almost as lucky charms, and as his story unravels we find that his range travels progressively from children's literature – *Peter Pan*, James Elroy Flecker's *Hassan*, Kipling and other British imperial literature – to the final solemnities of T. S. Eliot's *Four Quartets*. He also makes clear that his exposure to evangelical Christianity in his orphanage years was powerful but meaningless. His use of biblical reference is generally ironic, as are his comments on *Hassan* and *Peter Pan*, and he spends a great deal of time wrapped up in his cynical knowledge that the ending of *Hassan* with its cosmic redemption, the heroism of imperial British literature, Peter Pan's Never-Never Land and the promises of Christianity are all false and misleading. His cynicism is only a slight veneer over his enormous expectations, however; he thinks, in fact, that an ending like that of *Hassan* would be very nice in his fated non-affair with Kitty. Haunted by the lost function of God, he perpetually although ironically associates the women who love him with God. He likes his ex-mistress, Tommy, best when she offers to forgive him in God's stead, and again and again he compares Crystal's love to the love of

God. Crystal's godliness is something he controls with his typical rigidity, but it is very strongly there:

> I simply was her. I had to have her there, like God. And by 'there' I mean again, not necessarily in my presence. I needed to see her regularly but not very often. She just had to be always available in a place fixed and control-led by me. I had to know, at any moment where she was. I needed her sequestered innocence, as a man might want his better self to be stored away separately in a pure deity. Did I want her to remain a virgin? Yes.
>
> (p. 60)

Her permanence and sequestered existence allow him to be in control, but in the case of Lady Kitty the opposite happens. Here the God figure takes on redemptive authority and becomes the strong being who will take care of everything, who will 'arrange it all'. Hilary's connection to this attractive manipulator is both trusting and mystical:

> Then as I walked along I began to think about Kitty: not to think anything special about her, but rather perhaps simply to think her, as a mystic thinks God, with a thought which goes beyond thinking and becomes being.
>
> (p. 293)

He perceives the quest she sets him on, the healing of Gunnar, with the intensity of a religious mandate, and finds himself capable of being slighted and used according to her command. At the end of the first cold interview with Gunnar, Hilary sees the whole thing as an illustration of his desperate life: 'The whole extraordinary business was over. And I was back where I belonged, where my childhood had condemned me to be, alone, out in the cold without a coat' (p. 269). But at Kitty's behest he tries again, obeying her in spite of the logical moral promptings which should make him act in another way.

Kitty's power over Hilary, even more strongly than Crystal's religious significance for him, illustrates something awry in his perception, and indeed his history is a showing forth of a trapped man idealistically endowing the objects of his perception with a symbolic power which his cynical surface belies. Murdoch projects a complete psychology here: Hilary as narrator leads us to a fully realized sense of his motivation as he limns his entrapment in a long established personality in which hatred and love, lying capriciously close together, struggle to be expressed equally. The source of both is inescapably established in Hilary's childhood from which, a true Peter Pan, he wills ferociously not to break free. The blind rage which had killed Anne and which emerges whenever he is crossed began with his boyhood badness – kicking apart flower gardens, trying to burn down the orphanage, attacking Aunt Bill – and keeps surfacing in his present. The piques of Peter Pan are very much Hilary's, as are Peter's underground world and the dreams of Never-Never Land.

The process of the novel is a process of unfolding that psychology and describing the events which jar him from the patterned rigidity that continues to imprison him. As he sees it, the great motive of change is Gunnar's reappearance in his life, and hence a revival of the long-past affair with its attendant guilt and destruction. A revival is hardly necessary, however, since Hilary daily lives the whole fiasco in his resentment and now habitual crushing of talent and ambition. Anne's death has given him an excuse for not progressing from an already established pattern of misery and rage, a too narrow apprehension of the world epitomized by his narrow interest in words and language. As his intelligence and the examination system were beginning to allow him an access to change, his wild love of Anne disrupted and expanded his narrow hopes; failure in that love drove him back to hatred and destruction, and his life's pattern was fixed. Murdoch's use of the London Underground, especially the Inner Circle route, is marvellously apropos of this character, who rides round and round the Circle route just as his mind circles and circles the routes so often travelled, which he, in despair, acknowledges to be absolutely his and infinitely repeatable.

Despite the circularity of his personality's travels, Hilary also manages by sheer force of events to change somewhat – but in a surprising way and not through the route of Gunnar's re-entry into his life and the exciting role Lady Kitty subsequently lays upon him. The first major breakthrough comes from Crystal, who, on hearing of Gunnar's return and Kitty's interference, decides to tell Hilary that she had slept with Gunnar the night after Anne's death. Her revelation in effect changes the past, breaking the rigidity and certitude Hilary has so mightily maintained: ' "Don't Crystal, you're killing me." It was indeed as if some bond with childhood had been broken, some bond which had lasted crazily preternaturally long, some innocence' (p. 256). Hilary sees himself and Crystal as lost in a maze – the maze of a sophisticated world for which by their deprived background and lower-class status they are unfit. He describes them as babes in the wood ('How lost, in what a wood' p. 182), lost in a situation based on his incurable 'cosmic trouble' (p. 109). Both feel that they must tread carefully to avoid losing each other, but in fact this loss is one of the healthy outcomes of the tale. From Crystal's confession to the moment when Hilary decides firmly not to tell her of his responsibility in Kitty's death, there is a gradual alienation, a feeling of separation which allows Crystal finally to marry Arthur.

Crystal's confession leads to another change as well, which does much to illuminate the closed-off areas of Hilary's psychology. Clifford Larr, a successful senior colleague at Whitehall, is a closet homosexual with a secret social arrangement with the unsuccessful Hilary. Hilary has allotted him Monday nights, and goes there to eat gourmet food (as he does on Thursdays at the

Impiatts') which he despises as part of the sophisticated world he and Crystal are forever shut out of. When Hilary visits Crystal, they doggedly eat English stodge at its most adamantly lower-class level, and when poor Crystal finds some nice bread at the health food store, Hilary loses his temper at her for getting something too grand, for breaking a rule. Food, which is a key in Murdoch's work (see also *The Sea, The Sea*), is here used with a comic structural genius which transcends its reality. Clifford knew Hilary at Oxford, knows about the Jopling affair, presented Christopher Cather to Hilary as a lodger for his flat and is obviously in love with Hilary. A man of stringent and discriminating aesthetic tastes, Clifford had nevertheless in the past treated poor Crystal kindly and was rewarded by her prompt falling in love with him. He withdrew fastidiously from the situation, but retained an ideal of Crystal as a virgin which he uses with puerile insistence as he argues against her marrying the unacceptable Arthur.

Hilary's relationship with Clifford is occluded and carefully not examined while it lasts. There is some hand-holding and a great deal of talk, with Clifford playing the role of confidant and advisor while Hilary declines to question him about his own obviously unhappy past. The signet ring which Clifford wears on a chain around his neck as an amulet commemorating a great lost love remains after his death, with Hilary quite ignorant of the story which had so attenuated the life of his already melancholic friend. As Hilary recounts absolutely everything in his much too exciting relationship with the Joplings to the sardonic Clifford, he is often driven to the brink of rage by the cool, dry, incisive responses he receives, but he is quite unable to understand the relationship, or Clifford's occasional vengeful outbursts. Murdoch thus very tellingly indicates Hilary's emotional limitations, his egomaniacal self-concentration which closes him off from any proper reading of the nature of human love; as Clifford puts it:

> 'Can't you understand human conversation? Can't you *read* it, can't you read *me*? I should have thought it would be easy enough.' He touched the side of my head gently.
> 'All right. Sorry.' This sort of thing had happened before.          (p. 281)

Clearly, Hilary's concentration on himself, his refusal to read other people or see them whole, and the narrow possessiveness of his love are the constituent elements of his destructiveness, and Clifford's case is particularly poignant. Irritated by Clifford and by a situation that appears to be closing in on him, Hilary tells him of Crystal's lost virginity, driving the idealist into a rage which Hilary should have foreseen. Rage countering rage, Hilary runs after Clifford who has gone to confront Crystal with the name of whore, bashes him against the wall, and tries to comfort a devastated Crystal. His physical and verbal violence lead directly to the much-threatened suicide of his friend, with the result that at the end of the action, with Crystal ignorant of his complicity in Kitty's death, he has no confidant and must face his guilt with an awful loneliness. Had he been able to read the situation from Crystal's point of view, or from Clifford's, much pain and Clifford's death could have been spared, but his actions point to a fatal insensitivity, an utter inability to concentrate, as Crystal's quotation from *Philippians* would enjoin, on things that are true, honest and just.

Clifford's is the most dramatic but not the only case of Hilary's failure to see the quality of what he is dealing with. In spite of her strange behaviour, he is astonished to find that Laura Impiatt thinks he is in love with her, nor does he see anything potentially dangerous or revengeful in the tiresome but insistent love which Tommy bears him. When a very minor character like Christopher's friend, Jimbo, brings him a cross or a plant, he is merely puzzled by the generosity, and as he flirts with Biscuit he fails to realize how quickly human hearts are given and what she might hope for from him.

But at Clifford's death enough has happened to allow for some greater transformation than the death of Kitty and the awful playing-out of a reiterated drama with Gunnar have accomplished. I do not intend to imply, of course, that Kitty's death and the circular re-enactment of Hilary's and Gunnar's destructive cycle have no serious effect. For one thing, the 'days' end; after that fatal Tuesday, there are no more quasi-chapters labelled 'Thursday', 'Friday', 'Saturday', etc.: 'It was later, later, later. There were no more days. I was pressing my key into the door of Clifford Larr's flat in Lexham Gardens' (p. 377). This late eight-page section is extremely well handled: Tuesday, the last of the 'days', had left Hilary and Kitty in the freezing water of the Thames, in one of Murdoch's typically intense and convincing descriptions of extremely dangerous, physical, panic-laden di-lemmas. Hilary's seeking out Clifford now, it becomes clear, involves his need for the companionship and clarity that only his friend can give him after Kitty's death, of which we now hear. Hilary obviously has not thought about Clifford since the Monday preceding that death when the scene with Crystal had taken place, and with his usual insensitivity he comes to see Clifford blithely forgetting the violence of that scene in the more brilliant light of his own new and dreadful misery. His shock on hearing that Clifford has committed suicide pushes him further into pain, and into a far deeper realiza-tion of guilt than that which he had experienced before:

> I sat in St Stephen's Church crying for Clifford as I had not cried for Kitty, and just then his death seemed even more awful than hers. Crystal had seen Kitty as a *femme fatale* luring me to my doom. In fact I had lured Kitty to her doom as I had lured Anne. But the world's will had mingled in our loves and the purest of chances had been present at those deaths. I could at least see that much now. Clifford had died differently, he had died of being unloved and uncared for, as if the door had been shut upon him on a cold night.
>
> (p. 380)

Hilary acknowledges that Clifford's actual death could have been part of a drama other than his, but he recognizes his own responsibility as well as his real failure, which goes beyond the deaths of Kitty and Anne: his failure to love adequately and see clearly.

At the moment of Clifford's cousin's announcement of his death, Hilary's eyes fall on the Indian miniatures he had always admired and had jokingly asked Clifford to leave to him in his will:

> 'I see. He – often said he would –' I stood for a moment looking through the drawing-room door at the miniatures lined up, leaning against the wall: the princess on the terrace watching the thunderstorm, the prince leaving his mistress in the moonlight, two girls of transcendent beauty striding through a garden, a girl rather like Biscuit braiding her hair. Presumably they were on their way to the sale room.                                     (p. 378)

These coveted miniatures elegantly image the contrasting frameworks of reality and mythology which have been so jumbled in Hilary's mind, and which are joined in the smoothly flowing details of Biscuit's personality. The romantic scenes of the miniatures, the frozen moments of beauty they represent, are part of a mythologized pictorial world to which Biscuit occasionally belongs – when, for example, she appears as a mysterious shadow seeking him for unknown magical reasons, when she appears with Kitty on horseback in Kensington Gardens, when Hilary and she happily play leap-frog together, when she stands in a golden brown sari with a hairbrush beside splendid Kitty in front of the Cheyne Walk fireplace. The source of Biscuit's mythology is Kitty herself, who with her rich charm and games of power appears to Hilary as a transcedent being, not the spoiled rich girl Arthur and Clifford see. And of course the real Biscuit, in her duffle coat, a lovely half-Indian dreaming of a man to carry her off to a romantic world where she can be free of servitude and establish her own mythology, is something far different from the world these miniatures so romantically, dreamily and unrealistically evoke.

Clifford's death finally separates Hilary from such images and mythologies. He does not now, as he did on Anne's death, resolve to create another cycle of misery in which he acts the central role, although he knows that he is not immune to such a cycle:

> I was older, I lacked the recklessness of youth and its generosity. When I was in the cold Thames I soon forgot about Kitty. The deepest me who knew of no one else was desperate to survive. The middle-aged are more careful of themselves. Would such a desperation, or such a mean carefulness, now at last and in this more awful need, guard me from the self-destruction to which I had earlier doomed myself? . . . Certainly I could better measure now, what had been invisible to me then except as a provocation to rage,

the amount of sheer accident which these things, perhaps all things, contained. Then I had raged at the accidental but had not let it in any way save me from my insistence upon being the author of everything. Now I saw my authorship more modestly and could perhaps move in time towards forgiving myself, forgiving them all. (p. 382)

Most importantly, this rumination takes place in St Stephen's Church in Gloucester Road, the church where, Clifford had told him, T. S. Eliot had served for many years as a church-warden. Hilary's contemplation of all of the deaths, including that of Mr Osmand, his teacher from long ago who first turned loving attention to him, is intermingled with the memory of Eliot's greatest achievement, the words and ideology of *Four Quartets*. This eight-page section or chapter of *A Word Child* concludes with a meditation which uses a combination of lines from that work to reflect back on the substance of the novel and on the progress of Hilary's being:

There was . . . a memorial tablet which asked me to pray for the repose of the soul of Thomas Stearns Eliot. How is it now with you, old friend, the intolerable wrestle with words and meanings being over? Alas, I could not pray for your soul any more than I could for Clifford's. You had both vanished from the catalogue of being. But I could feel a lively gratitude for words, even for words whose sense I could scarcely understand. If all time is eternally present all time is unredeemable. What might have been is an abstraction, remaining a perpetual possibility only in a world of specula-tion. (pp. 383–4)

In this novel where every work of art mentioned is weighed against the context of action, this passage takes on particular relevance: a giant step has been taken from *Hassan* and *Peter Pan* to the adult and profound recognitions of temporality in the *Four Quartets*, and Hilary for the first time is capable of seeing words as the vehicle of profound meaning, meaning that bears directly on his own misperceptions and now painfully increased knowledge. Not only has he escaped the bondage of his 'days', but words break out of their narrow bondage into the world of poetic statement.

Much earlier, in an argument over *Peter Pan*, Hilary had responded to Arthur in this interchange:

'It's better not to explain', said Arthur. 'Poetry is best of all. Who wouldn't rather be a poet than anything else. Poetry is where words end.'
'Poetry is where words begin.' (p. 88)

Ideas of circularity, the eternality of time, the equivalence of ending and beginning, the absolute value and elusiveness of words and a breakthrough into Julian of Norwich's ecstatic 'Sin is behovely, but all shall be well and all shall be well and all manner of things shall be well', all are rooted in Eliot's poem as they are in the substance of this novel, and the graduation from *Peter*

*Pan* to *Four Quartets* which illustrates the progress of the novel is one of Murdoch's most ingenious devices. Far from breaking in on the fiction, this reference to Eliot pulls together at a pivotal point a great deal of the novel's earlier material.

During the action, Hilary has two distinct accesses to the usefulness of reality and honest estimation: conversations with Arthur, and his LSD trip in which he comes up with the cosmic equation that forgiving equals being forgiven, an equation which during his more cynical, rational hours looks impossible. The LSD trip also brings him the words of both Julian (all shall be well, etc.) and Mr Osmand, the schoolmaster, the first to have loved him and who had taught him to conjugate the Latin verb *amare*, to love. The ecstatic love he turns towards this poor man during his drug experience is unfortunately obscured by the attendant craziness of that trip, and is another sorry example of the primary, accidental nature of the universe; sadly, this visit, which for Mr Osmand had been a desperate cry for help, has no effect on saving the man's life, nor does the illumination of the drug carry over redemptively into Hilary's life.

The equation of reconciliation and forgiveness is joined to Arthur's injunctions, but both are too simple-minded for the maze-trapped Hilary, who perceives the accuracy of such statements only much later, after the frantic cycle is over. Arthur's argument is indeed humble, and has much of the inarticulateness characteristic of someone like Tallis trying to describe the good:

> All right, I don't believe in God either. But I think one should try to stick to simplicity and truth. There may be no God, but there's decency and – and there's truth and trying to stay there, I mean to stay in it, in its sort of light, and trying to do a good thing and to hold onto what you know to be a good thing even if it seems stupid when you come to do it. You could help yourself and Crystal, you could help him, but it can only be done by holding onto the good thing and believing in it and holding on, it can only be done sort of – simply – without any dignity or – drama – or – magic –
>
> (p. 290)

One is also reminded of the reiterated need to abjure magic which recurs in Murdoch's fictions, and of Crystal's quotation from *Philippians*, 'Whatsoever things are true, whatsoever things are honest . . ., think of these things.' Keeping attention fixed on the high quality of truth is the only possible way out, as Arthur sees so clearly and as only bitter pain can teach Hilary.

Arthur is ineffectual as an agent of the good because of the power he allows Hilary over his life, and indeed one of Murdoch's strongest ways of getting across the quality of Hilary's character is her portrayal of his tyranny over others. She describes both Crystal and Tommy as watching him as dogs watch their masters for any hint of rage or disapproval; Arthur and Crystal start up guiltily from hand-holding when Hilary comes into the room; Tommy leaves Crystal's before her tiny allotted time is up because she has displeased him and received the slight nod which inexorably means her dismissal. Arthur argues but gives in, is plunged from elation to despair by Hilary giving or withholding his permission for him to marry Crystal, but persists with his sympathy and desire for reconciliation, even when he finds it hard completely to forgive, as he does after Hilary has insulted Crystal.

This humble character who points so clearly towards the good is interesting in that he acquiesces completely in order to achieve the possible happiness of family life and a bright future, something very rare in Murdoch but something Arthur and Crystal may earn through their discipline and humility.

Nevertheless, the tearful wedding which constitutes a closure of a sort absolutely ends the pattern of Hilary's life dependency on Crystal's suffering as a reinforcement of his own, and is, in this sense at least, a real closure. The future remains uncertain, and Tommy's final admission that she had written to Gunnar about Kitty and Hilary compounds the irony of fate and accident which comprises so much of the novel's action. Tommy's insistence that she will marry him meets teasing ambiguity from Hilary, who, unredeemed but a bit wiser, moves forward to an uncertain future where anything could happen, where old patterns from the past are broken into but not defeated, where cycles and circularity may or may not dominate.

Two structural features of this novel must be mentioned before leaving it: the intense and complex life of the Whitehall office is magnificently described and full of detail – the 'Room' Hilary shares with the superbly satirized Edith Whicher and Reggie Farbottom, kind Skinker the tea man, Arthur in his closet, the whole system of breaks, games and note-writing, the watchful presence of Big Ben, the carefully maintained hierarchy. Reminiscent of the SELIB offices of *The Flight from the Enchanter* or the Whitewall of *The Nice and the Good*, the atmosphere here resonates with a debasing comic reality which attaches itself to the mediocrity of Hilary's life. The other feature is the choric effect of the rock song 'Waterbird', with which Christopher and his former friends had made a brief reputation during the fly-by-night life of their rock group. Christopher, with his phony, paperback Buddhism, forms a constant frivolous periphery to most of the tale, and this silly song of loss and betrayal is a flimsy shadow of the real loss of Anne and finally Kitty, who becomes, ironically and sadly, the real waterbird of the novel as she loses her life in the icy Thames.

I have of necessity been parsimonious in talking about this superbly constructed novel, and indeed as I write about mature Murdoch, I must acknowledge my reluctant limitations. Yet for all its excellence, *A Word Child* pales somewhat beside the successes of *The Sacred and Profane Love Machine*, a bitter account of a man who gets away with everything, and, unlike Hilary

Burde, is not forced by fate and circumstances to live a life of remorse of the sort Hilary describes when everything lies in ruins around him:

> I had spoilt my talents and made myself a slave, not because I sincerely regretted what I had done, but because I ferociously resented the ill-luck which had prevented me from 'getting away with it'. What had impressed me really was not the crime itself but the instant and automatic nature of the first retribution, the loss of Oxford, my 'position' and the fruits of my labour. If I had indeed got away with it I could perhaps have recovered.
>
> (p. 381)

Blaise Gavender's commitment to mediocrity triumphs in a life which, unlike Hilary's, never even glances at the possibilities of open access to something better.

★

The process of reading *The Sacred and Profane Love Machine* (1974) is quite different from that of either *A Word Child* (1975) or *An Accidental Man* (1971). The latter two tend to hold in focus the central, titular male character, whereas *The Sacred and Profane Love Machine* only at first glance centres on the double loves of Blaise Gavender. Its deep structure is much more ambiguous, richly supplied with dualities and choices for sets of characters for whom the terms sacred and profane have extended meanings. Only because Blaise Gavender is so obviously caught between two women, Emily McHugh and his wife Harriet, does his problem appear to be the central issue; but while reading the novel the reader is more powerfully connected to the mourning Montague Small by all sorts of authorial devices. To put it another way, Blaise carries the external structure of the work while Monty dominates its internal rhythms.

The idea of doubling goes beyond Harriet-Emily and Blaise-Monty to include: the two sons, David and Luca; the two products of Monty's artistic imagination, Milo Fane and Magnus Bowles; Monty's two love-hate objects, the dead Sophie and Edgar Demarnay; and the two vaguely symbolic women, Pinn and Kiki St Loy. Every character apparently feels at every moment that he or she has a choice of love object, but the quality of decision is strained and contorted by surface caprice or deep subconscious will into directions not easily foreseen. As the characters live their actions they see their sense of choice as life-giving, redemptive and necessary; when choice is withdrawn, as it is from poor loving Harriet – who is progressively rejected, first by Blaise, by her second choice, Monty, by Edgar, by the children and finally by the fictional Magnus Bowles through his putative suicide – the result is despair and entry into a dark and desperate reality where the personality has no resources whatever. As in the case of *An Accidental Man*, the reader is kept in a confusing, negative world where exits close as the action proceeds, and the triumphs of such characters as Blaise and Emily are morally appalling.

The most important duality at the base of the novel springs from its concentration on the internal life as opposed to the lived, active external surface of life at Hood House, Locketts and Emily's two flats. A complete master of the ruminative style, Murdoch here combines external realism with the revelations of the subconscious displayed by dreams, and mixes both with moral and religious thought and symbolism. Considerably earlier in her career, in *The Italian Girl*, she had played an elaborate Freudian game with comic dream sequences, and dreams are often used in her other fictions, but here she endows them with an extended power of reflection on the characters who experience them. Each major character is introduced only very briefly in the external action, but with a detailed and fascinating dream which is both reflective of his psyche and subject to extended future variations as the dream life of the characters is reiterated through the pages of the fiction. David's dream pattern involves fish; Harriet begins with an intuitive dream of an illuminated child's face; Blaise dreams of a Freudian snake; Emily dreams of cat butchery; and Monty, whose inner life is most fully examined, first dreams of a piteous baby monster mourning its decapitated mother.

The inclination towards the violent or frightening in all these dreams reflects the terrifying levels of the unconscious which are appallingly open to these characters, who desperately try to ignore them and live on the quotidian surface of things. The psychoanalyst, Blaise, experiences the simplest and most transparent dreams, and reduces them all to his professional knowledge of the 'muck-heap' of human minds. Bored with listening to too many neurotic patients, he feels that dreams have lost all power to interest or move him, and indeed his job has made him a creature of the surface, a facile analyst who, as Monty discovered very quickly after a few psychoanalytic sessions with him, links everything to everything too quickly and easily. A practical therapist, he sees very little of the mystery of human personality and is merely an explicator of the characters who come to him. When he needs a more complex vision, as in the creation of Magnus Bowles, he goes to Monty, the artist, to receive the creation in steady installments as he requires them.

Monty's areas of contrast to Blaise are extensive, but the most interesting is that of dreams. Monty not only has the most haunting and varied dreams of any of the dream-ridden characters in this novel, but he is also capable of creating a necessary fictional person whose neuroses are carried almost entirely by the elaborate images of a complex dream life. Invented to cover Blaise's frequent absences from Harriet due to his *sub rosa* life with his mistress Emily, Monty's Magnus Bowles is conceived novelistically, chapter by chapter or dream by dream, as Monty creates new apparitions to fit the madness of what Harriet is supposed to accept as her husband's most difficult and incurable patient. Since Blaise spends a night a week with Emily, Magnus must exist in weekly instalments, and his continuous creation keeps Monty entertained even during his hard times of mourning for his dead wife, Sophie. Harriet receives these instalments from Blaise, forever unaware that she is responding to a fiction rather than a reality, as she indeed is in her whole relationship with her husband before the Emily revelation. The abyss that opens before her, therefore, would suggest that there is no secure external reality at all.

Magnus's most discussed dream is that he 'was a huge white egg floating in a sea of turquoise blue, and he was everything that was' (p. 91). Harriet sees it as a graphic and beautiful dream, whereas Blaise, with his usual tedious psychoanalytic slickness, associates it with compulsive eating and castration fears. But the most interesting commentary comes indirectly a few pages later, as Harriet talks to the Greek scholar, Edgar Demarnay, about his work on early Greek poets and pre-Socratic philosophers; in describing some of the earliest philosophic ideas, Edgar has this exchange with her:

> 'Parmenides thought that nothing really existed except one changeless object. And Empedocles thought that Love could fuse everything in the universe into a spherical god which did nothing but think.'
> 'That sounds like Magnus Bowles's white egg.' (p. 101)

The Empedoclean sphere of love and thought represents a pure ideal which sails away from the ken of any of these characters; they can hardly even perceive it as an ideal. Actually the image of Magnus's egg is a projected symbol of Monty's own half-conscious mind, and represents his separation, his intense, inescapable and dreadful concentration on his own mind and his self-enclosed solipsism.

The image is also playful, of course – a charming fancy made to amuse himself, his sardonic audience Blaise, and his innocent audience Harriet, as are all the accounts of Magnus Bowles's behaviour and dreams. In shocking contrast to these are Monty's own dreams, which haunt him as perceivable images even when he is not asleep. Most of them involve apparitions of the dead Sophie dressed as a nun, as a bride, as a wraith – young, old, terrified, mourning, in tears. When awake, he sees her apparition in mirrors, and in the whole dream pattern Murdoch subtly indicates an almost ghost-like aspect which is always close to intruding on reality. Locketts, the house Sophie and Monty shared and where Sophie died, is almost, if not literally, haunted by her presence, and Murdoch, by exploring Monty's conscious mind and his dream material, extends the atmosphere so successfully that the borderline between natural and supernatural wavers and becomes obscure. The reader is put into a strange and interesting position in terms of this issue, for he may choose to read it simply as Monty's spontaneous expression of guilt and remorse (the Blaise method of simplification) or allow it to extend into the mysterious reaches of psychic energy which I am convinced this novel is primarily exploring.

Many of the Sophie manifestations are only momentarily connected to her ghostly presence, as for example when Edgar, very early in the novel, thinks he hears her voice as he rummages in her desk looking for letters, only to find that it is Monty playing a tape of it. But the most significant manifestations occur when a conjunction of external reality and internal energy creates an eerie sense of mysterious realms lurking beneath the controlled quotidian. I am not of course suggesting that Murdoch is telling a ghost story or that this is, in effect or intention, a gothic novel, but she is, certainly, expanding perception and depicting the more awesome and terrifying reaches of the mind. One striking conjunction of external and internal images occurs when Monty dreams of Sophie standing like a priestess over him, only to wake and find that a woman is indeed there. It turns out to be Constance Pinn, who has come to seduce him if possible, and as she carries on in her attempt, her rather crass reality is suddenly dramatically contrasted to the ghostly image, seen by Monty in the mirror, of Sophie weeping in her wedding-gown.

Even more successful is the sudden haunting of a distraught and despairing Harriet by the spirit of Sophie, who could not, at the moment of haunting, be further from her mind. As Harriet, after Monty's cruel rejection, despondently wanders from room to room at Locketts, she suddenly hears Sophie's voice. The reader is aware that it is again the tape, this time being played for Edgar Demarnay, but for Harriet it is an echo of pure terror which attaches itself to a further eerie phenomenon:

> Harriet listened carefully and then with cold incredulous horror recognized that unique inimitable sound. It was Sophie's voice. Harriet ran to the door, ran back again. What had Monty done? Had he conjured up a ghost, had he that power? She was half willing to believe it. Or was Sophie really not dead but hidden somewhere in the house? Was that why Monty was so strange? Utter terror took hold of Harriet and she wailed with it. She ran out of her bedroom onto the landing and listened more intently. Now she heard Edgar's voice, Monty's voice, nothing more. Had she imagined that awful sound? Was she going mad at last?
>
> She stood in the darkness holding her heart. Then suddenly from below there was a strange wailing cry. And as Harriet stood there motionless with fear, it was as if a wind blew through the house, as if an airy shape passed through, passed by, and Harriet felt cold, cold. Something very cold and frightful seemed to have passed through the house and touched her in passing.
>
> (p. 269)

Harriet's sensation of coldness and her fear are traditional responses to ghosts, but Murdoch's double handling of the situation increases its subtlety. The reality of the tape, the ordinariness of Monty's and Edgar's voices and

Harriet's own overwrought state are part of another atmosphere, that of the genuine emotional complexity and tension of the confused Locketts situation. In sharp contrast to this realism are the wind, the airy shape of something passing and the cold. On the one hand, the ghostly passing can be seen as a release of psychic energy through Monty's confession to Edgar – the passing of a false object of attention, held too long and too absolutely in Monty's mind and now released, as are his tears; Harriet picks up this release as a curious embodiment and also feels the cold which has damagingly been held too tightly at the centre of Monty's personality. On the other hand, the manifestation can be seen as a ghostly essence that even an outsider like Harriet can perceive, something to do with the objective reality of the supernatural that reflects a psychic eavesdropping on the dreaming inner world of others.

This complex incident parallels an earlier, carefully placed literary backdrop designed to enhance the sad distance between dream and reality. Considerably earlier in the novel, a greatly confused and miserable young David Gavender had read from a Greek text of the *Iliad* open on Monty's desk the account of Achilles' attempt to embrace the ghost of Patroclus:

> 'even for a little while let us embrace each other and satisfy our hearts with grieving.' So saying he reached out his hands, but could not clasp him. The spirit like a vapour fled away beneath the earth, gibbering faintly. (p. 176)

This literary evocation helps define Monty's haunting by Sophie, a haunting so powerful that Harriet in her anguish picks it up, and it also parallels David's mourning for the innocence and happiness of his former life. His tears after reading this 'terrible image of bereavement and loss, winged by beauty' are very much connected to all the tears that flow in this novel, tears reflecting the loss and deprivation of loved or desired centres that are seen most poignantly through haunting ghosts, dreams and sustained fictions, which are all illusory and which all adamantly indicate the distance of all desires from the seeking soul. Images reflecting loss and separation attach themselves to and haunt the dreaming psyche, and the oceanic sense of mystery thus evoked holds this novel apart from and considerably beyond the controlled conceptual frames which the reader may through habit wish to apply.

Monty as a character remains instructive of the architecture of the novel, for his dream world is not limited to Sophie, and its extensions illustrate how broadly based and freely drifting Murdoch's conception of this and other characters really is. His affecting first dream of the weeping baby monster presents a desolate inner landscape in which even the monstrous reflects grief, and where the only beauty lies in the pictorial dream-tears themselves, described here as seed-pearls, elsewhere as beautiful crystals, and presented consistently throughout the novel as aesthetic objects. It is interesting that the reader's sympathy attaches to Monty through this image of dead and mourn-ing monsters, for Monty himself will prove a considerable monster in the subsequent action. Yet this novel is devoted to forgiveness of monsters – if only because so little else survives in the world. Thus Edgar at the end of the novel comforts a bereft David by urging that he refrain from judgement, that he forgive and be merciful to his father and Emily as they wipe out the traces of his beloved mother and build a snug, smug nest for themselves. Edgar, who carries with him the signposts of the good, will soon have to handle and forgive Monty's last piece of monstrous behaviour, but there can be little doubt of his capacity to do so after this conversation with David.

The same conversation reflects importantly on Monty in that David, extremely uneasy over his fading childhood image of Jesus, complains of his incapacity to pray or manage any contact with Christ, which would be a reversion to a childhood form taught him by Harriet and potentially able to help him through this crisis. Edgar argues that any address to Jesus may be primitive but:

> If it's natural to you to cry out 'Christ help me!' cry it and then be quiet. You may be helped. . . . That sort of truth is local too. I don't mean any relativism nonsense. Of course there's science and history and so on. I mean just that one's ordinary tasks are usually immediate and simple and one's own truth lives in these tasks. Not to deceive oneself, not to protect one's pride with false ideas, never to be pretentious or bogus, always to try to be lucid and quiet. There's a kind of pure speech of the mind which one must try to attain. To attain it is to be in the truth, one's own truth, which needn't mean any big apparatus of belief. And when one is *there* one will be truthful and kind and able to see other people and what they need.   (p. 314)

This fundamental Murdoch argument is not only a generous salve for the confused boy, but also a complete contrast to Monty's religious aspirations. When David asks whether any of Edgar's arguments about Christ had been discussed with Monty, Edgar replies, 'Yes, but – Monty is so ambitious. I daresay he's right to be for him' (p. 314). Monty's spiritual ambitions are indeed great, and again his dream visions are useful in marking his awareness of his manifold failures. One especially striking dream of spiritual limitation and failure involves a symbolic test in which he is asked to perform the apparently simple task of scooping up water in his hands, only to find that even this has a mysteriously correct mode that he is too unsaintly, too alienated from the true path, to perform. Hence he fails the test, and although he can smile ironically about it the next day, it marks his strong conviction of the hopelessness of the spiritual task.

In Monty's life, his failure as Sophie's husband represents his defeat in the profane world, a world in which his jealousy and tyrannical urge to power

destroyed their happiness and caused him to lose any capacity he might have
had to see her or her actions clearly. Because Sophie was completely secular
and lacked the religious component so powerful in Monty's make-up, he
assumed her separation from his spiritual aspirations; he is therefore astounded by her dream hauntings. While alive, she had mocked his non-
secular attempts, and his meditative techniques, although technically effective, remain spiritually sterile. Afflicted by a sense of failed spiritual vocation,
Monty is aware that the mechanical meditative disciplines by which he had
hoped to get rid of the ego have become mere exercises:

> He knew at least enough to know that this, in his case, was merely an
> experience. However much his technique might improve the enlightening
> spirit was absent. Except in dreams he had no teacher. It would have been,
> he felt, artificial, another occasion for lying. No, Monty did not imagine
> that he had, by his pains, won anything of value. He had not even glimpsed
> his freedom. The obsessions which made Magnus Bowles's life a misery
> simply travelled with him like dormant viruses. The gods, who had
> nothing to do with enlightenment, unplacated, undefeated, were still
> there.                                                          (p. 106)

Monty resists the idea that the profane and sacred might be closer together,
and instead of trusting either Sophie and their mutual love in the past, or
Edgar with his promise of conversations at Mockingham in the present, he
exits bitterly into a world of continued mediocrity, indicated by more Milo
Fane novels.

The quality of his exit is transmitted through his letter to Edgar, in which
he aggressively attacks Edgar's moral persistence and human connectedness:

> I have never, I think, impressed upon you how almost impossible I find it
> to communicate with anybody. . . . There are dull areas of egoism and
> failure which have no resonance and reflect no light. Such are my loneli-
> nesses, which I once thought that Sophie might cure . . . . Your nervous
> desire for intimacy and communion of souls, your urge to sidle up close and
> gaze into eyes and whisper into ears, has always filled me (excuse me, dear
> Edgar) with a disgust which prompted in turn the brutality which you
> have so suffered, deplored and enjoyed. I regard your blundering kindness
> and officious desire to 'understand' me simply as a rude trespass upon the
> fastidious integrity of my being. Your moral style sets my teeth on edge,
> just as your soggy so-called religion makes me want to vomit.    (p. 320)

For Monty, the utter inability to connect, as well as the failures of religion,
philosophy (the 'doubling of an already double world', p. 106), meditation
and ordinary, humble human relationships are conditions of a life which
shows no trust in any route, a life so set on denying the false and too easily
debased routes that it cannot follow any at all. His exit to Italy to visit the

television actor who plays Milo Fane, and his probable intention to write more murder mysteries about his attenuated hero, represent a refusal to move forward, a miring of himself in the mediocre which seems, sadly, the only possibility for most characters in this novel.

Yet Edgar, with whom the novel ends, as women suddenly, comically converge on him, does not collapse, and in spite of his self-effacing nature fights back. Sadly aware that Harriet would still be alive had he not been caught in the enchantment of Monty's need for him, he reflects honestly on his situation: 'I preferred a ghost to reality, he thought; and yet I could not then have abandoned Monty, he held me in a grip of steel. O rapacious ruthless ghost!' (p. 323). Most importantly, he now perceives a de-mythologized Monty whose moral style need not be measured as superior to Edgar's own:

> No, thought Edgar, no, I may be in the Neva but I'm damned if I'll drown! If I ever believed in divine grace now is the time to make a grab for it. Every little thing matters, yes it does, and if Monty thinks it is greed and not love that says this, well Monty need not be right. Monty is simply a chap with his own troubles, a chap just like me after all. (p. 328)

Edgar's persistence in the point of view that loving attention to every detail constitutes his central task is the most positive thing in this novel, and since the book ends with his assertion and hope for 'innocent frivolous unimportant happiness once again in the world', the reader is wryly buoyed by Murdoch's comedic device.

Yet the merest flitting backwards of the reader's mind to the other character in the novel who apparently pointed to a selfless good breaks any positive pattern projected by Edgar's courage in the face of his rejection by Monty. Inured to heartbreak and repeatedly tried by fires of unrequited love, Edgar has learned to carry on, to go forward without self-pity, but Harriet Gavender with her placid life of loving attention to the people and things around her (she is described as rescuing every insect in a lettuce), depends on reciprocity and support. When she is forced to realize that Blaise has not only deceived her for years in his affair with Emily McHugh but now has chosen Emily above her, she enters another world from which her innocence and apparent goodness had previously kept her. As she explains to Monty, whom she wishes to force into a loving relationship, substituting him for Blaise, she must acknowledge a new dimension of the terrible before her real adult life can begin properly:

> 'You can't – I think – imagine,' said Harriet slowly, 'what it's like – to be me – now . . . . It seemed perfect, a kind of perfection anyway. I would never have needed to grow up and change and see the world as terrible, for it *is* terrible, it is terrible in its nature, in its essence, only sometimes one

can't see. Some people never see. *You* have always known this, and I knew
you knew, long ago, something I could not name in you attracted me, and
it was this, that you *knew*. As Blaise never did. Blaise pretended to. He
played at it with his patients, but he was too self-centred and too fond of
pleasure really to see it. Blaise has always lived in a dream world.' (p. 237)

Monty's haunting knowledge of the terrible is not useful to him, nor can
his knowledge join with Harriet's in the consoling fruition she wishes, but
Harriet herself has been forced to see the duality of the world for the first
time. As a result, she dredges up a structure for herself, creating a series of
mythologies as a substitute for what looked like the single, simple world of
her happy marriage to Blaise. Emily refers to the pre-revelation Harriet quite
correctly as Mrs Placid, and indeed her life of calm happiness, punctuated by
no anxieties beyond wishing her son David were not going through adolescent withdrawal and hoping Blaise would be able to go to medical school if it
is what he wants, appears to be absolute. Yet her opening dream of an
illuminated child's face shows an uncanny ability to read or intuit a much
broader and more frightening area of experience than her conscious mind
understands, and as Blaise himself notes, her night fears and compulsive
collecting of a vicious dog-pack indicate a subconscious area of knowledge
where the terrible lurks.

    A study of Harriet's progress through the action of this novel is illuminat-
ing, and it is significant that she is cut off as she is still developing. The reader
cannot help questioning what would have been possible, and the use of
completely outside agents in her death – unidentified terrorists shooting in
the Hanover airport for unidentified reasons – raises a question about the
workings of causality in this book. Generally in Murdoch's work the death of
characters, even when apparently accidental, is linked to a version of moral
causality and can be meditated upon within that compelling framework. But
in this case, the reader is still very absorbed in Harriet's activity within
despair, her ability to spawn plan after plan to keep herself, in spite of her
hysteria, afloat in the terrible world in which she now lives. The accidental
nature of her death is an indifferent external act which reminds the reader
how completely sheer chance can take over in a world which is entirely out of
the control of its inhabitants. On the surface, then, the machine-gunning of
Harriet is a casual act which goes no further in the moral realm than allowing
her a last, splendid, saintly act – covering the child Luca with her own body in
a moment of terrified bravery. But in the system of foreshadowing which so
skilfully binds together pieces of this fiction, Harriet's death has been subtly
prepared for and can be seen as a horrifying projection into the real world of
the inner wishes and feelings of Blaise and Emily. In Blaise's early remembrance of his affair with Emily he had wished Harriet dead, and Emily's final
joy in her death is quite undisguised; moreover, Emily in one of her intermin-

able early quarrels with Blaise says that she feels like a terrorist with a machine-gun. The early references prepare subtly for Harriet's death: externally it is capriciously and senselessly enacted by terrorists; internally and mysteriously it functions as another example of subconscious psychic projection, this time on the part of her husband and his mistress. Again, as so often in this novel, the eerie and uncanny enter obliquely into the ordinary world of action.

Harriet aligns herself from early on in the book with the idea of sainthood, and until she is tested her overload of love is an apparent good. Her natural moral companion is Edgar Demarnay, whose habituation to misery has advanced him beyond her in wisdom. After the disastrous drinks party during which Blaise defects to Emily's side, Edgar and Harriet are, not entirely ironically, described as pacing the room like Socrates being instructed by Diotima. Both of these characters are flawed however – Edgar in his blind desire to own Monty, Harriet in the very fact of never having been tested – and the process of Harriet's test presents Murdoch's dissection of spontaneous and unwilling frailty even in characters whose urge to love and be selfless is very highly developed. Harriet's first reaction to Blaise's revelation is to feel that the past has been absolutely changed but nevertheless to set in motion a machine for forgiveness which will put her, as she is soon forced to realize, into a position of power. She says exultantly that she feels she is living in a myth, and her tactics for survival do involve creating a mythological world with herself as mediator at the centre. Previously she had felt that she was living in a real world where Blaise, loved and trusted, held the centre, but now that the past has been destroyed, her creative fecundity spawns a new myth. When Blaise's final defection breaks the myth of her power to free and forgive, she creates a mythology of love and pain centred on Monty, then states herself willing to create one around Edgar. Finally she turns to and is foiled by the 'last one' – the genuinely mythical Magnus Bowles.

As Harriet is progressively stripped of mythology she is pushed closer and closer to the dreadful emptiness at the real centre of things, and forced to admit that the image of saint that she had nurtured in herself and that Blaise and Monty urge on her has been a chimera, a false role that she cannot play in the absence of loving supports. If she is rather vain about a possible access to sainthood, she is also confident of her ability to be magical; as Luca puts it: 'I love you. I saw you that night in the garden, and I knew you were magic like in dreams' (p. 160). A serious reader of Murdoch can see the signs of danger in this, but Harriet feeds fully on such images, and it is necessary to see too that demonic little Luca longs for a mythology to make his bizarre and ugly life more bearable. Harriet dies in flight to her soldier brother, Adrian, and it is noteworthy that her military father and brother had throughout her life represented a standard of behaviour against which she set her actions: 'She recalled Adrian saying, when some incident was being bemoaned, "but soldiers are supposed to be shot at, it's their job". Harriet was determined to stay upright now in the gunfire' (p. 131). Again, Murdoch foreshadows Harriet's death when her myth-building resources are running out and the casual gunfire of the external world cannot be stood against.

Harriet, who is so much a creature of love, concentrates particular attention on paintings, and although Murdoch's title most obviously calls up Titian's great painting in the Borghese Gallery in Rome, entitled since the end of the eighteenth century 'Sacred and Profane Love', Harriet's real attention falls on Giorgione's picture in the National Gallery in London of Saint Anthony and Saint George. The picture is compositionally parallel to the Titian, with two essential characters separated and held to their sides of the canvas by a central fulcrum which is relatively insignificant in itself, but on which Murdoch as authorial control in the case of the Titian, and Harriet as fictional commentator in the case of the Giorgione, concentrate sudden intense attention. In Titian's painting the figures of sacred and profane love (called in the seventeenth century *Beltà disornata e Beltà ornata*) are separated by a little boy (not quite a *putto*, but not unlike one) playing in a fountain. In Murdoch's fiction, Luca becomes this child and is invested with demonic drawing and separating powers which torment one woman and reward the other. In Harriet's apprehension of the Giorgione, her attention is drawn not so much to either saint, each of whom is busily performing his major saintly action, but to the tree which divides the canvas:

> There was a tree in the middle background which she had never properly attended to before. Of course she had seen it, since she had often looked at the picture, but she had never before felt its significance, though what that significance was she could not say. There it was in the middle of clarity, in the middle of bright darkness, in the middle of limpid sultry yellow air, in the middle of nowhere at all with distant clouds creeping by behind it, linking the two saints, yet also separating them and also being itself and nothing to do with them at all. (p. 41)

Feeling something prophetic in her peculiar interest in the tree and her inability to withdraw herself from the picture, Harriet, still ignorant of Blaise's double life, evinces still another proof of her intuitive nature.

The point of division between Blaise's two lives is much emphasized in this novel and takes many forms: metaphorically in the child in the Titian painting, the tree in the Giorgione or the bridge which divides Emily from Harriet, Putney from Blaise's habitual London; literally in the boy Luca, who bridges the division between his mother and Harriet, and in Blaise himself, the fulcrum on whom rests the life design of the two women. Throughout the years of his affair with Emily Blaise has successfully compartmentalized the two women, and the idea that Luca, a major separating figure, could also join the two in a single composition had not occurred to him, as it necessarily does after Luca's excursions to Hood House. The elegant beginning of this novel, with several characters looking at the strange, motionless boy in the garden, quietly flows into an identification of the mysterious alien as Luca, the uniting figure who also assists in the separation or alienation of the two women. The blurring of the distinction between union and separation, between singleness and doubleness which Luca gradually effects, is part of the progress of the novel. As Blaise puts it to Monty when he has just discovered Luca's secret and mysterious visits: '– it's the separation being – broken through –. . . . It's the two worlds, suddenly one sees – they're really – one world after all' (p. 109).

They are one world, one painting or canvas, only through the illusions of will created by Harriet and Blaise – Harriet in her moral urge to reconcile and unite, Blaise in his greedy attempt to have everything and get away with his self-serving duplicity. Blaise has long thought of himself as a man of two 'truths' – one external, open and good, symbolized by his happy marriage to Harriet and the existence of David as an ideal son; the other internal, secret and wicked, symbolized by his affair with Emily and the birth of the illegitimate, off-centre, demonic son Luca. Blaise's interpretation is simply and obviously the embodiment of the title, and as Murdoch explores his mind his faltering uncertainty about his real allegiance is seen as a struggle between internal and external, a repetition in almost too simple terms of the major pattern of this book. It is also a psychoanalytical presentation of Blaise's secretly powerful animal or sexual nature as opposed to his conscious moral behaviour. He mourns for his lost goodness where a steady allegiance to Harriet would have held him, and indeed she carries in her person the qualities that he recognizes as morally vital – goodness, love of the conventional Christian God, generosity, forgiveness. Emily on the other hand represents his interior self, and it is interesting that for him the sacred and profane are divided in much more coarse and simplified terms than they are for Monty. Blaise's internal self lacks any spiritual dimensions – such things have been explained away long since by his psychoanalytic habits of reduction – and is entirely concentrated on the sexual.

He and Emily have what they call a secret world of special things, unnamed devices to increase their sexual pleasure, and their absorbing, unimaginably peculiar sexual practices form the powerful bond between them. They are described as paired automatically and absolutely in physical essence (which for them constitutes soul) like animals in the Ark, and Emily in her shrill arguments with Blaise repeatedly accuses him of having lost faith too quickly in marrying Harriet, of betraying through the continuation of the marriage his true inner self which her own relationship with him celebrates. Reflecting on the quality of his relationship with Emily, Blaise thinks, 'Even at the first meeting he had felt . . . like an animal who had thought that just *his* sort of animal did not exist anywhere in the forest – and then had suddenly met one'

(p. 59). This sense of a common animal nature is paralleled by the image of the dark enclosed cupboard of his mind as opposed to Harriet's open sunniness. He had discovered in the affair with Emily that

> Sin was an awful private happiness blotting out all else; only it was not sin, it was glory, it was his good, his very own, manifested at last. This was the dark cupboard all right, only it was not dark, it was blazing with light and as large as the universe. Everything he had done before seemed feeble, shadowy, and insincere.                                         (pp. 59–60)

The loss of Harriet means his complete withdrawal into the morally unambitious and self-indulgent life he so obviously craves. Blaise, as the novel describes him after Harriet's death and his marriage to Emily, feels free and relieved, reduced to an inner world of fantasies, and utterly separated from the moral life.

Yet the two issues – that Blaise should so desperately wish to have both of the worlds represented by Emily and Harriet, and that he should settle down with such reprehensible self-satisfaction with his inner sexual being – are not presented in this novel as genuine puzzles or problems. Again the title is illuminating – for him the split between the sacred and profane is only a machine, and its mechanical nature is very much emphasized. By contrast, Edgar Demarnay too is troubled by sexual fantasies and spends much of his life in a state of unrequited love, but at the same time he is a man of genuine spiritual discipline. For him the choice of an inner life is not simply mechanical, although he sees and regrets his own machine-like qualities. He consciously makes distinctions of the sort that the coarser Blaise cannot handle or explains away with the typical ease of psychoanalysis. Whereas Edgar lives an external life in which internal urges have through pain been translated into coherent and, apart from the serious error with Monty, essentially generous actions, Blaise's fantasies damage many people. It is hard to believe in Blaise's genuine doubleness of spirit, and his obvious happiness after Harriet's death shows the degree to which the juggling of the two women had been a machine purring on conventionally in his psyche, even though he was not particularly interested in the extended disciplines it should have demanded.

Emily is fond of telling him that she is a Eurydice figure: 'You've killed me and sent me to hell, and you must descend to the underworld to find me and make me live again. If you don't come for me, I'll become a demon and drag you down into the dark.' (p. 81) Her whole complex of imagery – the underworld, the demonic and the world through the looking-glass (p. 221) – reflects Blaise's need to go inwards to dark hidden areas to find his real and predominantly sexual being. His descent to her hell is redemptive, and Emily's role as a demon pulling him to his dark nature is fiercely sustained throughout the novel. Blaise's descent to the underworld with Emily and his bringing her back to life limit his being, as does Monty's final reversion to the monstrous (which so consistently defines him throughout the fiction) in his treatment of Edgar and his escape to Italy and more bad detective fiction. At the end of the novel both men have chosen ease and mediocrity, and the double effect on the reader is devastating.

In spite of the title's surface applicability to Blaise, he is little more than a device, an expedient to plot and structure, whereas Monty dominates the mysterious and oceanic sense of the novel. Although each in his separate way reflects the contrast between the sacred and profane, the novel also suggests that Blaise represents the profane and Monty the sacred. Blaise knows himself to be an *homme moyen sensuel* (a common Murdoch type), though he has intellectual and moral ambitions beyond the type – and the choice between two women handily defines his limited inner life. Monty is much more complicated and even his choices are doubled and redoubled: between just estimation of Sophie and a fair acknowledgement of Edgar, in both of which he fails; between mediocre literary production and a life dedicated to spiritual or moral development; and in the crassest terms, between his fictional creations, Milo Fane and Magnus Bowles.

Although it is at most points difficult for the reader to sympathize much with Blaise, Monty's grief and self-knowledge make him more attractive, and through the warm and loving characters, Harriet and Edgar, Murdoch pulls us towards a hope of amelioration or change for him. In taking Monty to Mockingham, Edgar hopes not only for his own happiness but also for Monty to turn to serious fiction and eschew the frivolous, popularly successful Milo Fane murder mysteries. Emotionally, however, the reader is convinced that Monty's lived life, and the one that really counts, lies in his attempts and failures in human contact – with Sophie, Harriet, David and Edgar. His one open success, a brief afternoon in bed with Kiki St Loy, qualifies as success only in its uncomplicated brevity and its temporary usefulness in unlocking his too enclosed mind. This small relief fails to satisfy or console the reader who longs for more, and Monty's brutal withdrawal from the scene defines much of the unredeemed desolation with which this novel ends.

Blaise's activity, on the other hand, constitutes not only the most straightforward exemplification of the title, but also the progressive and continual sense of doubling in the novel; therefore in spite of his relative simplicity, his coarse-grained spirit and his essentially negative character, the book can rest structurally on his being. In a final brilliant doubling device, Murdoch ties together father and son, present and future, sexuality and destruction by two evocations of the Actaeon myth which illustrate the external working-out of internal, subconscious data. Blaise's Emily has cats, his Harriet dogs; compared to Harriet's growling and paranoid pack, Emily's animals look very domestic, and there is a curious crossing-over of the innocent and demonic. Harriet has collected her animals, as Blaise knows all too well, out of deeply concealed fear and as extensions of her highly intuitive nature. Like the hounds of Actaeon, they come to represent the demonic sexual reaches of Blaise's personality, and just as Harriet perceives that personality as innocent and love-worthy, so she interprets the dogs as receptacles of her love. Their potential viciousness eludes her, and she welcomes the night protection they afford, completely oblivious to their function as subconscious projections of Blaise's animal nature and her own desperate fears.

In the Actaeon myth, Actaeon the hunter comes upon Diana bathing, and his punishment for breaking unawares into her chaste concourse is to be changed into a stag and torn apart by his own hounds. In Murdoch's doubling of the reference, young David Gavender is the first to become Actaeon, taken secretly by the mysterious Pinn through heavy underbrush to a point where he can feast his eyes on seven bathing nymphs – girls from the special school where Emily had taught, Pinn now works and Kiki St Loy is a student. Kiki is David's Diana, and as he watches the naked girls in the fountain she becomes the centre of his inexperienced sexual desires and fantasies. He does not, however, play out the myth to its horrifying conclusion; instead the scene is presented as the first step in a sexual initiation to be completed by his going to bed with Pinn, minutes before Harriet's dogs go for Blaise. In this initiatory sequence Pinn plays a major part, as she obscurely does in the entire novel. As she appears to Blaise, Monty and David, she constantly identifies herself as a kind of priestess, a semi-sacred source of knowledge, transcending her char-woman origins. She is mysterious, meddlesome, irritating and often ironically right about situations, but her intrusions and phony mysticism are difficult to work into any realistic frame: she reminds me of the mysterious gypsy of *The Sandcastle* in being too peculiar, too obviously planted as a vehicle for extending the subconscious data. Nevertheless, in a novel so interested in varieties of demonism, her bizarre character works suprisingly well. She is there near the end of the book to show Monty's human failure and to identify him as a monster, and she is extremely useful in effecting David's rite of passage.

The second part of the Actaeon myth is enacted by the dogs and Blaise, and is set precisely against the completion of the first part, with Pinn and David in bed at Hood House as the dogs attack Blaise outside the kitchen door. Sharing the myth between father and son gives it a curious resonance which involves a contrast between innocence and guilt. David's adolescent, anti-sexual fastidiousness collapses in the face of the vision of nymphic chastity at the fountain, and his initiation into a sexual mode of being is perceived as innocence *en route* to guilt. His father who once, like David, longed for an innocent sexual self in marrying the chaste Harriet, has long since entered the corrupt animal phase where the brilliant vision of goddesses has faded to duplicity and debased sexuality. Unlike the original Actaeon myth, this enactment separates the vision of chaste Diana from the guilt of the man consumed by the hounds of his psychological state, and the essential double-ness and separation central to the novel is once again stressed. The sense that David's touching innocence will gradually, through time, become identical to his father's coarse guilt is very much part of the book's pessimism, and is proven by the simultaneity of David's happily undergoing his first sexual experience as the dogs go for darkened, debased Blaise.

Murdoch had foreshadowed this event in her account of a television programme from the Milo Fane series, where Monty's cool detective care-fully and ruthlessly severs the Achilles tendon of one of his murderous victims. When Harriet's famished dogs smell blood from Blaise's wrist, cut as he tried to break into locked and bolted Hood House, they unleash their always ready aggression; the black Ajax, the most untrustworthy of the dogs, bites and severs Blaise's Achilles tendon, rendering him incapable of flight, then makes for his throat as all of the dogs pounce. Blaise's moment of narrow escape parallels Harriet's moment of death at Hanover airport, and his survival as opposed to her death is merely and shockingly accidental: the reader, of course, wants the opposite to happen, but this novel is not written for the consolation of the reader. That Blaise is punished, his internal self externalized through the dogs, is as much as we are given.

There is something very elegant in this structuring around the Actaeon myth, in its doubling between David and Blaise, and in the mythic power of its evocation, as though some moral value has been infused in the novel by remembering the myth and by its oblique and dual working-through. Mur-doch's tactful restraint, as well as her refusal to make the myth work in a traditionally accepted way, makes a point about the interior subject matter of the novel. Although the most outrageously external of the characters, Blaise involuntarily participates in one of its subtle internal patterns, and the pecul-iar release of psychic energy always occasioned by the evocation of great myths functions through him as a moment of revenge much desired by the reader. Blaise as a character is a type of Actaeon at his most guilty and yet – a significant element in the myth – naive and bewildered and helpless. That Murdoch chooses to end with Edgar rather than Blaise reflects her desire to put the subject matter slightly askew, to revert to someone more highly developed and above all to inflict a modified comic closure. As woman after woman comes to Edgar to make an appointment to see him in Oxford, he enters a more amusing, considerably more minor, world, and successfully deflects our attention from Blaise and Monty, the contrast between whom forms the central task of the novel. Murdoch obviously intends her closure as a game, and a bitter one; it asserts the ascendance of the mediocre life and the hopelessness of most moral endeavour.

VIII

# CIRCULARITY VERSUS PROGRESS IN THE RELIGIOUS LIFE

A study of *The Bell* and *Henry and Cato*

Between *The Bell* (1958) and *Henry and Cato* (1976), Murdoch wrote thirteen novels and two plays, not to mention extensive work in philosophy and dramatic versions of two of her novels, and there can be no doubt that significant development took place. Echoing Murdoch's own statements in various interviews to the effect that novel-writing is a craft at which the practitioner becomes more skilled with practice, one can validly assume that *Henry and Cato* is the better book. Certainly it is a much denser, more complex work which accomplishes its extensive tasks unobtrusively, and with apparent ease achieves the mysterious sense of endless reverberation which has consistently characterized Murdoch's style since *An Accidental Man* (1971). By comparison, *The Bell* is thinner and its skeleton shows; every device in that novel contributes tightly to the end in view and speaks to its specific purpose, making the book feel more narrowly contained and obviously controlled than the later one.

I have chosen to compare the two works for a number of reasons, some better than others. First of all, *The Bell* is Murdoch's first approach to the style which I believe will define her reputation as one of the foremost novelists writing in English in the twentieth century. Its coherence centres on the spontaneous activity of the characters rather than on a too tightly expressed ideology, although in fact there are so many ideological points of view expressed, all of them oddly convincing during their expression, that discriminations are complex and exceedingly (even excessively) interesting to make. The reader feels absorbed in much more than the well-spun plot and is persistently hard at work, as he must always be in later Murdoch. The circularity of *The Bell*'s structure, in which Michael Meade in his middle age repeats a pattern of behaviour which in his youth condemned him to years of guilt and unhappiness, is much more predictive of the dramatic and terrible *déjà vu* of *A Word Child* (1975); I have nevertheless chosen to set *Henry and*

*Cato* against this early work (it is Murdoch's fourth novel) even though the structure is quite different, primarily because both novels' most important thematic concerns are with the characters' basic apprehensions of religion. Although Murdoch's work has always inclined towards religious scrutiny even when apparently dealing with an all too secular milieu, the inclination to concentrate on religion as a major subject was present very early and has been predominant in the last few novels.

I think, as the title of this study shows, that Murdoch is primarily a religious writer, and that the easiest and most pointed way of making this inclination evident is to examine how she works within a religious framework which is obvious and unconcealed, rather than oblique and indirect as in many of the novels. By pitting *The Bell* against *Henry and Cato*, and in the next chapter the more mysterious novel, *The Unicorn* (1963), against *The Sea, The Sea* (1978), it should be possible to see not only the nature of Murdoch's development as an artist from her early period to the most recent great novels, but also the extended range of her thinking on a subject with which the current historical period is ill at ease.

Critics have described Murdoch as inexorably falling into an opposition of two basic character types as a way of defining many of her structures – the aspiring saint versus the would-be artist – but it is frequently more accurate to talk about a person immersed in the sacred as opposed to one completely subject to the profane. *The Bell* and *Henry and Cato*, conveniently for discussion, make parallel use of these types, but they are less obtrusive than several other comparable elements in the two novels, and one can see the mileage Murdoch gains from the contrast without having to concentrate also on that other major subject of hers, the unworthiness of the contemporary artist and the paradoxes of art. Of course Dora in *The Bell* and Henry in *Henry and Cato* are artists *manqués*, and are principally interested in art in a failed professional way, but they are not practitioners, and interest in art is for them a version of religious attention in a world in which the outward, lingering signs of Christianity hold no particular interest for them. Opposed to them are Michael Meade and Cato Forbes, both men with a religious vocation who define their lives in terms of their allegiance to the Church and to Christ. Both of these latter two also have homosexual inclinations which they sadly and unsuccessfully fight and which they place in an either/or relationship to their Christianity.

In both novels Murdoch explores the labyrinth of sexuality and spirituality whose subtle interactions are so confusing and often so damaging. Her choice of homosexuality in both books is interesting in that is is the mode of sexuality which has been questioned and largely disapproved of in the Christian tradition, and about which much guilt can accumulate. Both novels feature a character who comments on the problem, and both of these commentators are deeply involved in ideas of the spiritual life. James Tayper Pace in *The Bell* disapproves of homosexuality simply and outrightly, and point-lessly drops anti-homosexual remarks as in his uncharitable references to Nick Fawley, who he claims looks like a 'pansy'; when an embarrassed Toby Gashe goes to him to confess his very slight flirtation with Michael, James is shocked and has no machinery for understanding or forgiving the belea-guered and only slightly erring Michael. In his sermon on the good, he sees the whole issue, indeed the whole of moral life, as very simple:

> We should consider not what delights us or what disgusts us, morally speaking, but what is forbidden. And this we know, more than we are often ready to admit. We know it from God's Word and from His Church with a certainty as great as our belief. Truthfulness is enjoined, the relief of suffering is enjoined, adultery is forbidden, sodomy is forbidden . . . sodomy is not disgusting, it is just forbidden. (p. 133)

In this sermon, James is probably consciously attacking Dora's sexual carelessness, and reflecting on that of Nick Fawley and, unconsciously, Michael. His reversion to the Law is certainly not a ringing example of Christianity's putative allegiance to mercy, and his entire sermon is an ambiguously handled statement. On the one hand, his idea of a disciplined following of an external good as opposed to directing energy to the infinite delights of egotism is very much a Murdochian statement, and his handling of it has the confusing double ring of accuracy and reductiveness. His later analysis of Michael's misdemeanour – and from the point of view of his limited knowledge of Michael's past and present behaviour it is hardly more than that – obviates the continuation of Michael's spiritual aspirations. This kind of negative judgement, inherent in established Christianity and of which James is so pure a spokesman, cannot be seen as other than destructive to both the secular and the spiritual life. Poor Nick Fawley, in angrily catechizing Toby about his relations with Michael and Dora, describes the virtuous James as the 'only available saint' (p. 262), but his statement reflects only his own inclination towards guilt and a guilty relationship to Christianity as opposed to James's simple, untemptable nature, not any noteworthy truth about the real thrust of the novel.

Very unlike James in theological temper is the Roman Catholic priest, Brendan Craddock, in *Henry and Cato*. Whereas James is obtuse, Brendan quickly perceives the nature of the relationship between his fellow priest, Cato, and the clever delinquent boy called Beautiful Joe. Brendan is a theolog-ically more sophisticated character; moreover, he reflects a real change in Murdoch's apprehension of Christianity and the possibilities of the religious life. He does not assume that Cato's homosexual longings are blameworthy or unusual; he focuses rather on Cato's naive egotistic belief that he is the only person in the world who can 'save' Beautiful Joe. For Brendan the only important issue is Cato's hurtful or helpful behaviour in respect to Joe, and he castigates his colleague's lack of humility and failure to believe in the functioning of a separate providential agent. As he sees it, the state of being in love is automatically a powerfully egotistical one, in which major substitutions take place. Brendan, as I pointed out in Chapter II, is one of Murdoch's characters of the good, and a voice to be listened to; the direct and passionate truth and irreversibility of his arguments reflect both the quality of those arguments and the texture of the character himself. Unlike James Tayper Pace in *The Bell*, Brendan Craddock speaks at great length but does not sermonize, and rather than merely reflecting an abstract theoretical system, his words bear the force of a personality which lives out to its spiritually necessary end the content of his arguments.

Brendan's intelligent passion in outlining the real and necessary in the traditional language of Christianity depends on a sophisticated sense of the higher spiritual reaches of his Catholicism, so that for him the breaking of questionable Levitican and Pauline rules like those forbidding homosexuality is not at all important, as it had been for the more naive James. Like the Abbess in *The Bell*, Brendan concentrates the force of his argument on the nature of the spiritual life taken at its highest, but unlike the Abbess he is not protected by the cloister or by years of unworldliness – and above all he is perceived as a real character with real depth. The danger he sees in Cato's behaviour has to do not only with Cato's pride in his ability to reform Beautiful Joe and make him happy, but most significantly with the confusion of images and the dangerous paths of substitution Cato's mind automatically falls into. In both Cato's speculative daydreaming and his awful hallucinations while Joe's prisoner, Brendan's fears turn out to be quite right: the face of the Redeemer becomes the face of Beautiful Joe, and the spiritual erotic energy directed during his seminary and priestly years towards Christ is now entirely concentrated on Joe. Cato's spiritual vagaries receive, through Brendan's intelligence and generosity, every chance that advice or well-meaning, with their attendant insufficiencies, can deliver. Cato is, moreover, set against the background of a Christian organization – the Roman Church – which in its internal workings has seen the spiritual history of many Catos. He is balanced in the fiction by the secular Henry, whose fervent, unexamined desire to destroy an established historical past apparently contrasts sharply to the atavistic conversion which had led Cato to the Christian Church in the first place. In simpler outline, *The Bell* takes up some of the same points, with one crucial difference: the apprehension of Christianity is more confused, the religious community cannot agree among themselves and the multiplicity of points of view in this general confusion leads to a task laid rather too heavily on the reader – the task of discriminating among arguments which all at first appear acceptable. Michael Meade in his longing for piety is differentiated from his secular balance, Dora Greenfield, but he is also without powerful personal support (the Abbess, although endowed with real spirituality, talks to him too seldom, too briefly and at the wrong times) or powerful, subtle arguments directed to his aid, of the sort that Cato has if he could only begin, as Brendan puts it, to 'try at least to use [them] now in relation to yourself' (p. 366).

Every argument Michael knows, develops or hears applies to him: his conviction that the good are powerless, the Abbess's contention that all failures are failures in love and that the way is always forward but never back, James's conviction that the moral life can and should be simple, his own sermon which argues that the human being must know himself and work with the material given him. The multiplicity of routes is intrinsically confusing and reflects the diversity of points of view among those living in or on the fringes of the religious community at Imber. Within the community, some members who want to shoot pigeons and squirrels are opposed by vegetarians offended by the slaughter of the innocents. Some of these latter even disapprove of Peter Topglass ringing birds and Dora picking wildflowers. The community divides into factions over arguments about man's labour within nature, which complicates the problem of buying or rejecting a mechanical cultivator. That they are all, except naive James, deeply unsettled becomes obvious at the climax of the book, and it seems evident that Murdoch is deliberately delivering a picture of the difficulties and probable impossibility of setting up a utopian religious community for those who, as the Abbess describes it, are in search of a non-cloistered working life endowed with spiritual significance:

> although it is possible, and indeed demanded of us, that all and any occupation be given a sacramental meaning, this is now for the majority of people almost intolerably difficult; and for some of such people 'disturbed and hunted by God', as she put it, who cannot find a work which satisfies them in the ordinary world, a life half retired, and a work made simple and significant by its dedicated setting, is what is needed. Our duty, the Abbess said, is not necessarily to seek the highest regardless of the realities of our spiritual life as it in fact is, but to seek that place, that task, those people, which will make our spiritual life most constantly grow and flourish; and in this search, said the Abbess, we must make use of a divine cunning. 'As wise as serpents, as harmless as doves.' (pp. 82–3)

In contrast to the failures of Michael's group, the community which genuinely works is the one within the convent walls, where the wise Abbess and her cloistered nuns evidently live in simplicity, joy and devotion. In the few contacts the uncloistered characters have with them, they are pictured as filled with gaiety and wisdom, entirely contented, like creatures from another world. When a sister, Mother Clare, strips to her odd nunnish underwear to rescue Catherine and Dora from the lake, she looks distinctly peculiar, almost otherworldly, a condition that her vows dedicated her to.

The distance between her world and secular Michael's is vast. Bowing under the guilty burden of his failures, he expresses the problem of the gap between spiritual aspiration and human defeat after a conversation with the Abbess:

> How well she knew his heart. But her exhortations seemed to him a marvel rather than a practical inspiration. He was too tarnished an instrument to do the work that needed doing. Love. He shook his head. Perhaps only those who had given up the world had the right to use that word. (p. 238)

The practical, workaday secular-religious community, although it tries very hard, does not seem capable of the high ideals the Abbess urges, and the strain of loving one's neighbours too often shows. In that community, Nick is an outsider, Dora is disapproved of, sermons contradict each other directly, moral arguments uncharitably arise.

The real problem among Michael's community involves their inability to deal with other than the perfect and ideal; their one point of unity lies in the admiration they all feel for Catherine Fawley and the symbolic association they all, but particularly James, make between her and the new convent bell, both shortly to be installed inside the cloistered walls. The attachment of Catherine's personality to the bell is carefully worked out to encompass the concluding ironies: the bell as the voice of love and a symbol of purity had, in its conventual history, always been gainsaid by the labyrinthine power of human sexual love. Thus the medieval story of its mysterious flight into the lake because of the unchastity of one nun parallels the new bell's unceremonious tumble into the water as a result of Nick's ministrations. Catherine, who has identified the bell's symbolism with her religious desires, rushes into the lake in a suicide attempt, overwhelmed by guilt over her comparative unchastity in loving Michael. The violent, obsessive quality of her action suggests not only a deep mental instability, but also a negative violence within Christianity itself unless conceived very clearly in non-idealistic terms.

The London journalist, Noel Spens, cheers up erring, profane Dora by lecturing her against the would-be piety of a community like Imber:

> I can't stand complacent swine who go around judging other people and making them feel cheap. If *they* want to wallow in a sense of unworthiness, let them; but when they interfere with their neighbours one ought positively to *fight* them! (p. 187)

Noel is, of course, arguing from a point of view most unsympathetic to the community: he does not believe in God, but sounds rather like the 'sincere' man of British empiricism. The dangers of Christianity therefore send him into paroxysms of rage which are not intended to represent Murdoch's posture so much as another very real possibility in interpreting the peculiar and dangerous quality of religious belief in general. Certainly the reader is expected to see the hopeless problems of human community, and more specifically of the religious life, and Noel is one of the means to this end.

Dora keeps insisting through the course of the book that Catherine could not *want* to lock herself in the prison of the convent, but Dora does not, until after all the drama is over, know anything at all about religion (she gave up Christianity, we are amused to be told, when she discovered that she could repeat the Lord's Prayer quickly but not slowly). Nick and Catherine Fawley, unnervingly alike in appearance, both have a strong religious inclination, and for both this aspect is, as Freudian psychoanalysis has been telling us for years it must be, suspiciously close to their sexuality. The implication may be that success in separating these modes of intensity can occur either by being purely a sexual being, as Dora is, or purely committed to the sacred, as the nuns are and Catherine wishes to be. Catherine is able to repress the temptation of her love for Michael until the collapse of the bell ceremony, at which point her obsessional guilt neurosis surfaces with grotesque power. The rigid practice of repression which both she and Michael attempt in their very different sexualities is obviously unhealthy and absolutely destructive, and it is interesting to notice that both lives are crushed by what, in justice, are little more than peccadilloes – but peccadilloes subject to real, destructive Christian judgement. Nick as a schoolboy had originally been driven by the power of an itinerant evangelist's sermon to report to his headmaster his little affair with Michael, who was then his teacher, thus ending the latter's dream of becoming a priest; a cynical and embittered Nick as virtuous sermonizer drives Toby to confess the business with Michael to James Tayper Pace; Catherine is driven by the collapse of the bridge and the ruin of the bell ceremony, which she interprets as a divine judgement on the horrendous unchasity of her love for Michael. This sorry catalogue reduces the possibilities and definitions of the Christian life with chilly efficiency, so that Noel can easily and even justly write up his very witty, funny and devastating newspaper account which completely denigrates the whole religious experiment at Imber.

Murdoch uses this sexual material partly as sensationalist stuff which can bolster the argument of atheistic rationalists like Noel, and partly to show how easily more profound content can be caught up and destroyed by the strongly negative and basically superficial idea of the religious life that both the egotistically pious and the proudly rationalist hold – the idea that Christianity is perceived by its rules and behavioural exterior rather than in the hard-won life of inner discipline. Dependence on the exaggerated image of something like Catherine's purity is wrong in the light of simple human frailty, where one is never secure in any idea or belief: 'At any moment one can be removed from a state of guileless serenity and plunged into its opposite, without any intermediate condition, so high about us do the waters rise of our own and other people's imperfection' (p. 161). Michael and

Catherine are both ashamed of their imperfections because they feel they must interfere with the rigid and ideal patterns they have set for themselves and, in Catherine's case, the self-image that has been accepted. Both want to live tight lives in which their special destinies will be flawlessly lived out: the reader already knows of Michael's flaws and failures; Catherine's fall is a sensational surprise which underlines the errors they share in their conception of the spiritual life.

That conception, ironically, comes from the wisdom of the Abbess. It is not judgmental or negative, and always emphasizes the need to escape the past and attempt to live in a loving present with a sense of forward movement. But the Abbess is like an abstract exhortatory text, untouched by the world in which it exists and having only the authority of its detached wisdom. In this respect, her words are analogous to the literal text of Julian of Norwich's *Revelations of Divine Love*, a book central as a background to this novel and which Murdoch repeatedly refers to in her other works. Catherine has made it evident that her desire to become a contemplative was influenced by Julian's history and writing, and Chapter 12 of *The Bell*, which immediately follows Michael's 'mistake' in kissing Toby, opens with Catherine earnestly reading aloud from the *Revelations'* beautiful passages which show the anchoress's 'simple understanding of the reality of God's love' (p. 167). Julian's assurance that God will make all things well in spite of marred life in the world is quoted through one of her Showings of God: '*That which is impossible to thee is not impossible to me: I shall make all things well*' (p. 161). Unfortunately, this theology of God's power and man's impotence does not transfer to the anxious characters, who cannot give up their struggle with self or subdue their hyper-kinetic egos under God; instead they either fall into guilt through basically egotistic shame and failure or cause real destruction, as Michael does in brooding neurotically on himself and not heeding Nick's signals for help.

Nick is like many characters in Murdoch novels who savagely echo and pervert Julian of Norwich's famous phrase: 'All shall be well, and all shall be well, and all manner of thing shall be well.' The perversion is automatic, for the lines represent a terrible distance between the speaker and the God who in our period can scarcely be known. Nick sees himself as finished and shows his suicidal inclinations when he asks that the brake be released so that the lorry he is working on will run over him, and gives his version: 'All shall be well and all shall be well and all manner of bloody thing shall be well' (p. 209), and indeed, for contemporary man his twisting of the words appears to have a kind of direct truth. Before Nick's suicide, a seeking, hopeful Michael knows that all might still be well if he could break through his shame and the disastrous confusion of things and act simply towards Nick. His complete inability to do so, coupled with the foul timing of events in the world, shows how remote the state of grace is from personalities diseased by neurosis.

When Nick is dead, Catherine mad, the community broken up and Michael utterly destroyed by his inadequate love of Nick, the religious idea is clearly stated as the central recognition of the book:

> [Michael] thought of religion as something far away, something into which he had never really penetrated at all. He vaguely remembered that he had had emotions, experiences, hopes; but real faith in God was something utterly remote from all that. He understood that at last, and felt, almost coldly, the remoteness. The pattern which he had seen in his life had existed only in his own romantic imagination. At the human level there was no pattern. 'For as the heavens are higher than the earth, so are my ways higher than your ways, and my thoughts than your thoughts.' And as he felt bitterly the grimness of these words, he put it to himself: there is a God, but I do not believe in Him.                                    (p.312)

Michael, like most Christians, had associated his interpretation of life with the idea of a necessary pattern, a visible and comprehensible providential order whose design is automatically consoling and meaningful. This longing for order is a built-in component in western culture to which existential thought as well as conventional Christianity is devoted: Sartre, one of Murdoch's early subjects of study, subscribed to this longing and recognized its power. The horror of Michael's experience denies such coherence and comfort, and emphasizes what Murdoch sees persistently through her work as the unbridgeable space between human images of God as a pattern-setter and the ineffable nature of whatever, if anything, is out there in the divine distance. Michael's necessary lesson stresses the unknowability of God and bitterly asserts that the ways of God are higher and wholly other than that which human faith and desire for knowledge can fruitfully deal with. Michael's attempt to fit his life to a pattern has been wrong, pointless, destructive – and when he says 'there is a God, but I do not believe in Him', he is saying that his need to live a coherent life is eternally separated from the immense human need for large and mighty symbols. This particular alienation can be seen as Murdoch's definition of the ravages of Romanticism.

When Julian of Norwich's radiant belief in an absolute benignity even amid the pain of life is set side by side with Michael's recognition that God's ways are higher than man's, there is little contradiction; but a real savouring of the meaning of Julian's ecstatic belief that 'All shall be well and all shall be well and all manner of thing shall be well' involves a pointed discipline. All shall not be well in a world governed by the theories of personality that dominate our period, and for the mystic's words to have any value, major steps in a direction contrary to ours would be necessary. All cannot be well in a world in which separation from reality is inevitable because concentration on self obscures the necessary quality of transcendence in religious experience. Murdoch's people are world-immanent characters who often and bitterly acknowledge this limitation, but who feel trapped in a world where their undisciplined spiritual energy has no object of attention. The necessary quality of religious experience does, however, have possible outlets in the secular world, and interestingly, the most apparently profane and spiritually undeveloped character in the book, Dora Greenfield, is given most immediate access to them. Confronted with the bell, a beautiful object in which the power of viable religion and artistic production coincide, Dora can dimly perceive the quality of holy reality which the medieval bell-founder had perceived as he sculpted the images from the life of Christ. Much more consciously Dora knows this transcendence in art as she looks at her favourite paintings in the National Gallery, seeing them as real and perfect, as 'something real outside herself, which spoke to her kindly and yet in sovereign tones, something superior and good whose presence destroyed the dreary trance-like solipsisms of her earlier mood' (p. 192).

Art apparently has the power to draw the self out of the self which the Christianity imaged in the Imber community lacks. Its members cannot even properly perceive the specifically theological data of Julian's words, as Murdoch illustrates art's greater ability than theology's to call out religious feeling in the contemporary world. The brief, luminous glimpses of reality art gives are, as she later argues in *The Sovereignty of Good*, a sort of contemporary substitute for prayer which is not a workable source of grace for people who confuse religion and power, the idea of God with the idea of self.

Keeping pace with and helping to define the religious failures in the novel are the various sexualities – Catherine's and Michael's repressions, Nick's destructive revenge, Toby's initiations, the Stafford's obscurely troubled marriage, Dora's promiscuity and, perhaps most interestingly of all, Paul Greenfield's demonic possessiveness. A pale secular shadow in the religious community, Paul is not extensively developed and in certain ways remains a caricature; but like many other characters in the novel he too is trying in a perverted way to fabricate an ideal, purposive life through a futile combination of his sterilely elegant collection of art objects and bibelots which he perceives only as his possessions and his sexual tyranny over a wayward Dora. His poisonous, selfish anger and inability to see either art or another person clearly ruin the marriage, and his attempt to juggle his profession, the scholarly life and his recalcitrant and misunderstood sexuality contribute to the novel's total aura of chaos in community and the individual soul.

★

Michael Meade's grieving conclusion near the end of *The Bell*, 'There is a God but I do not believe in him', is basically a statement of utter and irremediable separation of the divine from the mortal: 'For as the heavens are higher than the earth, so are my ways higher than your ways, and my thoughts than your thoughts' (p. 312). The same idea will be wordlessly present in *Henry and Cato* where the kestrel, sighted by both Henry and Cato on different occasions, soars above the Ladbroke Grove wasteland and is specifically but ironically identified as a symbol for the Holy Ghost. When Cato, whose belief in God has been replaced by a dream of redemption and love with Beautiful Joe, stuffs his filthy cassock (his own consciously symbolic mark of himself as priest) into the rubbish tip, the kestrel swoops in a powerfully symbolic gesture:

> Then he saw the kestrel. The brown bird was hovering, a still portent, not very high up, right in the centre of the waste, so intent yet so aloof, its tail drawn down, its wings silently beating as in a cold immobile passion. Cato stood looking up. There was no one else around upon the desert space where already, after the rain, upon the torn and lumpy ground, spring was making grass and little plants to grow. The kestrel was perfectly still, an image of contemplation, the warm blue afternoon spread out behind it, vibrating with colour and light. Cato looked at it, aware suddenly of nothing else. Then as he looked, holding his breath, the bird swooped. It came down, with almost slow casual ease, to the ground, then rose again and flew away over Cato's head. As he turned, shading his eyes, he could see the tiny dark form in its beak, the little doomed training tail.
>
> 'My Lord and my God', said Cato aloud. Then he laughed and set off again in the direction of the Mission.                                    (p. 186)

Cato's laughter, following his ironic quotation of St Augustine's infinitely repeated brief prayer, 'My Lord and my God', is the laughter of a career dangerously set free from discipline and prepared to pursue a *vita nuova* of egotism. The swoop of the bird on its victim presents a nice parallel to Cato's original conversion, but what his mind cannot yet comprehend is the final doom of the religious life – the terror, darkness and death he is yet to experience, which will become his great teachers. Murdoch carefully points out that Cato's ecstatic early perception of the Trinity, his sense of having stepped out into the light and looked at the sun itself, is a misapprehension of the spiritual life which must be corrected in the course of events.

The spiritually much more advanced Brendan Craddock, one of Murdoch's characters of the good, differs radically from Cato's limited perception of the Christian problem. Writing with full awareness of the dark night of the soul to a distraught Cato, he says:

> We have to suffer for God in the intellect, go on and on taking the strain. Of course we can never be altogether in the truth, given the distance between man and God how could we be? Our truth is at best a shadowy reflection, yet we must never stop trying to understand. . . . There is a mystical life of the church to which we must subdue ourselves even in our

doubts. Do not puzzle your mind with images and ideas which you know can be only the merest glimmerings of Godhead. Stay. Sit. You cannot escape from God. (p. 161)

Later, in conversation, Brendan will argue that Christ represents a principle of change rather than of settled theology, and he will finally leave everything in his English life and intellectual order to go to India alone, without theology or traditional images, in order to follow the furthest reaches of the religious life and to enter an area of obedience where even speculation is disallowed. His final statement fearlessly accepts the limitations of human knowledge:

The point is, one will never get to the end of it, never get to the bottom of it, never, never, never. And that never, never, never is what you must take for your hope and your shield and your most glorious promise. Everything that we concoct about God is an illusion. (p. 339)

Brendan, like Michael Meade in *The Bell*, perceives the distance between man and God, but unlike Michael he is not driven to despair by it. Brendan faces no conflict between the blank face of reality and our rich desire for images, and we can see him as a steadily advancing character, changing and moving as the demands of the religious life impel him onwards. A telling distinction between *The Bell* and *Henry and Cato* comes from Murdoch's development of Brendan Craddock as a powerful character with an eloquent ability to recount the dangers and disciplines of the religious life. Contrasted to the briefly glimpsed Abbess of *The Bell*, he is the spokesman for the aloof pressure of the spiritual life, and his convincing portrayal reminds both Cato and the reader that that life is supremely important, not the bitter impossibility Michael Meade had seen it to be. Throughout *Henry and Cato* Murdoch confronts religious problems with a firmness not seen in earlier religious novels like *The Bell* and *The Unicorn*, and her luminous writing on the subject of spiritual experiences is a daunting and brilliant achievement – something courageously taken on and movingly absolute, whether she is talking about Cato's first wonderful apprehension of the Trinity, the darkness of his defeat after Joe's death, or Brendan's spiritual knowledge.

Cato and Michael Meade are far distant from Brendan and very much alike: both are caught in the conflict between messy personal desires and the unrewarding, even impossible demands of a strangely alien transcendence. The birds evoked in both books establish a connection both literal and symbolic between the natural world and the spiritual, and the hovering kestrel high above the wasteland of the grim present effectively illustrates the distance and separation so strongly felt by the spiritually restless characters. It is impossible not to notice the parallel between the alien transcendence of the divine and the highest reaches of art in *Henry and Cato*, as again Murdoch insists on her sense of reality and the artist's obedience to it. Again, she has set this novel against several works of art, most importantly against the German expressionist Max Beckmann's large triptych entitled 'Departure' in the Museum of Modern Art in New York.

This painting is most specifically connected to Henry, whose spiritual energies expend themselves on the secular and are split between his demonic desire to destroy his ancestral home, Laxlinden, and his very real love of art. The triptych possesses great spiritual significance, and Henry identifies the King of the central panel as the kingfisher – another Christian symbol. In his book, *Max Beckmann* (New York: Abrams, 1977), Stephan Lackner quotes Lilly von Schnitzler's letter of explanation which purports to be Beckmann's own interpretation of the picture:

> Life is what you see right and left. Life is torture, pain of every kind – physical and mental – men and women are subjected to it equally. On the right wing you can see yourself trying to find your way in the darkness, lighting the hall and staircase with a miserable lamp, dragging along tied to you, as a part of yourself, the corpse of your memories, of your wrongs and failures, the murder everyone commits at some time of his life – you can never free yourself from your past, you have to carry that corpse while Life plays the drum.
>
> And in the center?
>
> The King and Queen, Man and Woman, are taken to another shore by a boatsman whom they do not know, he wears a mask, it is the mysterious figure taking us to a mysterious land. . . . The King and Queen have freed themselves of the tortures of life – they have overcome them. The Queen carries the greatest treasure – Freedom – as a child in her lap. Freedom is the one thing that matters – it is the departure, the new start.          (p. 116)

The framing images of appalling suffering exist in sharp contrast to the luminous sea and sky of the central picture of boatman, king, queen and child – a secular reproduction of the Christian holy family, and a reflection of transcendent achievement.

The problem for Henry – and indeed for all the characters in the novel – is how to cross the borders of suffering to attain this transcendent image. Henry is a student of Beckmann, and has been fiddling around on a book on him as part of his attempt to get tenure at a bad little college in Sperriton, Illinois, where he has been teaching art history and in the process has had to learn some. The proximity of this fictional dull little town to St Louis, where Beckmann spent the last few years of his life, no doubt gives his project its novelistic *raison d'être,* but Henry as a character brilliantly models his life on his apprehension of Beckmann's style and career. He perceives himself as ill-treated, tentative, suffering, and in his insecurity he identifies with the strong masculine symbolism of this most assertive of painters. Equalled only by Rembrandt in the number of self-portraits he produced, Beckmann is a model for Henry, who constantly looks at himself in the mirror, mentally creating hard, romantic adjectives to describe himself: 'foxlike Henry', 'assuaged drunken Henry', 'harlequin Henry' (the latter a direct reference to a self-portrait by Beckmann). His enormous egotism is firmly sustained through this powerful stylistic device. Throughout the book he refers to the images of suffering on the side panels of the triptych, but the reader is increasingly convinced, especially because of the terms of Cato's ordeal, that Henry's suffering is neurotic, a barrier thrown up by a personality which has largely imagined its pain. As his mother, Gerda, says to him in the only real conversation they have, her own struggle with her marriage made her choose between her husband and her demanding child; the result was a special joy in her elder, kinder child, Sandy:

> I couldn't deal with both you and him. Sandy was all right, I think he sort of understood, and anyway he was independent. I hoped you'd be. You weren't. You were demanding then, you were terribly hostile. A child's hostility can hurt too. I couldn't reach you. I had my own fight, and my own tears. It was partly just a matter of energy. . . . Sandy was the only thing that gave my life any pure sense and any pure joy, but I never talked to Sandy. I never communicated with Sandy. I never told him what I've just told you. I never touched him or kissed him after he was twelve.

(pp. 301–2)

We first see Henry on a plane above the Atlantic delighting in the death of his brother, Alexander, the Sandy of Gerda's plaintive account. The elder son and heir to the Marshalson estate, Alexander is one of the puzzles of the novel. Neurotic, untrustworthy Henry gives no reason for hating him, except that Alexander apparently fitted into the Marshalson picture more readily than seething Henry and was obviously everybody's favourite. Alexander's interest in boats, cars and little else separated his sensibility from Henry's, but the ghost of the dead brother is strangely anonymous – and very much like the masked helmsman of the boat in the Beckmann triptych. He is a mysterious presence, separate from the action and yet necessary and ominously present. His ghostly recurrence in everyone's mind keeps making itself felt, yet his anonymity is never broken. For Henry he is a probably false object of envy and hatred; Gerda, who idealized him and mourns absolutely for this tall, red-haired son she never talked intimately with or touched as an adult, dreams of him as a great redemptive figure cut off from her forever and taken away on his yacht. Lucius recalls him only as a large, comfortable, indifferent presence, and Stephanie, who never met him, fantasizes the romance that could never have been. We discover late, after Henry and Colette's wedding, that the bird-headed servant, Rhoda, had had an affair with him and that he gave her the heirloom ring, the Marshalson Rose. But our most important piece of information comes from the priest, Brendan Craddock, whose authority the reader is very willing to accept. His account of a drunken Alexander, suffering and inwardly tormented, is a surprising detail after the neutral descriptions of his bland personality, bland room, bland flat in London. Whatever this man might have been in life, his death becomes a large symbolic issue haunting the novel.

The second half of the novel is entitled 'The Great Teacher', and the teacher is death. Murdoch, obviously interpreting the helmsman in the Beckmann triptych as death, is not interested in romantic readings of happy families sailing into the serene blue of the horizon; but in her heavily ironic denouement she depicts the newly married Henry and Colette on a punt in the lake, contemplating Colette's new pregnancy, a mimetic image of the Fisher King and Queen. The space between them and the transcendent serenity of the painting is as enormous as the distance between shattered Cato and the Christ he had once worshipped, and their apparent continuation in a viable world comes only from strong denials of reality from both Colette and Henry. Colette, when imprisoned in the darkness by dangerously criminal Beautiful Joe, had realized in her terror that her romantic childhood dream of marrying Henry – a dream with which she had been persecuting him and poor dazed Stephanie – has utterly gone, replaced by a darker, more adult recognition:

> She thought, I *ran* to Henry, I had to. And she saw his dark glowing eyes looking at her, and she wished for physical desire to distract her from her misery and terror, but it would not come. And she felt with a sadness that she had lost him, not because he did not want her, but because she did not any more want him. In this darkness Henry gave no light, he was just a young girl's empty dream.                                                    (p. 258)

Her subsequent intuition of guilty Cato as a soul in hell and her own remorse over Joe's death lie at the heart of the novel, and the quasi-cheerful note of future happiness, children and a calm life continuing the tradition of beautiful Laxlinden Hall is off-key indeed.

Henry's compromise is in many ways greater than Colette's, and involves a more complete recognition than hers. His egotism is not easily broken into, and indeed he survives in a comfortable world by retreating into that egotism. After the disaster of Cato and Joe, Henry reluctantly seeks out Cato at Brendan Craddock's flat. He is astonished and appalled by Cato's sneering reference to Henry as a tourist in the situation and by the bitterness of his new moral line:

> One realizes that there are no barriers, there never were any barriers, what one thought were barriers were simply frivolous selfish complacent illusions and vanities. All that so-called morality is simply smirking at yourself in a mirror and thinking how good you are. Morality is nothing but

self-esteem, nothing else, simply affectations of virtue and spiritual charm. And when self-esteem is gone there's nothing left but fury, fury of unbridled egoism. . . . I just hope and pray for you – may you never see what I see now, never know what I know now, never be where I am now!

(p. 295)

Henry flees from Cato to the consolation of art, and sits before Titian's 'Death of Actaeon'. As he looks at that great painting, he ponders how horror can be transformed into beauty, and even assumes that perhaps great artists do not know the horror of reality. Frantically he repeats Cato's prayer that he never see or know the dark fury that Cato's failures and actions have unleashed. The passage is extremely important:

Something frightful and beastly and terrible has been turned into one of the most beautiful things in the world. How is this possible? Is it a lie, or what? Did Titian know that really human life was awful, awful, that it was nothing but a slaughterhouse? Did Max know, when he painted witty cleverly composed scenes of torture? Maybe they knew, thought Henry, but I certainly don't and I don't want to. And he thought of Cato now with a horrified pity which was a sort of disgust, and he gazed into the far depths of the great picture and he prayed for himself – May I never see what he sees, never know what he knows, never be where he is, so help me God!

(p. 296)

One suddenly recognizes Henry's essential superficiality as he gazes at great art, his choice to see the beauty and ignore the pain. Thinking of Beckmann and Titian much earlier in the novel he had questioned why these artists were so arresting, why he loved Beckmann so; clearly he now has an answer which he chooses consciously and fervently to shut out from his life, repeating the words of Cato's prayer that he never see, know or be in the horror of pain and death the artists so absolutely depict. Choosing ease and consolation, he cannot begin to confront the profound question of how death and pain can be transformed into beauty. He buys his restoration of Laxlinden and his marriage to Colette by this compromise, and he remains wistfully aware of his limitations:

As a spiritual being I'm done for. The pity I felt for Stephanie was probably the only spiritual experience that I ever had. . . . Yes, I'm done for, thought Henry. Now I shall never live simply and bereft as I ought to live. I have chosen a mediocre destiny. . . . I have failed, but I don't care. I shall be happy. I never expected it, I never wanted it or sought for it, but it's happened. Apparently I am doomed to be a happy man, and I shall do my damnedest to make it last. (pp. 326–7)

Henry's recognition of failure in a higher task is oddly parallel to Cato's spiritual bleakness and to Lucius Lamb's dying knowledge, as well as to the feelings of defeat that encompass every character in this novel. This exciting, fast-moving book, with the wry illusion of happy marriage and new starts in its denouement, reflects Murdoch at her grimmest. Except for Brendan Craddock, the characters operate consistently at a level of failed ambition and personal defeat. All of them are ambitious to succeed at an idealistic level, and to a greater or lesser extent the course of action shows them a vision of the bleak truth behind these ambitions. Cato's final knowledge that morality and the spiritual life he had lived are merely cosmetic gives us a good place to begin, as does Brendan's much truer definition of the spiritual life and its identity with death. Brendan's point of view has been fully discussed in Chapter II, but it is important to connect his insights to the central idea of this novel about the Great Teacher:

> Death is what instructs us most of all, and then only when it is present. When it is absent it is totally forgotten. Those who can live with death can live in the truth, only this is almost unendurable. It is not the drama of death that teaches – when you are there facing it there is no drama. That's why it's so hard to write tragedy. Death is the great destroyer of all images and all stories, and human beings will do anything rather than envisage it. Their last resource is to rely on suffering, to try to cheat death by suffering instead. And suffering we know breeds images, it breeds the most beauti-ful images of all.                                                                    (p. 336)

Cato's ambition and image of himself as a priest were indeed limited, and as Brendan correctly points out to him, he had scarcely begun the endless journey the spiritual life involves. In the novel we see a Cato whose vanity and egotism centre on his near-homosexual relationship with Beautiful Joe. Even vain Henry is astounded by the egotism in Cato's letter asking for money to support the two of them, and the reader tires of Cato's endless litany acclaiming himself as the only means of Joe's salvation. Cato's loss of faith occurs obscurely, in conjunction with his increased interest in Joe, and shows the limit of his commitment to the rigours of the religious life. Until his imprisonment he looks as Henry will look at the end of the book – compromised, but perhaps heading for a personal, longed-for happiness. His sorry failure inevitably casts its shadow on the false image of happiness in the novel's ironic closure.

Murdoch's virulent undoing of his false ideal and her general attack on happiness are vital in considering reader response to this powerful book. Although *Henry and Cato* is a serious novel about the rigours of the mystic way and Cato's egotistic fall into the delights and horrors of the secular renunciation of that way, Murdoch is also closely attuned to an audience impatient of or indifferent to the religious life and more likely to delight in

Henry and Colette's doggedly happy marriage than respond to Cato's punishment or to Brendan going forward into the final stages of the saintly *via negativa*. Like Henry himself, novel audiences have a strong resistance to the knowledge of reality in its hardest forms; we huddle as he does before great art, praying not to know the horror that might be at its centre. The ironies of the marriage can certainly console, and Colette and Henry are generously conceived by Murdoch. Colette's identification with punts and fish reminds us of the Beckmann triptych, and certainly she rescues Henry from his romantic perception of himself as suffering and demonically destructive like the characters on the two side panels of the painting. Even more, Colette's utterly courageous rush to save Cato, combined with her frantic attempt to be brave before Beautiful Joe's demands, align her in a small but substantial way with the good. Her romantic vision of the saving power of her virginity, her image of herself as the lady of Laxlinden and her witch-like curses on the Stephanie/Henry engagement show her deep attachment to fantasy, but because novel readers are always on the borders of fantasy, we are more likely to go along with her girlish foibles than damn her false images.

Henry is another case entirely. In his first conversation with Cato, he explains that he is writing a book on Max Beckmann called *Screaming or Yawning,* a title based on an early Beckmann drawing (p. 66); this title gives the reader a good pair of responses to Henry's impossible behaviour: his criminal destructiveness in trying to destroy Laxlinden as well as his mother's and Lucius's lives, his constant romantic readings of and self-association with Beckmann's paintings, his sustained hatred of the dead Alexander, his perverse falling in love with Stephanie Whitehouse because of his triumph in being alive while Alexander is dead. Neurotic and self-obsessed, he leaps about Laxlinden and London in an orgy of rotten behaviour which indeed drives the reader to both screams and yawns. His excessive brooding on himself carefully shields him from perceiving outside reality, and he sees nothing clearly – not Beckmann, not Stephanie, not Cato, not his mother, not Lucius; everything is screened through his heavy curtains of romanticism and hatred. In this quality Henry resembles Austin Gibson Grey in *An Accidental Man* and is another example of Murdoch's Everyman, who is in truth so close to us as readers.

Henry sees himself as a hero (identifying with the great H's including Hamlet, Hannibal and Hitler, as well as with Beckmann's self-portraits), but is too anxious and uncertain of himself to define his intentions very well. Principally he sees himself as a kind of social saint, who will destroy the paternal legacy of the Laxlinden estate, distribute his enormous fortune to the poor and return to a humble American backwater where he and Stephanie will drink many martinis with his American parent surrogates, Bella and Russell. This ill thought out plan is merely window-dressing to his real motivations, and through Henry the reader is strongly compelled to see the futility and fraudulence of the intellectual life among the characters in this novel. Several of them sustain the myth that they are working on books, the substance of which they fail to enact. Henry cannot understand the basis of Beckmann's art, even though he knows a great deal about him and 'loves' him; Lucius Lamb long ago gave up everything except the fiction of writing a book on Marxist thought as he settled into the sparse luxuries of life with Gerda; John Forbes spends his sabbatical writing lecture notes and reading rather than writing a book on the Quaker history of his ancestors. Apart from these failed works, large projects like Henry's socialism and Cato's priesthood fall through. Except for the consistency displayed by Brendan Craddock's moral position, all disciplines seem intractably difficult. Henry's lucky emergence into the world of external happiness is unearned, but by the end of the book he knows this fact and himself much better than before the frenzy of the action overtook him on page three of the novel. Moreover, the audience, without idealizing him, is able to respond with a certain degree of relief to the small changes that have taken place.

The women in *Henry and Cato* are markedly different in quality from the men. None is engaged in an ambitious intellectual or spiritual project or knows much about painting and art history. The American Bella, whom we know only by Henry's report, is a college professor but not notably intellectual; Gerda, who lives daily with a seventeeth-century Flemish tapestry and a good collection of paintings and furniture, is evidently unversed in their provenance; Colette deliberately withdraws from her college because she eschews the intellectual life; Stephanie is wonderfully ignorant and totally vulgar. Yet the image of woman aggrandized as goddess and redeemer is one of the most powerful and interesting in the book – and again it is emphasized by a series of references to works of art. Although these women function without conscious knowledge of theories or absolutes, they play a consistent symbolic role, most often illustrated by the Laxlinden tapestry depicting Athena hauling Achilles up by the hair. Both Colette in her efforts to marry Henry and Gerda in her prevention of his marriage to Stephanie play similar roles of powerful woman over inadequate man, and Henry in the National Gallery ruminates on the power of goddesses:

> It was certainly dangerous to tangle with goddesses. Athena was a fearful authoritarian and very austere even with her favourites. Hera was thoroughly vindictive. Artemis and Aphrodite were killers. What poor thin semiconscious beings mortal men were after all, so easily maddened, so readily destroyed by forces whose fearful strength remained forever beyond their powers of conception. Surely these forces were real, the human mind a mere shadow, a toy.                                        (p. 96)

These human female powers prowling courageously through the novel – Colette, Gerda, Stephanie, even Dame Patricia Raven and the absent Bella – provide centres of control on the ordinary human level which are, as always in Murdoch, echoed by more profound and mythic ideas. Colette graduates from Athena to the Redeemer's face (for Cato) and the Fisher Queen (for Henry); Gerda is both Athena and, for Lucius Lamb, a Calypso who has kept him from his great work and reduced him to secret haikus; Stephanie plays a voluptuous Aphrodite.

Henry's cogitation on the goddesses takes place before Titian's large and beautiful painting in the National Gallery in London called 'The Death of Actaeon', bought by the Gallery after a large fund-raising drive at just about the time Murdoch was composing this novel. This impressive painting is, after Beckmann, the most important art object in the book; it is also described through Henry's consciousness:

> The immortal goddess, with curving apple cheek, her bow uplifted, bounds with graceful ruthless indifference across the foreground, while further back, in an underworld of brooding light, the doll-like figure of Actaeon falls stiffly to the onslaught of the dogs. A stream flashes. A distant horseman passes. The woods, the air, are of a russet brown so intense and frightening as to persuade one that the tragedy is taking place in total silence. Henry felt such intense pleasure as he looked at the picture, he felt so purely happy that he wanted to howl aloud with delight. (p. 96)

His joy in the work is the reader's one access to sympathy for him, and in this passage we have a fine example of Murdoch's painterly eye and splendid capacity to catch briefly and completely the tonal achievement of a great work of art. In symbolic terms, the passage contrasts Diana's sacred un-defiled hunt, powerfully in the foreground, with the horrible suffering and death of Actaeon, torn apart by the hounds of his own mind. This image of Diana, unlike the other goddesses invoked, is not connected to literal women in the novel even though the symbolism of the goddess subtly links to the general plot idea. Just as the Beckmann triptych connects to the secular suffering and successes of Henry's part in the plot, the Titian reflects most fruitfully on the essentially religious tale of Cato's suffering. Even so, how-ever, 'The Death of Actaeon' provides the reader with the novel's central symbol.

Titian's dramatic reversal of the myth puts Diana's otherworldly, chaste hunt in the foreground rather than either balancing it with Actaeon's death or substituting the more common image of the goddess and her nymphs bathing. Diana's purposiveness in the hunt here vitally overshadows Actaeon being devoured by the hounds, with the result that the viewer is forced to rethink the myth. In Titian's version, the divine concentrates on its activity, indifferent to the human suffering and horror which is obscurely linked to it by a human causal means: Actaeon has incorrectly stumbled on and seen the divine Diana bathing, and as a result of this vision must be torn apart by his dogs. Titian's contrast between the overbalancing fleeting image of the divine and the less central brown suffering of the human is enormous, and an excellent image for this novel, where at a deep, infrastructural level the absolute nature of reality (the divine) is so much more important than the Actaeon-like centre of its double tales of false suffering and human failure. Murdoch's trick of so often diverting the reader from this deep level is counterbalanced by the strength and intensity of the conversations about or references to reality and the religious life when they infrequently occur, and only the tendency of the novel reader to escape (all of us) makes so many readers fasten onto the ironic novelistic notion of happy closure in marriage as ameliorative.

The important fact which connects us to the symbolic message of the Titian painting is, however, that the novel ends where it had begun, with Cato walking into the dark rain with an object in his mackintosh pocket. The turn from gun to crucifix illustrates the dominant progress of the book, from violence to quiet, from emotional turbulences of all sorts to happiness or serious theological summing-up. The aesthetic elegance of the Spanish ivory crucifix with which Cato exits endows it with a certain value even apart from its having belonged to the spiritually advanced Brendan. It replaces both the humbler wooden crucifix (an ostentatious sign of Cato's false humility as a swinging priest?) and the gun with which the book opens, and adds to the primacy of the idea of the 'divine' to which the Diana allegory points.

In the progress of the novel, however, the gun appears to be central, inasmuch as it motivates a great deal of the action and leads to the first and major split between Cato and his beloved Beautiful Joe. For all its dramatic placement, however, it is only one of several talismanic objects of violence which become so important: the gun itself, Joe's knife, the section of piping Cato manages to unscrew in his black prison. These objects represent not only the level of social violence and threat from which all twentieth-century people suffer, but also a continuous counter-current against which old, traditional ideas fight. As instruments of physical violence, they align thematically with Henry's desire to commit a 'murder' (p. 59), a 'crime' (p. 86), a 'destruction' (p. 125) against Laxlinden, his dead brother and father and his childhood. In deeply ironic terms they are pitted against the impotent figures of Christianity, as Joe's knife lies on the table like a holy image on an altar, or as, stained with Henry's blood, it becomes a nasty counterforce to the crucifix.

Murdoch's evocation of darkness, raw fear and both casual and horribly spontaneous violence is among the best things in this excellent novel, which in process takes on something of the quality of a Graham Greene or Joyce Carol Oates production – something rare in Murdoch and, I suspect, not particularly intentional. Probably the best explanation in terms of design is not in the inclination towards sensationalism which earlier marred some of her novels, but the connection with the major idea of this novel expressed in the title of its second half, 'The Great Teacher'. The sacramentalized instruments of violence cause the death of Beautiful Joe at the hands of an hysterical Cato, and Brendan describes his death most clearly as a version of the redemptive death which is at the centre of traditional Christianity: 'We live by redemptive death. Anyone can stand in for Christ. . . . Death is what instructs us most of all, and then only when it is present. . . ' (p. 336). Joe's death certainly jells the action in its new pattern, where the egotistic characters have faced reality and been turned from their frenzied activity into new silence. The first half of the book, 'Rites of Passage', has set up this shift with an elaboration of rapid activity in which words like freedom and love have been hurled about in a farrago of emotion. Joe's death utterly changes Cato, as well as Henry and Colette, but it is not the only great teacher: we remember that the death of Alexander Marshalson has hovered behind the novel, and touchingly, Lucius Lamb is given final temporary prominence.

A much more minor character than Lucius, Cato's early spiritual advisor, Father Milsom, had written to Cato: 'Your task is love and love is your teacher' (p. 162). Illusions of love, divine and human, prove useless in this novel, but Brendan, and finally Lucius, see the love that Father Milsom evoked as identical with death. Lucius throughout the novel has meant to love Gerda properly and intended to marry her, but he perpetually escapes commitment and lives as easily and comfortably as he can. Like and yet so unlike Henry, Lucius slips into the easiest, most comfortable mode of life, allowing his talents to slip away unused. His haikus, to which his supposedly enormous poetic talent has been reduced, reflect his resentments – against Gerda whom he has loved so imperfectly, and old age, which has him relentlessly in its grip. In addition Henry, the new master, threatens his parsimonious comfort and becomes the enemy. As the denouement approaches, a now redundant Lucius has a stroke, collapses and takes up his notepad for a final haiku:

> So many dawns I was blind to
> Now the illumination of night
> Comes to me too late, O great teacher.

(p. 330)

Although the poem is obviously scrawled just a few moments before death, Lucius's end is not reported until the last page of the novel, when Brendan reports briefly but poignantly that as a young man Lucius had written a good poem called 'The Great Teacher'. He cannot recall its substance, but the shadow of some great lost human talent joins with the salient imagery to suggest to the reader that this novel is about the waste of human knowledge and talent, something wilfully and dreadfully thrown away by careless hands.

At a crucial point, Beautiful Joe enunciates an important principle to Cato: 'And a funny thing, do you know, it's awfully easy to frighten anybody. Not everybody knows how easy it is, but it's dead easy . . . Dead easy. Do it even with a knife . . .' (pp. 41–2). Joe's success at frightening Cato, Henry and Colette is ample proof of his boast, but the reader is cunningly led to believe that talent, aspiration, love and goodness are all too easily undone by the easy ability of any casual forces of the world to join with individual human weakness and fear to undo our loftiest and doubtless our best aspirations. Joe's insistence on fear reminds us of Dicken's Magwitch in *Great Expectations*, who uses the same techniques on a seven-year-old boy on the marshes, and one of the heart-sickening ways Murdoch's novel drives home its proof of human inadequacy has to do with such analogies and with the fact that Beautiful Joe is all too painfully correct when he estimates the childish fragility of humankind.

# IX

# THE DANGEROUS ROAD

## Magic in *The Unicorn* and *The Sea, The Sea*

'Only stories and magic really endure,' says Bradley Pearson, the artist figure in *The Black Prince*, attesting to the two crucial talents of his creator, Iris Murdoch. The statement is partly autoreflexive of Bradley Pearson's own work and his increasing knowledge of sad mortality, but it also raises the spectre of human vagaries in the ontological search. The uses of fiction and its relation to magical systems are perpetual subjects of concern in Murdoch's work, as she plays her enormous talents against the problems of belief and the special interests of her audience. All novel readers are of course dedicated to stories, and no amount of twentieth-century experimentation has been successful in removing the expectation that a good novel tell a good story. But the fascination with story lies very close to magical beliefs, and a lasting impediment against the credibility of the novel as a genre can also be seen in the audience's proclivity towards enchantment by fictional systems. Murdoch's persistent distrust of her own forms, her ironic turning aside of audience expectation and her insistence on plunging the reader into an alien atmosphere which inclines to frustrate and disappoint him all run counter to the tale-spinning talents which constitute fiction's magic, and which she so much mistrusts.

Although it is naive and wrong to accuse Murdoch of didacticism in any narrow sense, her primary thrust towards reality tries to expand the accepted frame of the traditional novel and to convince the reader that what is most contrived in her work, most authorially controlled and most magical, contributes to a larger function. The difficulty of trying to get a handle on this larger function is nowhere better illustrated than in the contrast between the two novels this chapter will explore. Structurally and generically they exemplify very different approaches to thematically similar basic materials. Whereas *The Unicorn* (1963) is an elegantly wrought, significantly artificial gothic novel with a tight endgame closure which skims the surfaces of tragedy, *The Sea, The Sea* (1978) is maddeningly realistic and extended, and refuses closure entirely: the reader feels that Charles Arrowby's diary will resume with the new demons of Fritzie Eitel and Angela Godwin, and with a trip to Japan opening new areas of action.

An early novel like *The Bell* frequently comes close to being a forum for moral ideas, but *The Unicorn*'s subject is magic and its relationship to both stories and religion. The directions of these two early novels, which first showed the Murdoch reader her intense interest in religion, are very different: whereas *The Bell* involves the moral life and its possibility under a wished-for divine dispensation, *The Unicorn* is only secondarily interested in the moral being of its characters. Its real subject is the sources of magic in the human mind and that magic's translation into action once a context has been provided for it. The irony of Murdoch telling this self-conscious and stylized tale, replete with all of the visual and tonal magic of the gothic mode, joins nervously with the various magics which so influence the characters and so confound their and our judgements and ontological longings. When Murdoch specifically chooses to examine the related phenomena of magic and religion later in *The Sea, The Sea*, her techniques are yet again different, and one confronts the problem, so central to Murdoch's mature fictions, of the powerful effect of an almost hidden infrastructure. As in the contrast between *The Bell* and *Henry and Cato* discussed in the last chapter, the earlier novel reveals much of the material of the later, but the later operates with a profundity and subtlety towards which the reader must work delicately as he reads and rereads in an attempt to arrive at the infrastructural bases of the work. To put it bluntly, *The Unicorn* is a good book which diagnoses the confusions and desires of the spiritual life; *The Sea, The Sea* goes far deeper in both characterization and religious thought, and by understanding Murdoch's extensive fictional devices we can apprehend with increasing clarity its apparently hidden centre. The reader's quest in *The Sea, The Sea* is more difficult, but it also offers greater rewards.

*The Unicorn* has received a great deal of critical attention (the best essay on it is still A. S. Byatt's excellent analysis in *Degrees of Freedom*, 1965), but remains a mysterious and, I think deliberately, puzzling book. Like its later counterpart, *The Sea, The Sea*, it is about obsession and its relationship to love. Both novels are set in a pointedly hostile but very beautiful landscape; both echo Valéry's 'Le cimetière marin' in their evocations of the sea; both centre on houses with an unreal and alien atmosphere; both contain miraculous rescues by spiritually interesting agents; both have a mythical identification of the central woman – the unicorn as opposed to the phantom Helen of *The Sea, The Sea*. In both are a Maid Marion and symbolically named places; in both are serious extended conversations about magic and mystery religions; and in both we find specific descriptions of the good seen as a distant source of light towards which the characters, in their various ways, scramble. But for all these similarities, Murdoch's task has changed as have her structures. The contrast in narration between the whole, contained tale told in *The Unicorn* and the obsessive diary form of *The Sea, The Sea* describes the very different strategies of the two novels.

As the narrative of *The Unicorn* proceeds, from subjective entrance into Marion Taylor's mind to general objective description to subjective analysis from the mind of Effingham Cooper and back again, a subtle distinction is set up between these two secular outsiders, striving towards some elusive inner knowledge in ways almost unknown to their conscious minds, and the inhabitants of the strangely spiritual landscape in which the action is set. A psychomachia is being carried on in which Marion and Effingham undergo the landscape as part of a ritual passage which will allow them to return to the ordinary realm of the real world touched obscurely by what they have participated in. The curious quality of this book is mental and symbolic, and one feels strongly that Marion and Effingham are the only real characters – that is, characters belonging to the quotidian world – in the tale. Everyone else exudes an eeriness, like spiritual beings of a good or an evil propensity, although 'reading' the other characters can be very difficult, as Marion and certainly the reader find out instantly. At the centre of this group is the ambiguous imprisoned unicorn, Hannah Crean-Smith, on whom all attention is turned. A tale, an image and an object of contemplation rather than a character, Hannah demands interpretation, and the entire novel turns on this act of interpretation. Her quiet, compulsive escape into the untouchable silence of death at the end of the novel ends the activity that had sustained it. Without the unicorn, the other characters are forced out of the claustrophobia and concentration of the spiritual life and into their own destinies: the secular life of the ordinary world for Effingham and Marion, death and final quests for the inhabitants of the spiritual landscape.

Hannah's being is ultimately untouched, uninterpreted and persistently misunderstood through the progress of the novel. So far is she from definition, in fact, that it is doubtful whether she can herself fathom the destiny she enacts. The traditional association of the unicorn is with a Christ hunted by mankind who cannot begin to understand their motives in doing so, and then suffering in captivity as a human soul. Hannah's mystery certainly evokes this association, but like every other interpretation, it offers only a clumsy and partial approach to the heart of the matter. Murdoch, even at her most symbolic, is never out of touch with the multifarious aspects of realism, and Hannah also functions as an ordinary sinful human being, and one whose self-images, including that of a godly Christ identification, are as much a fiction as are the many ways the other characters try to apprehend her.

The ingenuity of each interpretive approach to Hannah's tale gives each character his or her own particular identification. Apart from the outsiders, Marion and Effingham, the characters range from those who aspire to the good – Denis Nolan and Max Lejour – to those whose function is primarily aligned with evil and the demonic – Gerald Scottow and the absent and invisible Peter, husband to and punisher of Hannah. Every character, regardless of his definitions of her, loves Hannah, even, arguably, the demonic Gerald Scottow, whose arguments about her destiny and spiritual place so confuse the secular Marion, who above all wishes to see Hannah freed to an ordinary life in the world. The most interesting activities in the novel occur when a character is working on his definition: Effingham's courtly love ideal for example, which, when he ultimately sees it as betrayed by Hannah, turns easily into debased Freudian analysis, or here as in Max's definition of courtly love's Platonic meaning and the way he connects it to beauty, suffering and the good, in one of Murdoch's eloquent definitions of her own thought:

> Plato tells us that of all things which belong to the spiritual world beauty is the one which is most easily seen here below. We can see wisdom only darkly. But we can see beauty quite plainly, whoever we are, and we don't need to be trained to love it. And because beauty is a spiritual thing it commands worship rather than arousing desire. That is the meaning of Courtly Love. Hannah is beautiful and her story is as you say 'somehow beautiful'. But of course unless there are other virtues, other values, such worship can become corrupt. . . . Recall the idea of Até which was so real to the Greeks. Até is the name of the almost automatic transfer of suffering from one being to another. Power is a form of Até. The victims of power, and any power has its victims, are themselves infected. They have to pass it on, to use power on others. This is evil, and the crude image of the all-powerful God is a sacrilege. Good is not exactly powerless. For to be powerless, to be a complete victim, may be another source of power. But Good is non-powerful. And it is in the good that Até is finally quenched, when it encounters a pure being who only suffers and does not attempt to pass the suffering on. . . . I may be suffering from my own form of what you call romanticism. The truth about her may be quite other. She may be just a sort of enchantress, a Circe, a spiritual Penelope keeping her suitors spellbound and enslaved.                                      (pp. 114–16)

Max, an undeveloped character whose inactivity kept me from classifying him as one of Murdoch's characters of the good in Chapters II and III of this study, represents a level of thought and an interpretation obviously at odds with Effingham's worldly inclination to fall into slick Freudianism. His idea of Até is central to Murdoch's examinations of suffering in her early novels (see also Simone Weil's *Cahiers* on this subject), and the idea of good as non-powerful fits well into the larger definition one later spells out from an examination of Tallis Browne in *A Fairly Honourable Defeat* (1970).

It is also true, as Max recognizes, that even his unillusioned Platonic thinking lies near the possibility of romantic consolation. His longing for a pure being must be corrected by his knowledge that Hannah may just be 'a spiritual Penelope', that the attempts all the characters so busily make to interpret her could be merely part of a losing game. Although no definition comes through clearly and Hannah disappears into the anonymity of death, the reader remains convinced that the various definitions of her being frequently participate in partial truths and lead to actions connected to a positive good. Not only Max's truth-telling eloquence, but also Marion's vivid sense of life in a real world, Hannah's touching belief in God and Denis's profound religious attention to all things lead to this conviction. Yet it is equally true that each of these persuasive particulars contains its own negation. Max admits that he 'meant all my life to go on a spiritual pilgrim-age. And here I am at the end – and I haven't even set out' (p. 118). Perhaps in the ambiguity of the ending when he is left alone with Alice, that pilgrimage may take place, but one doubts it – the shadow of his own death is too dark, even though the fuel of Hannah's death and her tribute to him provides him with material if he should choose, correctly or incorrectly, to use it. The reader can only fictionalize and conjecture here, as he has been doing all along. Similarly, Marion's allegiance to the real world is tainted by what Max calls

> That rag freedom! Freedom may be a value in politics, but it's not a value in morals. Truth, yes. But not freedom. That's a flimsy idea, like happiness. In morals, we are all prisoners, but the name of our cure is not freedom.
>
> (p. 114)

Seen as a romantic notion in Marion's life, freedom is contrasted to Hannah's spiritual discipline, which is broken into all too easily by the threat of Peter's return and her sexual submission to Gerald Scottow; her destiny is marked not by spiritual advancement but by murder and the defeat represented by her suicide. Even Denis Nolan, so close in every respect to fulfilling Max's stringent definition of the good in his loving, non-doing behaviour, breaks the pattern he had so firmly held by uselessly killing Peter, by, as he puts it, hating as well as loving.

These characters, confused by the spectre of Hannah's suffering, by the play of their own minds and by the often charming and certainly interesting evil of Peter Crean-Smith and Gerald Scottow's demonic tyranny, push themselves as far as their natures will take them, discover as much as they can about the reality which Hannah's existence presents to them. But the incompleteness of their spiritual visions as well as their failures to see all that is there defines the limits of the spiritual life. Hannah is a talismanic object on which they bring all the force of their symbol-making powers. References to courtly love, philosophy and belief in God combine with much more romantic and magical stuff from folktales and medieval lore. Hannah's capacity to look like a medieval princess is not lost on her audience, and her life's transition from realism to a figure in local folklore about whom superstitions and predictions abound increases her status as a magical symbol. The novel plays with the magic number seven, and the characters appear to have gathered in the separated and closed circle of the landscape so that the folkloric superstition that something stupendous will happen after seven years of imprisonment can magically come true. It does so, in a climax which includes some of the most interesting aspects of gothic literature – heaviness of tone, dark sick atmosphere, violence, embattled house, stylized fear in which hysteria keeps rising, murder, suicide, eruptions in nature – but the ending does not satisfy expectation nor mold the tale into a contained and explainable thing. In the midst of the carnage of its closure there are few clarities.

It is nevertheless useful and even necessary to try the obviously futile game of defining just what the various characters represent and where they have arrived by the end of the novel. First, the trio closest to the good. Hannah's indefinability is absolute, and she suffers not only from her own obsession with guilt and the spiritual life but also from the obsessions the other characters transfer to her. It is, however, possible to identify her in a limited way as a large symbol of the human soul perceived as it acknowledges its limitations and tries to break away. Hannah describes herself by analogy, talking about Denis's beloved salmon:

> He *will* show you the salmon pool, I expect. Have you ever seen salmon leaping? It's a most moving sight. They spring right out of the water and struggle up the rocks. Such fantastic bravery, to enter another element like that. Like souls approaching God.                                    (p. 51)

The moral and spiritual prison Hannah exists in requires the spiritual bravery she is talking about, and her attempts and failures to be a Christ-unicorn, to leap towards the divine, to make it to the other element, trace the history of the human soul, concentrating on its task although ultimately handicapped. Denis, with his equally disciplined concentration on the things and details of the natural world, represents a luminous approach to the good, and in spite of his failure in hating and killing Peter, his is the real and extended quest at the end of the novel. As he goes off with the dog, Tadg, and his fish, he carries as much as he can of the tale that has been told – the suffering and guilt, the Até which he accepts and will try not to pass on, thus perhaps defeating the cycle of evil. Like Murdoch's characters of the good, Denis goes into the obscure unknown, unlike the secular Marion and Effingham, who return to civilized, sophisticated life. Max completes the trio of characters with strong, positive, spiritual identifications. Unlike Denis, he does not concentrate on the creatures of the world but on the knowledge attainable through the scholarly life. This life cuts him off from relationships, and he is an onlooker rather than a participator in the action. His scholarly work has taken him far, however; he combines the mere knowledge of Plato and Aeschylus with a brilliant ability to extrapolate from the theories of reality a kind of gnosis about the world of the present. His route is seen as a possibility; his contact with Hannah cannot harm her, and it ultimately denies the consolation of obsessively defining her.

Deeply opposed to these characters are Peter Crean-Smith, the punishing demon who had originally been harmed in some unnamed crippling way by Hannah throwing him over the cliffs, and his well-trained creature, Gerald Scottow. Peter is a negative god figure, playing out self-consciously a symbolic offstage role as absolute as Hannah's, and as difficult to define. He is connected to the concept of Até, the passing-on of suffering which is seen as the principle of evil in the novel, and yet as an instrument of necessity, as the just judge, his role is crucial. Hannah submits to his judgement as to something not evil but necessary. Much less ambiguous is Gerald Scottow, one of Murdoch's demon figures. Terribly attractive to both sexes, Gerald uses his considerable talents to tyrannize and hold power over a series of victims, of whom Hannah is the chief. Very much Peter's instrument, his real capacity lies not so much in his role as prison-keeper as in his soul-destroying propensities. By his sexual power he has subdued Jamesie Evercreech to his will and made Jamesie become the broken and lost creature that he is. Hannah's failure of nerve and sexual submission represent the same sort of pattern, the difference being that she is spiritually much more advanced than the young Jamesie. And of course, Marion's sense of being broken and her willingness to submit to him is a still junior version of these two. Scottow's death at Hannah's hands is difficult to work on because of our necessary failure to know Hannah's mystery. The admirable Denis Nolan has tried to fight against this demon, and to stop Gerald's seduction of Hannah; he was thrown down the stairs in an ignominious defeat, and his killing of Peter is seen as an act of hate which mars his spiritual intention. If Max is right in saying that good is non-powerful, then the violence of the book's ending must be seen as a commentary on how confused and desperate and wrong evil causes even the most advanced souls to be.

In the middle range of characters, those who do not approach the terms of either good or evil, we have still to deal with ambiguity. The distinctly weird and very gothic Violet Evercreech represents a negative spirit of power, conventionality and zeal for punishing the guilty. Her greed for power and money is controlled up to the last section of the book by her sense of participating in Hannah's imprisonment and approving of her punishment: there is something ruthless and puritanical in her conception. Alice Lejour is an interestingly neutral character – the one person who phlegmatically refuses to make an image about Hannah. A gardener and a botanist, she is like a Denis without spirit, even though she longs after that spirit, a longing attested by her jumping on him some years before. Pip Lejour, a minor predator and the original partner in Hannah's adulterous deception of Peter seven years ago, ought to have spirit and yet is curiously without it. He is

described as somehow not up to his role, and indeed everything he does –
poetry-writing, fishing and hunting, watching Gaze with his binoculars,
coming finally to beg Hannah to go off with him, committing suicide quietly
after all the activity is over – is marked by a sort of lifelessness, and he can
easily be seen as an obscurely failed spiritual being.

Marion Taylor and Effingham Cooper, on the other hand, are examined
more closely and taken far beyond these minor characters. They return to the
ordinary world determined to forsake the mythology of the spiritual life
which they have just lived through and to throw themselves into such
anti-spiritual pursuits as Freudian analysis and dancing at weddings. Effingham, in attempting to close himself off completely from the whole thing,
very firmly makes it into a fiction and denies Hannah's reality:

> It had been a fantasy of the spiritual life, a story, a tragedy. Only the
> spiritual life has no story and is not tragic. Hannah had been for them an
> image of God; and if she was a false God they had certainly worked hard to
> make her so. He thought of her now as a doomed figure, a Lilith, a pale
> death-dealing enchantress: anything but a human being.          (p. 317)

Leaving the spiritual landscape and going back to his London office and his
clever Elizabeth also involve something much more important than closing
himself off from both the reality and the images of Hannah: it indicates the
loss of his central vision, the one thing in his gothic adventures that was
more than an act of the spiritual or literary imagination. Marion (herself
mythologized into Robin Hood's Maid Marion and tamer of the unicorn) has
a minor sort of religious apprehension in her sexual union and overall
experience with Denis, but the central and real revelation of the book occurs
to Effingham.

The issue is, of course, the near-death experience in the bog from which he
is miraculously saved by Denis, who comes walking rapidly across the
treacherous place as if by magic. But all magic is deliberately and carefully
withdrawn from this experience. Denis arrives because he knows the paths
and his donkey also knows them; Effingham has a profound spiritual insight
into the nature of reality not through a mythic exercise but because he
confronts his own death. There is no mythology, no fantasy, no magic as the
bog gradually sucks him down. Face to face with annihilation, Effingham is
forced to think of himself as non-existent, and his resulting apprehension of
the universe, from Murdoch's always stringent point of view, is true:

> Perhaps he was dead already, the darkening image of the self forever
> removed. Yet what was left, for something was surely left, something
> existed still? It came to him with the simplicity of a simple sum. What was
> left was everything else, all that was not himself, that object which he had
> never before seen and upon which he now gazed with the passion of a

lover. And indeed he could always have known this for the fact of death stretches the length of life. Since he was mortal he was nothing and since he was nothing all that was not himself was filled to the brim with being and it was from this that the light streamed. This then was love, to look and look until one exists no more, *this* was the love which was the same as death. He looked and knew with a clarity which was one with the increasing light, that with the death of the self the world becomes quite automatically the object of a perfect love. He clung on to the words 'quite automatically' and murmured them to himself as a charm. (p. 198)

This hard, clear vision of the reality of love in the death of the self constitutes the real spiritual truth of this novel, but it fades all too quickly from Effingham's awareness as he returns to a world where the ego and its fantasies can function. In Hannah's sitting-room after a hot bath and whisky, he sees Hannah, Marion and Alice as three angels, a sort of Orthodox Trinity. Hannah shortly becomes his Beatrice, and he feels the intensity and truth of his vision slipping away in the presence of objects he can romanticize and mythologize. He tries to hold on to it, but returns ineluctably to the ordinary world of egotism:

He could not in memory determine how long the vision had lasted. It might have been only a minute or only a second; and it had faded utterly with the return of his will to live. Yet he felt that it was in some sense still there, hidden in the core of the nightmare object. He must fix his attention upon it before it was engulfed and darkened and made as black as the bog itself. (p. 203)

Drunkenly he attempts to explain it to the women but he manages merely to sound hysterical, and the sudden energetic speed of the novel's endgame, where he fails so dismally, takes over. His final clumsy and egotistical fall into reductive Freudian theorizing and jealous resentment of Max's inheritance from Hannah are very disappointing, but they are part of the ordinary man's refusal to open that part of the psyche into which the spiritual has access. His return to the world, to London, to Elizabeth, marks his exit from a more luminous space.

Distinguishing the source of that luminosity is Effingham's and the reader's special task in the novel. His confrontation with death reveals directly the love that informs the universe and which all human systems merely play with, and by contrast the beautiful image of Hannah is indeed doomed to annihilation. Her gothic world, in which her life becomes a legend, is controlled very carefully by Murdoch's magnificent tonal effects. The claustrophobia of the dark, gloomy house; the fey 'black' maids; the literary echoes of what Jamesie at the end calls the Vampire Play and which evokes LeFanu and Emily Brontë; the constant sense that everything is off-key, sick and cloying; the atmosphere of the hostile landscape and the sea, always of major importance in Murdoch, which cannot be swum in; the mysterious inscrutability and fear aroused by many of the characters: all these indicate that Hannah's setting is deeply wrong. Indeed, it exudes a demonic power which annihilates all possibility of a white magical solution to the Hannah problem. Apart from Gerald Scottow and the Evercreeches, most of the characters live self-indulgently in a would-be theurgic universe in which Hannah appears to be the magic talismanic object calling down the divine powers. But the tone of the book radically argues otherwise, and its inevitability is marked by the death of the central figures who keep the fiction afloat, the destruction of both positive and negative magic and an acknowledgement that most of the structures of the spiritual life are or become demonic.

The passing of the vision of Hannah and the death of her talismanic power are juxtaposed to Effingham's momentary knowledge, his intense and true gnosis in the face of his own death in the bog. This brief and bare glimpse replaces the cloying tone and turns all the heaviness of the novel to its proper place as an intensely interesting part of the fictions which human beings ordinarily and automatically construct around themselves. Significantly, neither of the two great adventures of the spiritual life – the false gothic quest or the true vision of reality before death – is carried by Effingham back into his life except as fiction and fading memory, and in his self-satisfied departure for London he is an image of the reader who leaves the content of this novel behind him as he emerges from its insistent and claustrophobic tone into his own life. The novel can be seen as a momentary excursion into strange psychic territory in which very clear distinctions have been made, distinctions which the reader may also pervert and romanticize and which will no doubt slip away as he leaves the book's intensity and enchantment.

★

In an informal interview on BBC Radio 4's Kaleidoscope in November 1978, Iris Murdoch, discussing *The Sea, The Sea* for which she had just received the Booker Prize, pointed out that what she was particularly signalling in the novel was that 'the road to goodness is a dangerous road'. In both *The Unicorn* and *The Sea, The Sea* we have characters obsessively on that road and unable to sustain its dangerous demands. The extreme contrast in structure, however, makes the spiritual quests of the two novels appear very different, inasmuch as the aspect of formal tale in *The Unicorn* places Hannah Crean-Smith at the centre, whereas James Arrowby, the Buddhist quester in *The Sea, The Sea*, only gradually emerges from the egotistic tangle of his cousin Charles's first-person narrative. Subtly in the wings from page four of the novel, James is slowly and steadily revealed so that his presence can unravel mysteries and lead us to so much that is almost surreptitiously worked on in this difficult and often daunting novel. The story of Charles Arrowby's life is the ostensible subject of the book, and the reader gives it his immediate allegiance; but as in the case of the medieval idea of the *alieniloquium* (a speaking of things other than those it purports to do, which is fiction's strength and perhaps its bane), there is a sustained questioning of the spiritual life, a study of the devastation of magic in all its forms and a profound psychic landscape whose symbolic quality very slowly, in small, subtle steps unfolds. James is its vehicle, and on him rests the deep infrastructure of the book.

Murdoch has long been master of the unobtrusive detail which suddenly, on the second or third reading, becomes resonant with meaning and continues to expand even further in subsequent more intensive studies. *The Sea, The Sea* is a long book, even more replete with detail than earlier novels. This always strong and remarkable quality is here magnified to a level of almost limitless enrichment which adds to the complexity of the work and to the subtle difficulties of its attainments. As Murdoch's work becomes stronger, more dense and more difficult to deal with at the ordinary novelistic levels the reader is well versed or conditioned in, as responses to *The Sea, The Sea* have attested, special demands are made on the act of reading itself. Murdoch boldly asks for this attention and endlessly rewards the discipline required. As we watch the often tedious tracing and retracing of Charles Arrowby's obsession with his childhood love, Hartley, we are also called on to see the masses of subsidiary material which inform the text. The multi-layering, allusive, detailing technique is extremely interesting, in that much of its stress is on straightforward realism and hence on the details of Charles's life and memories; this emphasis is counterbalanced by an undertone at once demonic and connected to the spiritual reaches of the good, and it behoves the reader to sort out, distinguish and connect context with undertone. Unlike *The Unicorn*, where magic and the supernatural held so strongly to the centre, *The Sea, The Sea* is about a typically arrogant show business 'personality' and his crazily sophisticated friends – a milieu we cannot call unrealistic. Manically self-interested and untrustworthy, Charles Arrowby's first-person, diary-entry narration functions as a steady interference in our apprehension of both present and past events; his is a surface buzzing which tries to keep the real sounds from being heard. Yet from the beginning, magic and the supernatural seep in at various levels, and deep, irrational terror at what might lie in a nearby supersensible world is always on the fringe of the action.

Charles Arrowby as narrator presents another of Murdoch's risky, maddening first-person male voices. He almost outdoes even Bradley Pearson from *The Black Prince* in irritating egotism and self-revealing comedy as he writes his book whose form is so pretentiously and self-consciously difficult for him to define; he begins by calling it memoirs, diary, 'recollection in tranquillity', philosophical journal, and moves up to autobiography, feeling smugly that certain of his character sketches are so interesting (although

admittedly untrue to their subjects and incomplete) that the whole thing may
be a kind of novel. Later, having been forcibly taught a degree of humility, he
will move back again to the idea of story or journal, but he will never manage
what he had planned to do at the beginning – to work towards a coherent
form:

> Of course there is no need to separate 'memoir' from 'diary' or 'philosophi-
> cal journal'. I can tell you, reader, about my past life and about my
> 'world-view' also, as I ramble along. Why not? It can all come out naturally
> as I reflect. Thus unanxiously (for am I not now leaving anxiety behind?) I
> shall discover my 'literary form'. In any case, why decide now? Later, if I
> please, I can regard these ramblings as rough notes for a more coherent
> account.                                                          (pp. 2-3)

As in *The Unicorn*, the significance of form is great, but whereas in the earlier
book the conventional form of a well-shaped gothic novel was an ironic
means of depicting the divisions of fiction from reality, *The Sea, The Sea*
from its beginning fights against all the strictures of novelistic formal ideas.
From the first two paragraphs to its deliberate and extended refusal to end,
the novel strives to illustrate that its only approach to novelistic aspirations
lies in the deluded and muddy mind of its untrustworthy narrator.

Although Charles tries to persuade through his discussions of form that an
ordered and structured way of observing his past and contemplating his
'unanxious' present is perfectly possible, the first two paragraphs have already illustrated that as a diarist he has only the flimsiest hold on his material.
His diary begins with a superbly written and observed seascape lying in the
May sunshine, the first of many extended almost animistic descriptions of the
sea and of natural objects which fill this artfully languorous novel. The reader
of these minutely observed details is transported backwards into the blisses of
the romantic novel, and even in this first paragraph, a Pavlovian response sets
in. The shock of the second paragraph shatters that response, as we see the
recalcitrant and always vaguely frightening world break the smooth elegance
of artful description:

> I had written the above, destined to be the opening paragraph of my
> memoirs, when something happened which was so extraordinary and so
> horrible that I cannot bring myself to describe it even now after an interval
> of time and although a possible, though not totally reassuring, explanation
> has occurred to me. Perhaps I shall feel calmer and more clear-headed after
> yet another interval.                                              (p. 1)

Notice that the 'horrible' thing is excluded from the diary until considerably
later, after it has been absorbed by Charles's unwilling psyche. In the third
paragraph, a ruminative and orderly tone is again established, but through-

out the entire first part of the novel entitled 'Prehistory' and beyond, an alternation between formal control and the interruption of the order by various appalling and frightening or extraordinary incidents will occur in the 'entries'. The smooth elegance of form is projected whenever Charles can mold, shape and all too often belie his material, but the interruptions illustrate disorder and a breaking of control, which are interestingly paralleled by a literal breaking of objects.

Obviously Charles wishes to make his life into a whole art object, and he expends a great deal of energy in doing so; equally obviously, the necessary nature of the world will not allow him to succeed. Again as in several previous novels, Murdoch uses art to argue against its own possibility in one of her central paradoxes. As a literary theorist, she expressed her view to Bryan Magee on a BBC interview in 1978 shortly before *The Sea, The Sea* was published:

> And somehow, we live in a literary atmosphere. When we tell stories or when we write letters, we are making a form out of something which might be formless, and this is one of the deep motives for literature, or for art of any sort: that one is defeating the formlessness of the world. . . . one is cheering oneself up and consoling oneself, and also instructing oneself, by giving form to something which is perhaps alarmingly formless in its original condition – a sort of rubble. It is as if we live in a kind of rubble world, and we are always making forms.

Charles in constructing his art form tries to hide from himself and his reader that he lives in a 'rubble world', and his failures at concealment are often funny and frequently eerie.

The breaking in of the real world on the crafted form was a major idea in *The Black Prince*, and in certain ways *The Sea, The Sea* is related to that novel. Here, however, Murdoch extends her boundaries to an area including the development of the eerie, even as she illustrates richly that realism is the most accurate tool for the criticism and use of art. We find out very quickly that it is as impossible for the jealous, neurotically anxious Charles to order a carefully exclusive diary as it is to control his life or maintain the unanxious role of a retired Prospero. As horrible interruptions persist – an ugly green vase on the landing is smashed, a large numinous mirror is knocked down and broken, a face peers at him mysteriously in the night through the window of an inner room in his house – the reader fears with Charles the intrusion of the uncanny. When he return one night from the Raven Hotel and actually sees a figure in the house, we like him are almost ready for ghosts, only to find that a very real person, the vengeful discarded mistress, Rosina Vambrugh, has been the culprit. With a thankful return to the ordinary, Charles learns that she has been doing the smashing, which is also a symbolic smashing of his wished–for innocent solitude by the guilt of his past. Rosina picturesquely set out to haunt him and like the actress she is, she has done so in dramatically effective terms. Similarly, others are going to break his artificial solitude, to crowd his house and confront him with the manifold spectres of his past.

Two aspects of his hauntings, however, defy such rational explanation. The first is his account, many days after its occurrence, of the 'horrible thing' that happened in the second paragraph: his contemplation of the sea had been broken, as had the sea's smooth neutral surface, by a gigantic sea monster whose size, coils, head and mouth Charles describes minutely. This astounding, absolutely anti-realist apparition amazes the reader as much as it does Charles, who searches frantically for an explanation – a projection from the coiling worm he had just been watching? a giant eel? a nasty recurrence from a previous bad LSD trip? Only by the most subtle modulations through the whole novel are we gradually led to see that this is a projection of the subconscious, horrifying as the subconscious always is when it confronts us. We gradually find Charles almost surreptitiously mentioning the sea monster of jealousy; again and again we see his manic behaviour motivated and stirred by his monstrous jealousy. Even more interestingly, his concentration on the teeth and pink interior of the monster's mouth is repeated as he watches with loathing and irritation while Gilbert, Titus and Rosina sing, or listens nervously while Rosina talks. He sees that interior again in the sea monster in Titian's painting of Perseus and Andromeda, and his pointedly insulting comments about his cousin James's small, square teeth and 'inane smile' belong in the same category.

Yet the singing is one of the most positive and touching things in the novel, and Charles's separation from it stresses his ineptness at both community and harmony. His earliest happy memories of his beloved Aunt Estelle singing American pop songs and pretty things like 'Roses in Picardy,' as well as later ones of his love of Shakespeare and Lizzie are stirred by these songs. The glistening interior of mouths in singing is a deliberate perversion by a jealously unquiet mind of something that his conscious mind recognizes as beautiful, and this inclination to pervert and misperceive in an ugly way is part of the essential quality of this Murdochian Everyman. The sea monster as image does not die out until the last phase of the book, after Charles has miraculously escaped the violent whirlpool into which he had been pushed. Suddenly, trying to remember how on earth he had got out, he remembers that the sea monster with its green eyes (his subconscious of course remembered this requirement of Jealousy) was in the cauldron with him. A brilliant depiction of the wayward ingenuity of the subsconscious, this second appearance cunningly indicates the gradual return to Charles's conscious mind of the true situation: his cousin James, on whom the greatest intensity of his hyperactively jealous life had centred, entered the whirlpool miraculously to save him. The last part of the novel concentrates on James in an examination of whom Charles's jealousy finally dissolves.

The sea monster is not the only mysterious apparition, however. The second unexplained occurrence is the face high up in the inner room peering at him in the night. Rosina swears it was not she, and we are told that there was nothing to stand on which could elevate a face to that height. Again Charles tries a rational explanation: the reflection of the moon, but it does not seem to work and the thing remains a mystery. Later, the inner room becomes Hartley's prison, and the ghostly face takes on a subtle association with a series of dark-toned dreams about Hartley's death. In one dream in particular, Charles dreams that he wakes up to find that moon-faced Hartley has hanged herself with one of her stockings in the corner of the little inner room, and he immediately associates the height of her head as she hangs dead with the face that had peered at him through the window long before he realized she was living in the same village. Again we feel strongly that we are dealing with subconscious data, for although Charles has some vague nervous fears about being haunted by the mysterious Mrs Chorney who used to own the house, the explanation of the phenomenon must be linked to an unexplored precognition of the dread and fear he would feel once he actually felt Hartley restored to him. This is a darker region of the mind than the sea monster of jealousy had been, and one which links uncomfortably with aspects of the supernatural that Murdoch tactfully does not push. It is only late in the novel with James and his 'tricks' that we are forced back to this dangerous subliminal level.

Charles's striving towards form in his life and his art, then, is broken into at several angles, but these interruptions do not discourage him or modulate his energy. He persists in thinking that he can get rid of his past, clear his house of visitors and make his story and his life as he would like them to be. The miraculous return of Hartley he immediately connects to this clearing away of breakages and interruptions, and he manically starts working on restoring the story which had begun in his adolescence. Here his activity as fiction-maker is at its absurd height, and it becomes clear that he wishes to obliterate his entire adult life except for controlled, shaped memories, and join the radiant happiness of his childhood and adolescence to his recovery in advanced age of his innocence – the 'precious thing that has come with me, as if it were a talisman which I can now unwrap' (p. 4). In order to build a structure, the artist must discard unwanted materials, but in Charles's absurdly obsessive desire to discard over forty lived years from both his and Hartley's lives, and in Murdoch's forcing us to experience the excesses of the obsession, we see how futile and wrong-headed is any art or life which refuses to deal with the whole of the reality it experiences.

Again and again Charles will try to persuade a bewildered Hartley to disemburden herself of years of life and relationships in order to join him in his idyll of childhood and the golden world. Her muddled insistence on returning to Ben and resuming her perfectly ordinary lower-middle-class life indicates her stronger and more practical inclinations, but Charles does not give up. His desperate reiterations are funny, boring and madly obsessive, showing clearly how strongly human fantasy will fight against the powerful forces of reality around it. Murdoch uses a very interesting bit of symbolic action to reinforce this and connected ideas: Charles's house, Shruff End, is on a promontory out in the sea, but it is difficult after swimming to climb up the cliffs, to get an adequate series of toeholds without being swept back into the waves. There is an iron banister, but reaching it without some kind of rope can be intolerably difficult. Again and again Charles tries devices – ropes, curtains – but no knots will hold and the sea inexorably washes away all attempts, just as Charles's subjective desires and controls are all swept out into the ocean of the reality he tries so madly to banish.

There are two major issues in Charles's view of that art work, his life: the first and most interesting for his dreaming ego is his utter attachment to the sweet memories of his childhood; the other is his life in the theatre, the long middle years in which he lost his innocence and gained power and guilt. True to archetype, he longs for that innocence and wishes to banish experience; although in his ruminations he talks of myriad adult relationships, all the idealism of his emotional energy resides in his evocations of the far past. His touching recollections of his gentle and good father, his anxious mother, his glamorous Uncle Abel and beautiful American Aunt Estelle are luminously projected, and his happy memories are topped by his adolescent love for athletic Hartley whom he had childishly planned to marry and live with happily ever after. The dark spots in this picture inform his future life, and make him into a drivingly successful and competitive adult who will take on guilt and experience only because the beautiful childhood picture has been marred. First, his beloved father with his manifold virtues was not a successful man, a factor which crushed the entire family as they compared themselves to wealthy Uncle Abel. Abel also married a rich and charming woman, while Charles's father married a humble, puritanical Maid Marion who worked as a secretary on a farm before her marriage. Then Charles's only cousin James marred the picture: a nasty boy (if we are foolish enough to believe Charles) with uncommon and extended talents as well as a lot of money, James represented success on every level and awakened the deep sea monster of jealousy in his cousin which lasts through his life and so powerfully manifests itself in the action of this book. Finally, and to Charles's conscious mind most destructive of all, Hartley refused to marry him and ran away to find another life and another man. In his cogitations he accuses her of robbing him of his innocence and opening him to his lifelong distrust and hatred of all women except a heavily idealized version of Hartley and all Shakespeare's heroines, whom Peregrine Arbelow points out sharply to be fictions:

But they don't exist, dear man, that's the point. They live in the never-never land of art, all tricked out in Shakespeare's wit and wisdom, and mock us from there, filling us with false hopes and empty dreams. The real thing is spite and lies and arguments about money. (p. 163)

Certainly the adult Charles, for all his artful editorial attempts, ineluctably and comically comes through as an appalling fellow, and Murdoch makes it devastatingly clear that loving concentration on childhood cannot obliterate the real data of a human life. Murdoch acutely illustrates how the child is absolutely father to the man, and Charles's whole middle history can be seen as a revenge, a shouting back at the world which had recalcitrantly refused his deep childhood longings. It is impossible, however, to overstate how well Charles's childhood memories are described, how close they feel to the profundity of human experience in an audience who all, like him, are touched and driven by the dreams and injuries of their youth. But, as Murdoch is quick to point out, the possibility of retardation and permanent crippling lies at the heart of our attachment to the far past, and Charles's refusal to take responsibility for his adult life relates directly to his obsessive attachment to his past and his ultimate failure to grow up, to graduate from childhood.

In the same informal BBC interview from which I quoted at the beginning of this section, Murdoch quickly gave a few symbolic identifications: the theatre is the world, Charles is a naive, the sea is empty. These are not unexpected for anyone who has read the novel carefully, especially the knowledge that Charles is most wonderfully naive, but it is important and useful to note that Murdoch sees her places within a large symbolic framework. The theatre to which Charles fled from his childhood and from which he has now retreated to his solitary retirement represents both the world and his life in it: it is the entire long middle period of his experience which he wishes to exclude in his vain archetypal desire to get back to a golden age of innocence, happiness and a well-wrought whole. He is used to directing on the stage, and now wishes to take on a glorious Act V of his life. For all his naive inability to see his romantic nonsense, however, Charles eloquently communicates Murdoch's identification of the theatre with the lies and middle range of things which constitute real life in the world:

Emotions really exist at the bottom of the personality or at the top. In the middle they are acted. This is why all the world is a stage, and why the theatre is always popular and indeed why it exists: why it is like life, and it is like life even though it is also the most vulgar and outrageously factitious of all the arts. . . . the theatre, even at its most 'realistic', is connected with the level at which, and the methods by which, we tell our everyday lies. This is the sense in which 'ordinary' theatre resembles life and dramatists are disgraceful liars unless they are very good. . . . *What I needed with all my starved and silent soul was just that particular way of shouting back at the world.*

The theatre is an attack on mankind carried on by magic: to victimize an audience every night, to make them laugh and cry and suffer and miss their trains. . . . In other arts we can blame the client; he is stupid, unsophisticated, inattentive, dull. But the theatre must, if need be, stoop – until it attains that direct, that universal communication which other artists can afford to seek more deviously and at their ease. Hence the assault, the noise, the characteristic impatience. *All this was part of my revenge.*

(pp. 33–4; my italics)

The middle part of Charles's life – that is his real life in the theatre which is also the world – has been indeed a life of frenzied energy, lies and tyranny as he describes the theatre to be; and as we progressively patch together the pieces he gives of that life, it is evident how dependent his has been on women. The design of his history is fairly easily read: he loved his gentle father and has had loving relationships with a few men – the now dead actor, Wilfred Dunning, in particular, and the probably homosexual Fritzie Eitel – and for a while is pursued by Peregrine Arbelow and Gilbert Opian as their king of shadows, but his dependence on women is absolute. His glamorous Aunt Estelle began the procession, then his childhood love, Hartley, took over, and finally Clement Makin commenced the long string of adult relationships. He hates most other men as rivals, particularly his cousin James in a deep and jealous way, because, as he puts it when he hears that James and Lizzie had occasionally met over the years to discuss him, James was there before him with Aunt Estelle, and therefore probably with everyone else he cares for:

I daresay you knew Lizzie before I ever met her, you were there first, you were there before me, as you were with – as you were with – with Aunt Estelle and – and – with Titus – you'd met Titus before, he said he'd seen you in a dream. (p. 409)

Similarly, he hates Ben, who has long been married to Hartley; whenever someone else has been there before him as Peregrine Arbelow had been with Rosina, Charles ruthlessly takes over as he did in this case, pushing himself in front and coolly breaking up the marriage. Punishment for this act is, of course, one of the major lines of the novel.

Charles's first affair, and, as he reluctantly admits, probably the most important relationship in his life, occurred when Clement Makin, a famous actress twice his age, swooped on him when he was twenty years old and made him into the theatrical success he became. Although he was then still rocked by Hartley's defection, Clement represented what should have been a rite of passage into adult life, and when he told her of the Hartley business, she rightly ordered him to lock Hartley up in his toy cupboard and go forward into life. Charles's memoirs keep returning to Clement, saying frankly that the relationship was so absolute that in many ways she is the real subject of his autobiography. He claims that an account of their time together could fill a volume, and when he describes her death, he shows for the first time a real detachment in stepping outside of himself and into that terrible event. Although often mentioned and presiding like a spirit over the diary – Charles has after all come to the part of England where he is writing because Clement grew up there – she is completely eclipsed by what seems to be a return from the dead of Charles's childhood. Dead Clement remains irretrievably lost, whereas the advent of Hartley distracts Charles from his continuing string of women.

During Clement's life and after her death this steady stream of women flows on, although Charles, with false modesty, says there were really not so many. Most of them appear only as names – Jeannie, Doris – but two of them descend on Charles at Shruff End. One he is waiting and hoping for, as we learn with considerable amusement after his lengthy protestations about solitude and innocence and his spiritual amulet. Lizzie Scherer, a discarded mistress who did and does really love him, has, to Charles's rage, taken a house with the homosexual Gilbert Opian in an attempt to cope with her loss of the fickle Charles and live in innocent, non-sexual love. Charles, always eager to break any bond between one of his girls, as he degradingly calls them, and anyone else, succeeds in unhinging Lizzie by his half-promises and his power over her; he then with typical cruelty dismisses her because he has in the meanwhile found Hartley. Lizzie leaves Gilbert in any case as Charles manages another act in what is obviously an endless line of casual destruction. Lizzie's generous nature does not falter, however, but Rosina is another case entirely.

Charles long ago had wanted Rosina and remorselessly taken her from Peregrine – another casual and indifferent piece of selfish power. As in all his affairs except with Clement, he tired of her and passed on to the next girl, whom Rosina is convinced was Lizzie. Rosina's 'haunting' him and subsequent vicious threats are the first indication Charles has had that any of his actions might have consequences, and never does it cross his mind that Peregrine might also hate him. When Peregrine drunkenly warns him in London to beware, Charles sees it as nothing more than rhetorical. Here is Peregrine's almost transparent speech:

> You still have the *joie de vivre* of a young man. In your case it is nothing to do with goodness. You are ungood. It is just a natural endowment, a gift of nature, like your figure and your girlish complexion. But remember and beware – there are those who live in hell. (p. 166)

With his usual casual naivety, Charles, who has had ample proof of Peregrine's hell during that evening, pays no heed, and he is amazed when

Peregrine, under pressure from James, finally admits that it was he who pushed him into Minn's Cauldron to certain death:

> But, Peregrine, why on earth – did you really – why? . . . You mean – good heavens, you mean *Rosina?* . . . But Peregrine, you yourself *said* to me, more than once, that you were glad to be rid of the bitch – . . . But you yourself encouraged me to feel it was all right! Why did you bother to pretend, and mislead me? You can't blame me now – If you had looked more stricken I would have felt more guilty.                    (pp. 398–9)

This naive indifference to others, this selfish refusal to consider responsibility for another human being, typifies Charles's urge to power: he has loved his reputation as a tyrant and a tartar, and in directing people on the stage he has merely played out a representation of his control over them in their lives. Rosina and Peregrine both at separate times rail against his misuse of power and his loss of it on his retirement. Peregrine's onslaught is the more eloquent:

> You're an exploded myth. And you still think you're Genghis Khan! *Laissez-moi rire.* I can't think why I let you haunt me all these years, I suppose it was just your power and the endless spectacle of you doing well and flourishing like the green bay tree. Now you're old and done for, you'll wither away like Prospero did when he went back to Milan, you'll get pathetic and senile, and kind girls like Lizzie will visit you to cheer you up. At least they will for a while. You never did anything for mankind, you never did a damn thing for anybody except yourself. If Clement hadn't fancied you no one would ever have heard of you, your work wasn't any bloody good, it was just a pack of pretentious tricks, as everyone can see now that they aren't mesmerized any more, so the glitter's fading fast and you'll find yourself alone and you won't even be a monster in anybody's mind any more and they'll all heave a sigh of relief and feel sorry for you and forget you.                    (p. 399)

In spite of such attacks, it will be a long and often tiresome time before Charles can begin to relinquish power and achieve even a partial redemption; the fact that such a maddening character can do so at all is one of the generous triumphs of this novel.

It is evident that for Charles's life and self-identification the central art work is Shakespeare's plays, particularly *The Tempest* which gives him his vision of himself as Prospero, an identification that all of his actors and friends take on readily. Both Rosina and Peregrine vilify him as a negative Prospero, and when Gilbert temporarily becomes his 'houseboy' he acts like Ferdinand, cutting wood and cheerfully serving a harsh master in order to win his Miranda who in this case is Lizzie. Like Prospero, Charles sees himself as abjuring 'this rough magic', but he is generally confused about what the magic might actually be. Significantly, he separates 'ordinary' theatre from Shakespeare, whom he describes as *'quite different* from the others, not just *primus inter pares* but totally different in quality' (p. 36), and in describing his own life, he uses only Shakespearean material: identifying himself as Prospero, loving Lizzie in her resemblance to and playing of Shakespeare's boy/girl heroines and, finally at the end of the book, keeping, as one of two photographs from the past, that of Clement as Cordelia.

The world of illusion constructed by Prospero on his enchanted island has always led critics to equate Shakespeare himself with his last fey hero, and Charles, in his hubris, sees himself as stage magician, actor and playwright (although he admits his plays were small, ephemeral and written only for Wilfred Dunning), as his master had been. His last stage role was Prospero, and like many Murdoch characters he sees his present task in retirement to be that of changing magic into spirit as Shakespeare had so profoundly done. That Charles is not up to the identification or the task is risibly and quickly evident, because he does not understand either magic or the reality of the human beings who surround him. He has always seen manipulation of his friends under his personal power as a natural extension of his manipulation of them on the stage, and he believes that he can change and even revolutionize the lives and destinies of others. This false belief constitutes his only method of interpreting Prospero's magical manipulations, and like so many readers of *The Tempest,* Charles fails to see the sinister aspects of Prospero's almost negative power.

Believing that he has gained complete control over his London theatrical milieu, Charles finds himself, as he had wished, in an empty emotional space when he retires to the sea, but this void is quickly filled by Rosina and Lizzie, by the return of Hartley to his life and by the discovery of Titus, whom he intends to mold into a surrogate son. The latter two become the objects of his manipulation, the victims on whom his 'magic' is supposed to work. His first job is artistic and imaginative: he must make them into adequate receptacles for his transforming power, but he finds them stubbornly unbending to his will. The more extended struggle goes on between him and Hartley, a superbly constructed character who is completely the sort of woman her background and life would produce. Murdoch's precision in describing her is untainted by any condescension towards an ordinary, dowdy, ageing woman who has spent a quiet and vaguely unhappy average life. Contrasted to the eternally youthful Charles with his strong self-image, Hartley is instantly seen as an impossibility for Charles by both the reader and the other characters in the novel, and the depth of Charles's obsessions can be measured by her utter inappropriateness to the picture he is trying to build.

Not at all a candidate for metamorphosis, Hartley, whose adult name is simply Mary Fitch – a far cry from the romantic 'Hartley' of her and Charles's youth – wishes only to continue the life she and Ben have established. Their marriage is described as ordinary, and ordinarily miserable: when Charles eavesdrops one night, they carry on one of those monotonous marital quarrels Murdoch handles with such brutal accuracy here and elsewhere in her work. Ben's bullying and Hartley's repeated 'I'm sorry, I'm sorry' are obviously part of the established mood of the marriage, and Charles, eager for evidence that Hartley demands his redemption, does not see that it is exactly parallel to his bullying Lizzie and her reiterated 'I'm sorry, I'm sorry'. He pictures himself as a rescuing hero, and later, in London, his identification of himself and Hartley with Titian's famous painting of Perseus and Andromeda inflames him: Hartley chained to the rock of her marriage must be heroically saved by the magically flying Perseus, who descends on the devouring sea monster who is so obviously Ben. The connections of this interpretation to Charles's own sea monster and his persistent misreading of Ben's character are only part of his misapprehension of the whole situation.

When Charles has imprisoned Hartley in his inner room, the two actually have a conversation about redemption, but it contradicts Charles's romantic and deluded idea of saving Hartley. She talks about the religion of their childhood and her earned private conception of Christ in simple terms which define to a significant degree the marriage Charles is so determined to misunderstand:

> 'Do you believe in God?'
> 'No'.
> 'I think I believe in Jesus Christ. . . . I think I believe in the remission of sins. . . . Love redeems, that means something, doesn't it?'
> 'Well don't tell me you propose to redeem Ben by love! I'm getting sick of Ben. What about redeeming me?'
> 'No one else will redeem him, no one else will love him.'
> 'Jesus will love him.'
> 'No, you see, for Ben, I've got to be Jesus.'
> 'This is mad talk, darling, really mad. Just try to think a bit. Doesn't it occur to you that Ben would heave a sigh of relief if you left him? Damn it, you've left him already. You aren't all that necessary. He mightn't want to send you off, but he'll be jolly pleased now you've bolted.'
> 'You want to make him unreal, but he's real.'
> 'Real things become unreal when you enter into the truth.'
> 'Our love wasn't real, it was childish, it was like a game, we were like brother and sister, we didn't know what love was then.'  (pp. 301–2)

Hartley's moral triumph consists in her generosity to Ben and her clear view of the real situation between herself and Charles many years ago, but he typically persists in seeing her words as mad.

As we follow Charles through his long imprisonment of Hartley and his unshakeable belief that restoration of long lost innocence and happiness is imminent, it is impossible not to be reminded of Proust's *La Prisonnière* against the idea of which Murdoch plays so ironically. Just as the literary gothic mode serves negatively as a demonstration of false ideas of the spiritual life in *The Unicorn*, set literary ideas about love in the western tradition are here overturned. In Proust it is taken for granted that the lover's greatness and our sympathy for him are enlarged in direct proportion to his obsession with a love which is not reciprocated or requited; Murdoch shows how grotesque, cruel and even perverted is the romantic egotism which produces such a rule. Hartley imprisoned by Charles's unwelcome love becomes a desperate and pitiable figure – dirty, unkempt, smelly, full of lassitude and finally despera-tion – as she begs to return to the ordinary life she is used to. Murdoch's attack on the literary convention of the obsessed lover gives vivid intensity to the romance of ego and misuse of others which literature and those who toy with it can so often be guilty of. Again, she uses fiction to fight against its own traditional convictions, and realism to reveal reality.

In spite of Hartley's return to Ben, the death of Titus and a small reconcilia-tion scene with the Fitches, Charles persists in believing he can redeem the past and win back his youthful innocence, and only through Hartley's actual departure for a new life in Australia is Charles, faced with her empty house and finding his last letter to her hidden unread under the bathroom linoleum, forced to accept the defeat of his magician's attempt at change and manipula-tion. In Murdoch's description, the obsessed imagination works on its ma-terials endlessly, regardless of their resistance and in spite of the madness that such diligence so fully reveals, and ceases only when all possibilities are completely withdrawn.

Charles's other victim is the Fitch's adopted runaway son, Titus, who appears on the scene apparently only to check on whether Ben's jealous suspicion that Charles is his father might be true. He is received directly into the obsessional situation, and immediately feeds Charles's longing for a son, presumably so that Charles can relive the tender relationship he had had with his own father. There is much talk of a son for Charles in the novel apart from Titus's advent and his supposed 'adoption' by the man he had heard so much about while his parents fought: Lizzie points out that she would have married Charles long ago and that he could still father a child even though she could no longer bear it for him; Rosina in rage and hatred tells him that when he left her she was pregnant and reluctantly had a lonely abortion; the book ends with the teenager, Angela Godwin, plaguing him with letters offering herself as the bearer of a child for him before she goes off to Cambridge. When Charles tells an indignant Rosina that Titus is his 'son', however, her re-sponse hits the mark precisely:

You say you 'always wanted a son'. That's just a sentimental lie, you didn't want trouble, you didn't want to know. You never put yourself in a

situation where you could have a *real* son. Your sons are fantasies, they're
easier to deal with. Do you imagine you could really 'take on' that silly
uneducated adolescent boy in there? He'll vanish out of your life like
everything else has done, because you can't grasp the stuff of reality. He'll
turn out to be a dream child too – when you touch him he'll fade and
disappear – you'll see.                                                  (p. 315)

The horror of Titus's disappearance into death does indeed occur because
Charles in a dream-like fantasy has reached out and touched him, because he
has not taken proper responsibility and because Titus has entered the long
chain of causality which rules Charles's life.

Late in the novel, when the major action is over and Charles is left to
meditate, he makes the appropriate connections which show how his manipulation of Titus led to his death by drowning:

James's reaction to Titus's death had been 'it ought not to have happened',
almost as if he felt that it was his own fault. But then if it was his fault it was
my fault. There is a relentless causality of sin and in a way Titus died
because all those years ago, I had taken Rosina away from Peregrine. And
of course my vanity had killed Titus just as James's vanity had killed the
sherpa. In each case our weakness had destroyed the thing we loved.
                                                                         (p. 471)

Charles's early vain attempt to show himself a sporting equal to Titus meant
he did not mention that the sea was dangerous, a killer. Moreover, in a way
which will gradually become clearer, the demonism of James's rescue of
Charles from the boiling whirlpool into which the drunk and aggrieved
Peregrine had pushed him also becomes an uncanny cause for Titus's death.
Certainly at the moment of the drowning, Charles and James, absorbed in
metaphysical discussion, were not paying attention to the young man, who
earlier in diving off the cliffs had reminded Charles of Breughel's Icarus, a
precognition on which he had remarked, *Absit omen,* and had not warned
Titus. But something quite other haunts the supersensible reaches of this
book and is more than partly to blame for this apparently accidental death.

In all his thinking about himself and his power, Charles, who misunderstands much, has also underestimated Shakespeare. Prospero with whom
Charles so glibly identifies exists in *The Tempest* not only in his power over
Ariel and Caliban and the magical production of the staged wedding masque,
but as a powerful, nervously negative practitioner of white magic as it hovers
on the brink of either theurgic success or negative destruction. Prospero's
inclination to be a manipulator and a selfish avenger is never far from the
action of the play, and as a representative of the fascinating but complex
Renaissance idea of the magus, his position is more subtle and dangerous than
the ignorant Charles can recognize. Prospero manages narrowly to bring off

his intentions – modified revenge and a carefully tested marriage for Miranda and Ferdinand – but the magic of his materials is as dangerous as it is ultimately beneficent. Charles's hopeless naivety in reading his model, as well as his limited apprehension of Prospero as a character, neatly indicate his ignorance of the materials with which a magician, who in Renaissance thought is always a spiritual dabbler, works. Charles has been selfishly out to use transformational magic for his own ends, not to transform magic into spirit as he had so pretentiously stated as his aim at the beginning of the novel; that he is on a dangerous road and that it involves the whole of the moral and spiritual life does not occur to him, and we see his blindness inexorably mounting to the climax which Titus's death enacts.

★

Charles's cousin, James Arrowby, is a student of the dangerous road, and unlike the naive and largely unconscious Charles, he is acutely aware of its nature and dangers as well as of its task in seeking goodness and evoking the whole of the spiritual life. James is one of Murdoch's most subtly developed characters, and his spiritual discipline and practice of Tibetan Buddhist rigours only slowly emerge through the interference of Charles's narration. Charles not only hates James with jealous intensity, but is also ignorant of his cousin's enormous accretion of Buddhist lore and determined to perceive him only through his own spite. Violently competitive, Charles was cheered up by Wilfred Dunning's statement years ago that James seemed to be a disappointed man, and gradually Charles's own successes have made James's areas of shining expertise less threatening. Nevertheless, this prejudiced and self-centred narrator persists in negative judgements of James, and in spite of Charles's belief in his now customary power, James spontaneously and invariably comes out on top in terms of both intelligence and sensible action whenever he and Charles share a scene or a conversation.

James, kept in the wings from page four of the novel, served in the Green Jackets during the war, and through the army went to India and then Tibet. After the war, instead of returning to England and the successful life he was so obviously built for, he developed a career as a professional soldier, a far cry from what such a talented man could have achieved. Charles was delighted:

> I felt obscurely cheered because I intuited that James had taken a wrong turning. I was by then just beginning to do well in the theatre, my 'will to power' was bringing in results, and Clement was in my life like a travelling carnival. So cousin James was to be a soldier. Uncle Abel said that it was only temporary and he was doing it so as to have more time to write poetry. My mother said that Uncle Abel was whistling in the dark. It did not seem to occur to any of us then that the army too is, and traditionally, a road to power and glory. (p. 64)

Although the surface of this response reads simply as another statement of Charles's jealous triumph and an acknowledgement that James could certainly make an acceptable and even glorious career in the army, there are other ideas lurking which will become clearer as the subliminal aspects of the novel slowly develop. Charles is successfully establishing himself as a stage magician, but James too is secretly establishing himself, in a way that Charles intuits as a 'wrong turning'. His estimation of James's situation is based on a worldly comparison between himself and his cousin, but we find, through reports of James's having become a Buddhist as well as the reference here to poetry-writing, that his life has taken a turning quite unusual for a soldier.

When we actually meet James well into the 'diary', it is under odd circumstances and in a place which instantly becomes symbolic. After a drunken evening with Peregrine in London, Charles treats his hangover by going to the Wallace Collection where he perceives the paintings as reflecting his own life. In Terborch, Nicolaes Maes, Domenichino, Rubens, Greuze and Reynolds he finds portraits of the women in his life except for Hartley, Rembrandt provides a Titus which remarkably resembles the real Titus Fitch when he finally comes onstage, and there is of course the Titian 'Perseus and Andromeda' which symbolizes his version of the Hartley situation. The effects of the hangover put everything into peculiar perspective, and the hammering of workmen takes on an eerie quality which reminds him of the Japanese theatre. The gallery is miraculously empty, and is clearly meant to be a neutral space endowed by the mind of the perceiver and made into a symbolic inner place. The sense of eeriness and doom, the hammering which connects to both heartbeat and *hyoshigi*, and the dramatic entrance of James combine to take this scene into a psychic area where one questions external reality:

> I began to walk away down the long room and as I did so the hammering of the workmen down below seemed to be becoming more rhythmic, clearer, faster, more insistent, like the sound of those wooden clappers, which the Japanese call *hyoshigi,* and which are used to create suspense or announce doom in the Japanese theatre, and which I often used to use myself in my own plays. I began to walk down the gallery and as I went my hangover seemed to be turning into a sort of fainting fit. When I reached the door at the end I stopped and turned round. A man had come into the room by the other door at the far end and was standing looking at me through the curiously brownish murky air. I reached out and put one hand on the wall. Of course I recognized him at once. He was my cousin James.
>
> (p. 171)

Murdoch's realism projects an adequate explanation of this brown-toned, eerie meeting through Charles's hangover, but we meet the doom-ridden *hyoshigi* repeatedly throughout the novel: in the beating of Charles's heart, in the hammering here, in the clicking of the bead curtain on the landing at Shruff End, in the tinkling of the pendant glass 'ornaments' in the hall of James's flat. The novel is of course about doom and suspense, and more. The most important activity and conversations in it occur when Charles and James meet, and are characterized by James's extraordinary knowledge, his moral and spiritual development and his almost palpable connection with some other realm. When we learn of his rescue of Charles and set it against Titus's death, he takes on a new dimension, and we are forced to realize that this spiritually highly developed man has indeed taken a wrong turning as Charles had so long ago intuited. In the rescue of Charles, as earlier in the death of his sherpa, he succumbs to the power of his brand of potent magic: the dangerous road to goodness for a man like James who takes a spiritual route is more subtly tempting and finally more devastating than the egotistical path Charles has so blindly followed.

But this is to overtake the novel's delicate progress. James takes the dizzy and hungover Charles to his flat in Pimlico, another place whose symbolism is intense. In this far from neutral setting their first conversation of the novel occurs, a conversation during which James absorbs the diverse data of Charles's life and begins to talk intelligently and abstractly about it. On the subject of the autobiography Charles is busily writing, James puts his finger on the central problem of inaccuracy:

> We are such secret inward creatures. . . . Most of what we think we know about our minds is pseudo-knowledge. We are all such shocking poseurs, so good at inflating the importance of what we think we value. The heroes at Troy fought for a phantom Helen, according to Stesichorus. . . . If even a dog's tooth is truly worshipped it glows with light. The venerated object is endowed with power, that is the simple sense of the ontological proof. And if there is art enough a lie can enlighten us as well as the truth. What is the truth anyway, that truth? As we know ourselves we are fake objects, fakes, bundles of illusions. Can you determine exactly what you felt or thought or did?
>
> (p. 174)

Having followed Charles through 175 pages of private, self-centred interpretation, the reader is more than ready for James's vocabulary, but even more significantly his conversation on the perils of autobiography gives us two key ideas which are deeply functional in this novel: the image of the phantom Helen, and the book's first discussion of the ontological proof. That Hartley is a phantom Helen will only slowly dawn on Charles as he actually loses her, confronts her empty house and begins a long series of cogitations on the real, as opposed to his fantasized, long, agonizing relationship with her. Hartley as a phantom Helen is analogous to Hannah's mythology as the unicorn in the earlier novel; both images have their sources in human misuse of others, in the powerful human desire to create a mythology of another person in ead of letting her live in her own free being.

The ontological proof is of course related to this dangerous idea of the worshipped object being endowed with power beyond its real capacity, and we will find that James in his disciplined spiritual life has tried long and ultimately unsuccessfully to free himself from attachments and the power his mind can endow them with. Power is his disease, as in a very different way it is Charles's, and even in this first, impressively intelligent, conversation we will finally by hindsight find that James's desire for power is quietly enacted. As he listens to Charles's manic story of Hartley and his proposed rescue of her, he inquires the name of the runaway son, Titus, and although he is full of sound advice on Charles's illusions about the Hartley–Ben marriage, it will later become evident that he is playing with the possibility of restoring Titus to the scene in order to control it in some way.

The two most important scenes between Charles and James are this subtle first one and the last one which occurs at Shruff End during an evening visit before James's 'journey', which is a willed death. In the interim scenes, James is always a source of intelligence, acute analysis and sensible action; he lives naturally and completely in a world he knows very well, naming flora and fauna, admiring the stones and rescuing flies and moths; finally he is instrumental in rescuing Hartley from her imprisonment. Ironically, the Titian painting justly fits this rescue and not Charles's fantasized one: Hartley is indeed Andromeda, but Charles is the sea monster which his own possessive jealousy projected from his subconscious, and the rational James is heroic Perseus. All Charles's friends like James instantly, and the reader, maddened by Charles, understands quickly that James is a central character of impressive moral and personal characteristics. The intelligence of James's remarks, their enormous cultural evocations which Charles so comically does not catch and his impassioned sense of the truth of situations are all geared to draw the experienced Murdoch reader's sympathy and attention. In the midst of Charles's sustained madness, James shines very brightly.

In many ways close to being a character of the good, James cannot for a long time be suspected of the magical demonism which so sorrily ends the tale proper, before Charles's prolonged meditations take over at the end of the book. Yet his type is recognizable for students of Tibetan Buddhism, and his failure on the dangerous road to the good is one of the hardest, saddest *exempla* in all of Murdoch's work. Unafflicted by narrow self-interest or vanity, James is seen living in his Pimlico flat amid an enormous untidy mass of Tibetan materials, as well as Chinese and Buddhist objects of the greatest value – solid gold Buddhas, jade and porcelain items, all in an apparently indifferent muddle with odd objects such as bits of stone, mud, feathers, tied together in small incomprehensible bundles as far as the incurious Charles can see. The peculiar animistic and fetishistic, indeed almost primeval nature of

Tibetan Buddhism is of course behind all this, and we gradually recognize in this wise man the spiritual discipline of an adept. In his final conversation with Charles, again a masterpiece of wisdom fraught with confessions of failure, James talks of the tricks of the adept – the Indian rope trick, raising bodily warmth, walking indefinitely without stopping for food or drink – and carefully distinguishes between them and the life of the good from which he sees himself still utterly separated: 'Goodness is giving up power and acting upon the world negatively. The good are unimaginable' (p. 445). Aware that 'tricks' are dangerous and that this aspect of religious power is negative, James describes his own inclination towards the ontological proof and his use of religion to provide power for himself. As a result of his misuse of spirituality, he has made himself into a negative magician who has very little choice except to complete the game, to try to break what last attachments he had, and to die.

The annals of Buddhism are full of men of James's type – highly developed adepts who go off the rails – who are, as Murdoch describes James, genuinely spiritual beings but who finally do not quite make it; as Charles will say much later, there are spiritual beings but no saints, and James's attempt has been too dangerous and too closely aligned to magic and power. In his final conversation with Charles, James talks eloquently about the demonism always at the fringes of religious thought and the magic the human mind can project on such thought through the ontological proof:

'Of course,' said James, on whom the wine seemed simply to have the effect of speeding his utterance, 'you are right to keep using the word "superstition", the concept is essential. I asked where does the one end and the other begin. I suppose almost all religion is superstition really. Religion is power, it has to be, the power for instance to change oneself, even to destroy oneself. But that is also its bane. The exercise of power is a dangerous delight. The short path is the only path but it is very steep. . . . The worshipper endows the worshipped object with power, real power not imaginary power, that is the sense of the ontological proof, one of the most ambiguous ideas clever men ever thought of. But this power is dreadful stuff. Our lusts and attachments compose our god. And when one attachment is cast off another arrives by way of consolation. We never give up a pleasure absolutely, we only barter it for another. All spirituality tends to degenerate into magic, and the use of magic has an automatic nemesis even when the mind has been purified of grosser habits. White magic is black magic. And a less than perfect meddling in the spiritual world can breed monsters for other people. Demons used for good can hang around and make mischief afterwards. The last achievement is the absolute surrender of magic itself, the end of what you call superstition. Yet how does it happen? Goodness is giving up power and acting upon the world negatively. The good are unimaginable.'

(pp. 444–5)

Despite his discipline, James has allowed his 'lusts and attachments' to 'compose his god'; not least of these is his attachment to Charles and to power over others, and herein lies his spiritual failure. Although he is aware that religious thinking produces its own images of gods and demons, he is subject to the existence of demons which his mind projects. As he tells Charles, his great failure in the past sadly perverted the spiritual discipline which had originally taught him to play the physical 'tricks' common to the Buddhist adept. Years ago he attempted to cross a stormy mountain pass in Tibet with a beloved sherpa whom he called Milarepa, after the great medieval Tibetan poet-monk whose animist passion for the landscape and spiritual attainments won him a kind of sainthood. It is subtly evident that James pursues the Milarepan ideal in his studies and no doubt in the notebooks of poetry he leaves behind to be unread by the non-adept and unknowing Charles who thinks Milarepa might be an Italian poet; it is also clear that his failures have to do with attachments and the practice of tricks which he describes as 'a less than perfect meddling in the spiritual world [which] can breed monsters for other people'. In the snowy pass he had tried to raise his bodily temperature adequately to keep both himself and the sherpa alive, but he failed and the boy died: 'He trusted me. . . . It was my vanity that killed him. . . . The payment for a fault is automatic. . . . They can get to work on any flaw. . . . I relaxed my hold on him. . . . I lost my grip. . . . The Wheel is just' (p. 447).

These are his final statements to Charles, who in the last pages of the book compulsively extends a habit he had picked up earlier of echoing James's eloquent words as they apply so perfectly and uncannily to his own situation. Although James appears to have spent long years in repenting of his misuse of power and the death of the sherpa, he cannot avoid a direct repetition of behaviour, a plot device reminiscent of Murdoch's habit elsewhere of catching her characters again years later in patterns of action from which they cannot release themselves. Two things are subtly at issue in James's sorry fall – the miraculous rescue of Charles from Minn's Cauldron, and the subsequent death of Titus. The death of Titus is the more remote and tentative issue, and introduces conjecture and eerie puzzlement into the text. James is early described as an uncanny finder of lost objects, a talent he has had from his shining and brilliant boyhood, but Charles also nervously feels that James knows altogether too much: how, for example, had he heard about the death of Charles's father when both his own parents were dead and he off on secret missions in Tibet? How did he know of Charles's retreat to his house by the sea? His knowledge is on the edge of being uncanny, although there is always too a sense that it could be perfectly natural. Having asked for Titus's name, James is completely unsurprised by the young man's presence in Charles's house when he himself arrives for Whitsun week-end; it is rather Titus who is amazed and stares at James, muttering about having seen him in a dream. The idea of James's supersensible powers drawing the innocent Titus by invading his mind with a dream image is very strong here, and James later seems to take such an activity for granted; upon Titus's death he feels the responsibility and the remorse as strongly as Charles does, and sees the event as something involved with his power and his inability to 'hang on'. Titus's death replays for him the death of the sherpa long ago.

James has lost the ability to hang on by the exhaustion attendant on his superhuman rescue of Charles, as we learn later in the story. As Charles, who has just found his mnemonic note to himself describing his miraculous, even unbelievable rescue from the whirlpool by James, thinks over the dramatic events of those climactic days, he patches together a remarkable analysis of the complex situation of his own survival and Titus's death, composed of memory, conjecture and a reiteration of James's always prophetic words. The passage is crucial to the novel:

> I had not questioned James properly because he had become ill immediately afterwards, he had had some sort of collapse and retired to bed. Why was he so exhausted? Because of what he had endured in rescuing me, the physical and mental energy which he had expanded in that unimaginable descent. I recalled his words about 'those things that people do, they can be jolly tiring'. No wonder James was knocked out and seemed to have lost his grip. But then . . . 'I relaxed my hold on him, I lost my grip'. Whom had James been speaking of as I fell asleep that night, his sherpa or perhaps . . . Titus? How was it that Titus had come to me just then? Why had James so pointedly asked for Titus's name? A name is a road. And why had Titus said that he had seen James 'in a dream'? James had always been the finder of lost things. Had he stretched out some tentacle of his mind and found Titus and brought him here and kept him as it were under his care upon a binding thread, a thread of attention which was broken when James became so strangely ill after I had been lifted from the sea? James's reaction to Titus's death had been 'it ought not to have happened', almost as if he felt that it was his own fault. But then if it was his fault it was my fault. There is a relentless causality of sin. . . . And of course my vanity had killed Titus just as James's vanity had killed the sherpa. In each case our weakness had destroyed the thing we loved. And now I remembered something else which James had said. White magic is black magic. A less than perfect meddling in the spiritual world can breed monsters for other people, and demons used for good can hang around and make mischief afterwards. Had one of these demons, with whose help James had saved me, taken advantage of James's collapse to seize Titus and crash his young head against the rock?
>
> (pp. 471–2)

Charles's rationalist western mind, so separated from the real but eerie power mystical thought can project, immediately interprets this spontaneous analysis as madness, but within minutes he reads the letter from James's doctor P. R. Tsang reporting the sacred, magical, willed death of his cousin. Tsang's reverent account of James's quiet departure refers to the Buddha-smile on the dead face, as it had so often been in life; unknowing Charles had with typical condescension called it an 'inane smile' and described it as part of James's 'lowered occluded face'.

At this second climax in the novel, the reader is being hit hard and fast by material from which the rational mind turns vehemently, and Murdoch to satisfy such minds again provides realist explanations: James really died of a heart attack; Titus's death was an accident, as Lizzie had so clearly pointed out; Charles was rescued by a freak wave, as James himself had suggested, although no amount of examination of Minn's dreadful Cauldron really allows for such a rescue. Through James's dabbling in eastern mysticism, however, a clear and frightening entrance is opened into a world of demons of the mind and supersensible, superhuman powers which reflect the religious magic our empirical background shies away from. This eerie magic is a major presence in the novel: it is practised seriously by a thoughtful and intelligent character, and it provides a vocabulary for dealing with events which can scarcely be handled by more rational means.

Although she gives a just description of James and his function as a magician of the religious life, Murdoch is not advocating our necessary belief in magic, demonism or Tibetan disciplines. But she insists that they exist as temptations, and that religious practice, despite its positive disciplines and insistence that one clear the personality of selfishness and set out on the dangerous road to goodness, is all too easily perverted: white magic is black magic, as James says, and the reader's sorrow upon recognizing James's failures is overwhelming. Reading Murdoch teaches her serious audience to discriminate in reaching towards the good, and through most of the novel we regard James with pleasure as an arch-discriminator as pointedly observant of the human scene as Brendan Craddock in *Henry and Cato* and often close to the nameless good Murdoch advocates; he seems a candidate for the highest moral honours bestowable.

The powers James secretly practises connect to an extended vocabulary of demonism which is a necessary part of the novel. In discussing the Tibetan concept of *bardo* with Charles, James argues that 'very few people are without attendant demons' (p. 385), and the novel focuses on an illustration of these demons as they are projected, principally by the Arrowby cousins, but also by the demonic aura of every being. In James and Charles's last conversation, James points out that even the charming creatures of the natural world are thus plagued:

'Did you know that dolphins sometimes commit suicide by leaping onto the land because they're so tormented by parasites?'

'I wish you hadn't told me that. Dolphins are such good beasts. So even they have their attendant demons'.          (p. 443)

The fact that the dolphins' demons are real parasites and not just spiritual constructs illustrates Murdoch's most careful ambiguity in this book: demons appear to have an external reality, and coming from others as an exuding of essence they may have; but as Buddhism teaches, attendant demons are actually projections of personality, like Charles's sea monster. They play out the reality of failed and imperfect beings and illustrate something we are all plagued with. So terrible are the effects of these demons that only an emphatic magical language can deal with them adequately; hence the language of demonism which haunts the world of the two magicians of this novel – the religious James with his Buddhism and the secular Charles with his Shakespeare.

In one of his many ruminations over Hartley and their doomed relationship in the 'Postscript' of the novel, Charles explains the aura of demonism thus:

> there was some sort of demonic filth which had gradually corroded everything, and which seemed to come, without her fault, from her, so that for her sake, for my sake, we had to part eternally. And I seem to see her now, forever disfigured by that filth, untidy, frowzy, dirty, old. How cruel and unjust. Without her fault. The only fault which I can at all measure is my own. I let loose my own demons, not least the sea serpent of jealousy . . . and I know that I quietly belittle her, as almost every human being intentionally belittles every other one.
>
> (pp. 492–3)

The point of contact of one's personal demons with those of another human being is impenetrably difficult to see clearly: does the 'demonic filth' come from Hartley or is it part of Charles's hopeless subjectivity? How much can a first-person narrator see beyond himself? What real statement can he make about the reality of others? Having watched Charles through the larger sections of the book entitled 'Prehistory' and 'History,' we would have to answer these questions with devastating negatives. But as he see-saws to and fro in the limping final, aformal section of the book, going over and over the material, trying all possible angles of conjecture and rumination, there emerges a gradual partial redemption of this all too self-centred man. Repeatedly during the novel, Charles had asked the question, 'Who is one's first love?', and in answering it had led us and him up many blind alleys. Asking Peregrine who his first love was, he was told that it was an Uncle Peregrine, only to discover later that there was no such man: Peregrine's first love is an image of himself, which of course is where Charles's own impassioned attention is placed. The entire string of women from Aunt Estelle on merely illustrate his way of loving himself, and the loss of Hartley is the loss of one of his self-created demons.

Living contemplatively in James's flat during the last twenty-seven pages of the book while, as the subtitle to the last section indicates, 'Life Goes On',

Charles tries conscientiously to examine the bizarre events of the recent past dispassionately. Although he constantly slips back into egotism and a belittling of others, he keeps trying to abjure the magic and see the truth. In the process, his urge towards power over others subsides, and he becomes considerably more objective than we have seen him. He has also given up all attempt at form or the creation of a consistent art work. The progress of the diary here is jerky, full of non-sequiturs, often contradictory. But to replace any loss of formal control we have a daily vision of a man working with real human impediments and yet very, very slowly going forward. He rejects the novelistic shape of an ending which his morning visitation by four seals had given him and which earlier he would have seized on as artistically apropos, and accepts the formless, anti-artistic, shapeless reality of life instead:

> That no doubt is how the story ought to end, with the seals and the stars, explanation, resignation, reconciliation, everything picked up into some radiant bland ambiguous higher significance, in calm of mind, all passion spent. However life, unlike art, has an irritating way of bumping and limping on, undoing conversions, casting doubt on solutions, and generally illustrating the impossibility of living happily or virtuously ever after. . . . I felt too that I might take this opportunity to tie up a few loose ends, only of course loose ends can never be properly tied, one is always producing new ones. Time, like the sea, unties all knots. Judgments on people are never final, they emerge from summings up which at once suggest the need of reconsideration. Human arrangements are nothing but loose ends and hazy reckoning, whatever art may otherwise pretend in order to console us.                                                         (p. 477)

There are indeed some loose ends to be tied up, like the happiness of Lizzie and Gilbert, Gilbert's successes in the theatre and Peregrine's death at the hands of terrorists in Northern Ireland (as Charles had said earlier, 'there is a relentless causality of sin', and Peregrine also pays). But as Charles struggles with interpretations of Hartley and James, it is clear that 'judgments on people are never final', as indeed ours on him cannot be. Just as we watch him going forward into real insight, paying attention to others, generously giving money and time to people in a world to which he has never given a thought, and becoming a wise Prospero without demonic dependence on the magic of power and manipulation, the novel takes an abrupt turn and ends with the opening of new possibilities and likely regressions. The demon casket which has been mentioned several times in the course of the novel as one of James's spookiest treasures is accidentally opened:

> My God, that bloody casket has fallen on the floor! Some people were hammering in the next flat and it fell off its bracket. The lid has come off and whatever was inside it has certainly got out. Upon the demon-ridden pilgrimage of human life, what next I wonder?                         (p. 502)

Any idle or romantic expectation we may have been building up of Charles's conversion to the good is jolted by the book's ubiquitous study of demonism, and Murdoch in her clever apparent meandering to this abrupt conclusion clearly indicates that he could go in either way – towards a better selfless self, or towards more demonic shenanigans with Angela Godwin and Fritzie Eitel. The latter has been doing an on-again-off-again film of the *Odyssey*, and his return to Britain and Charles reminds us that Charles's odyssey, despite his chest pains, is not over until he dies, and no diary can go that far.

★

Among the most impressive things about *The Sea, The Sea* are its landscape, its natural setting and the interiors in which the action takes place. I mentioned earlier the powerful symbolism of the brown-toned, miraculously empty Wallace Collection where James and Charles meet for the first time in the novel. The same kind of evocative symbolism characterizes all other spaces, both natural ones and rooms. In this novel, as in the theatre where Charles has spent his life, everywhere is a symbolic stage set for action; as Charles builds up his description of his house, Shruff End, he specifically mentions the landing of the first floor as a haunted space waiting for action and this is merely a hint for a necessary reading of all other settings. In this, as in so many other ways, comparisons with *The Unicorn* are inevitable and important.

Connected to this strong sense of a place's symbolic power is the title itself, *The Sea, The Sea*, which may first echo in the reader's mind as 'Thalassa, Thalassa', the famous cry of Cyrus's Greek mercenaries in Xenophon's *Anabasis* when after a long overland march through parched Asia Minor, these Mediterranean lovers of the sea at last come to the Black Sea. Relief and delight at finally reaching an ardently wished-for place inform the cry, and the sheer joy in shouting 'the sea, the sea' indicates Charles's initial mood as he smugly delights in his new solitude and the work of art he will finally form of his erratic life. The undoing of this false ideal is one of Murdoch's intentions in the novel, where the sea is detached, neutral and empty, a force which cannot be subdued by Charles's ropes and which indifferently kills Titus. In all his magnificent descriptions of seascapes, Charles is unable to control or command this vast empty force which resists all imprints. The sea, always an important symbol in Murdoch, is not a place of rest, peace and knowledge for Charles, nor does it provide spirit after his parched life; his development and gradual moral advancement take place not here but later in James's London flat. Similarly the sea is not at last a place of joy or relief for Titus, who also cries out 'the sea, the sea,' for it remorselessly kills him; nor for James, who repeats the quotation and shortly undergoes a final dreadful failure under its enormous neutral power.

Even more interesting as a literary echo for this title is the line, 'La mer, la mer, toujours recommencée!' from Paul Valéry's 'Le cimitière marin.' In his notes on the poem (reprinted in Volume I of the Pléiade edition, 1957), Valéry called this work 'un monologue de "moi"', and Charles's autobiographical *oeuvre* certainly follows this definition. The French poet's prolonged meditation before the eternal aspects of the sea and the death symbolized by the marine graveyard is deliberately evoked both by Murdoch's title and by the frequently mentioned *cimitière marin* of Charles's local village, Narrowdean, whose church graveyard overlooks the sea and contains the interesting and quirky gravestone of a sailor named, simply, Dummy. The deaf and dumb long dead sailor reflects the silence and ineloquence of the sea, in deep contrast to the constant buzz of Charles's verbiage. Valéry's poem gives poetic proof of the sea's indifference to the mind of the *moi* which sees it as eternal and divine and keeps trying to interpret it. Murdoch's novel works towards a conclusion analogous to Valéry's where the mind breaking its bondage to the objects of contemplation forms the excitement of the final stanzas. Having in stanza 21 referred to the problem of Zeno's paradoxes, and hence the gulf between man's necessarily limited being and his longing for infinite knowledge (a problem close to the heart of Murdoch's novel), Valery's *moi* turns to the real world of lived experience rather than remaining in the bounds of the soul's naive attempt to exhaust Zeno's vast infinity, which Valéry images by the mesmerizing sea and graveyard. The attempt to leap to divine knowledge which also dominates *The Unicorn* and *The Sea, The Sea* is Valéry's theme, and his turning in the last stanzas from it to life's present reality is echoed by Murdoch's ideological movement in the novel.

Similarly, the poem's connotation as described by Valéry in his commentary of 1933 is of extended interest in dealing with *The Sea, The Sea*; I quote again from the Pléiade edition of Valéry's complete works:

On s'éloigne . . . des conditions 'naturelles' ou ingénues de la Littérature, et l'on vient insensiblement à confondre la composition d'un ouvrage de l'esprit, qui est chose *finie,* avec la vie de l'esprit même, – lequel est une puissance de transformation toujours en acte.

(One separates oneself . . . from 'natural' or naive conditions of Literature, and comes insensibly to confuse the composition of a work of the spirit, which is a *finite* thing, with the life of the spirit itself – which is a transforming power always in motion. [My translation])

Murdoch's paradox is nicely expressed here – the realization that the work of art is a limited thing whereas the reality it imitates, the whole human being, is infinite and always in motion: 'La mer, la mer, toujours recommencée!' As Murdoch well knows, good art must live with this paradox and must constantly fight, as she does through Charles's continuing reality, with the *chose finie* of a too narrow mimesis.

From Murdoch's empty sea of reality into which Charles's busy mind keeps pouring questionable content, we move to the landscape itself, and from there to the major place of the novel – Charles's house, Shruff End. The beautiful landscape, composed of rocks and a vast inland into which Charles rarely ventures, is alien, and in its formation of Minn's Cauldron absolutely dangerous. This is an uncomfortable place where the characters are sternly tested, but the natural objects are deceptively charming – the great yellow rocks, delicate seals and stunningly beautiful stones which are collected by Charles, examined by James and on two occasions made into talismanic objects: one stone is given to Hartley and left behind at her flight; the other requested by James and left on his desk when he dies. There are real places in this alien and symbolic landscape, however, all curiously connected to blackness: we are told that Shruff means black; the pub is called The Black Lion; the local hotel is The Raven; the village itself is named Narrowdean, but a signpost spells it Nerodene (black village) which aligns it with this general pattern. Hartley's bungalow is called Nibletts, which my Canadian childhood causes me to connect with black licorice candies, and at the end of the action at Shruff End the house is finally sold to a Dr Schwartzkopf. In fact, the world of this novel is dominated by black and yellow, the colours of Charles's clicking bead curtain, with a predominance of black; probably we are being nudged towards western and Buddhist death symbolism.

Shruff End itself is a house of many strangenesses. Charles loves it at first glance, in spite of its eerie inner rooms, its lonely separation from the mainland, its almost haunted landing and its resistance to his attempts to make it his own. Like the landscape, it has a weird power, and as Titus, Rosina and Gilbert say, it seems to be a nasty place with 'bad vibes'. The novel presents it as a fey but appropriate setting for the action, and it fits well with Charles's foolish ambitions and obsessions. This mysterious place, when considered in conjunction with the automatic imposition of supernatural material from James's life, becomes a spiritual setting. The fictional black names of its surroundings stress its very obscure placement in the north of England (Cumbria?); it is a nowhere where Charles confronts the obsessions and guilts of his life. In this it is like the Tibetan *bardo* which James had described to Charles:

'Some Tibetans', said James, 'believe –' He corrected himself. He now always spoke of that country in the past tense as a vanished civilization. 'Believed that the souls of the dead, while waiting to be reborn, wander in a sort of limbo, not unlike the Homeric Hades. They called it *bardo*. It can be rather unpleasant. You meet all kinds of demons there.'

'So it's a place of punishment?'

'Yes, but a just automatic sort of punishment. The learned ones regard these figures as subjective visions, which depend on the sort of life the dead man has led.'                                                                    (p. 384)

Charles's retirement from the world of the theatre which is life itself is like an entrance into *bardo*, and at Shruff End the long shadows of causality are enacted. He goes through a 'just automatic sort of punishment' for his misuse of many people, and the gathering of the characters from his past is reminiscent of *The Tibetan Book of the Dead*'s descriptions of the first phases of post-mortal life. The interesting and always important thing in Murdoch's hint in this direction is that the living and the dead are kept in carefully distinguished categories – although in the last pages of the book Charles begins seeing women, whom he thinks are the long dead Clement, on London streets and on underground escalators, a reminder of his earlier habit of thinking he saw Hartleys everywhere. Realistically, Charles is not in *bardo*, but in a world where consequences are uppermost – the world of old age, despite his protestations against such an idea, where the accumulations of a life's guilty activity visit him. Murdoch's hints about supersensible worlds notwithstanding, the occasionally wise Charles of the last twenty-seven pages of the book talks about memory and association and the reality of life in the world as opposed to post-mortal universes:

> Anything can be tarnished by association, and if you have enough associations you can blacken the world. Whenever I hear a dog barking I see again Hartley's face as I last saw it, all wrinkled up with pain, then going strangely blank. Just as, whenever I hear the music of Wagner I remember Clement dying and weeping over her own death. In hell or in purgatory there would be no need of other or more elaborate tortures.        (p. 493)

The novelistic advantage of Shruff End is that it isolates Charles, drives him in on himself and leads him to autobiography. This most fanciful of all realist forms can, in the hands of someone as ruthlessly accurate as Murdoch, mediate between the real and the absurd, between the ordinary vagaries of human experience and its ties with a world of knowledge which has many faces. Her ability to expose these faces and make her reader acknowledge the many paths in *The Sea, The Sea* has to do with her use of this peculiar place in both a literal and a symbolic way. The experience of reading the novel involves our entry into and exit from various worlds, and the ambiguities attendant on such a process produce an unnerving effect. The purely rationalist reader will be the least satisfied because of the unsettling effect of the magical data, which can be talked about but not denied. Shruff End may be an ordinarily eccentric house, but it feels disturbingly otherwise, and the human mind with its longing towards symbol will certainly find material to work on. Early in the novel, Charles quotes James: 'Everything is full of gods' (p. 69), a reference to the pre-Socratic Thales; indeed in the process of reading one feels one is in an ancient world where constant converse with the divine is close at hand through nature, places and certain human beings.

On two occasions in his northern landscape Charles experiences the sublime, a subject on which Murdoch has written two essays: 'The Sublime and the Good' (1959) and 'The Sublime and the Beautiful Revisited' (1960). Charles's sublime involves the starry skies and an almost mystical apprehension of the universe as he sleeps out on the rocks near Shruff End, and it is very interesting to see the subtlety of Murdoch's approach to this subject. On the first occasion, Charles sleeps outside in order to avoid Rosina, who has invaded his house determined to have an interview; as he lies thinking about his Aunt Estelle and his father, he watches the stars until he falls asleep, waking to find

> the sky had utterly changed again and was no longer dark but bright, golden, gold-dust golden, as if curtain after curtain had been removed behind the stars I had seen before, and now I was looking into the vast interior of the universe, as if the universe were quietly turning itself inside out. Stars behind stars and stars behind stars behind stars until there was nothing between them, nothing beyond them, but dusty dim gold of stars and no space and no light but stars. The moon was gone. The water lapped higher, nearer, touching the rock so lightly it was audible only as a kind of vibration. The sea had fallen dark, in submission to the stars. And the stars seemed to move as if one could see the rotation of the heavens as a kind of vast crepitation, only now there were no more events, no shooting stars, no falling stars, which human senses could grasp or even conceive of. All was movement, all was change, and somehow this was visible and yet unimaginable. And I was no longer I but something pinned down as an atom, an atom of an atom, a necessary captive spectator, a tiny mirror into which it was all indifferently beamed, as it motionlessly seethed and boiled, gold behind gold behind gold.                                    (pp. 145–6)

A better description of the reason-defeating aspect of the sublime as described by Kant would be hard to find, but because of the poetry of the description and the access to the heart of reality which is granted Charles, it is impossible not to feel that a spiritual dimension has also been profoundly evoked: the real sublime of nature causes the beholder to approach a mystical experience. Charles awakens to grey dawn and fear, and then has another dark dream about Hartley. Placed between reminders of his guilt with Rosina and his present vile obsession with Hartley, the sublime experience is unearned, something freely given, and the impression is that the luminous world of nature which Murdoch describes with increasing brilliance as her career advances lies waiting to give transcendent experience to anyone who can see.

The second experience of the sublime occurs on the night Charles hears of

James's death and is overwhelmed by a sudden new knowledge of his cousin's occult powers. Charles, who has never paid just attention to James and indeed did not even question how the teenaged boy might have borne the sudden violent death of his beautiful mother in a car crash, begins to see important things about him, spontaneously giving us a sudden insight into the love that actually existed between the two cousins, although obscured by Charles's endemic jealousy. He also gives a precise estimation of why James had to die:

> Religion is power, it must be, and yet that is its bane. The exercise of power is a dangerous delight. Perhaps James wanted simply to lay down the burden of a mysticism that had gone wrong, a spirituality which had somehow degenerated into magic.                                    (p. 474)

After the shock of the various news, Charles cannot sleep in the house but again lies out on the rocks looking at the 'billion billion stars' and seeing 'into the vast soft interior of the universe which was slowly and gently turning inside out. I went to sleep, and in my sleep I seemed to hear a sound of singing' (p. 475). This time he wakens to the sound of the four seals, the first he has seen since coming to Shruff End: 'as I watched their play I could not doubt that they were beneficent beings come to visit me and bless me' (p. 475). Both the sublime of the starry sky and the charm of the seals contribute to a profound religious experience for Charles which is in deep contrast to the route taken by his cousin. Again it is an animistic nature, a sublime but very real universe, which blesses, and compared to his cousin's demonism, this free gift to Charles, although temporary, must be seen as the greater way.

In spite of the realities and various ambiguities of the settings, there is one other aspect which no study of this novel can afford to overlook. Charles inhabits his spaces completely, which is what makes them so liable to symbolic interpretation, and in doing so he eats a lot. Murdoch's characters love their food and drink and can often be interpreted to a degree through them, but Charles is, as James had indicated in his first letter, a food mystic. No day, however extraordinary, is reported without a full account of every bite and swallow taken, all accompanied by Charles's bossy insistence to his reader that there is only one absolute way of cooking or eating anything. Having abjured his power over the stage, Charles picks it up here on this obsession which so amazingly and comically prepares us for his obsession with Hartley. The food business is an interesting device, not only for characterizing Charles and his lust for power, but because it is such a complete anchor to a heartily real world, a handy thing to have in this book where the sense of the supernatural presents such a severe counterbalance.

As a character, Charles is stretched out between his comic absoluteness about food and his inclinations towards a mysticism of the 'moi' for which he tends to use Platonic language. Both he and James constantly mention caves, and although we might be unwilling to believe that Charles is really in *bardo*, there can be little doubt that mentally and spiritually he is wandering in the darkness of Plato's cave, perceiving only shadows, though he talks confidently of a distant source of light which he considers, foolishly, to be Hartley's radiant presence throughout his life. As a cave-dweller he, through Murdoch's myriad devices, very quickly becomes an Everyman – his special case merely illustrates the blindness in which human beings live:

> What an egoist I must seem in the preceding pages. But am I so excep-tional? We must live by the light of our own self-satisfaction, through that secret vital busy inwardness which is even more remarkable than our reason. Thus we must live unless we are saints, and are there any? There are spiritual beings, perhaps James was one, but there are no saints. (p. 482)

In the last few pages of the book, Charles questions whether 'perhaps in a way James and I had the same problem?'. The answer obviously is yes: both these failed magicians, in wildly different ways and infinitely separated in terms of self-knowledge, seek the light of the sun. The difficulties of attaining light and the sad distance of the human mind from the greatest object of its desire are the subject of this subtle novel.

# X

# THE NEW MURDOCH

## Protraction and alien forces in *Nuns and Soldiers*

It is frequently difficult in philosophy to tell whether one is saying something reasonably public and objective, or whether one is merely erecting a barrier, special to one's own temperament, against one's own personal fears. (It is always a significant question to ask about any philosopher: what is he afraid of?) Of course one is afraid that the attempt to be good may turn out to be meaningless, or at best something vague and not very important, or turn out to be as Nietzsche described it, or that the greatness of great art may be an ephemeral illusion. . . . That a glance at the scene prompts despair is certainly the case. The difficulty indeed is to look at all. . . . It is very difficult to concentrate attention upon suffering and sin, in others or in oneself, without falsifying the picture in some way while making it bearable.                                   (*The Sovereignty of Good*, pp. 72–3)

Bradley Pearson in *The Black Prince* pointed to the significance of a comparable question and problem, What does the artist fear?, in perceiving what a writer is up to, and Murdoch, although persistently arguing for a strict differentiation between philosophy and the novel, consciously parallels their effects on their readers. 'A philosopher's thought suits you or it doesn't. It's only deep in that sense. Like a novel' (p. 2), says dying Guy Openshaw in *Nuns and Soldiers* as he debunks the 'dance of bloodless categories' in his former idol Wittgenstein's thought. As Murdoch in 1970 and earlier worked out her ethical philosophy in *The Sovereignty of Good*, she produced a vocabulary which her twentieth novel, published ten years later, reflects with a clarity and evocation that her other recent fictions have only touched on or shadowed. Here in *Nuns and Soldiers* (1980), characters of the good are finally but reluctantly separated from love and shared activity in an ordinary world of muddle and sin which they sadly renounce in their necessary and cold discipline, and the novel sets this barren renunciation, with its association with death, against the protracted warmth of worldly characters whose lies and egotism occupy so many extended pages of this pointedly unbalanced book.

As in the case of its predecessor, *The Sea, The Sea* (1978), *Nuns and Soldiers* is in relatively small measure about the subject of its greatest area of expansion, in this case the protracted relationship almost tediously rehearsed between Gertrude Openshaw and Tim Reede. This bourgeois surface with its overflow of tears occasionally skirts the domain of women's fiction in a frenzied concentration which succeeds in deflecting attention from the novel's centre. It is in this sense a 'falsifying [of] the picture in some way while making it bearable' – that is, the kind of distortion which the philosopher must guard against, although it can constitute an interesting and justified technique for the novelist to play with on the surface of a larger intention. The real centre of *Nuns and Soldiers* is large and multiform, far beyond the image of warm marital happiness for its two most obvious protagonists. It includes such issues as God, philosophy and at-homeness in the world, all seen as alien elements which must be rejected in the spiritual quest; their replacements are, in the light of this novel's stern scrutiny, Christ, the serious uses of the novel as a genre, and homeless alienation. The background of *Nuns and Soldiers* is nothing less than the cosmos whose themes are death and eternal loss, and whose terrifying presence lies behind the fiction not only in simple structural terms through the use of a minor character – the astrophysicist, Gerald Pavitt, with his big telescope and nameless cosmic discovery shadowily referred to as something which may mean the end of everything – but also through the repeated references by the main characters to mankind's nervous necessary connection with an infinite universe they cannot understand.

Although the particularity of Tim's and Gertrude's cogitations seems major, these two characters are severely offset by cosmic invocations, illustrated by Guy's wistful death-bed knowledge that the cosmos is closed to us and that his thoughts can never 'wander in infinite spaces' (p. 5). Tim himself, an interesting experiment in richly extended characterization, recognizes that his final parting from Daisy has cosmic overtones, and that his attempt to unravel it by fitting it to a form – the formula of Papagena and Papageno in *The Magic Flute* – belies the radical and absolute sense of his departure:

> The 'form' of his experience was, he supposed, his resolution to leave Daisy. And he said to himself, it's like the *Magic Flute* after all, except that something has gone wrong and the music is being played differently and Pappagena and Pappageno [*sic*] are not to be saved after all, they have lost each other in the darkness of their ordeal and are never to be reunited ever in any paradise by any god. Yet he knew too that his experience was more than this 'form', that it was absolute, some kind of ultimate phenomenon, some kind of truth, not as it were God, but the cosmos itself, gentle, terrible, final. It was also a vision of death.                            (p. 386)

Most crucially for the infrastructural organization of the novel, however, Anne Cavidge perceives her veridical vision of Christ, who showed her the universe in a small grey pebble, as a gift from the cosmos:

> Anne felt it [her incurably burnt finger] now against the hard cold surface of the stone: the stone in whose small compass her Visitor had made her to see the Universe, everything that is. And if it is so small, thought Anne, beginning thus a sentence which she was never able confidently to finish.
>
> There was no God, but Christ lived, at any rate her Christ lived, her nomadic cosmic Christ, uniquely hers, focused upon her alone by all the rays of being.                                                    (p.500)

Christ's identification with Cosmos (really, *as* Cosmos) had been a commonplace of the Christian centuries from as early as Chalcidius' fourth-century commentary on the *Timaeus*, and was a splendid illustration of the Christianization of the microcosm-macrocosm theory. Anne's visionary Christ, however, does not span the poles in his glory but appears as a small, ordinary, defeated man (compare Tallis Browne, the High Incarnation in *A Fairly Honourable Defeat*) whose message is discipline and failure, and whose image encompasses not infinite spaces but the small and even banal – the humble pebble as symbol, and the demand that the individual follow his unrewarded path through selfless love and responsibility to death. The cosmic connection is not lost in the ambiguity of his treatment, however, for although this Christ may be simply a vision, his searing reality scars Anne permanently beyond the aid of antibiotics, and his cosmic manifestations haunt the background of the novel.

For the secular Tim who amid his ignorance and failures carries much of the book's substance, Christ appears in various indirect guises, all connected to Tim's distance from and approaches to the externally real and true. Much of Tim's activity is unconscious and muddled, particularly in his painting where his subjects frequently approach profound areas of possible speculation of which he is only dimly aware. Thus he paints several series that he does not at all understand: animal paintings illustrative of the organic warmth which is so important in this novel, mesh and net paintings of mathematical precision, paintings of people whom he calls spectators at a crucifixion (although no crucifixion is ever depicted by Tim who does not choose to suffer if he can help it), paintings of the cosmic myth of Leda and the swan, and most interestingly, good sketches of a particular rock formation in France. This conjunction of rock and circular pool Tim labels the Great Face, and sees it as beyond nature, a numinous presence of undoubted external divinity, and a reminder of the divine in him. Its function parallels the work of Christ on Anne, and assists Murdoch in using Tim as a link between Christ and nature.

In describing the manifold beauties of the French landscape, Murdoch evokes an animist sense of the divine, and with reference both to the Great

Face's shimmering pool and to Tim's salvation of himself through leaf collages after his parting from Daisy, the word 'donation' is used to describe the free giving by nature of its organic products to be worked upon by the ever active psyches of the characters. Tim's project of decorating a bunker-like church for a harvest festival involves his use of the natural beauties of the world – berries, leaves, weeds – and has as a backdrop a large banner reading JESUS PARDONS, JESUS SAVES. Although the simple fundamentalism of the religious sect is not interesting to Tim, the presence of the image of Christ in the midst of organic reality and humble hard work is central to Murdoch's subtle laddering downwards of the cosmos from vast conceptions, through sublime nature in the Great Face, to the simple organisms of animals and leaves and weeds. This control of cosmic ideas through the vast, then to the animistic religious, then to the simple uses of nature defines the progress and perhaps the purpose of *Nuns and Soldiers*. Its principal point echoes what Murdoch has always tried to teach: that one must work towards a reality that exists truly and externally in the world. To domesticate Christ and associate him with humble mankind, nature and the task of the individual is also a way of balancing the terrors of the cosmos and of keeping a stern perspective on the romantic and aggrandizing instinct of the human mind to go against this natural reality towards theoretical ideas. Anne Cavidge's ruminations about her 'nomadic cosmic Christ' point the only route for homeless alien characters of the good in Murdoch's work:

He was defeated, she thought, the way to Jerusalem was not a triumphal progress. He was a failure, a pathetic deluded disappointed man who had come to an exceptionally sticky end. And yet: 'Weep not for me but for yourself.' Could she, knowing what she knew of him, of all his failure, all of it, tread that way after him? Could she relive his journey and his passion while knowing that he was after all not God? And she remembered the 'wonderful answer' which had made her Visitor laugh and call her 'witty', when she had said, 'Love is my meaning'. And she remembered too in an odd way something which the Count had said once about his own love and its object. 'I did it all, I enacted both sides of the relation, and this could be done because she was inaccessible.' And Anne cried out in her heart to her living Christ, 'Oh Sir, your yoke is heavy and your burden is intolerable.' And she was answered in his words, 'The work is yours.' (p. 500)

Opposed to this Christ, the imitation more than the worship of whom is a model for Murdoch's ethical thought, is the idea of God, a theoretical being whose existence is provable only by the ontological proof. Murdoch has frequently pondered this subject and exemplifies it in the above quotation by recalling the Count's happy theoretical love for Gertrude before Guy's death, a love which could exist only because he 'enacted both sides of the relation, and this could be done because she was inaccessible'. The concentration of the religious mind on the inaccessible and perhaps unreal object of worship imbues that object with power and psychic energy, as James Arrowby eloquently explained in *The Sea, The Sea*, but God for Murdoch is only a theory, an abstract something entirely enacted and materialized by the psyche of man and therefore non-existent. Christ's historicity, on the other hand, his enactment of life and preresurrection failure, separate him from the aspect of theory that surrounds the persona of God, and Murdoch's subtle connecting of him with nature itself materializes him in an oddly traditional way as the spirit of the cosmos. Anne's Christ deliberately deflects worship and pity, denigrating the period of his own suffering, and projects responsibility onto the living individual, the person seeking moral and spiritual amelioration amid the details of the time-and-space-ridden universe: '"The work is yours".'

God, persistently denied in this novel, is seen as an alien element produced by the theory-centred operations of the mind as opposed to the reality of experience. In fact the three rejected elements which are extensively treated in *Nuns and Soldiers* – God, philosophy (especially Wittgenstein) and at-homeness in the world – all appear as powerful, even overwhelming forces which, like the bourgeois content, distract attention from the true centre. Thus Anne Cavidge sees herself as having erred in her conventual pursuit of God and in her attempt to escape the mess and muddle of the world. Her necessary return to that world causes her pain and a considerable measure of confusion, but only through them is she enabled to take steps forward towards the good she yearns for. Gradually she learns a vocabulary for dealing with the non-existent God, perceiving that the necessary moral nexus forces one to act 'as if there were God'. She also comes to understand that her quest for the good which she had previously called God spoils her for any activity other than that quest, and she realizes now that the discipline of a pointless, repeated prayer can keep her directed outwards to the void. Two passages are essential in showing how she can use the concept of God without theory or fantasy. The first occurs as she addresses the suicidal Count:

'Your life doesn't belong to you', said Anne. 'Who can tell where his life ends? Our being spreads out far beyond us and mingles with the being of others. We live in other people's thoughts, in their plans, in their dreams. This is as if there were God. We have an infinite responsibility.'    (p. 446)

The other is part of her final ruminations before leaving for America and the Poor Clares:

She had been right after all, and the events of the last year had confirmed it, to think that she had been irrevocably spoilt for the world by God. And spoilt, and rightly spoilt, even though she no longer believed in Him. St Augustine had prayed by repeating simply again and again My Lord and my God, my Lord and my God. Anne felt now that she too could pray so in her utmost need, calling upon the name of the non-existent God.   (p. 499)

We learn through Anne what Murdoch expressed in *The Sovereignty of Good*: 'One might say that true morality is a sort of unesoteric mysticism, having its source in an austere and unconsoled love of the Good' (p. 92). Anne's task, however, is humbler than this, because what is most feared and guarded against in this novel is a vitiation of the idea of the good, and Murdoch is at pains not to push Anne too far in the direction of sainthood. In the last few pages of the novel Anne, sitting in The Prince of Denmark pub, hears that Daisy has gone off to America in search of her innocence, and thinks thus soberly about it: 'It was a quest suited to human powers. Perhaps after all, Goodness was too hard to seek and too hard to understand' (pp. 503–4). Murdoch's often repeated statement that there are no saints certainly indicates that Anne's fears are justified, but there can be no doubt that the hopeless quest will go on in her life.

It is instructive to set Anne's humility and drive towards the good against the demonic nay-saying of Carel Fisher in *The Time of the Angels*:

> People will endlessly conceal from themselves that good is only good if one is good for nothing. The whole history of philosophy, the whole of theology, is this act of concealment. The old delusion ends, but there will be others of a different kind, angelic delusions which we cannot now imagine. One must be good for nothing, without sense or reward, in the world of Jehovah and Leviathan, and that is why goodness is impossible for us human beings. It is not only impossible, it is not even imaginable, we cannot really name it, in our realm it is non-existent. The concept is empty. This has been said of the concept of God. It is even more true of the concept of Good. It would be a consolation, it would be a beatitude, to think that with the death of God the era of the true spirit begins, while all that went before was a fake. But this too would be a lie, indeed it is the lie of modern theology. With or without the illusion of God, goodness is impossible to us. We have been made too low in the order of things. God made it impossible that there should be true saints. But now he is gone we are not set free for sanctity. We are the prey of the angels.   (p. 186)

Carel has fallen into a fissure created by his own reality-seeking being, assuming that the impossibility of the task means that demonism must be substituted for holiness. Knowing the reality of the problem leads him to perversion and fury, to a position directly opposite to that taken by Tallis Browne in *A Fairly Honourable Defeat*, Brendan Craddock in *Henry and Cato* and Anne Cavidge in *Nuns and Soldiers*. The primary difference between Carel's truth and theirs deals with the fear Murdoch expressed in the quotation which began this chapter: the fear that 'the attempt to be good might be meaningless', or, even worse, its value non-existent. *Nuns and Soldiers* scrupulously distinguishes between the theoretical idea of the non-existent God and the stringent concept of the good which exists even though human beings like Anne, or Guy, or the Count can barely endure even the beginnings of the ardours demanded by the quest.

Certainly such difficult and faltering steps forward as Anne's are in obvious and dramatic opposition to the idea of happy at-homeness exemplified in the finally idyllic marriage of Gertrude and Tim which supplies the novelistic surface of *Nuns and Soldiers*. The novel as a bourgeois product has always served certain expectations of hero and heroine, and there is more than a touch of irony as Murdoch first shocks us with and then protracts this central relationship. The reader's impatience with the pair, particularly with the voracious Gertrude, is part of the strategy of the novel, as it had been in the case of the extended obsessions of Charles Arrowby in *The Sea, The Sea*. But the consolations of Gertrude and Tim's marriage, their home-making happiness and their final delight in a tribal society, originally set up by Guy, satisfy the conventional hunger of readers for traditional material. Murdoch delivers it with a vengeance, but the major moments in any novel – the beginning and ending – are here given to more significant characters, Guy and Anne, and to more important themes, death and Christ. The at-homeness and warmth which the bourgeois world longs for and tries so energetically to obtain are opposed to death, to the task of Christ, to the cosmos itself. The visionary Christ pointedly repeated the biblical words, 'Birds have nests and foxes have holes, but the Son of Man hath not where to lay his head', and the characters who are in varying ways on the path towards the good – Anne, the Count, the dying Guy – must reject the hope of being at home in the world and wander through a cosmos of uncertainty, as Christ had done, towards death, which Anne's Christ claimed as one of his names. The opposition of the reality of cosmic homelessness to the bourgeois longing for at-homeness is one of Murdoch's major themes in *Nuns and Soldiers*.

Nevertheless, the rejected elements of God and at-homeness supply important reference points against which sterner realities can be set. A third strong element of spurious interest early in the novel is the philosophy of Wittgenstein which had so fascinated Guy Openshaw, and which, as he confronts the hard reality of death, is also seen as theoretical, alien, and hence reduced from its initial godlike role in his life. Guy's frustration at the philosophical enterprise is rehearsed in his opening conversation with the Count: he calls Wittgenstein an amateur, an oracular voice, and describes his analysis of language as 'Linguistic idealism. A dance of bloodless categories after all' (p. 2). Wittgenstein's 'naive and touching belief in the power of pure thought' (p. 1) was negated long ago for Guy by the philosopher's naive skepticism about man's technological possibility of reaching the moon.

When theory touches reality as it does in Wittgenstein's skeptical error, the theory dies as its abstract nature demands.

Yet the first word of the novel in Guy's dying mouth is 'Wittgenstein –', and for a reading public long tantalized by the chimera of Murdoch as philosophical novelist, the temptations towards narrow Wittgensteinian interpretation are enormous. Murdoch has fought long and hard against such a tag and such a tendency to reduce her work to sterile formulae and philosophical preoccupations. At the same time, her broad allusive frame within the novels has kept her publicly aligned with certain philosophers, and Wittgenstein has kept bobbing up in the novels as a witty and often significant point of reference. From the early criticism of her first novel, *Under the Net*, the tendency was to talk about the net reference as having its source in Wittgenstein's *Tractatus*, and because of the use of philosophical debate in that novel Murdoch's reputation as a philosophical novelist became inerasable, and continues to be so in an unjust and clichéd way. Certainly the persistence of philosophical allusion cannot justify this, and it is true indeed that Murdoch's great achievement as a novelist is in old, purely novelistic issues like character, description, plot and technical brilliance. To the degree that there is a philosophical issue in her work, it is Platonic and moral, and functions at the same absolutely background level as her serious use of Shakespearean references or paintings. Although critics have talked a great deal about Sartre and Kant, the ultimate working-out of her fictions is much more concentrated on causality and the peculiar structures of human personality.

In no way negligent of the traps critics often fall into, I myself concocted a Wittgensteinian reading of *Nuns and Soldiers* on the basis of Guy's interest in that philosopher. It was remarkably easy to do, and I stubbornly followed the reading at its narrowest level for a long time: although it caused a jarring in interpretation, I felt like a triumphant puzzle-solver, the one thing the critic cannot be except in an ironic way when one is dealing with something as ambitious and multi-levelled as a Murdoch novel. Nevertheless, I culled the images of the net and picture from the *Tractatus Logico-Philosophicus*, as well as the ideas of tribal language, family resemblance, the chess game and forms of life from *Philosophical Investigations*. In this novel where a painter does net pictures, where the social setting comprises an extended Jewish family who share the same tribal 'language' and whose moral similarity constitutes easy communication in a shared *Sprachspiel*, where Gertrude and the Count cannot play chess because of a failure of communication, the set-up looks dangerously tempting, even though Guy dies fairly early in the novel and thereafter no mention of Wittgenstein is made. Murdoch, however, says firmly that the chess game is only a chess game and the family only a family, and although I share the current critical fashion of finding Wittgenstein's combinations of images radiant with meaning, a significant adjustment has to be made. The most important discipline – and this expands beyond *Nuns and*

*Soldiers* to the art of reading novels in general – is to avoid the simple habit of tracing an allusion and then expanding it to fit a critical theory. For of course it is equally true, and much more true to the actual effect of the text, that chess games and tribes and nets and language and pictures are also abiding images without philosophical connection, and the affective result of reading *Nuns and Soldiers* is to drive the reader back to the traditional novel, both in memory, as Murdoch evokes the techniques of the form during the period of its greatness, and in fact, as her calling on Scott (an example chosen randomly from among many in this novel) leads one back to the delights of rereading *The Heart of Midlothian*, with its extended pleasures and allusive largess. The major problem in pushing the philosophical effect beyond its intended usage into theory is that it denigrates and even denies the richness of the reading experience, a vital aspect of the enjoyment and apprehension of the work of art that current critical fashions are rendering secondary and even forgetting.

Most unconscionably, to say that the combinations and hence much of the basis of the book is Wittgensteinian is to accuse Murdoch, as critics have been all too ready to do, of playing secret games against her readers, of concentrating on philosophical theory at the expense of what she has again and again shown herself to be most dedicated to: engaging the attention by stressing characters and the real story. It is significantly the duty of her readers to allow the books to speak their own intention while we listen carefully to them, and to keep the text from being embroiled and sold short by the exciting limitations of theories.

It should be fairly obvious that the alien elements which look so comforting in *Nuns and Soldiers* – God, bourgeois happiness, the theoretical pleasures of philosophy – are there to cast a certain light, to show how people concentrate on ideas excessively, as do critics, before they fall into the rigours of true experience; above all, these elements are not depicted as central theories to take the reader's mind away from the experience at hand, which is replete with all the pleasures and scope the novel as genre has always celebrated. Keeping Murdoch's ideology in the right place should not be as difficult as it has proved to be, and from first to last in criticism of her work, the greatest mistakes have occurred when the philosophical references certainly present and functioning at a minor level become so haunting to the critic that the forefront and centre of the novels are both ignored. The inclination to see the novels as exercises in philosophy no doubt stems from the critic's desire to enlarge the boundaries of his commentary by whatever means possible, and to track down and identify, if not compete with, the mysterious reaches of the artist's imagination. In both intentions there is a deep gnostic desire and an impulse to place the use and value of literature in an intellectually respectable sphere.

Probably the critic's largest area of anxiety is that literary texts, so utterly valuable to those of us whose temperaments are attuned to their far-reaching achievement, can too easily be reduced to simple pleasure and entertainment as opposed to extended to a larger moral and spiritual function. The result can be both mystification and demystification, and unfortunately in the tendency many of us have had in commenting on Murdoch, the direction has been towards mystification, towards making general readers feel that the material is too complexly out of their ken. This disservice is emphasized by the fact that there is a great deal of difference between various intensities in reading a Murdoch novel: reading it once through quickly can certainly be a mystifying and confusing, if fascinating, experience. Studying it by a great variety of devices – and this book has traced only a few – is an immeasurable and rewarding experience, and as I indicated in quoting Nabokov on the quality of detail in great novels in the first pages of this study, it is the rereader who will be most rewarded by Murdoch's splendidly allusive and complex though *not* reader-alienating work. Nevertheless, there are paradoxes here, not least involving the sense one has in reading that there are two central *loci*, one having to do with the rich, character-driven life of the novel which comprises an inevitably interesting story and a good read, the other evoking mysterious moral depths that one must work on: the work for the spirit of my study's title.

The spokesman for the judges of the Booker Prize in 1978, Sir Alfred Ayer, rightly pointed out that *The Sea, The Sea* is not about Plato, and it is not, except for the occasional evocation or idea; nor, similarly, is *Nuns and Soldiers* about Wittgenstein. The force of allusion can certainly, in dealing with some sections of any Murdoch novel, throw the attention momentarily towards a philosophic idea or particularly an image, but the 'dance of bloodless categories' which Guy Openshaw finally sees philosophy to be is indeed opposed to the crowded, extensive life of a Murdoch novel. She deserves more than the cliché of 'philosophical novelist', and it should be remembered that in the case of a character with a partial philosophic bent like Guy Openshaw, Wittgenstein had once, when Guy was an idealistic undergraduate, provided a partial key to his mind, but not to this entire novel, and certainly not to Murdoch as artist, whose work cannot justly be read in this narrow way.

★

The extended and acknowledged profundity of this latest novel, *Nuns and Soldiers*, is in deep contrast to the comic currents of the first novel, *Under the Net*, and the best way of talking about Murdoch's latest style is to revert to a brief sketch of how that style developed. In Chapter V, I talked about the atypicality of *Under the Net* despite its thematic introduction to her subsequent work. Her zigzagging development through mixtures of ruminative novels, technically brilliant experiments and the quasi–gothic, to the full, mature style ushered in by *The Nice and the Good*, indicated how many styles she actually had at her disposal, and her particular expertise in these various styles showed that she had within her talent many possible directions. The variations and experiments of her mature style, from 1968 on, have occupied much of this book; it is now important to note that *The Sea, The Sea* (1978) appears to have created a partially new mode which is shared also by *Nuns and Soldiers*. Murdoch seems, in other words, to have become a new sort of novelist recently, and the *aficionado* must rearrange his expectations of the reading experience.

For all her experiments and changes in style, the one steady aspect of Murdoch's novels has been their speed. Although there has been a gradual, continuous lengthening of the novels, page counting has never been important because the energy of the action sweeps plot and reader along with hurricane force. *The Sea, The Sea* altered that, and in doing so puzzled many of her strongest fans. Some, reading the novel for the first time, argue that Charles Arrowby is such an impossible man that their negative feelings about the book come from his antics, but he is no worse than Hilary Burde of *A Word Child* or Bradley Pearson of *The Black Prince*. The problem is really one of defeated expectations, for Murdoch has concentrated in *The Sea, The Sea* on slowing down the action and extending both description and rumination. Throughout her career she has shown a strong tendency towards protraction, and her most lasting effects have to do with this inclination which counters her equal proclivity to speed. *The Sea, The Sea*'s greatly expanded descriptions and extended reportage of thought change the reading experience and slow the action. On the surface, one can say that this protraction is largely a function of the drawn–out nature of Charles's obsession, but it is in fact a stylistic change, a brooding on the natural world with an animistic intensity which has always been present in the style but is here developed to a new extreme. The resultant slow–down changes the whole quality of reading, makes us more languorous and in touch with the subtle effects which the rapid surface of the other books often deflected, at least during the first reading.

For subtlety is Murdoch's goal in this slower mode, as is a connection with the descriptive elegance of the early nineteenth–century novel. There is, of course, nothing softly sentimental in this surprising reversion, for it is mixed with occasional speed and the contemporary instinct for the bizarre whenever they are needed, and in *The Sea, The Sea* we are so frequently surprised by the action that it is very easy to forget that this slower pace is stylistically foremost. But in *Nuns and Soldiers*, with its switch to the omniscient narrator and its new quietness of action, it becomes clear that *The Sea, The Sea* was not an anomaly but a new turning. There is no lack of plotting or skimpiness in the development of this style, but rather a pervasive sense of a beautifully subtle world of nature and an endless, generous concept of the workings of the mind.

These elements have always been present in Murdoch; as in all her previous shifts and changes, the principal issue is one of stress: she simply enlarges and extends something she has handled well in narrower ways elsewhere. As usual she does not in changing her stress jettison the other areas of style she has established: thus plotting in *Nuns and Soldiers*, although not at all frenetic remains a powerful factor, and this retention of strong plot-movement makes the first reading of the novel difficult in a new way. The eager desire to know what happens next struggles against the languorous extensions and protracted subtleties in a way peculiar to Murdoch and not always in accord with the reading preferences of her anxious audience. Readers are strangely stubborn about their expectations, and in this new turning with its demand for patience, its increasing Proustianism and its spatial luxuries, reader response will no doubt hesitate at first.

Yet the reading of *Nuns and Soldiers* for the old Murdoch hand is replete with thematic pleasures connected to the enjoyment of her earlier books. To list only a few: we have jewellery gift-giving as in *The Unicorn*, the use of Augustine's prayer as in *Henry and Cato*, a great deal of Polish matter evocative of *The Flight from the Enchanter*, preoccupation with concepts of the just judge reminiscent of *The Nice and the Good* and *A Fairly Honourable Defeat*; so dense is the design of the book in fact that such evocations appear to occur on every other page. The most significant ones, however, involve the title itself: nuns remind not only of *The Bell* but lead us into an expanded examination of the idea of Julian of Norwich whose luminous words are never far from any Murdoch novel. And soldiers bring to the foreground a gentlemanly discipline which Murdoch touched on in brief references to Harriet Gavender's father and brother in *The Sacred and Profane Love Machine*, and developed somewhat more extensively in Felix Meecham in *An Unofficial Rose* and in the superficial qualities of James Arrowby in *The Sea, The Sea*.

The titular plurals of *Nuns and Soldiers* are meant to set up the binary contrasts which have always, from her novelistic beginnings in *Under the Net*, fascinated Murdoch. Although the ostensible nun is Anne Cavidge fresh from the convent, and the figurative soldier the honourable English Pole, Peter Szczepansky, nicknamed the Count, Murdoch makes it clear that these two 'moral oddities', as Manfred North is to call them at the end of the book, are balanced by more profane characters. We learn with some surprise that Manfred (not to mention the vain Gertrude herself) also considers Gertrude to be oddly virginal and chastely nun-like despite her marriages and need for masculine love, and Tim Reede is described as in his confused way soldiering along. The enormous distance between the moral discipline and austerity of Anne and the self-indulgence of Gertrude parallels that between the Count and Tim, and Murdoch's often used contrasting terminology of sacred and profane is once more called on and examined in the light of the various subject matters of the novel.

The disciplines of the cloistered religious life and of soldiering themselves reflect further binary qualities of the novel, and as Murdoch studies the religious Anne Cavidge and the secular Count a progressive image builds of the disciplined austerity of the good. One of the primary purposes of this study has been to describe the conditions of the good as Murdoch depicts them, and to examine how her definitions, achieved through the presentation of a few characters of the good, affect the nature of her fiction. Characters of the good are a rarity in Murdoch's work: she is much more likely to describe characters whose inclination is sadly incomplete or whose failures on the quest are uppermost, as she had done so dramatically with James Arrowby in *The Sea, The Sea.* Here in *Nuns and Soldiers* we have not merely one character of the lonely good, usually the maximum endowment for a novel, but several who are on the road: Anne, Guy, the Count, perhaps Manfred, perhaps Gerald Pavitt, perhaps even the hidden character, Balintoy – although they are developed in various ways and often mysteriously obscured from interpretation. Characters *are* very mysterious here, and one senses that their mystery is oddly connected with virtue rather than with the demonism Murdoch has so often studied.

Chiefly, of course, Anne and to a lesser degree the Count are seen as in process towards the unattainable good, and Anne finally goes furthest on that lonely and hopeless route through her disciplined ability to break away from the London scene and Gertrude's voracious desire to enclose everyone in the warm circle of her love: 'It's like a sheepfold with the sheep gathered in', says Gertrude, and Anne replies swiftly, 'Or a playpen with the children in it' (p. 467). This exchange does much to explain the extended central argument of a novel which contrasts the consoling illusion of home and permanence with the sharp reality of death and eternal partings. Not only is the serious quest for the good here defined in terms of insecurity and homelessness, but its opposite encourages the perpetual childishness we see in Tim Reede. The idea of retardation in childishness has been a very powerful one in Murdoch's work, and here it is examined with interesting and ambiguously generous results.

While the Count and Anne rigorously seek the good, Tim and Gertrude seek happiness. Throughout the action, all central activity is commented on by the novel's milieu – the extended Jewish family, more or less alienated from their Jewishness, over which Guy Openshaw has presided as a paterfamilias. He calls them *les cousins et les tantes,* and their number extends to distant relatives, orthodox Jews, Christianized Jews, non-Jewish members by marriage and miscellaneous friends. This extended family is unified in a tribal way, and indeed they use the term tribe; they speak the same language which here involves bourgeois virtue and kind relatedness, and they serve as an audience to the central action. Their estimation, expressed through the rather negative Mrs Mount, that Tim Reede seeks a mother in Gertrude just as years ago she had sought a father in her marriage to Guy, illustrates the sensible overview, as their conversations always do. The interesting thing about them is that the group is composed of decent people whose commonsensical kindness and generosity indicate a high level of civilization held as a positive attainment. Their comments on the affair and subsequent marriage of Tim and Gertrude could be sneeringly destructive and expressive of a feeling of betrayal of the much loved, much lamented Guy, but in general they are not, and there is a positive feeling of a potential extended inclination towards good in society, an idea rare in Murdoch's work.

Tim and Gertrude's search for happiness dominates the action and constitutes the central plot-line. In heavy contrast to this profane version of nun and soldier, Anne and the Count offer their own awkward and pallid search for at-homeness in the world which in the ironic context of the bourgeois level of this novel is the equivalent of happiness. Although both are under private moral orders, life in the world automatically muddies their tasks, and a longing for happiness hits both of them at a confusing erotic level. Significantly, they are described as having similar physical characteristics – colourless fair hair and cold blue eyes; both are thin and only hesitantly buy new clothes or think about their physical being. The Count is bony and awkward, ill at ease in the English world: he compensates with a soldierly continental habit of stiff, heel-clicking, formal behaviour. Both are essentially alienated from the milieu into which they half wish to fit. Unlike the Openshaw tribe, which crisscrosses and fits together, they speak another language, not to each other but privately, in their minds and in the loneliness which defines both their lives.

The Count lives in the political world of Poland's past, and as he listens to Radio 4 every night until sign-off or lies sleepless in bed, he reviews the horrors of Polish history which had so dominated his father's active life; when he sleeps, he dreams of the holocaust in the Warsaw ghetto. In love with Gertrude for years, he now, having overhead Guy's dying wish that Gertrude might marry him, lives in hope of a life warmed and integrated by love: but even here he shows his private obsession, imagining Gertrude with him in Warsaw where he could show her the landmarks of Polish disasters and talk about wars he did not fight but must relive. The haunting, unremitting horror of his mental replaying of the tragic violence of Poland's history isolates him from his London milieu; it is something he cannot talk about with anyone, not even Guy who, to the Count's puzzlement, does not even seem to have any books on the subject of Poland in his well-stocked libraries. His obsession with this central aspect of his Polish family's political wretchedness and Poland's national suffering keeps him in a tight prison and guarantees his inability to win Gertrude. The impossibility of his love for her is sadly asserted when she wishes to play chess with him in France, and he reluctantly has to point out that he plays so well that they would simply be playing different games. The novelistic point of this reflection is clear: Gertrude and the Count are from different tribes, and cannot get their game together. It makes sense that the Count, in losing all hope of marrying Gertrude, would contemplate rational suicide or departure for beleaguered Northern Ireland whose political history Murdoch has elsewhere compared with Poland's: physical removal from the scene simply parallels the lonely alienation which has plagued him since childhood. His inability to fit into English society and his sense of having no country except in Poland's suffering stress his homelessness at the civic and national level, and this politico-historical obsession cuts him off at the level of happiness from those who do feel at home in the world – especially Gertrude.

The Count's civic self involves stern moral discipline, as does Anne's religious attachment, and we see him paying attention to every small moral and social detail: from carefully refraining from taking a drink until Gertrude offers it during the 'evenings' while Guy lies dying, to scrupulously extending every kindness to guilty Tim even though doing so means that he may lose his one great chance to win Gertrude, his heart's desire. When he realizes that nothing can help Tim, he leaves the studio, smiling up at the rain as his hope revives; the important thing for the morally precise Count is that any personal happiness can come to him only if the whole situation has been treated with humanity and justice. Although he wants Gertrude very much, his moral accuracy never falters.

Anne shares this quality: she falls in love with the Count but never, not even by the flicker of an eyelid, allows her love to be seen; and never does she permit this love to interfere with the moral commitment she feels to Gertrude's happiness. When Tim's guilt in the Daisy affair seems palpable, she plays what she feels is a hateful role in watching Daisy's flat and seeing Tim's guilty entrance. Her moral accuracy parallels the Count's and in some ways goes beyond it: as a result, she is open to accusations by the other characters of coldness and cruelty as well as of prejudice and possessiveness. It is important to note that one of Murdoch's structural tricks involves the fact that of the entire Openshaw circle, only Manfred North sees Anne clearly, and given his hidden aspect as an observing Horatio who sees the entire action spread out before him, it makes sense that he would love the sustained secret nunhood in Anne and perceive as well as identify with her goodness. Murdoch's clever withholding of this information until the end of the novel, combined with her simultaneous revelation of the Balintoy character associates these two men with hidden paths of the good which the formal limitations of the fiction have not been able to explore. The fact that Manfred is always in the background performing virtuous deeds should not be taken lightly.

Like the Count, Anne absents herself from occasions that could help her win her beloved's heart, and when she, Gertrude and the Count go to France, she allows the two of them as much time alone as possible, acting as their servant and assuming that they will surely marry now that Tim's guilt has been established. Again like the Count, she is overcome with joy when circumstance seems to play into her hands; a battered Tim turns up at the French house, and she and the Count flee to England. She does not foresee how little Peter needs in order to be made happy by Gertrude, however. Although he will be meagrely content with his role as *cavaliere servente* to the delighted, voracious Gertrude and his civic self rejoices in the new Polish Pope, Anne with her religious quest towards an insatiable good goes off into a homeless world. Both will live not for themselves, but as servants: he to the bourgeois world, she to the poor and homeless whom the Chicago Poor Clares help.

The fascinating aspect of these two characters as they relate to the central action of the book is their alien aspect and fundamental unworkability within the novelistic frame. Not only are they alien to the family atmosphere of the novel's context, they frustrate the very idea of fictional character. Their cold control and the Count's inarticulate awkwardness do not add up to any concept a conventional reader might have of a character: Manfred is right in calling them 'moral oddities', and when one tries to fit the Count to his fictional forebear, the awkward wonderful Pierre of *War and Peace* (the novel Anne starts reading when she finally finishes *The Heart of Midlothian*, where she too seems to have a novelistic avatar in Jeanie Deans, a stringent and disciplined character whose single-minded devotion to a cause is rewarded in ways denied to Anne), his meagreness as a character becomes clear. Murdoch has long specialized in odd and alienated characters, but she here makes the Count and Anne extraordinarily central, and is obviously struggling to domesticate such beings in our sympathy by stressing their desperate inner intensities and private anguish. This difficult undertaking is put under additional strain as each falls in love with an unattainable person, and with overwrought stress and anxiety tries to enter the alien world of the bourgeoisie. At these points they too join in the long, self-indulgent passages, so characteristic of this novel's central style, in which characters in love brood selfishly on their total abandonment to an almost medieval lovesickness. The effect is jarring, if only because the awkwardness which comes from their alienation makes them unable to deal with the emotional frenzy Murdoch uses in describing the state of being in love.

The interesting result of the depiction of these two characters can at first glance appear to be a major flaw in the novel. It reflects, however, a condition in Murdoch's paradoxical thinking about both realism and the good. Fairly early in her career, in *An Unofficial Rose*, Murdoch put Ann Peronett, a character of unconscious good, at the centre of the novel with unsettling results. To place a character of the good in such a dominant position, given Murdoch's definitions, means a central lack of vitality, and although *An Unofficial Rose* is not a failed novel, it falters under this weakness. In Murdoch, characters of the good tend to be well integrated only in areas which are, although major, peripheral to the energy of the novel, because their stern discipline and self-denials are anomalies in the self-indulgent middle range of human life which it is fiction's task to illuminate.

Any novel adhering to the great Tolstoyan novelistic tradition as Murdoch's late work clearly does, belongs to a generous form which tries to reach its reader's heart, and Murdoch is certainly a generous writer. But the moral distinctions she presents to a contemporary world with no great admiration for such disciplines automatically mean that characters who represent the stringent good cannot be extremely sympathetic in the traditional sense. Murdoch's main point in *Nuns and Soldiers*, made much more openly and clearly than in any of the earlier novels, is that although the characters of the good, the characters in quest of hard reality, may yearn for a place in the comfortable middle space of the world, their essential state is one of alienation and separation. The warm world of so much of this novel centres on the Openshaw circle, on Gertrude and even for a while on the wonderful character, Daisy; here personality and character reside as they do in that smaller soldier, Tim. The life of the novel also lies here, and although characters like Anne and the Count have access to that life and can exist in the novel's frame, they cannot in conventional terms succeed. What I am saying is that Murdoch, given her conditions, could not have succeeded in engaging her audience in a totally friendly way with the problems and virtues of these two characters; the paradox of their inclusion necessarily involves failure at an apparent but, I think, only superficial level.

★

The case of Guy Openshaw reinforces the idea of alienation and separation which the Count and Anne play out, and his movingly described death presses home from the beginning the theme of eternal departures and farewells. In the last stages of cancer, Guy has withdrawn from his friends and wife to the lonely meditations of the dying. Although he sees none of his family except Gertrude and even with her has only one real conversation, about his desire that she marry again after he is gone, he does engage in serious conversation with the two obvious outsiders of his circle, Anne and the Count. The novel opens with him talking to the Count, and in this conversation and his talk with Anne, he subtly sets up the co-ordinates of the entire novel. Although Anne and the Count are not at home in the worldly social milieu where the Openshaw group does much to welcome them, it is significant that these outsiders cannot participate in Guy's present world either. The Count's alienation from the dying Guy is almost complete, as he listens, filled with pity and surreptitiously looking at his watch, to what he reckons to be Guy's irrationality. Anne manages much more in her conversation with the dying man before she too withdraws in terror. Both the Count and Anne are frightened lest Guy enter some terrible sealed-off territory in their minds, and therefore neither can go very far into his lonely experience.

As Guy tries to explain his longings to the Count, he appears to be wandering, but is really speaking accurately in broken unfinished phrases about the difference between the worlds of the living and the dying; he uses the Wittgensteinian concepts of the game and the tribe, but the Count picks up only a civic issue, Guy's Jewishness as opposed to his own Polish anti-semitic background. And as Guy fumbles with his tight, gnomic phrases in his final longing for knowledge, the Count, seeing this struggle as a failure of rationality, stumbles blindly:

> 'That one knows anything at all . . . is not guaranteed . . . by the game . . .'
> 'What – ?'
> 'Our worlds wax and wane with a difference. We belong to different tribes.'
> 'We have always done so', said the Count.
> 'No – only now – Oh – how ill's all here. How much I wish I could –'
> 'Could –'
> 'See it –'
> 'See?'
> 'See it . . . the whole . . . of logical space . . . the upper side . . . of the cube.'
> (pp. 5–6)

Separated as Guy now is from the language of the tribe of the living, his conversation is reduced to small phrases full of private meaning: 'Hey hey the white swan', 'the upper side of the cube', 'she shouldn't have sold the ring', 'logical space'. This narrowing of his world signals a cessation of communication with his survivors; they react by supposing his mind clouded by medication, which indeed it is to a degree. Guy's small stockpile of reiterated phrases confuses even his beloved Gertrude and the Count, but it obviously represents the nearest approximation he can manage to the few central truths he now lives and prepares to die with. Although these phrases are gnomic, all but one are explained at the end. (As critic-sleuth, I wasted a considerable amount of time trying to track down the unexplained 'Hey hey the white swan', first through Elizabethan miscellanies, then through the philosophy which so tantalized Guy. Here I found the white swan of medieval logic, which may be a possibility. Then I remembered that in Shakespeare's Stratford there was a pub called the White Swan, and since the Shakespearean

referential frame is strong for Guy, I pondered that. And of course England is
full of White Swan pubs. I thought of and rejected early Yeats and a possible
connection to Tim's paintings of Leda and the swan, and reluctantly decided
that it could be a deliberate trick on Murdoch's part, trying to leave untouched some of Guy's mystery. The alternative is that I am obtuse.) To the
extent that it is possible, the unravelling of the phrases for the reader illustrates Guy's desire for accurate knowledge, and in the case of Jessica's ring,
his involvement in ideas of rejection and alienation. Gertrude says of him late
in the book that he always identified with Shylock, and on another occasion
he is described as feeling, as Jews have always had to, that he ought to have a
bag packed, ready to flee at a moment's notice.

Like all language in the Wittgensteinian scheme, Guy's phrases represent
the user's attempt at accuracy but reflect the unbridgeable distance between
words and the things they represent. And because, as Wittgenstein argued in
*Philosophical Investigations*, the only universality language can manage comes
through use and shareability, the phrases reflect how utterly different is the
language game of the dying from that of the living tribe, who do not share
Guy's use and cannot put his words together into sense. Although alienated
from communication by the lonely process of dying, Guy is aware of a
greater alienation to come, an alienation that already renders Wittgenstein's
theories futile and meaningless. In fact, Wittgenstein is for Guy what God
had been for Anne, a theoretical substitute for the reality which he will soon
find in death as Anne is to find it in her visionary Christ's radical statements,
especially in his claiming death as one of his names. As Guy tells the Count:
'Death and dying are enemies. Death is an alien voluptuous power. It's an
idea that can be worked on. By the survivors.' He further points out that
'Suffering is such muck. Death is clean' (p. 3), and says that one must fear
especially and only the *Ereignis*, the actual event of death. The Count will not
or cannot enter into such a conversation and stands watching the falling
snow; his failure defines and introduces the separation which this book
concentrates on examining.

In talking to Anne, however, Guy's extended rationality is present and
easily perceived. He recognizes through her former vocation an access which
he could not manage with the Count, and a real conversation on death and
eternal partings takes place. Guy is very much one of Murdoch's characters of
the good, whose direct looking at annihilation does not seek the consolation
of *lux perpetua*. His critique of Christianity is of central importance to the
novel, and reflects Murdoch's thought on false comfort:

Judaism is a sober religion, teaching, prayer, no excesses. But Christianity
is so soft, it's sentimental and magical, it denies death. It changes death into
suffering, and suffering is always so interesting. There is pain, and then,
hey presto, there is eternal life. That's what we all want, that our misery

shall buy something, that we shall get something in return, something absolutely consoling. But it's a lie. There are final conclusions, one is shortly to be reached in this house. Eternal departures take place. Suffering has the shifting unreality of the human mind. A desire to suffer probably led you into that convent, perhaps it has led you out again. Death is real. But Christ doesn't really die. That can't be right. (p. 66)

Happily married, polymath Guy had lived at ease in the world despite his probings towards truth and reality, and his death shows the essential lie of serene at-homeness. His departure into the void is something he is prepared for, although he does long for the one consolation of being judged justly. In a life dedicated to accuracy, this would be a logical conclusion, but when it looks dangerously for a moment as though Anne might be put in the position of judge she panics, and he retreats again into his lonely dying world of gnomic utterances and broken sentences.

Nevertheless, his critique of Christianity's softness opens the way for the area of Anne's personality which is of such major importance in this novel – its aspect of a life given over to religious contemplation. Whereas Anne crucially fails to engage sympathy as a character when she tries to enter the muddled erotic life of the world, she is extremely interesting and sympathetic as a spiritual being; and one of Murdoch's points seems to be that the two aspects cannot coexist. The unselfing achieved through fifteen years in the cloistered convent never quite leaves Anne, and as she herself is to put it, she has been spoiled for the world by a God she no longer believes in; she sees the alien whiteness of her face in the mirror and thinks of herself as invisible, a white underground grub. And when Christ appears to her in a veridical vision – Murdoch's riskiest moment in the novel – he is a reflection of that hidden-from-the-world paleness: 'He had a strangely elongated head and a strange pallor, the pallor of something which had been long deprived of light, a shadowed leaf, a deep sea fish, a grub inside a fruit' (pp. 289–90). This is certainly not the Christ of Guy's account, the originator of a soft and magical Christianity of redemption and forgiveness, nor is he what Anne's private revision of Christianity might expect. Dressed in yellowish-white trousers and shirt with plimsolls on his naked feet, he is strangely ordinary in spite of his beautiful eyes and mouth. His blonde tribal resemblance to both Anne and the Count not only indicates that all three serve the same discipline, but also provides a convenient rationalist explanation for his appearance as hallucinatory.

The conversation between Christ and Anne, which occurs on pages 290–4, is an illuminating central aspect of the novel. About basic Christian doctrinal facts, both he and the angels who herald him in Anne's dream are casual and indifferent. To Anne's desperate question to the angels about the existence of God, she receives a casual 'Yes', and when she asks Christ whether there is salvation, his reply is 'Oh yes', but 'he said it almost carelessly.' On issues of his history and the moral life, Anne's still too conventional beliefs are entirely denied by this ambiguous apparition. Concentrating as Guy had said Christianity always has on the idea of suffering, Anne looks at Christ's hands for the scars of his wounds only to find them unmarked, and as he explains how ashamed his disciples were of him on the journey to Jerusalem, he puts suffering in its proper place: 'Yes, pain is a scandal and a task, but it is a shadow that passes! Death is a teaching. Indeed it is one of my names' (p. 291). This wrenching of Christ from his traditional identification with life to an equivalence with death is only part of Anne's lesson. She begs for the great things of conventional Christianity – to be saved, to become good, to be made clean – but these are treated coolly and negatively. She is told 'You must do it all yourself, you know' when she asks for instructions on the route to salvation, and Christ adds, 'As for salvation, anything you can think about it is as imaginary as my wounds. I am not a magician, I never was. You know what to do. Do right, refrain from wrong.' When she frantically says she wants to be made good, his sad response is 'Oh, I'm afraid that's impossible'; when she says 'I want to be made clean like you promised, I want to be made innocent, I want to be washed whiter than snow,' he tells her literally to wash herself at the kitchen sink, ironically showing how sentimental her traditional metaphoric desires are.

The vision's revelation connects to the central nexus of Murdoch's thinking about the good and the nature of the moral life: death, reality and a just image of Christ are closely connected; the psyche goes forward to the great teaching which is given only by death rather than by the consolations of suffering; the good is not attainable; clean innocence which the spirit longs for is impossible and even sentimental; absolute human responsibility resides in the continuous flow of disciplining oneself to act rightly rather than in any hope of an outside redemption or miracle. As Christ puts it, 'You must be the miracle-worker, little one. You must be the proof. The work is yours' (p. 293).

The substance of this list connects Anne's vision to the major ideas of *Nuns and Soldiers*: Guy's death and knowledge, and the assertion of homelessness, alienation and separation so crucial to the novel's teaching. Puzzled by what the vision shows her, Anne longs to place it somewhere, to domesticate this strange being who seems so real and put him in a comprehensible place. Christ answers that desire by paraphrasing *Matthew* 8:20 and *Luke* 9:58: 'Where do I live? I live nowhere. Have you not heard it said that birds have nests and foxes have holes but I have no house?' (p. 292). Anne, in a sudden flash of understanding borrowed from Julian of Norwich says, 'Oh, Sir, you have a home! . . . Love is my meaning' (p. 293). This substitution of an abstract psychic home for the literal place she had earlier been searching for illustrates the novel's tendency to point beyond its action to a higher realm which, paradoxically, it also distrusts. In fact, the whole visionary sequence combines the abstract and concrete in an ambiguous way.

In the hands of a less skilful novelist, a vision of Christ received by an ex-nun would be somehow tied to orthodoxy and send Anne running back to the community of the convent and the bosom of the Church, but the intelligent agnosticism with which it is treated here is complex and pointed. Although the vision had begun with a dream, Anne remains sure it was a real event; her years 'inside' have given her some acquaintance with the hysteria of those who receive the stigmata, and she is aware that the whole thing could be a projection of her own unconscious. In trying to reach out to touch Christ, however, her finger brushes his sleeve, leaving a searing burn which will not heal, and although Murdoch leaves room for the reader to interpret this as religious hysteria, there is also a strong feeling of some sort of theophany or intersection of the supernatural and natural. At several points in *Nuns and Soldiers* there are subtle parallels between Anne and the intense experience of the historical Mary Magdalene: in her early promiscuity which is abandoned in the service of God just as the Magdalene had turned from whoredom to Christ, in her secularization after leaving the convent which causes Gertrude to identify her, when she gives her jewellery, as Mary Magadalene in reverse, and now in her irresistible desire to touch the resurrected or reincarnated Christ. The traditional 'Noli me tangere' (do not touch me) the original Christ had addressed to Mary Magdalene on the morning of his resurrection became a major iconographical image in Christian art; it is here enacted by Anne's stumbling reach towards Christ and her incurable burn.

If Anne has experienced a real theophany as she tends to think, it is not a showing of a universal Christ to mankind; it is, rather, a personal and private revelation, meant to educate Anne alone. She leaves it instantly to indulge her frustrated love for the Count, and does not allow it to invade her mind completely; she also sees it as particular rather than general, and knows that one of its functions is to increase her already considerable distance from the consoling idea of God:

She had wondered whether belief in God would ever return, sweep over her one day like a great warm wet cloud. Now she felt more absolutely godless than she had ever felt in her life. Her good was her own, her evil was her own. Yet *he*, her early morning visitor, was he not something? Perhaps indeed it was he, with his luminous eyes and his enigmatic witty talk that had shaken her and shaken the last remnant of faith out of her soul. Had she understood? A little. Who was he? She felt that he had truly come from a distant place. And it came to her that he was real, that he was unique. She was an atom of the universe and he was *her own* Christ, the Christ that belonged only to her, laserbeamed to her alone from infinitely far away. At least she had seen him once; and now perhaps the grace of

prayer would return to her. Would it return now, a new and different kind
of prayer? (p. 304)

Like Guy's death, which had shown the lonely separation inherent in one's
knowledge of the blank face of reality, Anne's apprehension of Christ is not
to be shared and not conducive to standard generalized interpretation. It
becomes part of the private vocabulary of her experience and another factor
in her alienation. Anne's Christ does indeed teach her, but he also represents
one of his names which is death, in that he signals her loss of the Count and a
secular life. Anne can see the contrast between his spiritual being and her
erotic violence, and she feels herself 'surrounded by irresponsible spiritual
forces' (p. 303), including a black, shapeless, demonic creature crouching on
her darkened stairs. Again, ambiguity surrounds this dark thing – it feels like
a demonic force, but Anne also thinks that it may be a large sick dog. Christ's
visit and the death–like realities he teaches her also remind her of her own
eternal parting from the beautiful gentle nun she loved in the convent: Christ
is to Anne as death had been to Guy, a showing of failure, loss and separation.
All in all, the whole experience is aimed at drawing Anne out of herself, in the
Murdochian sense of taking her from self-indulgence to a higher reality
which is, in this case, a more stringently defined secret nunhood which must
be seen as a step on the dark path of the good.

The most striking thing about Anne's unredemptive vision is its ironic
connection to Julian of Norwich's *Revelations of Divine Love*. As Anne and
Christ talk, they revert to archaic forms, most of which are direct quotations
from the *Revelations*; Anne's most intelligent moments in the conversation
occur when she picks up phrases from Julian. Anne's Christ also knows the
text, but his contexts and meanings are very different. Julian is obviously a
model against which Murdoch has set Anne, and Julian's medieval Christianity forms an ironic background for Anne's religious knowledge. Julian's
Showings of Christ in May of 1373 were received by her joyfully as universal
truths, and written out, pondered over and rewritten at greater length so that
she could share with her 'even-Christians' the teachings she had received
from the mouth of the visionary Christ. Julian remarks how she was given no
Showings of the particular, but everything for the general case, explaining
the nature of Christ's redemption of the human soul. In every way opposite
to Anne's Showing, Julian's reflects a community of shared belief and an utter
certainty of divine reality through the images of Christianity. Julian's Christ,
unlike Anne's, says that he will do all things in order to make all things well,
including one last mysterious miracle. Even sin has no real horror for Julian
since her Christ will look after that too: 'Sin is behovely,' but 'all shall be well
and all shall be well and all manner of things shall be well,' as Murdoch
characters have with ironic frustration repeated in novel after novel. That 'sin
is behovely,' however, is a maxim Murdoch's people never mention and
cannot deal with.

Julian's Christ is above all a being of action and responsibility, and he
encourages a human resting on his divine power to perform what looks
impossible to the human mind. Julian's message of reassurance to her even-
Christians states that faith in Jesus is enough; Anne's Christ on the other hand
is quizzical and non-authoritative. He reminds her that he is not a magician,
and that 'the work is yours', and as Anne tries to identify him accurately, his
authority seems slight:

> He still seemed to her at times like a sprite, a fairy thing, a lost vagrant
> spiritual being. Perhaps he was in some sense local, a little god left behind
> by a lost cult which even he had forgotten. Or was not his 'locality'
> determined rather by the whole universe beaming its radiance in upon the
> monad soul? She remained persuaded that he was *her* Christ, hers alone.
> He's all I've got, she thought.
>
> (p. 354)

The miracle that will make all well cannot reside in this slight projection of
the spiritual energy of one person, and the greatest lesson Anne learns is that
she alone is responsible, as is every human being in Murdoch's work, for
whatever shall be well in the world.

The issue on which Julian and Anne agree in visionary terms is the size of
the universe. When Christ quizzes Anne about what he has in his hand, she
answers confidently, 'A hazelnut', since this is what Julian's Christ had
shown as the essence of all things. Anne's Christ does not answer to Julian's
text here, but rather shows a stone like the pebbles Anne had brought from
the Cumbrian beach where she and Gertrude had gone after Guy's death. The
incident is reminiscent of Theo's horror at the stones on the Dorset shingle in
*The Nice and the Good*, where the jumble of matter seemed impenetrable and
the confusion of the one and the many too great. Anne's version of the same
problem of beach pebbles fits into the frustrating and alienating game aspect
of *Nuns and Soldiers*:

> Anne picked up a stone. They were so similar, yet so dissimilar, like
> counters in a game played by some god. The shapes, very like, were never
> exactly the same. Each one, if carefully examined, revealed some tiny
> significant individuating mark, a shallow depression or chipped end, a
> short almost invisible line. Anne said to herself, what do my thoughts
> matter, what do their *details* matter, what does it matter whether Jesus
> Christ redeemed the world or not, it doesn't matter, our minds can't grasp
> such things, it's all too obscure, too vague, the whole matrix shifts and we
> shift with it. What does anything matter except helping one or two people
> who are nearby, doing what's obvious? We can see so little of the great
> game. Look at these stones. My Lord and my God.
>
> (p. 107)

In terms of the complex world imaged by this book, Anne's apprehension of
the hopelessness of understanding the whole is correct, yet when Christ

presents her with a small gray stone as an image of the tiny particular which is
everything, she is shocked at how small it is and wants what Christ calls a
'wonderful answer' (p. 292) to the whole of the universe. Julian too had been
appalled by the universe as a hazelnut, but her interpretation was entirely
different: for her it made generalization easier; for contemporary Anne it
means that total attention must be paid to the pointless particular, and that
such attention is incomprehensible but significant.

Since Anne's Christ claims that he is not and never was a magician, his
presence denies the wonderful unifying answer Anne is seeking, and it is clear
from the context of this novel that if all shall be well, it shall be so only
through moral discipline and whatever virtue is available in human beings
who face the blankness before them with love and humility: the major thing
about Anne's Christ is that he won no victories and promised no miracles.
The last few pages of the novel are given to Anne, who sits in the Prince of
Denmark pub and reflects on her state. Unlike Julian who became an anchoress ardently teaching her even-Christians, Anne must go out into an
impersonal void. She realizes that she left the convent because it had become a
home, and Christ's Showing taught her how true was the biblical passage:
'Birds have nests, and foxes have holes, but the Son of Man hath not where to
lay his head.' Like a true character of the good in Murdoch's canon, however,
Anne recognizes how quickly the idea of 'void' itself might be an illusion (p.
498) and that being an anchoress in the world might have no meaning. Her
sense of vocation and of being providentially sent to Gertrude must also die as
image after romantic image necessarily collapses.

The persistent idea of Christ which haunts late Murdoch novels is interesting in that although he is recognized as probably a mere image or model, his
authority persists in an odd, negative way: 'There was no God, but Christ
lived, at any rate her Christ lived, her nomadic cosmic Christ, uniquely hers,
focused upon her alone by all the rays of being' (p. 500). Christ's 'failure' is
the failure of the good in the human milieu; recognition and even a just,
tempered love of that failure, with the subsequent individual human responsibility it implies, are the lessons Anne learns. The thought sequence
leads her to remember her conversation with the dying Guy, who realized as
Christ had done that suffering is less important than death where our real
education lies:

> We want our vices to suffer but not to die. Purgatorial suffering is a magical
> story, the transformation of death into pain, happy pain whose guaranteed
> value will buy us in return some everlasting consolation. But there are
> eternal partings, all things end and end forever and nothing could be more
> important that that. We live with death. With pain, yes. But really . . .
> with death.                                                          (p. 500)

The consolations of suffering are imaged for Guy in the moving idea of purgatory: 'But purgatory, suffering in the presence of the Good, what joy. Computerised suffering, suffering with a purpose, with a progress – no wonder the souls in Dante plunge joyfully back into the fire' (p. 68); and they are ironically enacted in Anne's fight with the killing sea in Cumbria where she discovers, like a 'damned soul', that the issue constantly close at hand is annihilating death rather than redemption and reward.

The distance from Julian's sublime vision of redemption to this grim acknowledgement is measureless, and the reversal of terms shows the distance between the late Christian middle ages and our secular but morally significant time as Murdoch perceives it. In Julian's world, the large general *dicta* of Christ take the soul through simple faith to the truths of God and the Church; in the contemporary world Murdoch works on, the words Guy spoke to Anne are major, imitating as they do the argument of *The Sovereignty of Good*:

> We specialise, don't you think? . . . We are selectively decent, if we are decent at all. We each have one or two virtues which we cultivate, not much really. Or we pick a virtue which always seems to help, to mediate goodness somehow, as it might be resolution, or benevolence, or innocence, or temperance, or honour. Something not too large, not too impossibly hard. . . . We are not really very versatile when it comes to being good, we are awfully limited creatures. . . . Our vices are general, dull, the ordinary rotten mud of human meanness and cowardice and cruelty and egoism, and even when they're extreme they're all the same. Only in our virtues are we original, because virtue is difficult, and we have to try, to invent, to work through our nature against our nature –. . . . Vices are general, virtues are particular. They aren't in a continuum of general improvement.
> (pp. 68-9)

For contemporary mankind, generalization cannot lead to a large apprehension of a Christ-centred universe; rather, it illustrates the vicious state of things. What is general for a period which has lost its traditional beliefs is not the redemptive vision of Christ who will make all things well but the acknowledgement of universal vice; what small salvation there is lies in the particular, in the limited, specialized attempt to be accurate in whatever small areas can be handled. One is reminded once again of Hugo's words in *Under the Net*: 'God is a task. God is detail. It all lies close to your hand' (p. 258). In *Nuns and Soldiers*, good is even more stringently defined in terms of its limitations and unreachability. At the end of the novel, Anne takes on the theme in grim terms: 'Perhaps after all, Goodness was too hard to seek and too hard to understand' (p. 504). Nevertheless, *Nuns and Soldiers* makes clear that the only route for characters of the good is Christ's: the narrow painful way of guaranteed failure which leads to death (Guy's unwilling path) or to the self-abnegating, life-denying service Anne seeks in America.

★

Meanwhile the real life and energy of the novel lie elsewhere: Tim and Gertrude seek happiness and apparently find it. After his second ordeal in the French canal, Tim comes through the tunnel which looks like certain death to forgiveness and joy in Gertrude's arms. He finds in life what 'soft' Christianity conventionally promises: the ability to tell everything as though in the presence of God and to receive the remission of sins. The contrast between him and Guy is everywhere present, but nowhere more strongly than here. Having escaped from death into life, he can achieve a redemption that Guy knows death denies, and with Gertrude as his God Tim enters a world of joy. The route to that world is neither straight nor easy, however, and on its way both Tim and Gertrude change enormously; the most interesting progresses in this novel involve their transformations. Although the whole process is a parody of Christian ideas, Murdoch handles it with considerable generosity.

Gertrude is a fascinating study of the psychology of her great literary forebear, Hamlet's mother, after whom she is named. Like that confused character, this contemporary Gertrude goes from a worthy and marvellous husband through a period of terrible grief ('like Niobe, all tears') to an unworthy and rather shamefully happy second marriage. Gertrude's psychology is accurately and subtly reported with the great detail and attention which characterize the style of this novel, as she attempts to juggle her surprising new love for the unimposing Tim with her loss of the admirable Guy. Throughout the novel's events we are constantly being told that her mourning continues and coexists with her pleasure in Tim:

> Her strange love for absent Guy had not diminished, it had even perhaps increased, but it was purged of much of the painful anxiety and bitter speculation which had made it earlier almost like a hostile calculating love, a love relation in which he was angry and she resentfully compliant. . . . Now she felt more gently and naturally separated from Guy, more able to look towards him quietly and tenderly; and she rested in the certainty that her connection with him would remain alive and subject to change as all living things are, as long as she herself existed. . . . After a while she was even able to talk about some of this to Tim, and about how her mourning had to go inside her marriage. She was not worried any more about the 'time scheme', or about what in this connection 'the others' would think. Guy had died in December, Gertrude was to wed in July, with mirth in funeral and dirge in marriage.                              (pp. 278–9)

It is interesting to compare the extended analysis of Gertrude's paradoxical grief and joy, her 'mirth in funeral and dirge in marriage' with Shakespeare's Gertrude, for in this comparison more than at any other point in Murdoch's work one can see the difference between the novel and drama as genres, and perhaps suggest one reason why Murdoch's talents were not completely served when she herself turned to drama in *The Three Arrows* and *The Servants and the Snow*. The often sympathetic but sometimes boring protraction of Gertrude's early sufferings in *Nuns and Soldiers* illustrates Murdoch's peculiar and often contradictory strength, which lies in amplification and meditative brooding on the moment by moment changes in an active and realistically continuous psychology. Shakespeare's Gertrude is by comparison a thumb-nail sketch, where relatively few but very compelling speeches are made by Hamlet, Claudius and her in order to limn the nevertheless powerful character. When Charles Arrowby in *The Sea, The Sea* points out that Shakespeare is 'quite different from the others, not just *primus inter pares* but totally different in quality' (p. 36), he is presenting a case for the peculiar genius of Shakespeare in elevating drama to a more verbally crucial form than it ordinarily is. Murdoch's characters frequently claim to dislike Shakespeare on the stage where he is reduced to tricks as Peregrine Arbelow accuses Charles of doing in *The Sea, The Sea*, and indeed one can argue that Shakespeare's unique strength in the tightly controlled and spatially limited verbal form of drama constitutes at least a part of his greatness. The contraction necessary in the writing of drama does not particularly suit Murdoch's style, and although she can use dramatic devices as she frequently does in her novelistic conversations, her talent is ultimately too limited by the form.

At any rate, Shakespeare's Gertrude is well served by Murdoch's psychological study, and, as with Anne Cavidge being set against Julian of Norwich, an earlier source illuminates and contrasts with the progress of the novel. Although the basic condition of Gertrude's personality reflects Shakespeare's depiction, Murdoch's character takes an entirely new turning, and the Gertrude we see at the end of the novel has been metamorphosed into one of Murdoch's least attractive set characters – the emotionally voracious, middle-aged, middle-class woman. From a sympathetic character wretchedly watching Guy die and mourning miserably afterwards, she becomes progressively greedy and possessive: first and understandably, she wants Anne 'forever' by her side in what the two refer to as their 'indestructible chariot'; when she has secured Tim after separations and reconciliations, she wants the Count too as her *cavaliere servente*, and demands that a disappointed Anne fit in happily with the group. When Anne says the Count is heroic in being contented with little, a new Gertrude speaks, 'You call it little to be loved by ME?' (p. 465). Her confidence is based on a version of love which is obviously at the extreme opposite of the disinterested love implied by Julian of Norwich's phrase, so important in this novel, 'Love is my meaning'. Gertrude's love involves warmth and egotistical power, and when foiled by Anne's insistence on going away, her 'eyes flashed with anger, with exasperation, with her old eternal will to have her own way' (p. 469). Her inability to suppress her greed combines with her smug self-interest, and she knows that she will eventually get over even Anne's defection:

> How could she leave me, she thought again and again, how *could* she, when I needed her and loved her so much? Oh why can I not have everything, all that was given to me after Guy went. Anne was such a necessary being. This was another great grief to carry, one that would so very slowly diminish. The indestructible chariot in which she and Anne were to ride on through life had turned out to be an illusory vehicle after all. (p. 472)

This development of Gertrude's character is a disappointing diminution, but throughout, partly because of the choric effect of the Openshaw circle, the reader must be somewhat puzzled by the contrast between this character and the 'majestic Gertrude' perceived by Anne. In France after their affair has begun, Tim Reede contrasts the 'Gertrude of Ebury Street' with the naked sleeping girl in his bed, and although she is powerful and touching in her grief, the Gertrude of the Tim affair instantly loses the qualities she might once have had under the tutelage of Guy. Rather than a fault in the depiction of the character, this change seems to be a further comment on the Shakespearean Gertrude – the woman whose personality is moulded by the man she loves. When married to Guy, Gertrude shared in his magnificence and learned from it; when married to the weaker Tim, the lesser parts of her character emerge. Because Guy's presence as an austere, dying character of the good was so powerful early in the book, Gertrude's decline into the debased emotional greed which she calls love constitutes a sorry picture. One can understand all too well the dying man reading the *Odyssey* and contemplating a world when his journey is over and his Penelope regards her suitors. The ballad he recalls is bitterly pointed, as Gertrude later realizes:

> 'Nobody knows that he lies there but his hawk and his hound and his lady fair. His hound is to the hunting gone, his hawk to fetch the wild fowl home, his lady's ta'en another mate. . . . Many a one for him makes moan, but none shall know where he is gone. Over his bones when they are bare the wind shall blow forever more.' . . . No wonder Guy had become a stranger in the land of the living, withdrawn, and speaking a different tongue. His warm and loving wife could comfort him no more, nothing could comfort him any more. (p. 257)

This picture of Guy's sadly intelligent death and Gertrude's diminution is mediated to a degree by the charm of her relationship with Tim, a touching emissary from the pub called The Prince of Denmark, to stress the Hamlet connection. Although the ideological centre of this very ideological novel concentrates on important outsiders like the dying Guy, the austere Anne and the Count, the novel's real and living focus is on Tim Reede, also an outsider, but of another sort. A hanger-on in the Openshaw circle, Tim retains a filial relationship with Guy, with whose father and uncle he had originally had a financial arrangement. With neither family nor home of his own, Tim is grateful for his inclusion in the group and for Guy's emotional generosity, and his presence in the circle illustrates the open sense of friendly community which characterizes all of them. Known as a painter of uncertain talent, he is not questioned about his life; and although he once had brought Daisy to a gathering where she had acted badly and categorized them all as identical to the orchestra of china monkeys on the Openshaw mantelpiece, no one knows of his long-standing affair with her.

Foul-mouthed Daisy is the key to the action, for although Tim has a fringe relationship with the bourgeoisie, she is, as he points out, his home and his family. Their waifish bohemian life, centred in The Prince of Denmark, is a far cry from the accuracy and organization Guy imposed on his circle, and while Guy represents a high standard of civilized bourgeois life, Daisy and Tim reflect an aimlessly drifting existence on the dole and alcohol. Their struggle between drink and idleness as opposed to work illustrates a major theme in the novel, one which Anne Cavidge's judgement on the secular society she has newly joined constantly reflects, as she argues that they all drink too much or that Manfred drives too fast. Daisy and Tim's relationship has the staleness of generally unsatisfactory but habitual family life; thus Tim automatically, unthinkingly, runs home to Daisy when Gertrude calls a moratorium on their affair, and again, more damningly, when Daisy's existence becomes known and wrecks the marriage.

Daisy is one of the best drawn characters in the novel: gutsy, hilarious, touching, absolutely consistent, she is the true profane opposite to cold, guarded Anne Cavidge, and their meeting feels as morally inevitable as the fact that they dimly perceive each other's possible goodness. Daisy's fringe life with her unwritten novel, her flagons of wine and her straggling potted plants also contrasts to sleek Gertrude's well-defined place in a steady society; Tim's final parting from Daisy opens him in the end to a true contract with Gertrude and another world, although this is not part of his plan. All action in this novel is set against major works of art, and Tim justly perceives himself and Daisy as the comic characters in that great opera of farewells, Mozart's *The Magic Flute* – Papageno and Papagena. But as in every other case in *Nuns and Soldiers*, the art work is ironically denied. Papageno is here made better and wins the lofty Pamina, Papagena goes off as does Anne to the new world of America, and the ordeals of *The Magic Flute* are called on to assert a much altered, ironic conclusion.

Nevertheless, Tim's relationship with Daisy is basically destructive, and when he leaves the absolute at-homeness she had represented for him, he does so believing that he has also parted eternally from Gertrude. This condition gives his parting with Daisy a special quality typical of Murdoch's characters of the good: acting 'for nothing', with no hope of reward. Tim gives up Daisy not because he thinks he can get Gertrude back, but because he realizes he has not loved her enough, because he has merely used her and because their relationship is based on destructive selfishness. In doing so he goes out into an empty world, and his new courage is impressive. Rather than drinking and brooding on his suffering over the loss of both Gertrude and Daisy, Tim concentrates on work, making leaf collages, getting a one–day-a-week job at an art college in Willesden, decorating a meeting-house for a religious group's harvest festival. His resolution to part from Daisy and go homelessly, friendlessly forth into the world of work has the same basis as Anne's decision to go to America, and this apparently worthless man and habitual liar surprisingly exhibits some of the qualities of Murdoch's most positive characters.

Tim has been an anomaly from the start, a double character whose obvious tawdriness is often contradicted by strong positive activity. He wavers between sneaking food from the Openshaw refrigerator for his and Daisy's dinner, and his obvious love for the dying Guy. Described as a mediocre painter, he nevertheless has the ability to see accurately, a talent which unfortunately does not help him succeed in his work. His mediocrity allows Murdoch to use him as a vehicle for criticizing the undisciplined artist, in a passage reminiscent of Bradley Pearson's argument in *The Black Prince*:

> He went on trying, though he never tried very hard. Any artist who is not a beginner faces the problem of enlarging into a working space the line that runs between 'just begun' and 'too late'. The hard work lies in the middle when preliminaries are done, and the end is not yet enclosing the form. This is the space which longs to collapse, which the artist's strength must faithfully keep open. Tim was vaguely aware of this, but he was idle and lacked confidence. He was almost but not quite aware that he chose daily to remain mediocre. His efforts tended to be either 'sketches' or 'spoilt'. Yet he kept on drawing and in this activity something purely good, often mislaid, tended to come back. He knew nothing, he read nothing, but he kept on looking. Tim possessed by nature a gift yearned for by sages, he was able simple to *perceive!* (He did not realize that this was exceptional, he thought everybody could do it.)                              (pp. 124–5)

In describing the difficulties of the artist, Murdoch typically concentrates on the idea of the middle, where her realistic inclination has caused her to do her own hardest work. In the early novels, she sometimes compulsively submitted to closed form, but as her work matured, her talent can be described as concentrating on the open middle: the endings of the mature novels are almost always ironic and even irrelevant to the large, free central area of activity which defines her developed style. Tim, however, is unlike Murdoch; he lacks strength and discipline and is essentially too lazy to transform the good inherent in his ability to perceive well into a good art product.

Murdoch argued in *The Black Prince* that art and the moral life have the same sources, and Tim's moral folly in not telling the enamoured Gertrude about his liaison with Daisy directly connects to his final inability to be a good painter:

> He had always been good at dealing with profound and awful difficulties by a method which was no doubt connected (although Tim was unaware of this) with something which made him an indifferent painter. This method might be described as a systematic lack of thoroughness. As has been explained, Tim's work rushed blindly on from the stage where it was only a sketch to a stage where it was too late to bother. Similarly in moral matters, Tim felt it was not worth while to work out problems beforehand because after all one did not know what was going to happen and it might be that the threatened problem might not in fact materialize; then when events overtook him he was consoled by a fatalistic sense of helplessness.
>
> (pp. 201–2)

This 'systematic lack of thoroughness' which characterizes his art and the attendant mess of his life is in deep contrast to Guy Openshaw's order and desire for accuracy, as perceived by Anne:

> Guy too had wanted to keep out of the mess of life. His virtue was accuracy. That was his kind of truth. His desire for justice was his very private substitute for holiness. He worked for other men, he served his family, he was kind and generous and decent, but would have given himself no credit for that. His need for things to be precise and clean was a part of his secret judgement upon himself. Her idea that he had wanted to confess something to her now seemed like a piece of romanticism. Perhaps he had simply wanted to say certain words aloud to somebody: justice, purgatory, suffering, death. He had wanted to feel that their precise *meaning* was there somewhere, kept safe by someone, even just at one moment existent in thought. He lay there in the small last light of his mind, calculating, trying to get something clear, to get something right.
>
> (p. 241)

The particularity of Guy's virtue and the precision of his thought withdraw into death, and the muddle of Tim's life is left. As Guy had implied in the first conversation of the novel, he wants to see 'the top of the cube', his image for reality itself, and like Wittgenstein, whom he obviously follows even as he rejects him, he attempts even on the verge of death to pursue a final and accurate picture of reality.

Yet Tim too has had and has some vague inclination towards the exact and precise, which is connected to his art and, after his bitter lessons, to his love. The image of the net of theory and language which the mind places over reality had suggested the title of Murdoch's first novel, *Under the Net*, and it emerges again as an organic part of this novel's structure. References to meshes and nets abound, and the most significant connect to Tim's early and late painting. His spontaneous knowledge of the mathematics of form while a student at the Slade is described, and from this knowledge he goes on to painting a fanatical series of abstract 'net' pictures:

> He lived in a sea of graph paper. His squares became dots, pinpricks, then something invisible. It was (as someone said at the time) like a not very gifted savage trying to invent mathematics. It was as if he wanted to decode the world. His paintings looked like elaborate diagrams yet what were they diagrams of? If he could only cover *everything* with a fine enough mesh . . . If he could only *get it right*. Sometimes in dreams he thought that he had done so. No one liked these 'fanatical' paintings, and in the end for Tim they became a sort of sterile torment. Then one day (he could never explain how) it was as if the mesh began to bend and bulge and ever so quietly other forms came through it. When he returned to organic being it was as to something which had been vastly feeding in captivity. Everything now was plump, enlaced, tropical. Live existence which had been nowhere was now everywhere.                                              (pp. 125–6)

During this period Tim was unconsciously and in his untheoretical way closely analogous to Guy, who wished for precision and to perceive all of logical space. Completely intuitive and non-intellectual, Tim was not aware that his painting reflected a compulsive gnostic desire and, even more accurately, illustrated certain French speculations about the form of art that may have roots in Mallarmé, as Murdoch has suggested. Certainly it would be wrong to connect the nets to Wittgenstein whose directions were quite other than what is obliquely indicated here. The very obliquity of the statement is of central concern, for Tim is described as intuitively enacting a certain complex idea about art: he neither understands not speculates about it, and knowing somehow that it is major, he does not talk to Gertrude about it when he returns after his hard-won final happiness to such painterly combinations of mathematical precision and organic, bulging excess. The paradox contained here has, I think, much more to do with Murdoch's developing ideas about art which the present novel amply illustrates by its own paradoxes than with Tim's painting which is a small agent of it. The organic outbreaks and emphases in *Nuns and Soldiers* are allowed a certain illumination by what Tim tentatively and spontaneously does, and the aspect of secrecy and quiet waiting seems to me very much an analogue to the reader's need to wait and see what Murdoch will do with the problems of form and the life of the organic world of being in subsequent novels. Her account of

Tim's final artistic activity strikes me as significant in ways I cannot at present explain, and perhaps such explanation would be adverse to the effect:

> Sometimes he filled in mathematical patterns of which his 'animals' were part. . . . He had painted on big wooden panels with bright acrylic paint some purely abstract 'network' pictures which did not displease him. But then how did these networks connect with the organic forms which also spontaneously appeared? His thoughts about this were nonsense, and he never spoke of these deep things to Gertrude, but he lived calmly and patiently with the nonsense in expectation of, if not clarification, at least change.
>
> (p. 475)

Tim's present work lacks the obsessive quality of his earlier network pictures, and his calm waiting for some profound thing that his own mind is too muddled to predict cannot be seen as other than admirable and aligned to a kind of virtue, one that has subtly and secretly to do with the artist's apprehension of the problems of form.

The novel is also obviously using Tim and his artistic combination of the abstract and organic more simply as an illustration of its own structure. In his first conversation with the Count, Guy had described philosophical speculation irritably as 'a dance of bloodless categories after all' (p. 2), and *Nuns and Soldiers* which subtly opposes intellectual disciplines to lived experience is well served by Tim's combination. At every turn in the novel, the organic gives full illustration to and is more effective than the ideological, as for example when Anne throws herself confidently into the sea only to find that she cannot cope and nearly drowns. The act had been, as she interprets it later, a kind of vanity, an abstract belief in the power she had won by leaving the convent; her defeat and near death remind her that the external world is greater than her internal thoughts and image–creating capacities.

More poignant are the canal sequences in France where Tim undergoes his ordeals; indeed all the French landscape sequences are fraught with beauty and significance. The rushing canal itself invites abstract identification as an image of life: Tim's escape from the tunnel of death clearly parallels his emergence on the other side of his deadly moral failures into happiness and forgiveness with Gertrude. But the image is made stronger and connected to the old literary trick of pathetic fallacy in the presentation of the two dogs: the first dead, bloated dog, at first glance like a human being, is a terrible image of Guy, and recognition of this sends Gertrude into hysterical tears and Tim into a misery in which he wishes he were dead. The second dog, very much alive and struggling as it is swept towards the fatal tunnel is joined by Tim, whom it also symbolizes, and their emergence on the other side illustrates Tim's triumph and life as opposed to Guy's defeat and death. These powerful and touching sequences form part of the extensive machinery Murdoch deploys in making Tim, against heavy odds, into a sympathetic character.

Like the organic forms thrusting themselves out of Tim's network pictures, references to dogs recur throughout the novel, and cats are not far behind. Not only do we have the canal dogs, but the novel is framed by the year-long absence of the Prince of Denmark's yellow Labrador, Barkiss, from the pub: the last scene celebrates his return, and he obviously represents a principle of life. Tim himself is always associated imagistically with dogs: Daisy says she loves him almost as much as Barkiss, he stands like a dog, and his doggy attributes are frequently mentioned. The dark demon outside Anne's flat is described as possibly a large, sick dog, a factor which causes her to look pityingly for it. The Prince of Denmark's cat, Perkins, is the subject of a long series of cat pictures by Tim, and significantly these are the only original and successful things he does. Because they are frivolous and commercial, he is ashamed of them, but the point is that he is good at seeing cats and drawing them. When the Count in pity comes to visit Tim with Gertrude's letter, he sees a cat painting in the studio and recognizes the pub cat: for the first time in the book he relaxes his too controlled demeanour:

> The Count looked at the painting for a moment with pleasure, and his wrinkled brow relaxed as it had done in the pub when the cat jumped on his knee. Then he remembered the letter and rigidified himself. He stood at attention.                                                                    (p. 359)

The access to warmth and life given by these creatures is an important counterpoint in this novel where the principal characters of serious moral dimension act almost abstractly and are too often aligned to coldness, particularly Anne Cavidge. The moral dimension also can be seen as a net through which the organic thrusts itself.

Tim with his intuitive nature is entirely on the side of the organic, and therefore his greatest breakthroughs do not occur through thought, as Guy attempts, or soldierly discipline as practised by the Count, or spiritual insight as evidenced in Anne's vision of Christ. When alone in France and even after Gertrude's arrival, Tim feasts his ever alert eyes on a gorgeous landscape which, although cultivated, is apparently empty of people. Murdoch's extended and beautiful descriptions of this landscape are among the protracted strengths of the novel. Again, as in *The Sea, The Sea*, animist feeling is uppermost, and the light-reflecting rocks, parched fields and sudden streaking canal exude the excitement of Vaucluse and Provence. The marvels of this French landscape are in marked contast to Tim's gray-skied and grimy London, whose seediness reflects his unhealthy relationship with Daisy. Here in splendid France he will suddenly fall in love with a Gertrude subtly altered from her London self, and the two will dance a magic hay through a meadow of blue flowers. A sense of deep organic liberation replaces the tight mesh of London's controlled reality, and the two characters confront a new combination of happiness, muddle and lies. Tim and Gertrude, characters whose basic impulse is to resist the hard impact of reality, by their ill-thought-out actions actually choose the peculiar equivalence of this catalogue of qualities in which lies produce muddles out of which happiness blindly emerges. Yet their ultimate success is in a way a perversion of Murdoch's insistence elsewhere that the muddled and contingent in life be accepted, in that the two in their unlike ways dodge truths that would break through the rigid controls of form.

Murdoch's mistrust of form is played out in a negative way by Tim and Gertrude's mistakes as they refuse to confess their secret because of their shame at defying the form of the society to which Gertrude absolutely and Tim contingently belong. Through this shabby denial Murdoch frames in new terms her distrust of the pernicious and limiting effects of form as it relates to realism. Tim's manifold failures in facing any of the stern terms of the world are reflected by his habitual impulse to lie, and Daisy who knows more about him than any one keeps reminding him and us that he is a notorious liar. In the midst of the new glory of his affair with Gertrude, he tries stumblingly to describe his utter inability to fit into life in the organized, real world where moral commitments are thought about and enacted:

> Gertrude, I'm an awful liar − . . . I said I could speak French and I can't. . . . We haven't anywhere to go, we haven't anywhere to *be*, we're just impossible. We can't be together like real people are. Gertrude, I'm not real, don't rely on me. (p. 188)

But in the happy resolution of their relationship, Tim finally feels that he has been made real by his confessional truth-telling and Gertrude's godlike role in hearing and forgiving him, and from this point on he is able to merge with society as the smug, satisfied animal he so completely is.

But *en route* he is shown in an ambiguous light as his fears and qualities as an outsider dominate. From before the narrative time of the novel, he had recognized his desire not to be seen, to escape notice, and had learned from Guy the Greek word *lanthano* which he adopts as a motto: *Lanthano, oh lanthano* (I escape notice), he murmurs to himself in prayer. Like the other two outsiders, Anne and the Count, he half longs to be invisible and generally is so to the Openshaw group. Anne had achieved invisibility and a fading of personality in the convent, and even on emergence from it, she feels herself to be possessed of the 'invisibility of a nun'. Similarly, the Count's life has been characterized by the *lanthano* principle:

> He made out that he preferred to be alone. He felt that he was hiding, not waiting but hiding. He had friendly acquaintances, a fairly interesting job, but he was chronically unhappy. His unhappiness was not desperate, just quiet and steady and deep. His London flat became a place of solitude, a

citadel of loneliness, from which he began to assume he would never emerge.　　　　　　　　　　　　　　　　　　　　　　　　　　(p. 12)

These three who fit only marginally into the forms of society are all centrally related to Gertrude who, after Guy's death, is the fulcrum on whom the entire Openshaw circle is balanced. Loving all three contingent people, she wills strongly to draw them to her in a gradation arranged by her will. That she should choose as her major love object the comparatively worthless Tim provides Murdoch with a plot even as it illustrates the strange contrast between the disciplined and undisciplined life, between the inorganic and the organic, between those not made for happiness and those who are.

Tim is not, however, to be seen as contemptible on a grand scale, for his French experience wins him more than Gertrude. Like Charles Arrowby in *The Sea, The Sea*, he experiences the sublime in nature, for him an equivalent reward to Anne's vision of Christ, and his luminosity here, as well as his joy in the landscape, in Gertrude, in the dance, combine to make us pity him in the extended middle of the novel as a scapegoat who is unable to integrate himself into organized life. Daisy describes him as an habitual liar, and in dealing with Gertrude during the long, involved time of their troubles he is indeed an 'instinctive uncalculating liar . . . too lazy to think out his lies with care' (p. 333). Unlike the Wittgensteinian precisionist, Tim cannot state the case which would ally him to form and give him a handle on life. As he tells the Count:

> I've gone back where I belong. It's like magnetism or the force of gravity. I was never at home in your sort of world, well not yours, theirs, hers. I was in the wrong place. . . . It's no good, it's not just accidents or things one could remove or explain. It's my whole life, it's me, that's the trouble. Like I said, I live in a swamp. She comes from a different world where everything's just so and people know where they begin and end and what's the case and what isn't and what's right and what's wrong and all that. It's not my world. I made a mistake too.　　　　　　　　　　　　　(p. 361)

Like Anne and the Count, he speaks a different language from the integrated social tribe; he is hopelessly enmeshed in his own carelessness, lies, lack of discipline. But at the same time, he can picture the real in his cat drawings and sketches of the Great Face, and at his best, when he forces himself into genuine perception, he is a humble agent of the real. His relationship with Gertrude appears to set up what Wittgenstein described as a form of life, an endlessly interesting language which is also an absolutely shared *Sprachspiel*. Although Anne had warned that Gertrude would be bored with Tim, the two live in constant animated conversation, and ultimately Tim's sense of himself as an outsider dissolves in this communication with Gertrude. This is a generous ending for Tim and a resolution to the anxiety which perennially besets him. It is defined in terms of the paintings which lie behind much of the thought in this novel and which connect to the general nexus of images involving the possibility of seeing accurately. Tim has always used the paintings in the National Gallery in London as indicators of his intuitive moods and signals of reality. Early in the novel he had night-mares of going to the gallery to find the pictures dead and senseless; when he loses Gertrude through moral turpitude, the nightmare becomes real, and these paintings whose splendour had illuminated his life cease to speak to him. This image of despair and spiritual death is very effective, and as Gertrude and he are reconciled and their language flows, the pictures again become his beloved teachers.

In this interestingly contradictory novel, the warm access of joy which is granted Tim fights the cold austerity of the characters of the good whose alienation he had in his own off-centre way originally shared. But although Tim is far from moral discipline, his intuitive powers of perception – a sense of life in the organic world – align him in these particular terms with some aspects of that good. In spite of his palpable weaknesses, he is closer to the reader's comprehension than either Anne or the Count. It is fairly clear that the novel is making a statement about the nature of a fiction that chooses strong but diverse ideological material as *Nuns and Soldiers* does, and places it against an organic, intuitive force illustrated by animals, landscape and warm, rich characters like Tim and Daisy. The ideological characters – Guy, Anne, the Count – through death, spiritual discipline and civic obsession are cut off from the tribe, from that middle where the realist artist concentrates his attention and where life and communication exist. The result is that Daisy and Tim succeed very well and easily as characters, whereas Anne and the Count live in a difficult narrow realm only briefly interrupted by their defeated erotic desires.

Among the fruitful oppositions of *Nuns and Soldiers* is one closely related to the thematic material I have just been belabouring. Fundamental to Mur-doch's binary patterns of truth versus lies, formlessness versus form, it centres on a major principle in her theory of the novel: that of the accidental as opposed to the overdetermined. Late in the novel, as Gertrude and Tim count their blessings, the following passage occurs:

> They were talking and drinking. Tim was trying to tell the whole story, but there were so many interconnecting parts to the story and so many parts that did not connect at all, so many events which were over-determined, so many that were purely accidental, he kept darting about and breaking off and starting again, to present it all as a coherent picture was beyond his talents as a narrator, and they were both so pleased with each other's company that they could not concentrate. (p. 432)

This bewildering interweaving of the accidental and overdetermined may defeat Tim's power as a narrator, partly because here as in all aspects of art he does not concentrate enough, but Murdoch as master narrator has presented an apparently piecemeal narrative where the two opposite modes are held together in a state of tension, and determinism of structure is frequently denied. Hence she does not bother to try to control the compulsive and lengthy material of the Tim–Gertrude romance, does not try to limit her novel's middle. Yet when it comes to the formal necessity of closure, she ties things up by slickly granting Tim and Gertrude conventional novelistic happiness, while paradoxically exerting her real attention on the central religious personality of Anne Cavidge. For Anne, before whom the world in all of its numinous glory and disciplined austerity lies open, there is no closure, no sense of an ending. Here are the last words of the novel:

> The big flakes came into view, moving, weaving, crowding, descending slowly in a great hypnotic silence which seemed to separate itself from the sounds of the street below. Anne stopped and watched it. It reminded her of something, which perhaps she had seen in a picture or in a dream. It looked like the heavens spread out in glory, totally unrolled before the face of God, countless, limitless, eternally beautiful, the universe in majesty proclaiming the presence and the goodness of its creator.
>
> Anne stood there for a while. Then she began to walk through the snowy streets at random, feeling lightened of her burdens. Tomorrow she would be in America.                                          (pp. 504–5)

This double closure, with first the traditional closed ending tied neatly and put away, and the contrary open ending dominating, participates in many games of form, including the circular structure Murdoch has used elsewhere. The novel moves from November snowfall to November snowfall and enacts the cycle of one year; thus as usual Murdoch makes her ironic bow to form. But its protracted tracing of its middle works more like Tim's joyfully undisciplined narrative freedom with Gertrude, and gives Murdoch a means of aligning herself with the concept of the accidental which she finds essential to the true realist endeavour.

*

One way of talking about Murdoch's work as it stands in 1980 is to mention again the enormous difference between the first and twentieth novels, *Under the Net* and *Nuns and Soldiers*. The riskiness of the later work in pitching elements against each other and skating on the thin ice of experiments in ideology and realism is compensated for by the highly developed novelistic skills this practised author has accrued. A slow-moving cogitative book set against a plethora of great works – Julian's *Revelations*, Wittgenstein, *The*

*Magic Flute*, Hamlet, the *Odyssey* – *Nuns and Soldiers* makes no attempt to be fashionable or to woo the novel reader who wants fast, quick reads and easier experiments. Whereas *Under the Net* reflected the brevity and speed of Beckett and Queneau and subdued its philosophical material by limiting the amount used and hurrying its pace, *Nuns and Soldiers* deliberately declines from contemporary styles and inclines back towards the sort of novels its characters are always reading: *The Heart of Midlothian*, *Sense and Sensibility*, *War and Peace*, *Little Dorrit* and Proust. It is clearly in the great tradition of Scott, Austen, Tolstoy, Dickens and Proust that Murdoch wishes her best work to be placed.

Among the positive realities to emerge in *Nuns and Soldiers*, together with a new concept of Christ as model and the value of contingent muddled experience, is a strong concept of the novel as a genre. In an earlier period of her writing, Murdoch seemed all too ready to acknowledge the split in tradition between the novels of the genre's heyday in the nineteenth century and the more flimsy productions of the twentieth century. In a famous and often quoted statement from her 1961 essay, 'Against Dryness', she puts the case concisely and negatively:

If we consider 20th-century literature as compared with 19th-century literature, we notice certain significant contrasts. I said that, in a way, we were back in the 18th century, the era of rationalistical allegories and moral tales, the era when the idea of human nature was unitary and single. The 19th century novel (I use these terms boldly and roughly: of course there were exceptions) was not concerned with 'the human condition,' it was concerned with real various individuals struggling in society. The 20th-century novel is usually either crystalline or journalistic; that is, it is either a small quasi-allegorical object portraying the human condition and not containing 'characters' in the 19th-century sense, or else it is a large shapeless quasi-documentary object, the degenerate descendant of the 19th-century novel, telling, with pale conventional characters, some straightforward story enlivened with empirical facts.

During the period of writing this essay, Murdoch was, in her novels, giving free rein to her technical gamesmanship, and in spite of her sober undercurrents and intentions, her work came close to participating in these narrow, defeated categories.

In the last several novels, however, her assertion of style and seriousness have reflected an increasing alignment of her own fiction with the claims fiction made in the past. Her continually growing courage in risk, experiment and demand on the contemporary reader, who is unused to such responsibility as she thrusts on him here in *Nuns and Soldiers*, coalesces in an implied statement of her real connection with the great novelists of the nineteenth century. Although Murdoch would not claim to sound like artists from the past, she evokes them as our mentors; in general she has always argued that the artist is on his own, and must work out his own way independently of his admiration of his great antecedents. She has certainly done this, and in spite of her new alignment with the great past tradition, there remains a certain wistfulness about the consoling and redemptive achievements of earlier novelists, as opposed to her own frame which is morally and philosophically stringent and which introduces a new dimension into the art of the novel in general.

In evoking her allegiance to great works of the past, she also wrenches her particularized style from their hold. This insistence on her own function occurs not only as she places the Count against Pierre in *War and Peace*, but as she mentions any other past novels or great works in any genre. Thus Julian, Shakespeare, Mozart, Wittgenstein are all used but jarringly altered as Murdoch swerves from their achievement into what must irreversibly be her own. She ties *Nuns and Soldiers* to a rich cultural past which is infinitely admired by the characters, but from which they are alienated and which they must modify significantly according to the conditions of their lived-in present. Mixed with the ambiguous comprehension of her characters, who are like and yet essentially unlike their great forebears, is Murdoch's strong novelistic habit of infusing specific religious content into her work. Unlike any other contemporary novelist, Murdoch's particular, carefully developed style juggles an impressive amount of material, both hidden and overt, with unique technical expertise and with a versatile experimentalism which is often deliberately obscured under the realist bourgeois surface of plot and insistent character development.

In Murdoch's most recent development of the extended style in *The Sea, The Sea* and *Nuns and Soldiers*, she is much bolder in introducing both latent and open levels of discourse about the nature and function of novels themselves. In *Nuns and Soldiers* Anne Cavidge reads novels which had been banned in the convent in favour of more useful activity and, coming freshly to them after years of stringent, other-centred discipline, is amazed at their containing 'so much heterogeneous *stuff*':

> Anne had been reading *Little Dorrit*, it was amazing, it was so crammed and chaotic, and yet so touching, a kind of miracle, a strangely naked display of feeling, and full of profound ideas, yet one felt it was all true!   (pp. 53–4)

Dickens's combination of observation, feeling and details leads to truth, and Murdoch here states the basic function of the novel as an instrument of reality felt at a complex level of human experience. Murdoch's own recent developments take her work back to something like the detail and pleasure in the form which the novels read by these characters so completely elicit, and she now boldly implies the possibility of her own contemporary but extended style participating in the same aura of significance and achievement.

Murdoch does not sound like any of her antecedents, of course; she has step by step found her own way. This study has tried to follow that way through her always unexpected and often puzzling progressions. Although Murdoch's ideology has changed only slightly from time to time, her wide variety of forms, subtle indirect experimentation and continuous ability to surprise and enchant underline a development of increasing seriousness. At the same time, she is capable of subtle illustrations of the mysterious qualities of human experience as she strives to unite the paradoxes of reality and realism, the peripheral but major character of the good with the failed majority of characters who populate the middle range of the ordinary world. A specialist in drawing distinctions, Murdoch writes not to buoy the spirits of the reader but to teach him how to see, to perceive his obscure journey to or from the objective reality which lies endlessly far away from all of us. The trick of the novel as a genre had always been to take on such tasks unobtrusively, and Murdoch's teaching belongs in this tradition even as it occasionally departs from it. Her ambitions in relation to the traditional novel and in the moral aggrandizement of that form are extensive and unique in the late twentieth century, and her equipment for achieving and illustrating a very great deal has, in twenty novels, displayed itself compellingly.

★

This study has tried to give extended analyses of major Murdoch novels and trace the strong development of Murdoch's career through to the end of the year 1980. As this study goes to press, another novel is in progress, and predictions of possible future directions are tantalizing but impossible. Two areas that have been of primary concern to my work are beyond doubt important parts of Murdoch's continued concentration: the idea of the good, and the immeasurable ironies of the problems of form. With the publication of *Nuns and Soldiers* in 1980, it was clear that through the use of an unpretentious character, Tim Reede, whose muddle about his art and confusions of the moral life are primary, Murdoch produced a complex of imagery involving tight nets and meshes of form as opposed to rich, organic life which parallels but subtly alters her long-standing contrast between form and formlessness, or between lies and truth. The careful intermingling of the tightly formal and bulgingly organic in Tim's late pictures (which nobody likes and which do not pretend to be great art) is described as something deep and secret, but it also reflects a wider openness of approach to the problems of form. I hesitate to use this balanced intermingling as predictive, for although there are certain formal similarities between this and the previous novel, *The Sea, The Sea* (1978), the two are not comparable in direction and not liable to the same sort of interpretation. What she does in any given novel does not form the basis of the next. It is certainly true, however, that as Murdoch now conceives form, it has, in the last few novels, its direct echo in human personality, and is more dependent on the nature of character and the direction of event than it had been in her early novels. The switch from concentration on mechanics to the free deployment of character and story has for some time been absolutely complete.

Moreover, Murdoch's persistent interest in the disciplines of the characters of the good continues to provide a device of unshakeable authority against which the characters of the middle range can be set. Her attention to the entire panoply of people who clothe her novels is the compelling force which shapes the fictions, and as we watch these characters in the struggle of a life we all share in the violent confusion of the twentieth century, the perpetual idea of a moral imperative as shown by the touchstone characters of the good serves as a reminder of what we half wish to be.

Murdoch readers often ask why she so mercilessly causes them to undergo the horrors of the relentless causality of her tales, and although one can answer sardonically that she is merely trying to have us temporarily don the hair-shirt of reality, there can be no doubt that some of the novels are, particularly in denouement, more endurable than others. I have tried throughout this book to warn the reader against falling into romantic consolation as a result of occasional apparently happy endings in marriage which are, when examined, either savagely ironic or merely kind and indicative of mediocrity. But there is another way in which Murdoch's essential generosity has in her last two novels had an outlet, in that the experience through which her characters painfully and guiltily live is much more productive of amelioration than in some of the heart-sickening novels of the recent past, such as *An Accidental Man*, *The Sacred and Profane Love Machine* and *Henry and Cato*. Charles Arrowby, in the last fifty pages of *The Sea, The Sea*, wavers between profound insight and a foul belittling of others, but the reader ends the book feeling that some progress has been made or that progress is possible, though not assured as long as the character lives to meet his uncertain future. Similarly, *Nuns and Soldiers* projects a more positive view of society, has more characters of the good than any novel before it and indicates a sense of work-centred human possibility. I do not mean to imply that Murdoch has softened the stern area of reality which has been her central subject throughout her career, but to argue that the new protractive directions may involve a reunion with the past history of the novel where extended beauty and human potentiality do not deflect from the horror of the world, but make us more ready to accept it.

These are, however, conjectures and game-playing, and as I conclude this study, I do not know whether they constitute at all a just apprehension of Murdoch's future directions. We must wait and see.

# BIBLIOGRAPHY

## MAJOR WORKS OF IRIS MURDOCH

Note: A list of Murdoch's novels can be found at the beginning of the book.

### DRAMA

*A Severed Head*, with J. B. Priestley, 1964
*The Italian Girl*, with James Saunders, 1968
*The Servants and the Snow*, 1970
*The Three Arrows*, 1972

### LIBRETTO

*The Servants*, 1980. For the opera composed by William Mathias.

### POETRY

*A Year of Birds*, 1978. Engravings by Reynolds Stone.

### BOOKS ON PHILOSOPHY

*Sartre: Romantic Rationalist*, 1953
*The Sovereignty of Good*, 1970
*The Fire and the Sun: Why Plato Banished the Artists*, 1977

### MAJOR ESSAYS: A SELECTED LIST

'The Novelist as Metaphysician', *The Listener*, 16 March 1950, 473–6.
'Nostalgia for the Particular', *Proceedings of the Aristotelian Society 52*, 1952, 243–60.
'Vision and Choice in Morality', *Dreams and Self-Knowledge*, Aristotelian Society, Supplementary Volume 30, 1956, 32–58.
'Metaphysics and Ethics', in D. F. Pears (ed.), *The Nature of Metaphysics*, London, Macmillan 1957, 99–123.
'T. S. Eliot as a Moralist', in Neville Braybrooke (ed.), *T. S. Eliot: A Symposium for his Seventieth Birthday*, New York, Books for Libraries, Inc., 1958, 152–60.
'The Sublime and the Good', *Chicago Review*, 13, Autumn 1959, 42–55.
'The Sublime and the Beautiful Revisited', *Yale Review*, 49, December 1960, 247–71. [1959]
'Against Dryness: A Polemical Sketch', *Encounter*, 16, January 1961, 16–20.
'The Darkness of Practical Reason', *Encounter*, 27, July 1966, 46–50.

MAJOR INTERVIEWS: A SELECTED LIST

Frank Kermode, 'The House of Fiction: Interviews with English Novelists',
  *Partisan Review*, 30, 1963, 62ff.
Ruth Heyd, 'An Interview with Iris Murdoch', *University of Windsor Review*,
  1965, 142 ff.
Ronald Bryden (with A. S. Byatt), 'Talking to Iris Murdoch', *The Listener*,
  14 April 1968, 433 ff.
W. K. Rose, 'Iris Murdoch, informally', *London Magazine*, 8, 1968, 59 ff.
Michael O. Bellamy, 'An Interview with Iris Murdoch', *Contemporary Litera-
  ture*, 18, 1977, University of Wisconsin Press, 129 ff.
Bryan Magee, 'Iris Murdoch on Natural Novelists and Unnatural Phil-
  osophers', *The Listener*, 27 April 1978, 533 ff.
Jack I. Biles, 'An Interview with Iris Murdoch', *Studies in the Literary
  Imagination*, XI, Fall 1978.


MURDOCH CRITICISM

This is not to be construed as a bibliography of works on Murdoch. I have
included only those studies I consider useful or supplementary.

BOOKS (IN ORDER OF USEFULNESS)

A. S. Byatt, *Degrees of Freedom: The Novels of Iris Murdoch*, London, Chatto &
  Windus, 1965.
Peter Wolfe, *The Disciplined Heart: Iris Murdoch and her Novels*, Columbia,
  University of Missouri Press, 1966.
Wolfram Völker, *The Rhetoric of Love*, in German, Amsterdam, B. R.
  Grüner, 1978.
Richard Todd, *Iris Murdoch: The Shakespearian Interest*, New York, Barnes &
  Noble, 1979.
Frank Baldanza, *Iris Murdoch*, New York, Twayne Publishers, 1974.

MONOGRAPHS

Donna Gerstenberger, *Iris Murdoch*, Lewisburg, Penn., Bucknell University
  Press, 1975.
Rubin Rabinovitz, 'Iris Murdoch', in George Stade (ed.), *Six Contemporary
  British Novelists*, New York, Columbia University Press, 1976 (originally
  published as a pamphlet 1968).

ARTICLES (ALPHABETICAL)

Warner Berthoff, 'Fortunes of the Novel: Muriel Spark and Iris Murdoch',
  *Massachussetts Review*, 8, 1967, 301–32.
G. S. Fraser, 'Iris Murdoch and the Solidity of the Normal', *International
  Literary Annual*, 2, 1959, 37–54.
Howard German, 'Allusions in the Early Novels of Iris Murdoch', *Modern
  Fiction Studies*, 15, 1969, 361–77.

——'The Range of Allusions in the Novels of Iris Murdoch', *Journal of Modern Literature*, 2, 1971, 57–85.

William F. Hall, '"The Third Way": The Novels of Iris Murdoch', *Dalhousie Review*, 1, 1965, 306–18.

Linda Kaehl, 'Iris Murdoch: The Novelist as Magician/The Magician as Artist', *Modern Fiction Studies*, 15, 1969, 347–60.

Hena Maes-Jelinek, 'A House for Free Characters: the Novels of Iris Murdoch', *Revue des Langues Vivantes*, 29, 1963, 45–69.

Louis L. Martz, 'Iris Murdoch: the London Novels', *Twentieth-Century Literature in Retrospect*, 1970, 65–86.

Mary McCarthy, 'Characters in Fiction', *Partisan Review*, 28, 1961, 171–91.

William M. Murray, 'A Note on the Iris Murdoch Manuscripts in the University of Iowa Libraries', *Modern Fiction Studies*, 15, 1969, 445–8.

Jacques Souvage, 'The Novels of Iris Murdoch', *Studia Germanica Gandensia*, 4, 1962, 225–52.

### GENERAL WORKS OF LITERARY CRITICISM

This study implies a wide-ranging background in thought on the novel and contemporary critical quarrels. The following list should be seen as introductory to the issues; it makes no pretense at being exhaustive, and is meant only as an aid to readers who may wish to delve further into the setting of this kind of critical study.

M. H. Abrams, *Natural Supernaturalism*, New York, W. W. Norton, 1971.

Robert M. Adams, *Strains of Discord: Studies in Literary Openness*, Ithaca, NY, Cornell University Press, 1958.

Robert Alter, *Partial Magic: The Novel as a Self-Conscious Genre*, Berkeley, University of California Press, 1975.

Erich Auerbach, *Mimesis: The Representation of Reality in Western Literature*, trans. Willard Trask, Princeton University Press, 1953.

John Barth, 'The Literature of Exhaustion', *Atlantic Monthly*, 220, August 1967, 29–34.

—— 'The Literature of Replenishment', *Atlantic Monthly*, 245, January 1980, 65–71.

Roland Barthes, *Mythologies*, trans. A. Lavers, New York, Hill & Wang, 1972.

John Bayley, *The Characters of Love: A Study in the Literature of Personality*, London, Constable, 1960.

—— *The Uses of Division: Unity and Disharmony in Literature*, London, Chatto & Windus, 1976.

George J. Becker (ed.), *Documents of Modern Literary Realism*, Princeton University Press, 1963.

Leo Bersani, *A Future for Astyanax: Character and Desire in Literature*, Boston, Little, Brown, 1976.

Wayne Booth, *The Rhetoric of Fiction*, University of Chicago Press, 1961.

John D. Boyd, *The Function of Mimesis and Its Decline*, Cambridge, Mass., Harvard University Press, 1968.

Eugene Current-García and Walton R. Patrick, *Realism and Romanticism in Fiction: An Approach to the Novel*, Fairlawn, NJ, Scott, Foresman & Co., 1962.

Raymond Federman (ed.), *Surfiction: Fiction Now and Tomorrow*, Chicago, Swallow Press, 1975.

John Gardner, *On Moral Fiction*, New York, Basic Books, 1978.

Richard Gilman, *The Confusion of Realms*, New York, Random House, 1969.

Eugene Goodheart, *The Cult of the Ego: The Self in Modern Literature*, University of Chicago Press, 1968.

Gerald Graff, *Literature Against Itself: Literary Ideas in Modern Society*, University of Chicago Press, 1979.

Damian Grant, *Realism*, London, Methuen, 1970.

John Halperin (ed.), *The Theory of the Novel: New Essays*, London and New York, Oxford University Press, 1974.

Henry James, *The Future of the Novel: Essays on the Art of Fiction*, ed. Leon Edel, New York, Random House, 1956.

Frank Kermode, *The Genesis of Secrecy: On the Interpretation of Narrative*, Cambridge, Mass., Harvard University Press, 1979.

—— *The Sense of an Ending*, London and New York, Oxford University Press, 1967.

Christopher Lasch, *The Culture of Narcissism*, New York, W. W. Norton, 1978.

George Levine, 'Realism Reconsidered', in John Halperin (ed.), *The Theory of the Novel: New Essays*, London and New York, Oxford University Press, 1974.

Georg Lukács, *The Theory of the Novel*, trans. Anna Bostock, Cambridge, Mass., MIT Press, 1971.

——*The Meaning of Contemporary Realism*, trans. J. and N. Mander, London, Merlin Press, 1963.

Edwin Muir, *The Structure of the Novel*, London, Hogarth Press, 1928.

Vladimir Nabokov, *Lectures on Literature*, ed. Fredson Bowers, New York, Harcourt Brace Jovanovich, 1980.

Frank O'Connor, *The Mirror in the Roadway*, New York, Alfred A. Knopf, 1956.

Richard Poirier, *The Performing Self: Compositions and Decompositions in the Languages of Contemporary Life*, London and New York, Oxford University Press, 1971.

Robert Scholes, *Fabulation and Metafiction*, Urbana, University of Illinois Press, 1979.

Robert Scholes and Robert Kellogg, *The Nature of Narrative*, London and New York, Oxford University Press, 1966.

Charles Singleton (ed.), *Interpretation: Theory and Practice*, Baltimore, Johns Hopkins University Press, 1969.

Susan Sontag, *Against Interpretation*, New York, Delta Books, 1967.

J. P. Stern, *On Realism*, London and Boston, Routledge & Kegan Paul, 1973.

Wylie Sypher, *The Loss of the Self in Modern Literature and Art*, New York, Random House, 1962.

Tony Tanner, *City of Words: American Fiction 1950–70*, London, Jonathan Cape, 1971.

René Wellek, *Concepts of Criticism*, New Haven, Yale University Press, 1963.

Hayden White, *Tropics of Discourse: Essays in Cultural Criticism*, Baltimore, Johns Hopkins University Press, 1978.

Raymond Williams, *Culture and Society, 1780–1950*, London, Chatto & Windus, 1960.

Edgar Wind, *Pagan Mysteries in the Renaissance*, New York, W. W. Norton, 1968.

# INDEX TO WORKS BY IRIS MURDOCH

Note: Page numbers shown in italics indicate major discussions.

# NAME INDEX

Abrams, M. H., 127
Aeschylus, 17, 107, 112
Amis, Kingsley, 134
Auerbach, Erich, 32
Augustine, Saint, 17, 47, 252, 317
Austen, Jane, 345
Ayer, Sir Alfred, 315

Balzac, Honoré de, 31, 37
Barrie, J. M., 84, 216, 217, 223
Barth, John, xi
Barthelme, Donald, xi, 49
Baudelaire, Charles, 8
Bayley, John O., x
Beckett, Samuel, xi, 28, 81, 84, 134, 136
Beckmann, Max, 99, 254, 255, 257, 259, 261
Bellamy, Michael O., 40–1, 115
Bellow, Saul, 6, 49, 90–1
Bergman, Ingmar, 87
Bible, The, 26, 27, 182–3, 215, 221, 224, 249, 326, 330
Borges, Jorge Luis, 30
Bradley, A. C., 110
Bradley, F. H., 110
Breughel, Pieter, 288
Brontë, Charlotte, 88
Brontë, Emily, 151, 273
Bronzino, Il, 3–4, 99, 161
Byatt, A. S., x, 37, 133, 134, 139, 159, 266

Chalcidius, 308
Chaucer, Geoffrey, 62
Conrad, Joseph, 190

Dante Alighieri, 108, 139, 149
Dickens, Charles, 29, 30, 31, 38, 39, 40, 49, 88, 264, 345, 347
Domenichino, 290
Dostoevsky, Fyodor, 31

Eliot, George, 29, 33, 62, 79
Eliot, T. S., 51, 217, 223

Federman, Raymond, xi
Flaubert, Gustave, 31

Flecker, James Elroy, 217, 218–19, 223
Fowles, John, 6
Freud, Sigmund, 93–4, 152, 157, 207, 227, 268, 272, 273

Gardner, John, xi, 4
Giorgione, 236
Golding, William, 30
Graff, Gerald, xi
Greuze, Jean Baptiste, 290

Hampshire, Stuart, 52
Hardy, Thomas, 31
Heidegger, Martin, 62–3, 68, 69
Herodotus, 149
Homer, 84, 230, 299, 334, 345

James, Henry, 30, 39, 52, 83, 136
John of the Cross, St, 3, 22, 47, 78
Joyce, James, xi, 28, 30, 40
Julian of Norwich, 3, 78, 127, 249, 250, 317, 326, 328–31, 334, 345, 346

Kant, Emmanuel, x, 28, 157, 303
Keats, John, 32
Kipling, Rudyard, 217

Lackner, Stephan, 254
LeFanu, Sheridan, 151, 273
Levine, George, 39
Lukács, George, 39

Maes, Nicolaes, 290
Magee, Bryan, 156, 277
Mallarmé, Stéphane, 338
Marlowe, Christopher, 154
Medici, Lorenzo de, 108
Milarepa, 294
Milton, John, 18, 32, 99, 184, 197
Mozart, Wolfgang Amadeus, 307, 335, 345, 346

Nabokov, Vladimir, xi, 1–2, 28, 29, 30, 84, 91
Nietzche, Friedrich, 66